Westminster Pelican Commentaries
Edited by D. E. Nineham

Paul's Letters from Prison

PHILIPPIANS, COLOSSIANS, PHILEMON, AND EPHESIANS

Westminster Pelican Commentaries

Paul's Letters from Prison

PHILIPPIANS, COLOSSIANS, PHILEMON,
AND EPHESIANS

J. L. HOULDEN

The Westminster Press
PHILADELPHIA

© J. L. Houlden 1970, 1977

First published in 1970 by Penguin Books Ltd.

First published in 1977 in SCM Pelican Commentaries series
by SCM Press Ltd.

Scripture quotations from the Revised Standard Version of the
Bible are copyright, 1946 and 1952, by the Division of Christian
Education of the National Council of Churches, and are used
by permission.

Published by The Westminster Press ®
Philadelphia, Pennsylvania

PRINTED IN THE UNITED STATES OF AMERICA

Library of Congress Cataloging in Publication Data

Houlden, James Leslie.
   Paul's letters from prison.

   (Westminster Pelican commentaries)
   Includes bibliographical references and indexes.
   1. Bible. N.T. Philippians—Commentaries.
   2. Bible. N.T. Colossians—Commentaries. 3. Bible.
   N.T. Philemon—Commentaries. 4. Bible. N.T.
   Ephesians—Commentaries. I. Bible. N.T. Epistles of
   Paul. English. Revised standard. 1977. II. Title.
   III. Series.
   BS2650.3.H65 1977   227   77-24028
   ISBN 0-664-21347-2
   ISBN 0-664-24182-4 pbk.

Matri meae

Contents

Contents

Editorial Foreword

The general aim and scope of the Pelican Commentaries on the later books of the New Testament will be similar to those of the Pelican Gospel Commentaries. Each volume will contain an introduction designed to provide non-specialist readers with sufficient background information to enable them to understand the situation to which the author was addressing himself and the way his original readers are likely to have understood what he wrote. The more detailed information necessary for the understanding of individual passages will be provided in the body of the commentary.

As in the case of the Gospel Commentaries, the basic endeavour will be to elucidate the religious meaning of the text, but it is hoped at the same time to give the reader a fair indication of current scholarly opinion on the various historical, critical, and linguistic questions raised by each book.

Acknowledgements

I am deeply indebted to the General Editor of this series, Dennis Nineham, Warden of Keble College, Oxford, both for his teaching in the past and for his help during the writing of this book. He has made many suggestions and given constant encouragement. I also thank many friends, colleagues, and pupils for aid and interest, Miss Jane Clark for cheerfully and devotedly typing the manuscript, Miss Clare Nineham for reading proofs, and Mrs Patricia Richardson for making the index.

For corrections and improvements for this reissue, I am grateful to the Revd J. C. Fenton, Mr R. A. West and Mr D. Cook.

References, Abbreviations, and Technical Terms

The biblical text used is the *Revised Standard Version*.
The titles of the books of the Bible receive their customary abbreviations.
Biblical references are given by chapter and verse, and where necessary also by section of verse; thus Heb. 1^{3a} means the first half of verse 3 of chapter 1 of the *Epistle to the Hebrews*.
Articles in periodicals are cited by the abbreviated title of the periodical, followed by the volume number and/or its date, then the page number. Standard collections of documents are referred to by the editor's name or an abbreviated title, followed by volume and/or page numbers.

A.V.	*Authorized Version of the Bible* (1611).
CHARLES	*Apocrypha and Pseudepigrapha of the Old Testament*, Vols. I & II, ed. R. H. Charles (Oxford, 1913).
E.C.W.	*Early Christian Writings*, translated by Maxwell Staniforth (Penguin, 1968).
EX.T.	*Expository Times*.
HENNECKE	*New Testament Apocrypha*, Vols. I & II, ed. E. Hennecke/W. Schneemelcher (E. T. ed. R. McL. Wilson) (London, 1963).
IGN.	the letters of Ignatius, Bishop of Antioch, to be found in E.C.W. and L.C.C., I.
J.B.L.	*Journal of Biblical Literature*.
J.TH.C.	*Journal for Theology and the Church*.
J.T.S.	*Journal of Theological Studies*.
L.C.C.	*Library of Christian Classics*.
LXX	the Greek version of the Old Testament, the Septuagint, so called because it was believed to be the work of seventy-two translators working independently, and by a miracle producing an

identical version in seventy-two days. It differs considerably from the Hebrew text on which our English translations are based.

N.E.B.	*New English Bible* (New Testament) (Oxford, 1961).
N.T.S.	*New Testament Studies.*
NOV. TEST.	*Novum Testamentum.*
R.S.V.	*Revised Standard Version of the Bible* (1946).
T.D.N.T.	*Theological Dictionary of the New Testament.*
T.L.Z.	*Theologische Literaturzeitung.*
VERMES	*The Dead Sea Scrolls in English*, ed. & translated by G. Vermes (Penguin, 1962).
Z.N.W.	*Zeitschrift für die Neutestamentliche Wissenschaft.*

Other abbreviations include:

E.T.	English translation.
GK	Greek.
MS(S)	Manuscript(s).
OP. CIT.	the work of the author mentioned which has already been cited.
P46	a third-century papyrus copy of parts of the N.T.

General Introduction

THE PURPOSE OF THE COMMENTARY

That the writings of Paul the Apostle are obscure is a widespread opinion among those who have been exposed to them. To a certain degree the increasing use of translations into modern English has dissipated this impression. But in one way it has strengthened it. It has made it clearer than ever that many of Paul's assumptions and ideas are utterly foreign to us. Modern translations merely serve to remove the disguise of archaism and leave this alien quality exposed as a naked fact. The chief aim of this commentary is to guide those who are aware of this difficulty.

At certain points it would have been possible to alleviate it by sheltering behind the long and devout use which these texts have received. Whether we are Christians or not, all who have any links with the literature and religion of the western world (at least) have lived under their shadow. We are accustomed to ignore some of their strangeness because we are so used to them. In this book we have chosen to place their exotic quality firmly under the reader's eyes – partly because it is there, partly because it raises questions which ought not to be refused.

To make the same point in other words, the first aim is to let Paul speak for himself, freed from the effects of the assumptions with which we his modern readers approach him. From this point of view the commentary sets out to put the reader on his guard, so that he may be able to hear Paul himself more clearly.

Quite apart from the difficulty caused by the gulf between Paul's world and ours, there are in these writings many genuine obscurities of sense. Paul wrote for the moment, not for posterity. Sometimes, perhaps, he wrote in a hurry, without revising. After his letters were received by the particular people addressed, they were kept and used – and perhaps modified or damaged – in the decades before they were brought together into a more permanent collection. After that the repeated copying of manuscripts, in the early centuries, with little in the way of punctuation marks or spacing between words, gave ample scope for both ambiguity and mistakes. The commentary also gives guidance on the problems to which these developments give rise.

Some commentaries have a third aim: to stimulate the meditative use of the work in question. They set out to allow the reader to work slowly with his text, drawing as much profit as he possibly can from it and sometimes exercising his imagination upon it. This approach leads to a more diffuse kind of book than has been attempted here. But those who wish to use it for this purpose ought not to feel themselves hindered; for to know what the writer meant by what he wrote is a proper first step in the use of any work.

PAUL THE APOSTLE

Paul was a Jew, born probably a few years after Jesus, and he died in Rome, probably in Nero's persecution of Christians in that city in A.D. 64. He was a Jew of the Dispersion; that is, he was born in one of the numerous Jewish colonies to be found, by his time, in all the chief towns of the Mediterranean world. According to Acts 22[3] his native place was Tarsus, in Cilicia, in the southern part of modern Turkey. This chapter in *Acts* goes on to say that he was brought up in Jerusalem, at the feet of Gamaliel, one of the leading Jewish religious teachers of his day. In Phil. 3[5] he himself says that he was a member of the sect of the Pharisees, that is, the inner core of rigorous and observant Jewry. His letters bear ample witness to his Old Testament learning (including current ways of interpreting it), and to the depth of his Judaism; to forsake it meant a crisis which went to the roots of his being. Nevertheless he was utterly, perhaps chiefly, at home in the Greek language and wrote it with ease, so much so that he used the Jewish scriptures in their Greek version, the Septuagint (completed about two centuries before in Alexandria); and in his use of certain words Greek and Jewish senses are found side by side. In addition he seems to have had a smattering of the popular philosophy (chiefly Stoic) of the Greek world and a deeper knowledge of the religious speculation often associated with it.

This mingling of cultures need cause no surprise. Despite the strong self-consciousness of Jews and their reputation for keeping themselves apart (which Roman authorities generally recognized), in this age of religious syncretism they were far from immune from external influences. The Dead Sea Scrolls have shown that even in Palestine itself the penetration of Judaism by Greek-cum-oriental religious speculation was not at all negligible. It manifested itself in an imaginative search for answers to two questions: what is the structure of the cosmos? what is the plan of the world's history? Lack of evidence merely stimulated replies. There was an intense awareness of the angelic and demonic population of the heavens, and of the rich drama which God would unfold in the affairs of angels and men to demonstrate his omnipotent righteousness. In all this Paul shared to the full.

A few years after the crucifixion of Jesus of Nazareth, whom (as far as we can tell) he had not known, Paul experienced him in his living and exalted power (Gal. 1¹²⁻¹⁷). He was overwhelmed, transformed, and totally re-directed by this event. What led up to it we cannot say, except that in Acts 7⁵⁸ff. we learn that he was present at the martyrdom of Stephen, one of Jesus' first followers.

Out of this event Paul reconstructed his life. In its outward aspect he became a missionary for Jesus, with, at least to begin with, only modified acceptance by those who led the Church from its Jerusalem headquarters. He saw his vocation as the conveying of the 'good news' of Jesus to those who were not Jews. He therefore embarked on a prolonged missionary programme; partly preaching in new places, either in person or through associates, partly shepherding newly founded congregations and building up their life. Relations with Jewish Christians, who wished Gentile converts to observe the customs of Judaism (dietary laws, circumcision, etc.), were so strained that in due course a firm agreement with the Jerusalem apostles was both sought and found (Gal. 2¹ff.). Deeply relieved by this acceptance and peace, Paul organized a collection of alms from his Gentile churches for the mother church of Jerusalem as a token of mutual love (Gal. 2¹⁰; Rom. 15²⁵ff.; 2 Cor. 9).

About the rest of his life we know little from his letters, but from Acts 21ff. we learn that he was arrested in Jerusalem after Jewish opponents had raised a disturbance near the Temple. In due course, pleading Roman citizenship, he was transferred to Rome for trial. What happened between then and his death, perhaps over half a decade later, we do not know. Three of the letters dealt with in this volume may well come from this period of imprisonment, though it is impossible to be sure.

Inwardly, Paul had found the answer to a devout Jew's profoundest question: how may a man find acceptance with the holy God? From the moment of his conversion, in whatever terms he would at that early stage have expressed it, Paul was convinced that the answer to that question was: by relating himself to God by means of the person of Jesus Christ. But how does this reply come to be the answer to that question?

We must understand the considerations uppermost in Paul's mind. First, he had certain convictions about God. Not only is God the omnipotent Lord of the vast array of the cosmic hierarchy and the earth itself, but he is utterly righteous in his own being and in his demands upon man. He is also deeply concerned for man's salvation and expresses his concern by his attitude to human history. He displays neither detachment nor indifference. On the contrary, the progress of events is both crucial and purposeful; it works towards God's End. Already, long ago, he has taken the people of Israel into special relationship with himself (the Covenant), and ultimately that relationship is for all. It was the dream of Paul, as of many in Israel in this period, that in the end all nations might become the people of God. History was moving towards God's realization of that dream.

Second, he had convictions about man. Not only is man sinfully and wilfully alienated from God, despite the indications of his will which God has given (both conscience and the Jewish Law); he is also under bondage to demonic powers who stalk the universe and who use the Law, not as the means of man's obedience to God, but as an instrument of their tyranny. This alienation of man from God is common to all mankind – it is neither purely Jewish nor purely Gentile. It is the state of man as child of Adam.

Thus the cure for man's state is not merely that he should come to a better moral condition. That is part of it, but not the root of the matter. Before that comes his translation into a new status, a new pattern of relationships – with God, and so with the rest of mankind and with the universe as a whole. As far as the demonic powers are concerned man's need is simply deliverance from their control. And the same goes for the Law, which, good in essence, has gone sour for man and does him nothing but harm, frustrating and tempting him. As far as his neighbour is concerned, man needs to see him as child of some new Adam, who will be all that the first Adam so abysmally and tragically failed to be. And in relation to God, he needs from him no less than the effecting of this change; no lesser power can conceivably bring it about.

Probably because, despite Paul's share in the persecution of Stephen, Jesus had with great favour appeared to him and called him to his apostolic task, Paul saw in Jesus the unique agent of God for accomplishing all these things, the Son whom the Father had willingly given. He who had been ignominiously executed by Israel and Rome had clearly, as his followers claimed, been exalted by God to a position of cosmic rule. And if his vindication by God availed so freely for one such as Paul, was it not open to all the human race? Was he not therefore the desired new Adam, in whom all could find restored affiliation to God (Rom. 5$^{12ff.}$; 8$^{14ff.}$)?

For a man to come into this position required two things, neither of them a matter of merit or deserts or qualifications, both a matter of status and membership. The first was faith, and the second a place in the people of God. The two were closely related, for it was Paul's contention that, whatever Jews might say, the proper basis of membership of God's people (i.e. Israel) had never been observance of the Law, or physical descent from Abraham, but the quality which he called by a word of many senses: 'faith'. In his central use of the word, it meant for Paul that attitude to God which alone formed the possibility of true relationship with him: that is, total trust and openness, demanding nothing, boasting nothing, but simply awaiting his bounty. This quality was the secret at the heart of the true life of Israel herself – Paul sees it in the life of Abraham, right at the start (Rom. 4). But now it comes into its own. In Christ it has a visible, triumphant point at which to attach itself. In him it becomes openly the foundation for life in the people of God. So, in Christ, that people is re-founded on a new basis. The Church is one with him – his body, his bride; and Paul is his apostle, his ambassador. Because Christ's rule is already established in the heavens, the Church goes forward confidently to the fulfilment of God's plan, whereby the whole human race is to be brought to its true allegiance to the one Creator through her, in Christ. The new Adam will 'include' all mankind.

Such is the magnificent sweep of Paul's teaching. It is easy to feel that somehow it has cut loose from the realities of ordinary earthly life and from the realities of the life and death of Jesus of Nazareth. Would the teaching of Jesus, for example, as we find it in the Gospels, lead anyone to this estimate of his role? Yet those same Gospels were written by a Church which had seen Paul live and die; a Church which, if it did not always think in his terms, would not have dissented from his message. And is it not the case that the teaching of Jesus has that note of authority which Paul openly ascribes to him, and that it claims a universality of application which Paul's estimate does no more than bring out? Jesus' proclamation of the 'kingdom' or rule of God in particular carries exactly this meaning. The Jesus of the Gospels acts as one for whom the imagery employed by Paul is wholly appropriate. Indeed, it would be surprising if Paul was as ignorant of the Jesus of history as some hold. For Paul as for everybody, whatever the apparent extravagance of some of his language, the heart of the matter was the historic death of Jesus by crucifixion and his amply attested resurrection from the dead. But because these events were the acts *of God* they shape the context in which all men live; and to them men are to give faith in order to relate truly to God.

THE IMPORTANCE OF PAUL

Paul is important at two levels. At the level of events, it was he who brought the Church out of its Jewish cocoon. Despite the implications of Christ's teaching, institutionally the primitive Church in Jerusalem must have appeared, not only to others but also to itself, as *a* (rather *the true*) sect in Judaism. And when the question of the admission of Gentiles began to arise it seemed natural that their entry into the Church should be regarded as an entry into Judaism. In other words, the Church was that part of Jewry which believed that, in the person of Jesus, the Messiah had come and the promises of God were being fulfilled. By his mission, Paul shifted the physical weight of the Church, so that though Jerusalem remained the mother church to the end of his days, Gentiles were already beginning to predominate in the Church as a whole. When Jerusalem was largely destroyed by the Romans in A.D. 70 and the Christians there dispersed, this was no crippling blow to the Church. She was able to go on expanding. That she was well enough established in the Gentile world to survive this blow, while still containing many Jewish Christians, is primarily due to Paul. Without him this first storm might never have been weathered at all.

At the level of doctrine, his influence runs parallel. It was Paul who first provided a way of formulating the significance of Jesus which made it possible to universalize his mission. Though with emotional hesitations, apparent above all in Rom. 9–11 (cf. p. 286f.), Paul saw with luminous clarity that in Christ God had acted for all. And having seen this he followed its implications resolutely. For him Christ's Adamic role and universal lordship meant that there was a new directness and simplicity in man's coming to God and man's acceptance by him. Here Paul made it conceptually possible for the Church not merely to survive but to flourish increasingly as a mainly Gentile community, cut off from her original roots in Jerusalem and Israel. She need no longer see herself as merely an offshoot of that central stem but as the outpost of that heavenly kingdom whose life she already shared.

Paul also brought simplicity and directness into the relationship of the individual with God. However much some of his chosen images now strike us as too dependent for our taste on the culture of his time (talk of sacrifices and angelic powers and even of eccentrically functioning law-courts), the essence of his meaning is clear enough. The loving initiative of God has given freely to man that relationship with him which he vainly seeks for himself; and on that assured basis the good life, the life acceptable to God, can begin to grow.

Finally, Paul, the Hellenistic Jew, was able to go far enough in expressing the Christian gospel in terms congenial to Greeks to launch the Church's teaching safely on non-semitic waters. We have already mentioned the mingling of Greek ways of thought with Judaism. In a sense, therefore, Paul was continuing what Jews, especially in the Dispersion (e.g. Philo of Alexandria), had begun before him. But to him belongs the credit for setting about this task for the Christian faith; many were to continue with it after him. It was an essential task if the faith was to be expressed in terms that were capable of a conceptual refinement impossible in the framework of more conservative Jewish thought.

MYTHOLOGY, GNOSTICISM, AND APOCALYPTIC

Already we have referred several times to Paul's way of regarding the universe in which he lived. We have described the rich speculation with which this was surrounded·in the world – Jewish and Gentile alike – of his time. Time and again in this commentary it will come before us, and its details will need to be explained. Three terms frequently occur in this connexion.

First, *mythology*. In the sense in which the word is used here it refers not to fables about the gods and primeval times, but to the story which a society or culture uses to explain and identify to itself the universe in which it lives. In the world of the first century it was a highly pictorial story, the contents of which are elucidated by the other two terms dealt with in this section. Possible though it is for us to treat it simply as one type of religious imagery alongside others, one feature of it has particularly important consequences. In it the heavenly world was thought of as in many respects continuous with (though much more powerful than) this one. This continuity of the two worlds often led to the obscuring of the 'otherness' or transcendence which was inherent in the idea of God. It also encouraged a tendency to take interest in the sheer topography of the heavenly world, almost for its own sake. Both the movements which we go on to describe in this section have in them a strong dash of cosmic tourism, in which God himself is in danger of being seen as one (even if the greatest) item in his universe. In other words there was a built-in hazard in the religious atmosphere of the time, which hindered appreciation of the essential simplicity and immediacy of God's relationship with man. It was Paul's greatness that, despite his sharing the basic 'mental furniture' of his day, he was able to avoid this hazard. And it was his overwhelming sense of the directness of God's dealings with man, as revealed in Christ, which made this possible. He saw Christ as having overcome or eliminated all those intermediaries (like the expanse of the heavens, the angelic powers, and the Jewish Law) which the contemporary mythology placed between God and man.

Second, *gnosticism*. This word is both technical and vague. It has a narrow and a wide meaning. In its narrow meaning it describes the tenets of a group of deviationist Christian sects who flourished chiefly in the second century and whose literature has recently become much better known to us through the discovery of a whole collection in upper Egypt (see ed. R. M. Grant, *Gnosticism*). In its wider meaning it describes systems of religio-philosophical thought of the type entertained by these sects, wherever and whenever encountered. In particular it is used for signs of these views already visible before the sects themselves came into existence. It is, then, the designation of a cultural climate, compounded of oriental, Hellenistic, and Jewish ingredients, found in places as varied as the interior of Asia Minor and the monastery at Qumran in the desert of Judea. It is characterized by extravagance of speculation, concern for the esoteric, depreciation of the material, and extreme anxiety about salvation. We shall see how Paul partly shared, partly rejected, partly adapted, its contents and assumptions. He used it as one idiom in which to speak of the Christian gospel, often in order to refute those who tried to assimilate Christ into their system, as one element among many. For Paul the boot was decisively on the other foot, as *Colossians* in particular makes abundantly clear.

Third, *apocalyptic*. This term is used to describe a literary genre in Judaism whose prototype was the *Book of Daniel*, written about 165 B.C., and of great importance in Jewish religious thought in the succeeding three centuries. The *Revelation to John* is the best example of a Christian work written in this idiom, and shorter examples are to be found in the first three gospels (cf. Mark 13; Matt. 24; Luke 21). It is concerned with detailed portrayal of the heavenly world and of the impending action of God to vindicate his power over the universe. His struggle with evil forces will come to a terrifying climax, in which the sufferings of his own people will reach unprecedented intensity. Then will come his victory, in the winding up of the present world-order and the ushering in of his new dispensation. Judgement will be given and the people of God will receive his infinite blessings. It may be seen as a peculiarly Jewish form (especially in its temporal orientation) of the more general movement of thought to which the name *gnosticism* is commonly applied. There is no doubt that much of the content of Jewish apocalyptic was related to this movement and contributed to it.

CAPTIVITY EPISTLES

These letters have been traditionally grouped together because all come as from Paul the prisoner. There, it may be, the resemblance stops. We shall see reasons for wondering which imprisonment of Paul provides the occasion for the writing of *Philippians*, *Colossians*, and *Philemon*, and we shall show reason for thinking that *Ephesians* was not written by Paul at all but by a later disciple. In any case, the fact that they were, supposedly at least, written in prison is not among the more significant features of any of them.

Nevertheless to treat these writings as a group is not without sense. These four short epistles make a good introduction to the apostle's work, from a certain angle. They may not contain in its fullest form the heart of his teaching, but they well illustrate his true place in the New Testament picture of early Christianity. They provide a back-door into the study of Paul, with the advantages and limitations of that mode of entry. The grandeur of the front entrance is lacking, but much is revealed that is vital to the life of the house.

We see here both the genuine Paul and the refracted Paul. In the first three epistles we have the Paul of history, dealing now (in *Philippians*) with a church of his own founding and as intimately linked with him as any, now (in *Colossians*) with a church less well-known and exposed to serious doctrinal confusion, now (in *Philemon*) with a personal need and a pastoral problem. They give a richly varied sight of Paul the apostle in his most practical work.

In *Ephesians* we see, in all probability, the first fruit of pauline tradition. Already, perhaps thirty years after his death, Paul has become a name and an authority. And in *Ephesians* we see Paul already not only revered, but adapted, in order that he may speak to the needs of the writer's day. Pure Paul (i.e. Paul in his own writings alone) was to become the special possession in the first half of the second century of the heretical teacher Marcion who, discarding the Old Testament, made Paul his chief authority. In the main-stream of the Church it was a refracted Paul whose voice was heard – Paul seen also in the light of the *Acts of the Apostles*, the Pastoral Epistles (*1 & 2 Timothy* and *Titus*) and *Ephesians*. Of these works, Marcion had only the last in his collection (calling it *Laodiceans*), and it is our belief that in it already the process had begun of using Paul's authority to support teaching beginning to diverge a little from his own; necessitated for the correction of distortions such as Marcion was to produce, having emphases hardly warranted in his time, but at the later time of the deepest importance. Above all, *Ephesians* proclaims the authority of the Church and her leaders in the safeguarding of the great unity which Christ has established between man and God, Jew and Gentile. It is the beginning of that use and interpretation of Paul which has continued in the Church to our own day, though now the device of pseudonymity would be less congenial to our taste.

THE USEFULNESS OF PAUL

Our brief exposition of Paul's thought and of the intellectual climate in which he lived must prompt the reflection, especially in those encountering it for the first time, that such alien ideas generated in a culture so different from our own can have little to say to us. We have made no attempt to banish that reflection or to soften its harshness. But to make it a final reflection would be an act of superficiality or despair.

In the first place, the strangeness of Paul's idiom cannot disguise the fact that he is dealing with permanent questions of man's existence in the world in a way which is not only original but also profound. The rigour with which he refuses all easy remedies for man's moral ineptitude, the subtlety with which he explores man's relationship with a righteous God in a sinful world, the richness with which he develops the implications of Christ's person and role for the peace man longs for – all these features deserve to command respect from Christian and non-Christian alike, quite apart from the magnitude of his historical achievement in the development of the Church. Whatever his own personal attitudes to these matters, a man can find in Paul ample material with which to extend and deepen his consideration of them. And the man who does not already see these questions as momentous may find that exposure to Paul brings them closer to the centre of his thinking. It is then not difficult to see beneath the form of Paul's thought a concern with perennial issues which face man as man, in whatever culture or society he lives.

But can we see Paul not only as the one who directs us towards serious questions but as the one whose answers still commend themselves? Here we can expect to carry fewer of our readers with us. It is after all strange that man's right relationship with God should depend so much on a man who was once crucified in Palestine. We have said something about the way in which Paul came to believe that this was so, and the commentary will make his ideas clearer. Though he had adequate conceptual tools to hand for his use, it would be a mistake to suppose that this conclusion was one that imposed itself intellectually in Paul's day much more than in ours. But again, the strangeness of his idiom cannot disguise the fact that once we go behind it we can see the appropriateness of Paul's answer to the fundamental needs and dilemmas of man to which his questions draw attention. Though Paul is thoroughly a man of his time, the product of his particular background and training (what else could he be?), there is a certain simplicity and (in the scientist's sense) elegance about his doctrine which needs to be emphasized. Given the purposes of God and the needs of man, God's act in Christ, in the light of which man lives and can know God, is fitting rather than outrageous. Once more, then, Christian and non-Christian alike may see in Paul's teaching insights which go far beyond the local and temporary ideas of his time.

For the Christian believer there is a further element which greatly affects his reaction to Paul in relation to our own day. The believer lives within the tradition of which Paul was among the first members and of which his writings were the first literary deposit. Whether he nourishes his faith directly and continually upon the writings of Paul himself or inherits Paul more indirectly through the life and teaching of the Church, he is able neither to avoid developing the tradition derived from Paul (by bringing his own personal experience into contact with it) nor to escape the influence of Paul. He lives in a Church which Paul, in some ways crucially, helped to make. But the Church has never fossilized Paul and could not do so if she wished. Paul received anew is Paul interpreted anew. The pauline tradition continually develops, yet with observable continuity and connexions. We have suggested that *Ephesians* was the first visible evidence of that development. Christians in the Church, seeing it as the sphere within which God is active for the world, and recognized to be so, have no reason to resist the notion of constant development and modification of the tradition received. But right reception involves understanding, and a commentary on Paul is one tool for its acquisition.

It ought to be apparent then that the believer should not see himself as a slave to the letter of Paul, whose thought-world is not and cannot be his own. There is no obligation on the pious to abandon, in entering the world of scripture, the understanding of the world which is conveyed to them by the ordinary educational processes. We have presented the view that Paul is not an outdated speculative thinker but a profound analyst of man's permanent questions and a proclaimer of the good news which he sees as their answer.

The Christian believer, besides sharing with Paul the tradition of understanding the faith, shares also the experience of it as gospel – the 'good news' of true relationship with God who creates and renews his people. There is no obligation on the Christian to describe this experience in the same imagery as Paul, and some of it will be uncongenial and even, in a different world, misleading to him. But the conviction that God is essentially man's friend and not his enemy, a God of love and not of impossible demand or olympian remoteness, is good news, colouring a total outlook, for Paul and the modern believer alike.

There is one other special difficulty. These letters contain much besides doctrinal teaching, in particular ethical injunctions, mostly about domestic relationships between husbands and wives or masters and slaves (see Col. $3^{18ff.}$ and Eph. $5^{22ff.}$). Clearly these are at least interesting historically, both in relationship to the study of the ancient world in general and of the Christian Church in particular. But is there anything authoritative in these rulings for Christian life in a quite different society? Many Christians who can see that transient idiom can be allowed for in doctrinal statement may still feel that Paul's words on moral matters carry permanent validity. Non-Christians too may think that Christians ought to feel so obliged. But this can hardly be so totally; one institution prominent here (slavery) is absent from our society. But does relativism, in this case forced upon us by the march of events, extend itself to the questions of marriage and the relationship of parent with child? Here too we must adhere to the principle that Paul wrote as a man of his time for the needs of his day; and though in so far as his teaching derives from his central insights about God's relationship with man we shall read him with profit, where the social situation has changed (e.g. with regard to the subjection of women assumed in Ephesians 5) we shall not feel bound to perpetuate obsolete arrangements, or the duties to which they gave rise.*

Suggestions for Further Reading

A. Schweizer: *Paul and His Interpreters* (London, 1912).
A. Schweizer: *The Mysticism of Paul the Apostle* (London, 1931).
W. L. Knox: *St Paul and the Church of the Gentiles* (Cambridge, 1939).
W. D. Davies: *Paul and Rabbinic Judaism* (London, 1948).

* For further discussion of the questions dealt with in this section, with particular reference to the understanding of the Gospels, see D. E. Nineham, *Saint Mark* (Pelican, 1963) pp. 48–52.

R. Bultmann: *Theology of the New Testament*, Vol. I (London, 1952).
M. Dibelius: *Paul* (London, 1953).
J. Knox: *Chapters in a Life of Paul* (London, 1954).
J. Munck: *Paul and the Salvation of Mankind* (London, 1959).
H. J. Schoeps: *Paul* (London, 1961).
D. E. H. Whiteley: *The Theology of St Paul* (Oxford, 1964).

The Letter to the Philippians

Introduction

PHILIPPI AND THE PHILIPPIANS

Philippi lies about a hundred miles out of Salonika, just off the main road to Istanbul. No longer inhabited, it is a well-excavated site, having been worked by the French School in Athens over the past fifty years or so. Recent work has concentrated on Byzantine remains, and there is much to see from this period as well as from Roman times. More is to be seen from the Philippi of the second century A.D., a period of extensive building in the city, than from the town to which Paul came in the forties of the first century A.D.

It occupies an important position astride the main overland route from Syria and Anatolia to the west. In Roman times this road, which ran to the north of the modern road, was the Via Egnatia, one of the great roads of the Empire's communications system. It carried substantial military and commercial traffic and was a prime route for the spread of ideas. Paul, bearing his gospel along this road into Europe, was one of many who over the years brought oriental cults to the Latin world. The road ran from Byzantium (Istanbul) to Dyrrhachium (Durazzo) on the Adriatic coast, a crossing-point to Brindisi and so to Rome itself. The position of Philippi, and its role as the first staging-point inland from its port of Neapolis (Kavalla), nine miles to the south-east, made it a place used to receiving a stream of visitors of many races and types. It sits astride the old road in a narrow piece of land between marsh on the south-west and the Lakanis range on the east. The last outcrop of these hills forms the town's acropolis or citadel. At the foot of the acropolis is the theatre whose origins go back to the city's earliest days and on the opposite side of the road the forum, the centre of civic life.

In Paul's day the town was still in the relatively early stages of a new lease of life. As a place of any importance it goes back to c. 360 B.C. when Thracian colonists were settled there, and, more importantly, to its acquisition by Philip of Macedon a few years later. He developed it and gave it his name. At that time its importance lay in its strategic position and in the gold deposits which were found

31

in the area. But by the first century B.C. the gold had long since given out and Philippi was no longer even the chief city of the district.

However, in 42 B.C., the armies of Antony and Octavian (later the Emperor Augustus) defeated those of Brutus and Cassius in the vicinity of Philippi, and the victors made the town into a Roman colony. That is to say, it became an outpost of 'Romanism' in an otherwise unlatinized area (cf. Acts 16²¹). On top of its population of original Thracians and Macedonian Greeks was introduced a top layer of disbanded Roman soldiers. A few years later a contingent of transplanted Italians arrived to complete the picture. The language of official business was Latin, and the structure of the magistracy reproduced that established by Rome in Italian towns, with duumviri (Acts 16²⁰), praetors, lictors (Acts 16³⁵), etc. It was granted the privileges of the *ius italicum*; that is, a series of rights giving it a legal status on a par with Rome, a status which had been extended to the towns of Italy in the last century of the Republic. The effect of these rights, which were highly prized, was to give self-government and exemption from the supervision of the provincial governor, as well as certain special conditions of land tenure. In fact Philippi as a Roman colony was a place of considerable distinction. The people of such a place 'were apt to regard themselves as being *in* but not *of* the province where they lay'.*

Still, Philippi was not important enough to merit the title accorded it in Acts 16¹² ('first city of the region of Macedonia'), and, unless the text suffered early interference, the author has either allowed himself to exaggerate the status of the place where his hero first suffered at the hands of Roman authorities or he was not fully acquainted with the meaning of some of the technical terms he used. Macedonia was not a 'region' (*meris*), but a province divided into four such regions, each with its own regional council. Philippi appears in fact to have been in the *first* region, so that either an early copyist, by repeating two Greek letters, changed the sense from 'a city of the first region of Macedonia' to the present reading, or the author of *Acts* may have simply become muddled in the placing of his 'first'. But while there was no formal title, Philippi certainly was, as he says, the chief city of its *region*. This full reference to Philippi's status recognized the special importance of the place and the fact that here Paul begins to

---

* Sh erwin-White: *Roman Society and Roman Law in the New Testament* (Oxfor d, 1963), p. 94.

meet Roman power face to face. Perhaps Paul himself thought of Philippi in this way; apart from the reference to Ephesus in 1 Cor. 15³² it is the only scene of persecution which he actually mentions by name in his letters (1 Thess. 2²).

Philippians itself contains evidence that Paul was conscious of the city's 'Romanness'. In mentioning converts from Caesar's household (4²²), whatever precise meaning the term should be given (see p. 116), he may well be appealing to the city's Roman pride. The official Latin name of the town, *Colonia Julia Augusta Philippensis*, is reflected in Paul's term for its inhabitants in 4¹⁵, *Philippēsioi*, a form which is a Graecizing of the Latin rather than the ordinary Greek.

There is no doubt that its status as a Roman colony meant everything to this small country town; and it is no wonder that Augustus was reckoned its co-founder alongside Philip of Macedon. The epitaph of one of its citizens of the third century A.D. speaks of it as 'the creation of Philip and of Augustus the king, circled with her walls'. (See P. Lemerle: *Philippes et la Macédoine Orientale à l'Époque Chrétienne et Byzantine* (Paris, 1945) pp. 7ff.)

It is natural to suppose that at the time of Paul's visit the Roman element in the population (which Lemerle thinks likely to have been the most numerous) still retained its distinctive quality. But Greek culture must have been increasingly pervasive, overlaying the old but persistent Thracian elements. Philippi's position on a busy highway meant that its religious life was more diverse than might otherwise have been the case. Apart from the Thracian cult of Dionysus and the official cult of the emperor there is evidence of the mystery cult, Orphism, with its emphasis on the attainment of union with the divine, and of other similar oriental religions. The name of *Epaphroditus* serves as a reminder of this richly varied background (2²⁵). Paul was by no means the first to bring new teaching to Philippi.

Whether he was preceded by Jews in any number is uncertain. Acts 16¹³ᶠᶠ· is curiously ambiguous. Jewish worship depended upon male leadership, but only women are mentioned as present on this occasion; and Lydia, alone mentioned by name, is said to be a 'worshipper of God' – a Gentile adherent of Judaism who had not taken the step of full entry by baptism (that is, if the term is to be taken in its normal technical sense). But clearly, despite the apparent absence of men, this is an occasion of Jewish worship, though the place as well as the composition of the congregation gives rise to difficulty. The meeting takes place by the riverside (a mile or so outside the town), but it is not clear whether it happens in the open or whether the *proseuchē* (*place of prayer*, R.S.V.) is an actual edifice. The term is usually simply a synonym for synagogue and, apart from the fact that *Acts* otherwise uses the latter word, only the oddity of the absence of males, who were required for synagogue worship, causes serious doubt about its accuracy in this case. Whatever the truth, it does not sound as if the Jews in Philippi were very prominent; their sabbath meeting-place was some way out of the town.

However, the evidence of *Philippians* tips the balance the other way. At any rate when this letter was written Jews were sufficiently prominent in Philippi and sufficiently aggressive towards what they doubtless saw as a disruptive breakaway group to provoke one of Paul's most passionate and abusive outbursts ($3^{2ff.}$). Whether they were strong enough actually to attempt a judaizing counter-attack upon the Christians, who were probably mostly (wholly as far as we can tell from the names we know) of Gentile extraction, or merely stated their position firmly, we do not know for certain. To a Jewish congregation the spectacle of Gentiles apparently availing themselves of so much of the Jewish heritage, claiming to be the true Israel (3^3), while neglecting to undertake the yoke of the Law must have seemed wholly intolerable. If some of the Christians felt shamed into thinking better of the Law than Paul would allow it would not be surprising, and this might be the motive which leads Paul to spell out his doctrine on the subject (3^{8-11}).

PAUL AND PHILIPPI

In the New Testament we have information about the church in Philippi not only in Paul's letter to it (and momentarily in 2 Cor. 8^1 and 1 Thess. 2^2), but also in the *Acts of the Apostles*. In Acts 16 there is the story of the founding of the church there, and in Acts 20^{1-6} we hear of two visits paid to it later. The reader of the commentary may be surprised at the lack of references to these passages, and this calls for explanation.

Partly because it seems the straightforward thing to do, and partly because the book gives a vivid account of the early Church's history and we have no other such account, people have always accorded primacy to *Acts* in forming a picture of those days and especially in tracing the story of Paul's journeys. Where there appears to be difficulty in fitting together the account given in *Acts* and that in Paul's letters (the most intractable instance being the various visits of Paul to Jerusalem in comparison with Gal. 1–2*), preference has nearly always been given to the *Acts* account, and all efforts have gone into the attempt to fit such data as Paul's letters contain into that account. After all, *Acts* looks like a straight narrative and seems easy to interpret, and everybody knows how easy it is for letters to be confused or to omit the kind of detail which we need in order to make a proper historical account.

But despite its attractiveness this approach demands caution. We easily forget that Paul's letters are our primary source for the history of his life and work, and *Acts* is at best secondary. However difficult it may be in certain cases to see exactly what Paul means or how brief allusions to historical circumstances should be interpreted, that priority should always remain in mind. If anybody is to be 'fitted in' it is surely *Acts* not Paul. It would in any case be quite anachronistic to attribute to the author of *Acts* (whatever his good intentions) the kind of painstaking inquiry and aspiration after objectivity (itself a most complex concept) which we associate with modern historical research. Historian he may be, but such objectivity is unlikely to have been his aim or to have been within his competence. Moreover it is also improbable, especially for the earlier days, that much accurate information, even about the sequence of events, survived; the Church was a small insignificant society, expecting the end of the present world order very soon, and most unlikely to appoint an archivist in every congregation! It is not surprising that where the author of *Acts* wins good marks for accuracy is in the sphere of the institutions, customs, and laws of the Mediterranean world in which he lived.† (See Sherwin-White: *Roman Society and Roman Law in the New Testament* (Oxford, 1963).) A historian in our day, investigating the early history of a Victorian friendly society, now grown to considerable size, might well find himself faced with much the same situation; he would be better informed on the general circumstances of English Society at the time (e.g. the names of the Prime Ministers) than on the

---

* For a most useful and clear analysis of this tangled question, see G. B. Caird: *The Apostolic Age* (London 1955), Appx. A.

† Though for an example of muddle, see above p. 32.

exact duties and even the order of the first officers of the society, which in its first days kept its rudimentary records in notebooks long since lost. The difference between our modern historian and the author of *Acts* is that the former would probably admit ignorance, and perhaps give up the attempt to describe the period concerned altogether, whereas the author of *Acts* went on with his task.

Why should he have done this? Simply because other factors besides the desire to write history weighed with him and therefore influenced the way his book was formed. Foremost among these are certain theological convictions, i.e. beliefs about God and about the life, death, and resurrection of Jesus; and, secondly, a strong desire to show the life of the Church developing according to a particular pattern and in relation to certain key events, e.g. the Council of Jerusalem described in Acts 15, which were in various ways exemplary for right Christian life.*

Since this is not a commentary on *Acts* there is no space to deal more fully with this subject. But the passage in Acts 16 which describes Paul's first visit to Philippi raises one special difficulty which demands comment. The reader will notice that in this part of *Acts*, as in some others, the writer uses the pronoun 'we', with the apparent implication that he himself took part in the events concerned. It looks as if these passages (generally referred to as the 'We-source') have a greater claim to be authentic history than other parts of the book where the information is at least second-hand. But the correct evaluation of these sections is a matter of much dispute, and it is clear that the simple inference is not necessarily the right one. It is possible that the author is using a diary made by some other person; it is even possible, on contemporary parallels, that he adopts this style as a device to add verisimilitude to his story. Certainly, on any showing, the writer of *Luke–Acts* has assimilated this source, like all others, into the total frame of his book; as we can most easily see him doing with *St Mark's Gospel* as he uses it in the making of his own.

We mention this point only to reinforce our contention that it is not possible to use *Acts* as a wholly secure basis upon which to re-

---

* For the theological and compositional motivation of the writer of *Acts*, see especially: H. J. Cadbury: *The Making of Luke-Acts*, 2nd ed. (London, 1958); J. C. O'Neill: *The Theology of Acts* (London, 1961); M. D. Goulder: *Type and History in Acts* (London, 1964); ed. E. Keck and J. L. Martyn: *Studies in Luke-Acts* (London, 1968).

construct the history of Paul's activities, even in a section like the one that deals with Philippi, where we appear to have the account of an eye-witness. It is clearly a sounder policy to interpret *Philippians* (and Paul's other epistles too) without initial reference to *Acts* or, at most, to use *Acts* only in the light of a thorough investigation of its theology and methods of composition. Considerations of caution like these apply whether *Acts* was written close to the events with which it deals or some decades later. But clearly they apply much more strongly if, as many scholars are inclined to think, *Acts* comes from the very end of the first century or the early part of the second.

When we turn to the specific case here before us, that of Paul's relations with Philippi, we find that actual discrepancies, of the kind so tantalizing and frustrating elsewhere, do not exist. The account in *Acts* (apart from the brief reference to subsequent visits in Acts 20[1–6]) deals only with Paul's first visit to Philippi. The letter belongs, probably, to the end of Paul's life. It is not surprising therefore that none of the persons mentioned in *Philippians* (Epaphroditus, Euodia, and Syntyche) occurs in *Acts*. On one point the Acts account is confirmed by the epistles; I Thess. 2[2] and Phil. 1[30] both speak of persecution endured by Paul during his stay in Philippi; and it is natural to relate these references to the incident described in Acts 16[16ff.].

But having said that, and maintaining our preference for the epistles over *Acts* as evidence for Paul's life, we cannot help noting that there are certain significant differences between the parts played by Philippi in the two sources. It is a question not so much of discrepancies between the two in matters of fact as in the total impression conveyed. The writer of *Acts* fails to show the clearly central role played by the church in Philippi in Paul's view of his mission and in his affections. Both the evidence of *Philippians* itself and of the references to that church in 2 Cor. 8[1ff.] and I Thess. 2[2] indicate that this (together with other Macedonian churches*) was the crown and chief satisfaction of Paul's whole apostolate. His letter to them breathes an assured and secure relationship based on their own Christian maturity and reliability and on their constant love and support for Paul. The same cannot be said of his relations with the churches of Galatia or with the church in Corinth. In particular, in the great

---

* Besides Philippi, the only Macedonian church centres we know of are Thessalonica and Beroea, the latter only from Acts 17[10–15], the former from the epistles addressed to it, from Phil. 4[16] and Acts 17[1–9].

symbolic project of Paul's apostolate, the collection of money in the Gentile churches for the relief of the needs of the senior church in Jerusalem, the Philippians (and their neighbours) had played an exemplary part (2 Cor. 8$^{1ff.}$). Further, in Paul's letters there are more references to the Macedonian churches (commendations of them, intentions to visit them) than of any others; they were much in his mind. And the impression given by a passage like 2 Cor. 9$^{1-5}$ is that these churches give Paul his point of reference – they form his mental base as well as, for the time being, his physical one; though it may be simply that he uses the example of the churches from which he is writing to arouse emulation in those addressed – a natural enough ruse. Whether the author of *Acts* has succeeded in giving a fair or complete picture of the actual visits paid by Paul to Philippi, at any rate down to the time of his Roman imprisonment, we cannot say. What we can say is that he has totally failed to convey the dominant role played by this church in Paul's own estimate of his mission as we see it revealed in his own words.

Finally, Paul's coming to Philippi is often hailed by commentators as his first entry into Europe, and it is not always clear whose perspective is in mind when this statement is made. To see it thus would indeed have been possible in Paul's time, but it would have been nothing like so clear as for us. Neither Paul's epistles nor *Acts* shows any consciousness of such a view. For the latter there was certainly something of a new departure at this point in Paul's mission, but it consisted in his entry into Macedonia (Acts 16^9), and the significant thing about Philippi itself was its status as a Roman colony (Acts 16^{12}). Culturally, Philippi would have seemed as much a part of the Greek world as Athens, Ephesus, or Antioch. As far as the epistles are concerned there is no indication that the importance of Philippi for Paul himself came from its being the 'first-fruits of his European mission'.

AUTHENTICITY AND INTEGRITY

The reader of *Philippians* will find it difficult to believe that its authenticity is seriously questioned. It has all the marks of a highly personal and intimate letter – warmth of feeling, sensitivity to specific needs, references to individuals; and none of the marks of the pseudonymous imitator – generalized and platitudinous doctrinal statements, absence of references to particular persons. It seems to spring straight out of a close and living relationship. Yet there are those who pronounce otherwise. What grounds have they for their assertion?

Its most reputable basis in modern scholarship is to be found in the statistical approach championed, in relation to a number of author-ship problems in New Testament literature, by A. Q. Morton. His work on the supposed writings of Paul* yields quite definite results; that only *Romans, 1 & 2 Corinthians*, and *Galatians*, and probably *Philemon* (though it is too short for testing) are the work of a single author – presumably Paul – who in *Galatians* writes clearly about himself; and that *Hebrews, Ephesians, Philippians, Colossians*, the two Thessalonian letters, and the letters to Timothy and Titus come from six distinct hands. This last statement is made more tentatively than the first which is put forward as an assured result of scholarship. The basis for it is a series of tests, chiefly concerned with sentence length and the frequency of use of common words (*and, but*, etc.), which are held to be accurate revealers of identity of authorship.

The advantage of this approach clearly lies in its objectivity, once the right tests have been decided upon. It avoids the subjective elements in assessment of style which have produced – not only in New Testa-ment scholarship – such wide diversity of judgements from com-parably competent writers. However, the new approach has not at all points dissented from the results of older methods; *Hebrews, 1 & 2 Timothy, Titus*, and *Ephesians* have long been felt to be non-pauline (in descending order of certainty), and *2 Thessalonians* and *Colossians* (cf. p. 134) have also had a number of doubters.

The present writer has no qualification to assess the technical validity of Morton's work; but clearly difficulties arise when it is set in the wider context of pauline scholarship as a whole. The findings of a single approach cannot be allowed to overthrow the sound conclusions yielded by other methods. For example, if *Philemon* is (probably) by Paul, then the last part of *Colossians* (4⁷ᶠᶠ·) is also by Paul; the circumstances referred to in the two letters clearly dovetail with one another and names coincide (e.g. Archippus and Onesimus). To take our present case, *Philippians*, there is ample evidence of close parallels of wording and thought with the undoubtedly pauline epistles;† similarities best explained by identity of authorship. These

---

* A. Q. Morton and James McLeman: *Paul, the Man and the Myth* (London, 1966).
† See C. L. Mitton: *Ephesians* (Oxford, 1951), Appx. IV and V.

similarities are scattered throughout the epistle and it is very hard to believe that a passage like Phil. 3^{9-11}, for example, so similar to Paul's teaching in *Romans* and *Galatians* (and to nothing else in the New Testament except Acts 13^{39} which significantly fails to comprehend the full sense of the pauline terms used), comes from a hand other than his.

Morton is well aware of the objection to his conclusions on the grounds that letter-writing in antiquity was often done with the aid of an amanuensis, but he is unwilling to face its force (op. cit. p. 94). We just do not know to what extent some of Paul's amanuenses – and passages like Gal. 6^{11}, 2 Thess. 3^{17}, 1 Cor. 16^{21}, make it clear that he used them – sometimes were asked to write with considerable freedom on his behalf. After all, they were probably his close associates rather than professionals hired to do a job of no special personal interest to them. It is true that there is no reference to an amanuensis in *Philippians*, but the silence is in no way conclusive. Obviously, statistical arguments cannot distinguish between the work of an amanuensis writing with a certain freedom but close to Paul, and that of a pauline imitator writing perhaps years after Paul's death.

It is worth adding that not all critics working on the statistical approach have been brought to conclusions as drastic as Morton's, and some have seriously questioned his way of using the method especially in relation to such brief works as the epistles which form the subject of this volume. (See H. H. Somers in ed. J. Leed: *The Computer and Literary Style* (Kent, Ohio, 1966). For a critical view from the standpoint of another field, see S. Schoenbaum: *Internal Evidence and Elizabethan Dramatic Authorship* (Evanston, 1966), p. 196.)

If most scholarly opinion, whether on good grounds or bad, supports the authenticity of *Philippians*, the same cannot be said of its unity. Many writers have felt that the epistle we have is made up of a number of fragments of pauline letters, no doubt all addressed to Philippi, but sent at different times and coming together into a whole later, perhaps on the occasion of the collecting of Paul's correspondence with some of his churches, towards the end of the first century (see on 3^1-4^1 p. 95ff.). Readers will find that we do not consider the grounds for a fragment-hypothesis sufficient *in this particular case*, though we accept the view of the collection of Paul's letters which makes it both possible and plausible. It is not simply the negative consideration that there is such wide disagreement about where to place the seams between the various alleged letters and parts of letters; there is also the positive fact that certain themes (like exhortation to harmony, the place of suffering in Christian life, the note of joy and confidence) run through the whole epistle. Also, as so frequently, the partition theories are bound up with elaborate reconstructions of the exact course of Paul's relations with the church he is writing to; a procedure which is speculative and goes quite beyond the small amount of evidence available to us.

Instead of outlining the issues which arise in relation to this question here in the *Introduction*, we have preferred to discuss each as it arises in the course of the commentary, so that it can be fully assessed on its merits in its full context. This seems more realistic than the mere presentation of skeleton-schemes showing the various suggestions that have been made. But in brief, two arguments in favour of a fragment-theory deserve special attention; first, the change of tone at 3^2 from eirenical calm to what can be read as violent hysteria; and secondly, the relationship between the pictures given in 2^{25-29} on the one hand and 4^{10-20} on the other concerning the events in question (Epaphroditus' arrival and subsequent illness). In neither case do we think the arguments against the integrity of the epistle decisive, but we commend them to the reader's careful consideration. Certainly the two chief candidates for separation are the passages here in question: 3^1 (or 3^2) – 4^1 and 4^{10-20}. And in any case, clearly ch. 1–2 (and possibly 3^{1a} or 3^1 in toto) makes a single piece.*

PLACE AND TIME OF WRITING

In the *General Introduction* we have looked at the concept of a distinct group of captivity epistles and found it to be of limited utility (however convenient it may be as an aid to the classification of Paul's writings). When it comes to deciding the whereabouts of Paul's imprisonment in any particular case there is complete uncertainty. There is no cast-iron evidence of Paul's prolonged incarceration anywhere except Rome, though it would be hyper-sceptical to doubt that Paul was held captive in various places in Palestine, including very probably Caesarea, before he was shipped to Italy. So much depends upon the view taken of *Acts* and, as we have shown briefly

* See B. S. Mackay: *Further Thoughts on Philippians*, N.T.S., 7, pp. 161ff.; B. D. Rahtjen: *The Three Letters of Paul to the Philippians*, N.T.S., 6, pp. 167ff.

(p.35) there are strong reasons for suspecting that its narrative is highly selective and that non-historical considerations have affected the telling of the stories which are selected. We prefer not to tie our view of Paul's activity to the data of *Acts*, not because they are likely to be misleading at all points but simply because we do not know when they are, except in a small number of cases where comparison with the epistles is possible. The clear lesson of these cases is caution in accepting *Acts* as historical *tout court*.

That Paul had been in prison earlier than the final crisis which brought him to Rome, we know from 2 Cor. 6^5, which suggests that it had happened more than once, and from 2 Cor. 11^{23}, where he says that it happened to him more than to the Jewish Christian 'false apostles', with whom he is here so indignant. Unless 1 Cor. 15^{32} is to be taken literally, we do not know from his letters where these imprisonments took place. Those who hold that *Philippians* (and the other captivity epistles) was written in Ephesus at least have this shred of support; but the beasts there referred to, with whom Paul had fought, may well be human or demonic rather than zoological enemies.

But lack of evidence does not silence the many scholars who desire to reconstruct both the course of Paul's life and the order in which his letters were written, for the most part using *Acts* as a historical basis. G. S. Duncan's theory (*St Paul's Ephesian Ministry* (London, 1929)) that Ephesus was the place of imprisonment from which the captivity epistles (except *Ephesians!*) came, depends heavily upon this method and for that reason alone fails to commend itself to the present writer. If silence seems over-cautious, then let us say that Rome still has the best chance of being right, and in this commentary we have written as if this were so. But we must examine the arguments.

It has often been held that the affinities of thought and language of *Philippians* are with the earlier writings of Paul, like *Galatians* and the Corinthian letters rather than the supposedly late *Colossians*. But of course the early dating of these epistles depends wholly upon fitting them into the order of events revealed in *Acts*, and increasingly it is recognized as open to doubt. For one thing, it separates *Galatians* (early) from *Romans* (late), two letters which are clearly in close relationship as far as their thought is concerned.* And in any case

---

* See J. C. O'Neill: *Theology of Acts* (London, 1961), p. 97; C. H. Buck: *The Date of Galatians*, J.B.L., 70, pp. 113–22.

Mitton (op. cit) has shown that *Philippians* has equally close connexions with the whole of the pauline corpus. Perhaps this in itself is evidence for the view that the letters we have all come from a quite short period towards the end of Paul's life and that the attempt to stick to the dating implied by the *Acts* sequence of events is unhelpful. For our purpose the upshot is that *Philippians* can easily belong to the last period of Paul's life, his Roman captivity, about A.D. 58–60.

Secondly, it is likely that if Paul was originally arrested in Palestine and only subsequently transferred to Rome for trial, as *Acts* describes, the charges against him were probably those referred to rather vaguely in *Acts* (21^{28}; $25^{7\text{ff.}}$); that is concerning offences against Jewish Law. But in *Philippians*, though Paul shows clear animosity towards Jews ($3^{2\text{f.}}$), he nowhere refers to such charges as responsible for his imprisonment, unless his claim to former scrupulous obedience to the Law in 3^6 is an oblique thrust in that direction. This might appear to be evidence that *Philippians* comes from an earlier imprisonment, whether at Ephesus or elsewhere. But in fact he does not refer to any accusations at all, simply to what he sees as the purpose of his imprisonment in the divine economy ('for the defence of the gospel', 1^{16}). Those accusations may have been as *Acts* suggests, though the placing of full responsibility upon the Jews for all attacks upon Christians and the exoneration of the Romans is such a powerful apologetic motive in *Acts* that we are justified in raising a doubt; they may have related rather to what the Romans themselves would have recognized as trouble-making. We cannot say; and the evidence we possess on this matter throws no light on the date of the epistle or the place of its writing.

Thirdly, the question of the supposed journeys of Epaphroditus and others is relevant to this question, and we discuss it in the commentary on 4^{10-20} (see p. 112). It emerges from that discussion that though a place of imprisonment nearer to Philippi than Rome clearly eases the situation, we certainly cannot say that Rome is impossible or even unlikely.

As we show in the commentary, the references to the praetorian guard (or praetorium) in 1^{13} and to Caesar's household in 4^{22} do not tell very strongly either for or against Rome; but on balance we consider that they are in favour. The latter reference might impress the inhabitants of a Roman colony, especially if Rome is indeed the place of writing.

The reference in 2 Cor. 1^8 to sufferings in Asia (presumably Ephesus) is not relevant; there is no reference there to imprisonment and Paul endured sufferings of many other kinds, as we know from his own lists of them in 2 Cor. $6^{4f.}$ and $11^{23f.}$.

On the evidence of Acts $23^{33}-26^{32}$, the other good candidate for Paul's imprisonment, and so for the place of writing of *Philippians*, is Caesarea. But there are no arguments for this hypothesis that do not equally apply to Rome and it remains just an interesting suggestion, without anything very positive or distinctive to commend it. Its chief virtue is to help to demonstrate that the traditional favouring of Rome is by no means the only possibility.

So far as it goes, the evidence of Acts $28^{30f.}$ accords with that of *Philippians* that Paul enjoyed a relaxed régime in Rome (*custodia libra*), receiving visitors and corresponding freely. But we do not know that this did not happen elsewhere too.

CONTENTS OF THE EPISTLE

This epistle is so short that the best way to get an impression of its subject-matter is simply to read it through quickly, preferably in one of the current translations into modern English (e.g. the Jerusalem Bible or N.E.B.). But the reader may be helped if we provide a few pointers to its chief features.

The circumstances in which the letter was written colour strongly the first two chapters and 4^{10-20} in two respects. First, there is the fact that Paul is in custody. In 1^{3-18} and $2^{17f.}$ he considers the implications of this for his apostolate, both for its prospects and for its significance. Even if it were to lead to martyrdom, what is happening to Paul conforms gloriously to the pattern of Christ's sufferings ($1^{21, 29f.}$; cf. $3^{10f.}$) and has led to the effective spreading of the gospel ($1^{12-14, 18}$). Secondly, there is the making of plans for the future (1^{26}; 2^{19-30}). Consideration of these entails references both to the recent relations of Paul with the Philippian church, i.e. the receiving of their gift at the hands of Epaphroditus (2^{25-30}; $4^{10, 17f.}$), and to their kindness to Paul in the more distant past ($4^{15f.}$) as well as to Paul's sufferings when he was with them (1^{30}).

Interwoven with these passages about Paul's circumstances there is much in the letter by way of exhortation to the church in Philippi to preserve harmony and avoid dissension ($1^{27}-2^{18}$; $4^{2f.}$). The theological basis for this exhortation is the same as that which determines Paul's attitude to his own present predicament, the obedient suffering of Christ crowned by his triumph (1^{29}; 2^{5-11}); only in Paul's case it is more obviously the *fact* of Christ's suffering which is operative (1^{21}; $3^{10f.}$), in theirs the humble obedience which characterized his whole coming to the world as well as his death (2^{6-8}; but see 1^{29}). These two factors meet in the life *in Christ* which he and they share (1^{21}; 2^5; $3^{8f.}$).

But internal jealousies and bickerings are not the only threat to the peace and strength which are the most notable features of the congregation we glimpse in this letter. The other matter to which Paul draws their urgent attention is an external threat – from Jews who challenge their faith. From them Paul differs radically and uncompromisingly (3^{2-8}, $^{18f.}$). In reply to them, or rather in giving material for the Philippians to use in answering them, Paul adopts two positive lines of argument which for him are entirely fused with one another. First, he shows that man's supreme need, righteousness with God, is not to be achieved along the lines of Judaism (by being a Jew, devoted to the Law) but only by faith in Christ (3^{3-9}). And secondly, he knows that on this basis alone can man seek the consummation which is designed for him and which is open to him, the resurrection from the dead to God's eternal life (3^{10-16}, $2^{0f.}$; cf. 1^{20-23}).

Some commentators, notably Lohmeyer, think that the whole letter is addressed to a church which is undergoing persecution; but while 1^{29} and perhaps one or two other statements give some ground for this, to make a thoroughgoing interpretation along these lines means going well beyond the clear evidence.

Further Reading

We refer in the course of the commentary at the appropriate places to books and articles for further reading. Sometimes these amplify our own discussion, sometimes they are authorities for our statements. We do not propose to give here a comprehensive list of the works to which we have referred but rather to give aids for the discriminating use of a few of them.

The old, standard commentary on *Philippians* in English is that by Bishop J. B. Lightfoot, which was originally published as part of a series of commentaries on the Epistles of Paul in 1868. This remains a full and useful commentary. Its fame, however, has largely come from a dissertation on 'The Christian Ministry' which follows the commentary itself. This has played a major part in subsequent discussions on the nature and theological significance of the early Christian ministry (for which one tantalizing piece of evidence is Phil. 1[1]).

Recent commentaries available in English include Karl Barth's (London, 1962) which was first published in 1947, F. W. Beare's (London, 1959) and G. B. Caird's (Oxford, 1976). The first is not very full from the point of view of the reader requiring detailed explanation but is full of brilliant shafts of wisdom, some of them theologically provocative even if exegetically eccentric. It deals only briefly with the later sections of *Philippians*. The second commentary is full in every way and contains a thorough introduction. The last is excellent, lucid and concise.

Behind all modern commentaries there lies the fundamental work of E. Lohmeyer, both in his commentary (the 8th edition of the *Meyerkommentar*, published in 1930) and in his *Kyrios Jesus* (*Sitzungsberichte der Heidelberger Akademie der Wissenschaften* (1928)), neither of which has been translated. The most recent edition of the Lohmeyer commentary, which is extremely detailed, is that of 1964. It carries with it a supplement by W. Schmauch noting more recent literature. The fact that its main standpoint (that persecution and the idea of martyrdom dominate both Paul's mind and the situations of himself and the Philippian church) and its adoption of Caesarea as the place of writing are not generally accepted does not invalidate its usefulness. The latter work revolutionized the interpretation of Phil. 2[5-11] – the christological hymn – showing its separateness, its Hellenistic character, and its poetic structure (see ad loc.).

For the study of this crucial passage, R. P. Martin, *Carmen Christi* (Cambridge, 1967) is indispensable. It is an exhaustive and lucid survey of all the main scholarly discussions which have taken place on this subject and easily avoids being a mere catalogue of critics' names and opinions. Also valuable, especially on background, is Jack T. Sanders, *The New Testament Christological Hymns* (Cambridge, 1971).

On most of the questions to which the study of this epistle gives rise the discussion proceeds mostly in the learned periodicals. Recent numbers of *New Testament Studies* (Cambridge) contain numerous important articles on *Philippians* and we refer to them in the appropriate places in the commentary or in the introduction.

The Letter of Paul to the Philippians

¹ *Paul and Timothy, servants*ᵃ *of Christ Jesus, to all the saints in Christ Jesus who are at Philippi, with the bishops*ᵇ *and deacons:* ²*grace to you and peace from God our Father and the Lord Jesus Christ.*

        a Or *slaves.*   *b* Or *overseers.*

Paul opens all his letters with what appears at first sight to be an inconsequential variant of the formulae usual in letter-writing at the time.*

This is true of the general form; the naming of the writer, then of those addressed, and finally the expression of greeting. But even in these verses, which are much less elaborate than many of the greetings at the head of pauline letters, he embroiders the conventional shape with specifically Christian features. Paul has a great sense of the detailed significance of words and nowhere is this more apparent than in formulae of this kind, which most men would be content to dash off in the standard way without much ado. Even here Paul incorporates words which have ramifications stretching to the very heart of his theology.

For example, he and Timothy, his associate, are *servants* (better 'slaves') *of Christ Jesus.* They write, not because of any standing they possess in themselves nor by virtue of any office they hold in the Church, but on the authority of their absolute possession by their Master. It is a favourite idea of Paul's, one whose possibilities he frequently explores; see Rom. 6¹⁶⁻²³ and 1 Cor. 7²²ᶠ·. It appears in the heading of a letter only here and in *Romans.* Perhaps it looks ahead to 2⁷; the status of a slave is something he shares with the earthly Jesus, who now exalted and worshipped inspires this imitation on the part of his followers. The use of this image to describe the situation of Christians in general (as in *Romans* and *1 Corin-*

* For examples of ordinary letters of the period see G. Milligan, *Greek Papyri* (Cambridge, 1910). Typical openings are '*Hilarion to Alis his sister, heartiest greeting, and to my dear Berous and Apollonarion*' (p. 32) and '*Sarapion to our Heracleides, greeting*' (p. 39).

thians) probably means that here Paul does not use it to distinguish people like Timothy and himself who are engaged in the apostolic work. He may in fact be deliberately refraining from using any special title. However, there is some evidence for the opposite view; the use of the word in the openings of the *Epistles of James, Jude* and in *Titus* and *2 Peter* suggests that at any rate by the (later) time they were written it had acquired some degree of technical flavour. Even in Paul himself this way of using the word is not ruled out; in Col. 4^{12}, he seems to be singling out Epaphras to bear the title, 'slave of Christ', and this may imply its particular application to those actively employed in Christian work. Such a view is further supported if Paul is consciously recalling the application of the term 'servant of the Lord' in the Old Testament to great heroes, e.g. Josh. 24^{29}; 1 Sam. 3^{9}.

Whatever the truth of this, it is certainly the case that it is only in this letter, in *Philemon*, and in the two letters to the Thessalonians that Paul does *not* use the much more definitely technical title, which asserts and authenticates his own special function – 'apostle'. Perhaps in these cases Paul feels no need to include a reminder of his authority over his converts. They are among the best-known and most loyal of the fruits of his work. Nevertheless the fact that he does not formally state his title, in accordance with his usual custom, implies no weakening of the note of pastoral authority as he approaches the congregation in Philippi.

The Christians at Philippi are characterized by another of Paul's favourite terms for describing the Christian status; they are *saints in Christ Jesus*. The term translated *saints, hagioi,* is one of the Greek words for 'holy', but as used by Paul its meaning is influenced by the use of a comparable Hebrew word in the Old Testament, and the reference is not only, or even primarily, to moral goodness, but to the status of Christians as people chosen by God for special relationship with himself (cf. Col. 3^{12}; Rom. 1^{7}; 1 Cor. 1^{2}; 2 Cor. 1^{1}; 2 Thess. 1^{10}). In the Old Testament the Jews are described as 'holy' in this sense, especially in the period in the wilderness after the Exodus from Egypt, when God was thought to have chosen them as his own people (cf. the important verse Exod. 19^{6}, which was much used in the early Church, e.g. 1 Pet. 2^{9}; Rev. 1^{6}; also Deut. 7^{6}; 14^{2}).

As well as denoting relationship with God the word comes to imply the moral goodness which is to characterize that relationship (cf. Lev. 19^{2}; Isa. 6$^{3, 7}$); and with reference to the end of the world and

God's judgement it designates those who, having been faithful in persecution, will be admitted into the Kingdom and to a permanent share in God's glory (cf. Dan. 7$^{18, 22}$ and 1 Cor. 6^2 where Paul sees the Church as the true Israel which will receive the fulfilment of the promise in the *Daniel* passage).

If Paul has refrained from mentioning his own God-given office, he does now make a special and unique* reference to the officers of a congregation – *bishops and deacons* (*episkopoi kai diakonoi*), mentioned perhaps because they had organized the sending of money to him. The difficulty is to know how these terms should be understood. In ordinary Greek usage they would have meant something like 'overseers and attendants', and some scholars adopt some such translation here, doubting whether the words have any very specific meaning or any theological overtones. The early Christian communities, they suggest, are bound to have had some basic organization and officers of some kind, like any other comparable group, but nothing more than that should be read into this passage (see e.g. Beare, p. 50).

However, we know that within fifty years or so of Paul's day the terms found here were widely used by the Christian communities to describe their leaders, and profound theological significance was attached to them. For example, from *circa* A.D. 96 there is the statement in 1 Clement 42 (E.C.W., p. 45) to the effect that the apostles

appointed their first converts ... to be bishops and deacons for the believers of the future. This was in no way an innovation, for bishops and deacons had already been spoken of in scripture long before that; there is a text that says, 'I will confirm their bishops in righteousness and their deacons in faith'

(citing Isa. 60^{17} in its Greek form, but inaccurately so as to make the point better!). Cf. also the letters of Ignatius, Bishop of Antioch, writing a decade or two later: e.g. Trallians 3^1 (L.C.C., I, p. 99):

Everyone must show the deacons respect. They represent Jesus Christ, just as the bishop has the role of the Father.

In favour of the view that these terms had already begun to have at least a semi-technical force and perhaps some theological overtones in Paul's day, we may notice that the Qumran sect, as seen in the Dead Sea Scrolls, possibly provided a model for some aspects of early

---

* But see 1 Cor. 12^{28} (*helpers, administrators*) for a likely parallel, using different terms.

Christian organization (see Bo Reicke in ch. 10 of *The Scrolls and the New Testament*, ed. K. Stendahl (London, 1958)). Though admittedly church officials were not important enough for Paul to make special mention of them in the opening greeting in any of his other letters, we ought to allow for Paul's common tendency to give theological content to ordinary secular words and so to integrate them into a network of Christian vocabulary. That is to say, it is possible that the titles of these officers already bore the flavour of those aspects of the activity of God or of Jesus with which they were most naturally associated.

It is just possible that we ought to translate this phrase 'bishops-cum-deacons', i.e. rulers-who-serve. This would be wholly typical of Paul's conception of office in the Church, for example his own apostolic role (e.g. 2 Cor. 11³⁰; 12⁹), and it would accord with his description of himself here as a servant of Christ Jesus. It is of course closely related to the tradition of the teaching of Jesus (Luke 22²⁴⁻²⁷; John 13¹²⁻¹⁷).

Paul sends to his friends not the conventional Greek 'greeting' but the more Jewish *grace and peace* (see note below), both words of the utmost richness in his vocabulary. Together the words betoken the all-embracing and ultimate love and well-being with which God desires to surround man. They amount to an assurance that the Old Testament dream for the future is coming true (cf. passages like Isa. 2²⁻⁴; 11¹⁻⁹); the ground for this assurance being *Jesus Christ*, through whose life, death, and exaltation the new frame of existence has been set up. From him flow a community and an experience in which Paul and those to whom he writes alike participate. Notice that even in these opening verses Paul shows his persistent consciousness of this fact by reiterating at every turn the name of Jesus: the sole ground, setting, and object of the Christian existence within which Paul thinks and writes. But (as we shall see in 2⁶⁻¹¹), Jesus Christ is not only the one who *has* assured the grace and peace of God; he is also the one who *now* bestows God's gifts and mediates his relationship to his people. This present status and action of Christ are conveyed by the title *Lord* (*kyrios*).

৯৯

1

Christ Jesus: twice in this order; once, in v. 2, in the reverse order. It is not clear whether in a passage like this the order is of any significance.

In a letter addressed to what was probably a largely Gentile church it is probable that Paul would not make much deliberate play with the Jewish significance of Christos (= Messiah). In such a setting what was originally name-plus-title (Jesus Christ) becomes more and more a double name.

Timothy: appears from Paul's epistles as his most prominent associate. He is mentioned thirteen times, is in the heading of six letters, was important enough to be made the addressee of two pseudonymously pauline letters and to appear in the *Letter to the Hebrews*. He is by no means as prominent in the account of Paul's work in *Acts* as his place in the letters would lead us to expect. The mention of his name in the heading of a letter should not be taken to imply a share in its composition; in 2$^{19ff.}$ Timothy is spoken of in the third person. Rather, it demonstrates how intimately Paul links his associates with himself in his dealings with his churches. According to *Acts*, Timothy would be known to the Philippians from earliest days, cf. Acts 16$^{1ff.}$; 17^{14}; 19^{22}.

2

grace and peace: Paul uses these words in a thoroughly Christian manner, but the *form* of his greeting has interesting features. *Grace* (= *charis*) is a noun related to the verb *chairein*, which is used in this infinitive form in the standard Hellenistic epistolary address: 'A to B, greeting'. *Peace* is the standard Jewish and oriental greeting, e.g. Ezra 4^{17}. A greeting in double form has Jewish parallels, e.g. the contemporary 2 Baruch 78^2,* '*mercy and peace*' – a form used in reverse order by Paul in Gal. 6^{16}; cf. also 1 Pet. 1^2; 2 Pet. 1^2; Rev. 1^4; and for the Greek form, Jas. 1^1.

^{3}*I thank my God in all my remembrance of you,* ^{4}*always in every prayer of mine for you all making my prayer with joy,* ^{5}*thankful for your partnership in the gospel from the first day until now.* ^{6}*And I am sure that he who began a good work in you will bring it to completion at the day of Jesus Christ.* ^{7}*It is right for me to feel thus about you all, because I hold you in my heart, for you are all partakers with me of grace, both in my imprisonment and in the defence and confirmation of the gospel.* ^{8}*For God is my witness, how I yearn for you all with the affection of Christ Jesus.* ^{9}*And it is my prayer that your love may abound more and more, with knowledge and all discernment,*

* Charles, II, p. 521.

¹⁰*so that you may approve what is excellent, and may be pure and blameless for the day of Christ,* ¹¹*filled with the fruits of righteousness which come through Jesus Christ, to the glory and praise of God.*

The form of this passage again invites comparison with letter-writing conventions of the time, but here in the thanksgiving section it is less clear than in the opening greeting. The case for conscious use of an ordinary Hellenistic pattern (though it is admitted that Paul has here, as in the greetings, developed and enriched the customary forms of words) is cogently argued by Paul Schubert (*The Form and Function of the Pauline Thanksgivings*, Z.N.T.W., Beiheft XX (Berlin, 1939)). His survey of surviving parallels, most of them somewhat later than Paul, gives evidence that in serious and formal letters between people sharing a religious viewpoint an opening paragraph expressing thanks to the gods (or a particular deity) for some blessing related to the letter's subject, and going on to intercession, often simply for the good health of the person concerned, was common form. Paul's elaboration of the customary bare formalities is so great as to suggest the influence of other factors besides or instead of this one. A background in the piety and liturgy of Judaism is a clear possibility, especially when in two of the letters (*2 Corinthians* and *Ephesians*) we find the more obviously Jewish formula: 'Blessed be the God and Father of Our Lord Jesus Christ, who ...', cf. also I Peter 1³ff.. It is a striking fact that Paul begins every one of his letters with some variant of this pattern, except *Galatians*, where either he is too agitated to refrain from coming straight to his main point or, if Schubert is right, his relations with these Christians have been so damaged by their conduct that the common Christian mind, which the use of this formula presupposes, is no longer present.

The sonority and formality of these opening paragraphs may help to indicate the level at which Paul meant his letters to be taken. Their preservation, collection, and eventual canonization was doubtless far from his mind, but we may have here an indication that he wrote them intending more than purely ephemeral use.

The paragraph has three distinct themes which flow easily into one another; vv. 3–6 express thanks to God for the present state of the Philippian church; vv. 7–8 concern themselves with Paul's situation; vv. 9–11 are his prayer for the continued excellence of this congre-

gation. The whole is imbued with Paul's deep serenity and content-
ment as he contemplates this fruit of his apostolic work. In this letter
the tone is more consistently maintained than in others, though even
here Paul will later have admonitions to issue and complaints to make.
Some have been puzzled by this contrast between confident joy and
criticism, but it is a common feature of Paul's letters. In all cases,
including those (e.g. Corinth) where there was far more cause for
anxiety than at Philippi, the initial paragraph of thanksgiving, if read
alone, would give the impression that all was well. It might seem to
be a case of mere civility on Paul's part to start with pleasing remarks,
and he has even been accused of ingratiating flattery. It would be a
less superficial judgement to see here a practical example of that love
which is for him the crown and sum of Christian character, grounded
in the objective gift of God to his people and that relationship into
which through Christ he has brought them; Paul's thanksgivings are
the solemn expression of this fundamental theological conviction.
Far from his criticisms and complaints being evidence of a hectoring
and domineering attitude, they should be put firmly within the
setting of these expressions of confidence and hope. He is simply
recalling his converts to the way of life which their Christian faith
demands of them.

In no other letter does the corresponding passage show such an
intimate fusion of apostolic pronouncement and reference to Paul's
own personal situation – a further indication of his particularly close
and affectionate relationship with this church. Not that his role and
his personal affairs can ever be rigidly distinguished from one another.
Here his imprisonment and trial, far from being a source of frustrated
irritation to him, are a matter of *grace*, a privilege received. They are
wholly integrated into his purpose as an apostle, because they accord
thoroughly with the shape of a Gospel which has Christ's suffering at
its heart.

Lohmeyer saw the reference in v. 7 to the Philippians' being
partakers with Paul in the honour of undergoing his present trials as
an important piece of evidence for his thesis that the Philippian church
was at this time undergoing persecution and that Paul writes with the
specific aim of instructing and encouraging them in their crisis. There
is ample evidence in this letter of verbal opposition in Philippi (ch. 3),
much more of strong vitality in the church, so that for this reason,
as well as on general historical grounds, the existence of formal

persecution seems most unlikely. Paul's language in v. 7 is simply one example among many of the implications of that common life 'in Christ' which he sees with such vivid realism (cf. 2 Cor. 11^{29}; and Phil. 4^{14} where the tangible sign of their sharing in his sufferings is simply the money which they send to him).

The important MS., Codex Bezae (D), has an emphatic 'I' at the beginning of v. 3, yielding the sense: 'I for my part thank . . .'. Karl Barth (*The Epistle to the Philippians* (London, 1962), p. 13) took this as original, so that Paul is deliberately rebutting the Philippians' expressed anxiety about his situation: *his* attitude is quite the contrary, and the Gospel which enables him to look on his troubles as *grace* gives the explanation – though this does not prevent him saying how much he hopes to be released and able to visit them again. There is no unnatural striking of pious attitudes! This form of text has a vivid, spontaneous ring, but the MS. evidence against its being original is very strong.

Paul's prayer in vv. 9–11 is for the full growth of the love which this congregation has already displayed so conspicuously. He delicately notes those points where he sees room for improvement. It amounts to a need for greater maturity and balance in discriminating among the ideas presented to them and the pressures put upon them. He does not go into detail here, but in 3$^{2ff.}$ we see what is probably in his mind.

The goal is nothing less than their moral perfection, that they *may be pure and blameless*. It is worth noting the variety of causes which in their different modes of operation will bring about this object. Looked at in terms of the virtue which is to be displayed, their lives are to be characterized by *love*, the quality which epitomizes the Christian character (cf. Rom. 13$^{8-10}$ and 1 Cor. 13^{13}). It is the moral correlative of that relationship with God which itself gives rise to it in the believer. Looked at from the side of this fundamental relationship, Paul sees their ultimate perfection as *the fruits of righteousness*. The word *righteousness* signifies not so much moral rectitude as the 'right relationship' with God which he has established *through Jesus Christ*. Here we have the personal cause through whom their lives have been established in the way of perfection, from whom all their goodness derives. The *fruit* is not self-generated, not a result of private striving for moral improvement; it is a direct result of the relationship established with Christ and depends wholly upon him. This removes all

flavour of an upward struggle to conform to rigorous and impersonal
demands, and gives instead the quality of willing response to the
person of Jesus with whom the relationship has been formed.

The moral perfection is not an end; in two ways it looks to
an objective beyond itself. In the first place, Paul looks to the fulfilment of this hope in future events, within the terms of the historical
expectations natural to him as a Jew. *The day of Christ* (vv. 6 and 10)
refers to this; it is the time when Jesus will return in full and open
possession of Messianic power to round off the world order, judge
mankind, and recognize and receive his people. A reference to this
ultimate hope is another normal feature of the opening paragraphs
of Paul's letters. (Cf. 1 Cor. 1⁷; 2 Cor. 1¹⁰; Col. 1⁵; 1 Thess. 1¹⁰;
2 Thess. 1⁴ff.)

In the second place, the moral perfection of the believer looks towards God. The object is his *glory and praise*; that is, crudely put,
the believer desires to become a credit to God, one in whom God is
reflected (cf. 2 Cor. 4⁶) simply because God's 'godness' is his sole
concern and delight.

In effect, this introduction, with its reference to past, present, and
future, gives a solemn conspectus of the Christian dispensation, expressed in the quasi-liturgical form of gratitude to God for blessings
received and prayerful hope for both the immediate and ultimate
future.

తిం

3
my God: this is a specially solemn formula, with a background in the
piety of the psalms (e.g. 22¹; 63¹), cf. Rom. 1⁸; 1 Cor. 1⁴; Philem. 4.

in all my remembrance of you: the Greek (lit. 'in all the remembrance of
you') is not entirely unambiguous – the remembering may be on
Paul's part (so R.S.V. and most commentators) or on theirs, in which
case it is perhaps a gentle reference to the money which the Philippians
have sent.

5
in the gospel: lit. 'into, for the purpose of, the gospel': it is not a reference to their sharing in the mere acceptance of the preaching of Paul
but rather to their active participation in its furtherance.

the first day: i.e. the beginning of Paul's mission to Philippi, of which
an account is given in Acts 16¹²ff.

7

in my imprisonment and in the defence and confirmation of the gospel: his *defence* (*apologia*) is the technical term for his actual appearance in court which he expects shortly. The fact that he can tie this word with the phrase which follows shows how he regards his trial. The Roman authorities' way of phrasing his charge sheet would no doubt be very different from his. His trial will be a means of establishing the gospel; perhaps because he is confident of an acquittal which will strengthen the Church's position in relation to both the government and the Jews who according to *Acts* originally stirred up trouble for him; perhaps because he hopes to make converts by his testimony in court (cf. Acts 26[29]).

8

affection: lit. 'entrails'; but seen as the seat of the emotions, especially deeply felt loving sympathy. Thus 'heart' makes a suitable equivalent in English idiom, as indeed it did in the Greek of Paul's day. His word here probably depends upon the Jewish usage.

9

knowledge and all discernment: *epignōsis* and *aisthēsis* denote intellectual and moral insight respectively. As in 4[8] Paul may owe something to contemporary discussion about morals, inspired by the currently popular Stoic philosophy. In the case of *aisthēsis* in particular, the background is distinctly pagan rather than biblical.

10

approve what is excellent: or, in paraphrase, 'test and so come to approve the things that really matter'. *Dokimazo* is a favourite pauline word and in this sense he almost has a monopoly of its use in the New Testament (but see 1 John 4[1]). Compare especially Rom. 2[18]; the Jew thinks that in the Law he has a basis for learning true discrimination; Paul knows that the true basis lies in the love whose ultimate source is God (cf. Rom. 5[5]). *ta diapheronta*: lit. 'things which differ', but commonly for things distinguished by their worth or advantage to oneself.

11

fruits: (Gk singular) cf. Gal. 5[22] where the moral life of the Christian is again referred to by this image. There, however, though love comes first, other qualities are also mentioned. And the source of the fruit is the Spirit – the indwelling power of God which perpetuates the relationship God has formed with the Christian. Here that relationship is expressed in the term *righteousness*, which really belongs within the framework of Paul's common forensic metaphor – it is the condition of acquittal which God graciously gives through Christ. In both cases the reference is to the foundation upon which the moral life of the Christian is built. Alternatively: *the fruits* consist of *righteousness* (in an ethical sense).

glory and praise of God: i.e. given *to* not *by* God.

¹²*I want you to know, brethren, that what has happened to me has really served to advance the gospel,* ¹³*so that it has become known throughout the whole praetorian guard*^c *and to all the rest that my imprisonment is for Christ;* ¹⁴*and most of the brethren have been made confident in the Lord because of my imprisonment, and are much more bold to speak the word of God without fear.*

¹⁵*Some indeed preach Christ from envy and rivalry, but others from good will.* ¹⁶*The latter do it out of love, knowing that I am put here for the defence of the gospel;* ¹⁷*the former proclaim Christ out of partisanship, not sincerely but thinking to afflict me in my imprisonment.* ¹⁸*What then? Only that in every way, whether in pretence or in truth, Christ is proclaimed; and in that I rejoice.*

c Greek *in the whole praetorium.*

The solemn opening of his letter being now complete, Paul with abrupt change of tone turns to the substance of what he wishes to say to the Philippian Christians. In no other letter does he say so much about his own situation. It is clear that at this particular moment what is uppermost in his mind is his imprisonment, which he has already alluded to briefly in v. 7. But though this is his great concern he does not see it as an occasion for self-pity or anxiety, rather in its relation to the pushing forward of the Gospel. So natural to him was this way of regarding his situation that even in the brief reference to it in his formal introduction (v. 7) he cannot refrain from seeing it in this light. He is now quite explicit that his imprisonment is purely and simply a most powerful means of evangelism. To that fact all other considerations are wholly subordinate – both any suffering which he himself endures (this is simply ignored) and even the doubtful motives of some of those who are stimulated by his presence and situation to make Christ known.

The precise nature and cause of these doubtful motives are quite inaccessible to us. Presumably, though they refer to tensions within the church in Rome, Paul could assume that his audience would understand without more explanation. Most obviously (v. 15) it is a question of jealousy of Paul's startling success, perhaps on the part of the established leaders of the Roman church.

The section is dominated by a sense of evangelistic strategy, and in terms of that, Paul is triumphant. In getting himself put in prison, and in Rome above all, he has acted the Trojan horse, entering into the very heart of the Gentile world to which Christ had despatched him as apostle.

What Paul's achievement in altering the minds of *the whole praetorian guard* (see below) *and all the rest* (presumably, legal officials with whom he has come into contact) really amounted to is not easy to decide. It might be the case that he has won some kind of religious understanding if not conversion among these people. But if that were so he might well have had more confidence in obtaining a favourable judgement at his trial. Some have suggested that the new boldness (v. 14) of the Roman church resulted from just such an expectation, but this is unlikely; he would scarcely compliment them on their courage if all danger was about to be removed. It is more probable that we have a situation which looks rather different to the two sides sharing in it, and indeed the words of v. 13, taken strictly, demand no more than this. The lawyers and soldiers have come to see that his imprisonment is for reasons connected with his being a Christian (lit. 'in Christ'); that is, it has no political overtones and Paul is entirely harmless. And no doubt personal acquaintance has made it obvious that Paul is no criminal type but a man of deep and sincere religious conviction. There is no hint that any of the great matters later to trouble Christians in relation to the Empire, such as their attitude to the official cults, had yet even begun to be raised; it is likely that nobody of any great consequence in the legal machine had taken much notice of Paul's case. If this is so it confirms the impression given by *Acts* (e.g. 18^{15}; 26$^{31f.}$ – though the author no doubt has an axe to grind in these passages) that the matter was seen as the fruit of some kind of intra-Jewish dispute.

But if to those around Paul the realization that his *imprisonment is*

for Christ was simply a correction of their former impression that
his imprisonment was for sedition or some other criminal cause, Paul
himself clearly sees the matter in a quite different light, as v. 12 in
particular shows. Whether Paul's enthusiasm has led him to read
more into their perhaps more friendly attitude towards him than the
facts warrant, or whether he simply rejoices in the undeniable fact
that a mouthpiece of the gospel has successfully infiltrated to an inner
sanctum of the Empire itself, it is impossible to say, but the apostle
of the Gentiles might well record such an event with joyful satisfaction.
If this is the right explanation then no doubt in v. 13 Paul writes in
the character of the prophet who presents his message 'whether they
hear or whether they forbear'; he is not at all content to convince
those with whom he has contact that as 'in Christ' he is politically and
criminally harmless, but rather positively proclaims Christ (v. 18).
No doubt he met with varied reactions – probably much incomprehension and even hostility; this he does not tell us, and certainly
he mentions no conversions (unless 4²² overlaps with the groups
mentioned here). Enough that what he stands for, what he *is*, is truly
known, the witness made. His whole life in prison is like a great
speech of defence for the gospel which is on trial before the world.

ಬಬ

12
really: lit. 'more' or 'rather', probably with the twin sense that Paul's
fate has been advantageous rather than the reverse (as might have been
expected) for the advancement of the gospel, and that it has led to
greater growth than ever before.

13
become known . . . that my imprisonment is for Christ: lit. 'so that my bonds
became clear in Christ'. Lohmeyer translates boldly 'my bonds have
become a revelation in Christ'. N.E.B. has 'My imprisonment in
Christ's cause has become common knowledge'. Apart from the shape
of the clause, which R.S.V. turns out of its literal Greek order, the point
of interest is the meaning of *phaneros*. This adjective and its cognate
verb occur frequently in Paul in the sense of revelation by God, and
the word 'manifest' provides a not unsuitable translation with similar
religious overtones (e.g. Rom. 1¹⁹; 3²¹; 1 Cor. 4⁵). On the other hand,
though (e.g.) in 1 Cor. 3¹³ the *context* is theological, the word itself is
not concerned with the theological idea of the revelation of God; and
in 1 Cor. 11¹⁹ and 14²⁵ (where the phrase is the same as in our passage)
it would be wholly out of place to use 'revelation'. It would be quite

possible for Paul to say that his imprisonment was a 'revelation in Christ' (cf. I²¹) but it seems unlikely that his meaning is so strong.

the whole praetorian guard: lit. 'in the whole praetorium'. Unless we accept the possibility that Paul used this technical word loosely its interpretation is closely linked with the view taken of the place of writing. Like many military words, the Latin *praetorium* (originally, the general's tent in the camp) was simply transliterated into the common Greek of the Empire, and as Roman headquarters became more permanent and less military in character, so the word came to be used for any administrative building, especially the official residence of a provincial governor. For those who believe that the letter was written from Ephesus (e.g. Duncan) or Caesarea (Lohmeyer), the word has this accurate and well-attested sense. In the former case it refers to the headquarters of the proconsul of Asia, in the latter that of the procurator of Judea (cf. Acts 23³⁵). But if the letter was written in Rome, then either Paul uses the word loosely or he uses it for the barracks of the praetorian guard (*castra praetoriana*), or, in the very common sense, to refer to the soldiers themselves. Lightfoot argued for this view in a full note (op. cit. p. 99ff.) and R.S.V. adopts it.

14

in the lord: better taken with *brethren* rather than *confident.*

are ... bold ... without fear: Paul writes the two words concerned side by side. Courage in speaking the word was a virtue much admired in the Church's first years, and that Paul's imprisonment has been the occasion of its notable display shows that many of the Christians in Rome have seen the matter with the eyes of Paul.

of God: an early papyrus (P46) omits these words, and variety in their position in some other MSS. suggests that they were not in the original.

17

afflict: either by the pain caused through knowing their impure motives or by actual difficulties caused for him by the fact of their activity (e.g. objections on the part of the Roman authorities). It is almost certainly the former; he is pained (as for example in *1 Corinthians*) by their schismatic spirit, upsetting the fellowship of the Church.

I¹⁹⁻²⁶   PAUL FACES HIS SITUATION

¹⁹*Yes, and I shall rejoice. For I know that through your prayers and the help of the Spirit of Jesus Christ, this will turn out for my deliverance,*

²⁰*as it is my eager expectation and hope that I shall not be at all ashamed,
but that with full courage now as always Christ will be honoured in my
body, whether by life or by death.* ²¹*For to me to live is Christ, and to die is
gain.* ²²*If it is to be life in the flesh, that means fruitful labour for me. Yet
which I shall choose I cannot tell.* ²³*I am hard pressed between the two. My
desire is to depart and be with Christ, for that is far better.* ²⁴*But to remain in
the flesh is more necessary on your account.* ²⁵*Convinced of this, I know that
I shall remain and continue with you all, for your progress and joy in the
faith,* ²⁶*so that in me you may have ample cause to glory in Christ Jesus,
because of my coming to you again.*

Just as the fact that *Christ is proclaimed* entirely outweighs the confusion of motives from which it is done, so the fact of his life in Christ
entirely outweighs the confusion in Paul's own desires and his uncertainty about the future which confronts him. The primacy of
Christ, whether in overruling the sins of his followers or, more intimately, in filling Paul's horizon, is the link between this section and
the last. That is why he rejoices, despite the two kinds of confusion.

In his frank exposure of his most personal mental conflict, it seems
that he turned, at least momentarily, to the parallel between Job and
himself. Both were isolated under a shower of attacks; both firmly
assured of ultimate vindication of their cause by God. The quotation
from Job 13¹⁶ (*this will turn out for my deliverance*) is the first of a series
of statements which express Paul's unshakeable confidence that Christ
will burst through the apparent shackles of his circumstances –
whatever they turn out to be – and *will be honoured* in him. The uncertainty whether he is about to die (presumably as a result of an
adverse judgement in his trial, though how this accords with the
implication of v. 13 that he was now recognized as criminally harmless
is beyond our sight) drives him to a conflict of desires – between
death as that which will take him to Christ, and his concern for his
converts who need him and whom he wishes to see again.

Faced with these alternatives in this stark form, Paul has implicitly
expressed a view of Christian death whose accent is not wholly in
tune with that of passages written at a greater distance from the event
itself. For the effect of a number of pauline passages is to diminish
both the importance of death and a man's natural concern about what
lies in store for him on the far side of it: cf. Rom. 6⁷⁻¹¹ and Col. 3³,
which see the 'death' of the Christian as a past event, identified with

baptism (Rom. 6$^{1ff.}$ and Col. 2^{12}), and emphasize his present existence in the risen life of Christ; also Rom. 8^{38} where (physical) death appears as only one in a list of the Christian's impotent enemies. As a result of such attitudes, death and future life cease to be objects of anxious speculation.

But our present passage is not the only one where he places more emphasis on the significance of what is still to come rather than on what the Christian has already received. For example, 1 Cor. 15 is largely concerned with a series of questions about death, in face of which the Christian's present assurance is seen less in terms of an already-granted participation in Christ's risen life than as a guarantee for the future grounded on the fact of Christ's resurrection – what has happened to Christ *will* happen to him (1 Cor. 15^{22}). And even in the different emphasis of Rom. 6, the future element appears clearly in v. 8. Death remains as a real, even if the last, enemy (1 Cor. 15^{26}). 1 Cor. 15 might well be found useful for showing at greater length what is in Paul's mind as he writes our present passage, with its much more urgent tones. The divergence of these passages from the others, where what has already happened is uppermost, is easily exaggerated into inconsistency. Both emphases equally depend upon the overarching conviction of life in Christ, which is stated with as present a force as anywhere in v. 21; within that, the different moments and circumstances facing man will be variously highlighted but the conviction is nowhere impaired.

What Paul envisaged as the condition of a dead Christian – the being with Christ of v. 23 – is another and slightly different matter. 1 Thess. 4^{14} and 1 Cor. 15^{18} speak of it in terms of being asleep, an idea related to the Old Testament conception of life in the underworld (or *Sheol*) as well as to common Greek notions. But here again the all-important difference appears; it is a matter of being asleep *in Christ*. This is the prime theological conviction and it is seen as the common factor in all modes of Christian existence.

The other interesting point about Paul's beliefs as revealed in this passage is the implicit assumption that the return of Christ in power (the *parousia*) will not occur before his own death. In 1 Thess. 4^{17} he assumes the contrary; and in 1 Cor. 15^{52}, in the course of a letter where much is said in the light of an imminent *parousia*, again he seems to include himself among those still alive at Christ's coming who will be 'changed', i.e. transformed or transfigured into the resurrection-state without the intervention of death. In our passage the presumption is quite the opposite; yet the change passes without comment. Paul's whole theology of the believer's relationship with Christ makes the details of programme, so important to so many, in his day and since, a matter of relative indifference to him. (On the apparent oscillation between different schemes of eschatology, i.e. teaching about the end of the world and associated matters, see C. F. D. Moule, J.T.S., 15 (1964), pp. 1ff.)

This passage casts light on the question of eschatology also from the standpoint of Paul's ideas about man's nature and make-up. Many in recent years have held that Paul had the so-called biblical view of man (as described, for example, in Pedersen: *Israel I-II* (London, 1926) pp. 99ff.) and regarded him as a psychosomatic unity; that is, he meant all references to what we normally think of as parts of man (e.g. body, heart, flesh) as descriptions of his whole person from one particular angle. Thus to us the term 'flesh' usually denotes one part of man in distinction from other parts; but in the Bible, it is held, the word refers to the whole man regarded as a vulnerable, earthly creature, or, in more theological contexts, as alienated from God; in either case carrying the implication of weakness.

However true this account may be of the greater part of Old Testament usage, it has always been difficult to press all pauline (not to speak of other New Testament) passages into this mould, despite valiant attempts by those for whom 'Hebraic ways of thought' had acquired an almost sacred significance as the most fitting vehicle for biblical theology. It seems clear that already by Paul's time Judaism was well used to a variety of conceptions in this matter, so that man could be regarded as a soul, indwelling a body, separable at death, as well as in the older unitary way. And far from immortality of the soul being inconsistent with resurrection of the whole person, in-cluding the body, as a way of describing the future life, it was pos-sible to see them as successive phases in the eschatological programme. 2 Esdras 7⁷⁵, for example, has the two concepts side by side in this way. In these verses Paul gives evidence of both ways of regarding man. In vv. 22 and 24, to *remain in the flesh* involves none of the usual Old Testament implications of the word 'flesh'; it is simply the body seen as the temporary receptacle of the soul, which is the real centre of personality; at most it signifies 'earthly life' as a sphere of existence. In v. 20, however, we have Paul, significantly in a more theological context, giving much more positive significance to his body, as the scene of the honouring of Christ. Here the body is seen as no encumbrance to be shed but as the actual sphere within which, *whether by life or by death*, honour will be done to Christ. Paul is thinking, as in v. 29f. and at more length in 3$^{2-11}$, of that pattern of Christ's physical sufferings which the apostle 'in Christ' gladly reproduces in his own person by his own privations. (For a recent discussion of this issue see James Barr: *Old and New in Interpretation* (London, 1966) pp. 52ff.)

ന്റ

19

your prayers and the help of the Spirit: in pauline theology the two are closely linked, for the Spirit who indwells all Christians (1 Cor. 2$^{9-13}$) stimulates and supports their prayers (Rom. 8$^{15f., 26}$).

Spirit of Jesus Christ: the concept of the Holy Spirit is still (by later credal standards) unformed in the New Testament, and Paul expresses himself with notable imprecision, not so much in his references to the Spirit's role as in the way he names him. Rom. 8$^{1-11}$ displays bewildering variety within a short space, and v. 9 almost reproduces his wording here. There is no other example of it in Paul, though the shift from 'Spirit terminology' to 'Christ terminology' in 1 Cor. 2$^{13-16}$ shows some of the working which lies behind it.

deliverance: the word is *sotēria*, normally translated 'salvation'. For Paul this word almost invariably (together with its cognate verb) refers to the ultimate and cosmic saving act which God will complete at the end of the world. The Spirit will keep him in the way that will lead to this dénouement, and this assurance (which has in it nothing of the blind, fatalistic assurance sometimes encountered in sixteenth century disputes about whether justification by God could, once granted, be lost) is the ground of his joy. It is most unlikely that the word refers to hope of deliverance from prison.

20

eager expectation: apokaradokia – found only in Christian writers, and in the New Testament only here and at Rom. 8^{19}. Intensive in sense and entirely parallel to *hope (elpis)*.

that I shall not be at all ashamed: a common expression of humble piety in the Psalms (e.g. 25$^{3, 20}$; 31$^{3, 17}$; 119^{6}) and elsewhere (e.g. Isa. 45^{17}; 49^{23}; 50^{7}; Zeph. 3^{11}) related especially to one's standing in the sight of God. 'Not being ashamed' is almost equivalent to 'being accepted by

God'. The expression is concerned with relationship to God not with the possible reactions of public opinion. Especially as he contemplates the possibility of martyrdom Paul hopes for the closest identification between himself and Christ. For this ideal, cf. Wisdom 5^1; 1 John 2^{28}.

21

to me to live is Christ: close to but more intensive than Gal. 2^{20}. The concept 'life' is for Paul filled by Christ (cf. also 2 Cor. 4^{10}; Col. 3^3).

25

I know that I shall remain: despite his being torn as far as his own desires are concerned, the sober probability is that he will not die a martyr. And the likely disposition of God's providence supports this, for his converts clearly still need him. God is bound to act for the best interests of his people.

I^{27-30} PAUL CALLS FOR UNITY IN THE
FACE OF ATTACK

^{27}*Only let your manner of life be worthy of the gospel of Christ, so that whether I come and see you or am absent, I may hear of you that you stand firm in one spirit, with one mind striving side by side for the faith of the gospel, ^{28}and not frightened in anything by your opponents. This is a clear omen to them of their destruction, but of your salvation, and that from God. ^{29}For it has been granted to you that for the sake of Christ you should not only believe in him but also suffer for his sake, ^{30}engaged in the same conflict which you saw and now hear to be mine.*

At this point Paul turns from his own situation to the pastoral needs of the Philippian community, for which he has just shown such intense concern. First he urges them to unity in the face of opposition, which it is not easy for us to identify. Like v. 6, this passage is evidence for Lohmeyer's belief that the church in Philippi was itself undergoing rigorous persecution in the same way as Paul; v. 30 seems to say as much. But in the rest of the passage it sounds as if this is more a matter of long drawn-out antagonism than formal persecution by the Roman authorities; and much the most likely source of this opposition is Jews in Philippi (cf. 3^{2-11}). Their conflict is *the same*, not in kind (it is most improbable that the entire Philippian church is in prison like

Paul!) but in significance – like his, it is *for the sake of Christ*, a struggle after the likeness of Christ's own passion.

ଧଧ

27

Only: Paul raises a 'warning finger' (Barth). Just as his future is a matter of indifference to him, so it ought to be a matter of indifference to them. Now the alternative to his coming to them again seems to be not death (that has been virtually ruled out in v. 25) but simply his not finding an opportunity.

let your manner of life be: the verb used (*politeuomai*) is related to *polis* (city), and some commentators see in it a conscious allusion to the dual citizenship of those to whom Paul writes. They belong to the properly constituted *polis* of Philippi. They are also citizens of heaven, living incognito on earth; colonists of heaven, as Philippi was a *colonia* of Rome. The use of the same image in 3^{20} lends support to this interpretation, and it is not unlike Paul to use the word with this association in mind; but it remains that the verb is a perfectly ordinary word of the time meaning 'live' or 'lead one's life'. (For a defence of the richer sense, see R. R. Brewer, J.B.L., 73, pp. 76–83.)

in one spirit, with one mind: this theme is developed in Eph. 4^{3-6}. It would be a mistake to regard the use of these terms as signifying a rigid analysis of the human personality. *Spirit* (*pneuma*) and *mind* (lit. 'soul' – *psychē*) are alternative terms for man as a thinking and moral being. Paul's terminology in such passages is extremely fluid; cf. 1 Cor. 2^{10-16} where he passes without trouble from *spirit* to *mind* (this time, the Greek *nous*) simply, it appears, through the introduction of an Old Testament quotation (in 1 Cor. 2^{16}) which makes the shift desirable. Here we should probably see the implication that the unity of spirit is brought about through participation in the 'Spirit of God' (cf. 2 Cor. 13^{14}). 1^{15-18} and 4^2 throw light on the disunity which threatens the church.

striving side by side: an example of Paul's favourite metaphor, taken from the games (cf. 3^{14}; 4^3; 1 Cor. $9^{24\text{ff}}$.).

for the faith of the gospel: this is one of a few instances in Paul where 'the faith' is used in a sense approaching 'the Christian religion'. The distinguishing mark of this faith as distinct from other 'faiths' is the gospel – the good news of God's act in Christ for man's salvation.

28

This: i.e. their unity and courage. The Greek (*hētis*) is feminine by attraction to the noun which follows (*omen*).

a clear omen: the use of this word in the translation should not be taken as evidence of superstition on Paul's part! *Endeixis* is 'sign' or 'clear indication'.

to them of their destruction, but of your salvation: it is very hard to show in translation that the contrast Paul is making here is not between what the opponents see in the courage of the Philippians and what they themselves see in it, but between the twin result of it which is all too clear to the opponents (or ought to be so). The confusion which arises so easily in translation has also arisen in the textual tradition, whereby in some MSS. the genitive *your* became a dative ('to you') by attraction into parallelism with the earlier *to them*, yielding the sense 'a sign of destruction for them but of salvation for you'.

The antithesis here occurs again in 2 Cor. 2¹⁵ᶠ·, where it is the message of the apostle which has this dual effect on the two categories of hearers. Both words refer to the final destiny of the day of judgement; hence this perception – and that to which it refers – is *from God.*

29
it has been granted: the verb is *charizomai,* cognate with *charis* ('grace'). Its implication is to be taken seriously; there is divine gift and privilege in the endurance of suffering.

30
you saw: if this is read as a reference to some persecution which Paul had actually suffered in Philippi then Acts 16²³ᶠᶠ· may tell of the incident to which he refers (cf. 1 Thess. 2²).

2¹⁻¹¹   CHRIST THE MODEL OF HUMILITY

¹*So if there is any encouragement in Christ, any incentive of love, any participation in the Spirit, any affection and sympathy,* ²*complete my joy by being of the same mind, having the same love, being in full accord and of one mind.* ³*Do nothing from selfishness or conceit, but in humility count others better than yourselves.* ⁴*Let each of you look not only to his own interests, but also to the interests of others.* ⁵*Have this mind among yourselves, which you have in Christ Jesus,* ⁶*who, though he was in the form of God, did not count equality with God a thing to be grasped,* ⁷*but emptied himself, taking the form of a servant*ᵈ*, being born in the likeness of men.* ⁸*And being found in human form he humbled himself and became obedient unto death,*

even death on a cross. 9 *Therefore God has highly exalted him and bestowed on him the name which is above every name,* 10 *that at the name of Jesus every knee should bow, in heaven and on earth and under the earth,* 11 *and every tongue confess that Jesus Christ is Lord, to the glory of God the Father.*

d Or *slave.*

This is in many ways the most difficult section of this epistle and one of the most difficult in the whole New Testament. It is hard to make any statement about it which has not been the subject of intense and protracted scholarly controversy. But we may hazard two remarks which command general agreement. First, verses 6–11 are a separate unit from the rest and hymn-like in general structure and content. Second, while the subject of this hymn is doctrinal, in that it speaks of the nature and work of Christ, its use by Paul in the context of his letter is ethical – it presents Christ as an example of self-sacrificing, obedient, and humble behaviour. About many other questions there is no agreed position; e.g. it may be agreed that vv. 6–11 are hymn-like in structure, but uncertain exactly what that structure is; it may be agreed that this is in some way a separate unit, but uncertain whether it is by Paul or existed in the Church before him or even (though this would win little support) was inserted here by some later hand.

We can express the central problem of interpretation thus. Quickly read, or used devotionally without close attention to the detailed meaning of the words, the hymn (as we shall call it) may seem simply an impressive imaginative statement of the work of Christ and his divine lordship over the world. But once its terms are examined it becomes clear not only that certain words (see detailed notes) are difficult in themselves, but also that it is hard to decide to what world of thought it belongs. Where did Paul (or whoever wrote the hymn) find precisely *these* words and concepts to express his Christian faith? Do they come from the very first days in Palestine, just after the Church began? Are they the product of a mind influenced by a rather speculative kind of Judaism, of which we have other evidence? Or do they belong to the different world to which Paul himself was largely, though not solely, responsible for transferring the Gospel: the world of Hellenistic culture which covered most of the Roman Empire? The interpretation given to the hymn will depend upon the cultural associations which we see in particular words and phrases. If we can fix it in the right background we shall be in a position to see exactly what claims it is making for Christ and how theologically precise its terms are; and this in turn, especially if the hymn is taken as pre-pauline, throws important light on the kind of formulation and the degree of doctrinal sophistication current in at least certain parts of the Church, even in her first two decades.

But before looking at these questions we ought to examine the setting in which Paul places it. The end of chapter one is only a minor break in the sequence of thought. From 1^{27} to 2^{18} Paul is urging the Philippians to unity of mind and purpose and life, and in 2^{1-4} he is particularly concerned to move them to humility and self-sacrifice in their relations with one another. It is characteristic of Paul that in commending virtue he should appeal to the *person* and *work* of Christ – not to some saying or deed of his lifetime, but rather to his whole action in becoming man and dying a death which effected the reconciliation of man to God. (Cf. 2 Cor. 8^9 where financial liberality is urged in this way.)

Paul begins by mustering all possible features of Christian life (v. 1), which add up to a single message and yield a single inevitable conclusion: mutual deference and self-effacement. There is to be no competitive self-assertion, no attempt to dominate the rest, but rather the closest sympathy with their needs and interests. The decisive argument that this is to be the manner of life in the Christian community is that Christ, on the grandest scale and in unique degree, has behaved in this way: renouncing his heavenly claims, assuming the humblest human position, and dying a criminal's death. As far as this moral point is concerned, Paul could have finished the hymn at the end of v. 8, but he goes on to give the triumphant conclusion – that Jesus is acknowledged as Lord by the whole universe, to the Father's glory. That he should give the whole pattern of Christ's descent and ascent in this way is characteristic of him; for example it occurs in the passage already quoted (2 Cor. 8^9, using the image of wealth renounced and restored) and in 2 Cor. 5^{21}; cf. Eph. $4^{9f.}$. Unlike the passages in *2 Corinthians*, this one includes no reference to the benefit conferred on the Christian believers by the act of Christ. Paul did, however, quote the whole hymn for a purpose, and this is clear in the light of v. 5. For the universal lordship of Christ is the basis on which men are brought into relationship with him in the Church; and this relationship (being in *Christ Jesus*) is in turn the basis for Paul's moral appeal in this whole passage.

We now turn to questions raised by the hymn in vv. 6–11.

Structure

It is often said that the separateness of these verses can be seen from the fact that in themselves they are doctrinal whereas Paul uses them, in the context of his letter, to make an ethical point. The examples in the last paragraph show that this is an oversimplification. Paul often makes an ethical point with the support of a doctrinal proposition (cf. 2 Cor. 8$^{7-9}$; Col. 3$^{1-5}$). Also, he often sums up the work of Christ in terms of a 'descent–ascent' pattern. More to the point is the fact that this passage differs from the parallels to which we have referred by its sheer length, by its vivid language – and by its form.

Lohmeyer in 1927 (in *Kyrios Jesus*) began to popularize the view that the passage is poetic in form, in fact a christological hymn. But confidence in the rightness of this view, which has been almost universally accepted, is somewhat shaken by the considerable variations among the poetic patterns discerned by different commentators. Certainly it is impossible to see any of the ordinary Greek metrical forms here. It is safer to seek shape and balance in the arrangement of the phrases; by dividing them into groups, somewhat after the manner of the English Psalms, where lines fall into pairs or other groupings according to sense. Our passage falls fairly naturally into lines and into groups of lines which begin with suitable particles. This more modest assessment makes it easier to account for legitimate differences of opinion about the exact way the passage should be divided up.

The most widely accepted arrangement of the passage is that of Lohmeyer:

> Though he was in the form of God,
> He did not count as a thing to be grasped
> Equality with God,
>
> But emptied himself,
> Taking the form of a servant,
> Being born in the likeness of men.
>
> And being found in human form
> He humbled himself
> And became obedient unto death,
> (Even death on a cross).
>
> (End of first strophe.)

Therefore God has highly exalted him
And bestowed on him the name
Which is above every name,

That at the name of Jesus,
Every knee should bow,
In heaven and on earth and under the earth,

And every tongue confess
That Jesus Christ is Lord,
To the glory of God the Father.

(End of second strophe.)

The two strophes or parallel sections correspond naturally to the pattern of 'descent–ascent'. The last line of the first strophe is put in brackets because it spoils the pattern and may well be a pauline addition to the hymn; certainly it accords with his special emphasis upon the cross.

Other commentators divide the passage differently, notably Jeremias,* who sees a psalm-like parallelism in pairs of lines, each member of which makes roughly the same point in alternative words. This is a most plausible theory in that it is inherently probable that even if the hymn was composed in a Hellenistic church its author would be influenced by the Psalms; also it renders the absence of Greek metrical form understandable and acceptable, and coheres with strong Old Testament elements in the *thought* of the passage. So arranged, the passage reads:

I. Who, though he was in the form of God,
   Did not count equality with God a thing to be grasped,

   But emptied himself
   Taking the form of a servant.

II. Being born in the likeness of men,
    And being found in human form,

    He humbled himself
    And became obedient unto death (even death on a cross).

III. Therefore God has highly exalted him
     And bestowed on him the name which is above every name,

* Ed. J. N. Sevenster, *Studia Paulina* (Haarlem, 1953), pp. 146ff. See also E. Käsemann in ed. H. Braun, *God and Christ*, J.Th.C., 5, pp. 45ff., 'A Critical Analysis of Philippians 2⁵⁻¹¹'.

That at the name of Jesus every knee should bow (in heaven
and on earth and under the earth)
And every tongue confess that Jesus Christ is Lord (to the
glory of God the Father).

The three strophes refer to (a) the pre-existent, (b) the earthly, (c) the exalted Christ. The words in brackets are regarded as pauline additions; the first coincides with Lohmeyer's, the other two bring the passage into line with Paul's thought as expressed, for example, in 1 Cor. 15²⁴⁻²⁸. The last makes sure that any possible suggestion of Christ being a 'second God' is decisively ruled out. This arrangement has the advantage of bringing together pairs of lines which are rather awkwardly separated in the division made by Lohmeyer, e.g. the first half of strophe II.

Background

All questions concerning this passage are related, and as it is hard to discuss the background to the thought without expounding the thought itself, so the structure, as we have hinted, may throw light on the background. For example, some have seen such a strong influence of Old Testament form and imagery that they have been tempted to see behind our Greek version an Aramaic original. This may explain an oddity of Greek expression such as *kai schēmati heuretheis hōs anthrōpos (and being found in human form)*. It may also explain the fact that the passage falls reasonably easily into verse-like lines, and perhaps psalmic parallelism (see above), without being in anything like strict verse form; it is not poetry in Greek, perhaps it was in Aramaic. On the other hand, Paul shows that the piece was perfectly capable of use in Greek, probably as a liturgical utterance, and it could have started its life in that language and for that use.

The linguistic background does not in any case determine the cultural background. It is tempting to try and prove that such a piece as this is either Jewish or Hellenistic, and the evidence for either view will become clearer when we turn to expound the meaning; but it is quite false to seek the explanation exclusively in either quarter. It is more and more apparent that by the first century A.D. there was in varying degrees a mixing of the two cultures which renders firm pigeonholing both unnecessary and precarious. Which side bears greater weight depends largely upon whether the passage as a whole is seen as reflecting Old Testament patterns, such as the story of Adam in Genesis 1–3, or is taken to be making philosophical-cum-doctrinal statements about the person of Christ on the model of current Greek religious speculation. And a decision about *this* depends largely upon the elucidation of certain words, in particular *form* (*morphē*), and *thing to be grasped* (*harpagmos*). Our last two sentences need explaining; the explanation will become clear in what follows.

Meaning

The use of the term *morphē* twice in this passage (*form of God* and *form of a servant*) seems at first sight to be most easily explained along Greek lines. In terms of Greek philosophy we might take Paul to be asserting in v. 6 that Christ shared the divine attributes (so Lightfoot); others, also seeing a Greek background, take the usage to be looser and to mean in a somewhat undefined way that Christ shares the 'being' of God. The disadvantage of any interpretation of the word as signifying the substantial equality of Christ with God at the beginning of the hymn is that the first verse (v .6) of our hymn then becomes mere truism. If Christ is on a par with God, of course *equality with God* is not a thing he desires to obtain or worries about retaining; it is fully his.

So we turn elsewhere. There is much to be said for the theory that the dominant (though not the sole) inspiration for this hymn lies in the story of Adam, as it was interpreted at this period. The general grounds for this hypothesis are (*a*) the wide speculation about Adam at this time among Jews of different viewpoints and (*b*) the fact that Paul amply shows that this speculation was congenial to him and that the figure of Adam was a fruitful basis for his understanding of Christ's person and work (Rom. 5$^{12ff.}$; I Cor. 15$^{22, 45}$). Adam (Hebrew for 'man') was seen as both typical man and also the ancestor of the whole race. The stories about him in *Genesis* were scanned for illumination about the condition and fate of man in general and for further knowledge about Adam himself than their surface meaning revealed. This was done in accordance with the philosophical outlook and interpretative principles favoured by the scholar concerned. Thus Philo (the Jew of Alexandria who lived in the first century A.D. and was deeply influenced by a variety of elements of Greek philosophy) noted that Genesis 1$^{26ff.}$ and 2^7 contain two distinct accounts of the creation of Adam, and inferred that God created two primeval men, the one bearing the perfect image of himself, the other, made from the material of the world, being the ancestor of the human race. Whether this speculation is in any way related to Paul's seeing Adam and Christ in parallel as heads of fallen and redeemed humanity it is impossible to say, but at least there is some resemblance.

One of the fundamental statements in the *Genesis* story is that Adam was made in the *image* of God (Gen. 1²⁶). In the Septuagint (the Greek Old Testament) this is translated by *eikōn* – a word which Paul not infrequently uses of Christ, no doubt as part of the parallelism which he sees between him and Adam (cf. 2 Cor. 4⁴; Col. 1¹⁵; and in 1 Cor. 11⁷ it is used of the human male, as descended from Adam). There is however ample evidence to suggest that *morphē* could be used in the same sense and that it is therefore possible to see in the use of this word in the hymn an allusion to the Adamic parallel. It is not the author's concern to make precise philosophical statements about Christ's metaphysical status; he is merely alluding to the figure of Adam, with whom Christ has certain things in common, in order to show by contrast that there are other decisive things which Christ does *not* have in common with the head and father of the fallen human race.

If *morphē* is taken in this sense and the passage is Adamic, then the meaning of *harpagmos* is more easily decided. In itself it is a difficult word to define exactly, largely because of its rarity; it nowhere appears in the Septuagint or (apart from this passage) in the New Testament, and hardly occurs at all in Greek literature. Its commonest sense, *robbery*, is unlikely here, despite the Authorized Version. Much more probably it is synonymous with the far commoner cognate word, *harpagma*. This gives the meaning, *something which is seized*; but this step forward does not solve our problem, for it can be used in either a good or a bad sense. In the first case *booty* or *prize* would be reasonable translations, and the sense would be that equality with God was something which Christ already possessed, might have held on to, but in fact renounced. In the second case *prey* would convey the meaning better, and the sense would be that Christ might have snatched at an equality with God which he did not possess, but refrained from doing so. Which sense is chosen depends closely upon the interpretation of the whole passage and of *morphē* in particular. If the hymn has a strongly Hellenistic background and sees Christ on the model of a divine hero who descends to earth, with *morphē* bearing a quasi-philosophical sense, then the first sense is the more natural. But if the Adamic imagery is to the fore then the second is more likely.

A mediating position has been suggested, in the light of the undoubtedly common popular use of the word *harpagmos* to mean *a lucky find, a piece of good luck*. If this is right then the meaning of the hymn is that Christ did not exploit that existence with or in God which he possessed, but on the contrary renounced his claims, choosing the way of humiliation and simple obedience; his exaltation was not snatched, but received as God's gift only after he had trodden that path. This has the advantage of giving full value to the first line of the hymn referring to Christ's pre-existent status with God. This mediating position continues to see a strong reference to the Adam-story, especially to his attempt to reach divine status and so to the act whereby he overreached himself and brought about his downfall; Adam *had* considered equality with God a thing to be grasped (Gen. $3^{5, 22}$).* In contrast to him Christ made no such attempt but on the contrary renounced the heavenly status which he already possessed.

At this point it is clear that the picture of Adam (at any rate as seen in *Genesis*) is not enough to explain what is in the author's mind. He speaks of Christ as personally existent before his entry into this world, in the heavenly places, with God. This notion of Christ's pre-existence, arising so quickly in the history of the Church, here finds perhaps its earliest statement. But it is far from being the only one in the New Testament (cf. Heb. $1^{2f.}$, John 1^{1-14}, 1 Cor. 8^6). What are we to make of this difficult idea? In some passages it has more doctrinal value than in others. For example, in John 1^{1-14} it is used to express the thought that the mind and purpose (*logos*) of God towards man is eternally one and the same – in creation, in all the providential ordering of history, *and* in the activity of Jesus. But in other passages, including our own, it seems to be frankly mythological, i.e. to be part of a way of speaking in dramatic terms about God and heaven as essentially continuous with life and conditions in this world, however immeasurably greater and more impressive and powerful. Thus Christ appears, so far as the shape of the hymn is concerned, as rather like an angel who at a certain point descends to earth to accomplish a mission and return.

*As subsidiary examples of hubristic behaviour, the figures in Isa. 14^{13} and Ezek. 28^2 may contribute to the picture. Some scholars think that the divine claims of Roman emperors may be in mind.

In Hebrews 1, the position is much the same, and the writer takes trouble to safeguard the uniqueness of Christ by carefully differentiating him from the angels; he is in a category of his own – he is 'the Son'.

This kind of thinking did not arise spontaneously and without antecedents when Christians sought concepts lofty enough to do justice to their belief about Jesus. Already in the Old Testament the idea of Wisdom as a quasi-personal associate of God in the work of creation and in the history of Israel was prominent enough (Proverbs 8, Ecclesiasticus 24, Wisdom of Solomon 9). Both Paul and the *Epistle to the Hebrews* depend directly upon this concept, which brought with it the notion of pre-existence (1 Cor. 1^{24}; Heb. 1^3, cf. Wisdom of Solomon 7^{26})*. More obscure, both in date and in provenance, is the figure of 'the heavenly man'; perhaps partly Persian in origin, eventually at home in the more extravagant religious sects of the Mediterranean lands, probably discernible already in the figure of the Son of man in Daniel 7^{13}, this saving, judging figure may also contribute a little to the picture in our present passage. And we have already referred to the possible link with Philo's 'two-Adams' theory.

If the picture of Christ's heavenly origins given in the hymn strikes us as both obscure and uncongenial, two things must be said. In the first place, we must not try to squeeze a statement like this into the shape of later and more familiar doctrinal formulation; thus if our interpretation of *morphē* is right, then what later came to be defined as Christ's divinity, 'of one substance with the Father', is here stated most inadequately. Similarly this theologically crude (though imaginatively impressive and moving) picture of Christ's pre-existence needs much qualification before it can contribute to a satisfactory statement of doctrine about Christ's person (we have seen that the opening of *St John's Gospel* may begin to show the way). In the second place, though no doubt Paul saw Christ's role in the terms which he here uses (whether he wrote the hymn or not), it is not for him simply a piece of speculative theology-cum-cosmology; its chief point is Christ's obedience unto death and his vindication by God. This is made clear by the context in which Paul introduces the

* Cf. the Rabbis' conception of the pre-existence of the Law and other great elements in Judaism; it is a way of ascribing supreme religious importance (see G. F. Moore, *Judaism*, Vol. I (Harvard, 1958), p. 526; W. D. Davies, *Paul & Rabbinic Judaism* (London, 1948), p. 170).

hymn. And, what is more, it is the obedience and triumph not of a figure of myth, but of the historical figure, Jesus, so recently on earth.

There may be one final ingredient in the picture of Christ depicted here, and some commentators see it, rather than the figure of Adam, as the basic model which the hymn employs. It is the figure of the Servant of God as found in Isaiah 40–55 and especially 53; the righteous one, whose profound, intense, and undeserved sufferings are vindicated by God and who by his death justified many and bore their iniquities. As is well known, this figure was early seized upon as a key to the interpretation of Christ's work; perhaps Christ in his own lifetime interpreted himself in terms of it. Many New Testament writers make use of it, and what the New Testament began the Christian writers of the following centuries continued. Apart from the more common idea of vindication in 2⁹f·, which does not demand Isa. 53 as a background (though Isa. 52¹³ is relevant), the chief ground for believing that it may be involved in our passage is in the phrase *the form of a servant*. The difficulty is that the word for *servant* (*doulos*) is never used for the servant of Isa. 53 either in the Septuagint or in New Testament quotations from the passage (he is always *pais*) though it does occur in the associated passage, Isa. 49. The Old Testament background for *doulos* is much more general – it is used for prophets, and in general for pious, obedient servants of God. It is perhaps more likely that the word is chosen without any particular Old Testament background exclusively in mind, but simply as the word which denotes the lowest human status, the greatest possible contrast to the perfect, heavenly Adamic status conveyed by *the form of God*, to show the depth of Our Lord's humility and self-giving (cf. 2 Cor. 8⁹). Jesus renounced his heavenly claims as completely as this. It is also possible that the phrase *emptied himself* reflects Isa. 53¹² in which case it would have to refer to the humble suffering of Christ rather than to the act of becoming man, which would be more natural from its position in the hymn. And it is relevant that v. 9f. uses the same general Old Testament context by quoting Isa. 45²³. (For the comparison with Isa. 53, see further W. D. Davies, *Paul and Rabbinic Judaism*, p. 274.)

The logic is not worked out, but the result of Christ's obedience is that God has raised him to a dignity higher than that which he enjoyed before (the verb has the prefix *hyper*, so carries the force 'super-exalt'). Probably this is seen simply as a reward, though it is also shown to be in accordance with Scripture: cf. Isa. 45^{23} (also quoted by Paul in Rom. 14^{11}). This new status is described as the conferring of the name *kyrios* (*lord*). This constitutes the 'extra' which Christ has received; once more the passage should not be measured against the yardstick of later orthodoxy (precise doctrinal questions had not yet been posed and categories of speech were still flexible), but seen as concentrating upon the new dimension of Christ's authority signified in his new title. His authority is now cosmic in scope, and if looked at in the light of Isa. 45^{23} is also seen as the consummation of history; that passage speaks of the final and universal victory of God. This authority Christ already exercises, as a result of the obedience of the cross.

Why does Christ receive the name *kyrios*? The simplest explanation is to be found in the same passage in Isa. 45. There the name of God, Yahweh, is rendered *ho kyrios* – *the Lord,* as it is throughout the Greek Old Testament. And he is the one to whom every knee shall bow and whom every tongue will confess. In transferring the title (for in Greek it *is* a title rather than, as in the Hebrew equivalent, a proper name) to Christ, the hymn does what Paul does several times in his writings (cf. Rom. 10^{13}). Christ performs the role of God. Probably, the first application of this title to Christ came through the use of Ps. 110^1 as a scriptural witness to his exaltation; a verse quoted by such a wide range of New Testament writers that it must have been current in many parts of the primitive Church. But it may well be that these Old Testament texts are not all that lies behind its enthusiastic adoption. It was a term which had the advantages of ambiguity and bestrode cultural frontiers. Here for example in a passage that stresses Christ's universal rule it would be hard to exclude the common associations derived from its use in the emperor-cult. And if the emperor was *kyrios*, so also was the deity in many popular cults. What more natural then that Christ should be seen as *the* genuine *kyrios* who deservedly received all praise and honour? Paul says as much in 1 Cor. 8$^{5f.}$ (See further in Cullmann, *The Christology of the New Testament* (London, 1959), ch. 7.)

Authorship

Is the hymn the work of Paul himself or has he taken it over from earlier Christian use? The question is of some interest, because if the

hymn is pre-pauline (or even if it is only non-pauline) we have
evidence of the way some primitive Christians formulated their
belief about Jesus in the Church's first decade, and evidence that their
formulation both contained high and sophisticated claims (like pre-
existence and cosmic rule) and had already received this kind of
formal and dramatic expression.

The question cannot be finally resolved. On the one hand some of
the chief words (e.g. *morphē*, especially if it occurs as an alternative to
eikōn) are not those usually used by Paul. Also, the statement of
Christ's work contains no reference to the restoration of man to
relationship with God as its object and result, as uniformly in Paul's
statements about that work (e.g. 2 Cor. 8⁹; 5²¹), but only to Christ's
obedience and the acclaim which he received. On the other hand most
of the ideas in the hymn have parallels elsewhere in Paul's writings.
Thus the pre-existence of Christ appears in 1 Cor. 8⁶ and Col. 1¹⁵f..
The latter verse also agrees with what we have taken to be the most
likely sense of *morphē*. The picture of Christ as the heavenly Adam,
contrasted with the Adam of Genesis 1–3, is strikingly paralleled in
1 Cor. 15⁴⁵; the Christ of Philippians 2 accords well with this *last
Adam*. The self-emptying is an image analogous to the self-impover-
ishment of 2 Cor. 8⁹. It is true that the text in Isa. 45²³ alluded to in
v. 10 is, in its other use by Paul (Rom. 14¹¹), strictly applied to God
and not to Christ, but Rom. 14⁹ implies that the one includes the
other, and 1 Cor. 15²¹⁻²⁸ writes out the theological assumptions
involved at more length.

In other words there is no reason why the hymn should not be
Paul's own. He writes in different idiom from that of his ordinary
writing, as people do when they take to liturgical utterance. But even
if he was using what others had composed he needed to make few
concessions to the ideas therein expressed in order to see them as his
own.

Doctrinal Significance
Because this passage has played such an important part in the forming
of Christian doctrine it is important to see, on the basis of the best
interpretation that we can arrive at, how it can be legitimately used
for that purpose. In our exposition we have already found it necessary
to point out that confusion arises when this hymn (or any other
biblical passage for that matter) is read with the eyes of later doctrinal

formation. To do this is always to run the risk of attributing to words and images a precision or a sense which was not in the mind of the original writer.

We have suggested the area within which the reader ought to look for the original meaning of these verses and indicated the balance of probabilities. We shall now look at the way in which one of its chief themes – the self-emptying of Christ – has been used in Christian theology, and see how in the course of this use its words have been given new senses, made to answer new questions, and viewed in the light of concepts quite different from those of Paul's time. Then we shall make some remarks about the significance of the passage as a whole.

(i) The self-emptying of Christ

In Christian history the centre of the passage has understandably been seen as the idea of kenōsis (self-emptying). From the original writer's point of view it is likely that the exaltation of Christ to the position of kyrios was much more the climax and objective of the passage but as attention in the Church turned to the question of the mode of Christ's incarnation the verb in v. 7 obviously provided an important scriptural way of describing the mystery.

But the precise sense in which it has been read has depended on the presuppositions with which it has been approached. Thus while a casual reading would place the stress on a grand abandonment by Christ of his divine status and see in this act a real and moving condescension to share genuinely the human condition, there is no doubt that the theological outlook of (for example) the Greek fathers of the early centuries put severe limitations upon this natural way of reading the passage. If the incarnation is seen (as the Greek fathers did see it) as the taking of human nature by the Second Person of the eternal Trinity who in the process cannot and does not abrogate by one iota his full divine status, then his kenōsis consists simply of his fully conscious condescension to the human level just so far as is necessary for the reality of his life and work on earth. There is no question of abandonment of divine omniscience or omnipotence, merely a laying aside of them temporarily for specific ends. Thus, in the thirst of Jesus mentioned in the story of the crucifixion, there is no putting aside of the divine freedom from such limitations and weaknesses, as we might suppose, but rather a gracious identification of himself by Jesus with the ordinary sufferings of human nature, which he permits himself to experience in his human nature; genuinely, perhaps, but hardly in the most straightforward sense.

In more recent times (notably in the theology of Charles Gore) the concept of *kenōsis* has been used to answer quite different, modern questions about the incarnation, using quite different theological assumptions from those of the fathers of the early centuries. The new questions arise from our natural interest in the inner psychology and mentality of Jesus: what did it feel like to be the one whom the Creeds see as both God and man? how in practice does such a role work? While it seemed axiomatic to the fathers that the human Jesus retained to the full his divine attributes (such as omniscience), to more recent theologians this has seemed frankly impossible; it would render the incarnation quite unreal. How can Jesus be truly man, identified with the human race, if he is consciously *extra*ordinary in this way? The language of Philippians 2⁷ offered a clue. Christ at the incarnation *emptied himself* of such divine attributes as prevented his full and real identification with man. His knowledge of nuclear physics, modern Spanish, and the pattern of future events – all such things were left behind. This seemed to offer a psychologically plausible way of looking at the incarnate Christ.

It has won little acceptance. The chief difficulty is that it seems to make nonsense of the reality of personal identity between the preexistent and the incarnate Christ, by its notion of such massive amnesia. Nor does it easily provide a criterion for sifting which divine attributes Christ retained at the incarnation from those which he abandoned. In other words it raises the blunt question: is Christ being held to be divine or not? Many hold that the attempt fails, and perhaps at root this is because it attempts to raise new questions while retaining too much of the structure of traditional ways of thought about the person of Christ. And it is certainly using a very different idiom from the writer of the hymn in *Philippians* who is simply presenting the drama of Christ, even though it uses his word. It is, in other words, so far as it depends upon New Testament exegesis, a piece of anachronism.

(ii) *The hymn as a whole*
By now it will be clear that certain approaches to this passage are almost certainly unpromising. Even though Paul uses it as the theolo-

2$^{1-11}$

gical warrant for ethical exhortation, the hymn in itself does not have a moral message; it does not say 'Imitate the humble obedience of Christ'. Nor was it framed to make precise theological statements about the metaphysical nature of Christ. To that degree, ancient and modern expositors who have tried to use it in that way have been led into paths of obscurity rather than clarity. Whether its background is mainly in Hellenistic mythology and speculation, or in the Old Testament and Judaism, or, as is most likely, a mixture of ingredients from both sides, this is best seen as a dramatic, imaginative composition, lofty in poetic tone, the bearer of the fervent devotion of early Christian congregations. It tells in language appropriate to such a context the great story of Christ, who, through the voluntary choice of self-abasement, accepted the suffering of the cross, and was crowned by God with rule over the whole universe.

Dr R. P. Martin (in *Carmen Christi* (Cambridge, 1967)), after an exhaustive study of the passage, puts it firmly in this setting, alongside other similar formulations of the infant Gentile Church (e.g. Ignatius, Ephesians 19, E.C.W., p. 81). It is a poetic and mythological song to Christ, proclaiming that

life is under His rule and derives its purpose from the meaning which His incarnate existence gives to it. Above all, it assures us that the character of the God whose will controls the universe and human destiny is to be spelled out in terms of Jesus Christ. He is no arbitrary power, no capricious force, no pitiless, indifferent Fate. His nature is Love, and His concern for the world is most clearly expressed in the enthronement of Christ who came to His glory by a life of humble submission to His will and a complete obedience unto death. (R. P. Martin, op. cit., p. 311.)

I

if . . .: there is no verb in this clause and it has to be supplied. The sense is less likely to be abstract than to refer to the Philippians' situation; so not 'if there be any such thing as . . .', but 'if there be in you . . .'. However, a decision on this is largely determined by the interpretation given to the words rendered *encouragement* and *incentive*.

encouragement: the word *paraklēsis* also means 'consolation', and Paul makes much use of it in that sense, especially in 2 Cor. 1; but the translation given is probably better here. Paul is appealing to the insistent

82

pressure towards love and unity which comes from their life in relation to Christ.

incentive: this word (*paramythion*) has a similar range of meaning to *paraklēsis.* Paul hopes that their love (for him?) will encourage his readers to unity.

affection: lit. 'bowels', seen in Hebrew thought as the seat of the affections (cf. 1^8).

2

being of the same mind: a common theme in Paul (cf. Rom. 12^{16}; 2 Cor. 13^{11}).

3

count others better than yourselves: cf. Rom. 12$^{3,\ 10}$.

4

only: is not in the text, and some manuscripts omit *also.* The contrast is not meant to be softened, as in R.S.V., whichever wording is original.

5

you have: these words do not appear in Greek, and without them the translation is not entirely clear. The A.V. has: 'Let this mind be in you, which was also in Christ Jesus'. But the opening verb is likely to be an imperative (*have this mind*); and 'in you' is less likely than *among your-selves.* The last phrase then refers to the sphere of Christian life (*in Christ Jesus*). *This* points back to the humble disposition which Paul is enjoining. The relationship of Christians with one another is to reflect their relationship with Christ, and derives from it.

6–8

form: the English reproduces two different Greek words – *morphē* in the first two cases, *schēma* in the third. For the meaning of *morphē*, see the exposition above. *Schēma* technically refers to the outward shape presented by an object, and some see in v. 8 an implied distinction between the outward (human) appearance of Christ and his inner (divine) reality. But we suggested above that it is probably unrealistic to press such precise philosophical usage in the case of *morphē*, and the same may also be true of the second word. It is perhaps better to draw a third word, *likeness* (*homoiōma*), into the picture and strengthen the case for Old Testament background; a cognate noun is in Gen. 1^{26} and this word itself is common in the language of apocalyptic visions, e.g. Ezek. 1^{26}; 8^2. It may indicate, by allusion, the presentation of Jesus as the fulfilment of the Jewish hope for God's decisive intervention at the end of history. It is possible that this word, like the phrase which follows, is meant to imply that Jesus, though *like* man, was not exactly an ordinary man. Those who see in this hymn signs of a Gnostic-type 'redeemer myth' support this view, and see further evidence for it in Rom. 8² where Paul uses the same word: *in the likeness of sinful flesh* (see J. Knox, *The Humanity and Divinity of Christ* (Cambridge, 1967), pp. 31–3).

7

emptied himself: in the exposition above we suggested that there was no reference here to the death of Christ, but rather to the act of incarnation. This excludes one sense of the verb *kenoō: destroy* or *bring to nothing*. We do not come to that part of the drama till v. 8. Therefore the sense must be as R.S.V. gives it. However, this casts some doubt on the general line we have taken in interpreting this passage. If the pre-existent Christ is not seen as having metaphysically divine status, but rather as a perfect Adamic figure who avoids the sin of the ancestor of the human race, then the force of the self-emptying is somewhat reduced. It must be admitted that the word has much more power if the pre-existent Christ renounced an equality with God which he already possessed. *Then* the problem is not only to take the Adam imagery very strictly but also to give meaning to *hyper,* the prefix to the verb translated *exalted* in v. 9, which would most naturally imply that after his death Christ received a status higher than that which he before possessed, a status freshly conferred as a result of his obedience *unto death.* Perhaps it is unfair to try to press all elements in the hymn into too great a coherence.

9

name: this has the common Jewish overtones, whereby a person's name carries the idea of his position and role, and even embodies the potency of that position (cf. Acts 3⁶,¹⁶). The name in question is *Kyrios* (*Lord*).

10

every knee: it is likely that the universal homage is seen as being chiefly paid by the spiritual powers controlling the cosmos, according to the contemporary mythology. In Christ, they see and acknowledge their lord (cf. Col. 1²⁰; Rev. 5¹¹⁻¹³).

11

to the glory of God the Father: the Father has the ultimate sovereignty, cf. 1 Cor. 15²⁸.

^{12}*Therefore, my beloved, as you have always obeyed, so now, not only as in my presence but much more in my absence, work out your own salvation with fear and trembling;* ^{13}*for God is at work in you, both to will and to work for his good pleasure.* ^{14}*Do all things without grumbling or questioning,* ^{15}*that you may be blameless and innocent, children of God without blemish in the midst of a crooked and perverse generation, among whom you shine as lights in the world,* ^{16}*holding fast the word of life, so that in the day of Christ I may be proud that I did not run in vain or labour in vain.* ^{17}*Even if I am to be poured as a libation upon the sacrificial offering of your faith, I am glad and rejoice with you all.* ^{18}*Likewise you also should be glad and rejoice with me.*

Just as the opening verses of this chapter provide a hortatory setting for the christological hymn, so the passage which follows maintains the same tone. The logic is as follows: Paul begins by urging his readers to be humble, loving, and united, and then finds the basis and authority for this in the story of Christ's life and death, now decisively vindicated by God. The statement of this basis provides both a doctrinal ground for Paul's exhortation and a moral example which he applies: Christ acted as the Philippians are to act, and acted thus within the purposes of God. Finally, Paul goes on to repeat and extend his admonitions, but now introduces himself into the picture as the apostle responsible for these Christians and so able to claim their particular regard. As we have already found in this letter, Paul's apostolic role is at this point in his relationship with his church strongly coloured by his impending death. This in no way diminishes but rather intensifies the joy which he desires to share with them; and if he has joy enough to share with them, let them similarly have joy to share with him.

The passage opens with a verse which presents problems both of construction and of interpretation. The problem of construction is how to take the negative particle *mē* which appears in v. 12 (*not*). As this particle cannot be used with a verb in the indicative, the verb here (*work out*) must be an imperative, though in form it could be either. But settling that point does not settle all; there are two plausible translations, each carrying distinct doctrinal implications. First, we may take the negative strictly with the verb. This yields a rendering such as:

Wherefore, my beloved, as you have always been obedient, do not (as in my presence alone but now much more in my absence) work out your salvation with fear and trembling.

Such a rendering is cumbersome but does have advantages. It means, in particular, that Paul's teaching here is in line with his dominant idea: that man's salvation is brought about wholly on the initiative of God. He is saying that the Philippians, who have so far accepted Paul's teaching and acted upon it, are not to see themselves as working for their salvation by their own efforts (especially now when, in Paul's absence, they are trusted to adhere to his teaching); for God himself (v. 13) is at work in them to accomplish his good purposes.

However, despite the consistency of this view with Paul's main doctrine, most commentators have not adopted it. They have been persuaded by the structure of the sentence to choose a second rendering, even at the cost of having to come to terms with an apparent divergence from Paul's usual teaching. The constructional difficulty is simply that the negative particle is widely separated from the verb (*work out*) with which it must be, even if loosely, linked in terms of syntax. As far as sense is concerned it belongs more naturally with the phrase which immediately follows it – as in the R.S.V., given above. In other words Paul has expressed himself ambiguously, and we must simply accept the fact.

The result is that we have to take the imperative (*work out*) in the affirmative; and this is where the doctrinal difficulty arises. How can Paul, the great advocate of God's sole agency in the redemption of man, utter exhortations like this? Is it not wholly out of character for him to demand that Christians work for their own salvation? It is in fact not as difficult as it appears, and causes most difficulties to those more obsessed than Paul with the incompatibility of the roles of 'faith' and 'works' in man's right relationship with God!

There is one preliminary lexical point: Paul never employs the verb used here (*katergazomai*) in contexts where he is discussing the issue of 'works' versus 'faith' (i.e. whether man's salvation can be earned by his virtuous behaviour or only by his receiving of the free gift of God's grace). Despite its connexion with the noun *erga* (*works*), used in that discussion, this verb has much more the sense of *bring about*. So we do well not to allow our eyes to be clouded by questions with which Paul is not directly concerned here and which are too often seen in the light of disputes dating from much later times.

Our two verses, 12 and 13, must be taken together, and in fact have many parallels in Paul. Thus we can compare 1 Cor. 9^{27}, 10$^{1-13}$ and 2 Cor. 5$^{2f.}$ for warning against the danger of losing the gift of acceptance by God; and Gal. 5^{25} and Col. 3$^{3, 5}$ for the need to realize in moral life the implications of the Christian status which God has already conferred. Especially in the light of these latter passages there is no inconsistency here between the admonitions to the Philippians to bring about their *own salvation* and the statement in the following verse that *God is at work in* them. Paul never implies that God's purposes for man can be fulfilled whether man co-operates or not.

It is just possible that the *fear and trembling* (a commonplace of Septuagintal usage, which would have dropped off Paul's tongue as easily as ours) are to be directed not towards God; as our discussion suggests, but towards one's fellow Christians; in which case they spring not from awe at the divine but from respect and love for the human. This will be the case if the word translated *your own* (*heautōn*) should in fact be rendered 'one another's', so that the phrase re-inforces Paul's exhortation to mutual concern (cf. v. 4). However, the notion of awesome respect in the face of the human person is perhaps more redolent of modern humanism than of pauline ethics.

Here the emphasis in Paul's counsel moves to peace and content-ment – further aspects of that obedience of Christ which he has put forward as the comprehensive model for Christian life. That life is lived in the midst of a hostile world. To describe it, Paul quotes words from the Song of Moses (Deut. 32^5), in which the latter, on the eve of his death, reproached the people of Israel. Paul applies them instead to the pagan world; while, by contrast with the old Israel, the Church stands out as light in darkness.

The apostle need have no self-effacing modesty in relation to his church. On the contrary, even on the day of Christ's return in victory and judgement, Paul will point to his converts in pride as evidence that he has not *run in vain* – a fear expressed also in 1 Cor. 9^{27} and Gal.

2^2. His relationship with them is such that his death can be seen as involving them intimately. He describes it under the figure of a sacrifice. Their constant faith is an offering to God, and his death is added to that offering, consummating it and crowning it. Precisely this is to be the ground of the joy they share. For an extended exposition of Paul's doctrine that suffering and death typify and bring to a point the offering of the Christian life, and in particular the apostolic life, see 2 Cor. $11^{28}-12^{10}$ and Col. 1^{24}, where he makes explicit the relationship between Christ's suffering and the apostle's. Here it is Paul's last and deepest thrust in the campaign that he wages for unity and peace among his readers. *Participation in the Spirit* (v. 1), their objective status (cf. 2 Cor. 13^{14}), is the ground of his appeal, and Christ's life and death is the standing example. Their sacrificial life and death, in which he shares, is the fruit and the test of their relationship with Christ and their fellowship in the Spirit. (See L. S. Thornton, *The Common Life in the Body of Christ* (London, 1942), pp. 329f.)

ॐ

12

absence: not only his absence at the time of writing, but also his impending death, which will remove his apostolic aid and support (cf. v. 17).

salvation: see on $1^{19, 28}$.

13

good pleasure: man is the object of God's benevolent will not simply as an individual but in the context of God's purposive work in history.

14

grumbling: the apostle may see himself in relation to his church as parallel to Moses in relation to the people of Israel in the wilderness (cf. Exod. 15^{24}; 16^2; and 1 Cor. 10^{10}). Note his use of Deut. 32^5 later in this verse.

15

lights in the world: what Dan. 12^3 (LXX) applies to the people of God in the new world to come Paul uses for the Church here and now. Cf. Matt. 5^{14}.

16

the day of Christ: i.e. the second coming.

PERSONAL LINKS BETWEEN PAUL
AND PHILIPPI

^{19}*I hope in the Lord Jesus to send Timothy to you soon, so that I may be cheered by news of you.* ^{20} *I have no one like him, who will be genuinely anxious for your welfare.* ^{21} *They all look after their own interests, not those of Jesus Christ.* ^{22}*But Timothy's worth you know, how as a son with a father he has served with me in the gospel.* ^{23}*I hope therefore to send him just as soon as I see how it will go with me;* ^{24}*and I trust in the Lord that shortly I myself shall come also.*

^{25}*I have thought it necessary to send to you Epaphroditus my brother and fellow worker and fellow soldier, and your messenger and minister to my need,* ^{26}*for he has been longing for you all, and has been distressed because you heard that he was ill.* ^{27}*Indeed he was ill, near to death. But God had mercy on him, and not only on him but on me also, lest I should have sorrow upon sorrow.* ^{28}*I am the more eager to send him, therefore, that you may rejoice at seeing him again, and that I may be less anxious.* ^{29}*So receive him in the Lord with all joy; and honour such men,* ^{30}*for he nearly died for the work of Christ, risking his life to complete your service to me.*

This passage raises literary and biographical rather than theological or exegetical questions. It is the first passage we have met so far which casts doubt upon the unity of this epistle as we are accustomed to use it. A glance at Paul's other letters shows that he tends to put personal details at the end, and many commentators have come to the conclusion that these verses bring to an end *one* of Paul's letters to the church in Philippi. The rest of our epistle will then consist of parts of other letters which he wrote to the same church or of displaced parts of this letter (see Introduction, pp. 40f.).

This 'fragment-hypothesis' is not as unlikely as it may seem at first sight, even in the case of such a short epistle as this. It is highly probable that when the writings of Paul were first collected the unit which the collectors were setting out to assemble was not the isolated letter but the whole correspondence (or as much as was available or perhaps suitable for their purposes) with a particular church.* It was, after all, the churches who had been recipients of Paul's letters that

* See John Knox, *Philemon among the Letters of Paul* (London, 1960).

the collector had to deal with. If this is so then it is not surprising that some of the epistles as we have them look as if they are made up of a number of letters or parts of letters, and that sometimes the work of editing them into a single unit has been rather roughly done, leaving some of the seams visible. The editors may well not have been very interested in producing something that would look like a smooth literary whole, though they have taken the trouble to turn out a unit that in each case has the form of a single letter. Why this is so is not entirely clear; it is a point not satisfactorily explained on the basis of this theory of the editing of the pauline writings. An important virtue of the theory is that it draws attention to the moment of collection as of crucial importance for the works of Paul as we meet them in the New Testament, alongside the moment of writing to which attention has usually been exclusively directed.

But to return to this particular passage; perhaps it is not so clear in fact that these verses were originally the end of a letter. Where Paul does finish with personal details they usually appear in the form of greetings, but even these are by no means universal (see *Galatians*, *2 Corinthians*). In any case, on the fragment-hypothesis itself, we could be by no means sure that our endings of letters originally belonged where we now have them. In one case, Rom. 16, there are very strong textual as well as literary grounds for suspecting that this collection of greetings was not originally written for the letter to which it is now attached (see C. K. Barrett, *The Epistle to the Romans* (London, 1957) pp. 10–13). In our present case it is a matter not of greetings but of plans for the future, and there are certainly cases of Paul putting such material in the body of his writings: cf. 1 Cor. 4$^{17-19}$; 2 Cor. 8$^{16-19}$. The Corinthian correspondence is a particularly helpful parallel because it is another case of a church founded and closely shepherded by Paul. We conclude that it is by no means clear that we have here the end of a letter and that the following chapters did not originally belong where they are now placed. This can be said without deciding for or against the fragment-hypothesis in general or indeed about its applicability to other parts of *Philippians*. In the second half of the epistle we shall find other places where these considerations arise again.

There are also biographical questions. The most teasing is whether these verses throw any light on the location of Paul's imprisonment.

When the evidence is so slender there is of course a tendency to clutch at straws. Here, it is sometimes held, Paul seems to imply that Philippi is within reasonably easy visiting distance of his present abode. Epaphroditus has come to him, and with others will go to Philippi. To plan so many trips with such ease fits better with imprisonment in Ephesus or even Caesarea than Rome. But this may be either to underestimate the facility of Roman communications or to judge men of the first century in the light of our own expectations of travelling comfort. There are many examples from the past of men being willing to tolerate much harder conditions than would have faced a traveller from Rome to Philippi, and to move about a great deal despite them. Our passage leaves the question of where Paul was imprisoned quite open.

The other chief importance of the passage is the light which it casts on the inner working of Paul's apostolate. It is clear from references like this that it was a highly corporate enterprise, in which Paul was the leader of a team. But one feature of this team comes to the surface here which is often obscured, partly because it is not found in quite this way in the *Acts of the Apostles*, and partly because it goes against attempts to give a reasonably neat picture of the structure of the early Church. It is commonly held that there was a distinction between apostles (= missionaries) and the leaders of local churches established by them. The former were peripatetic, the latter static; the former belonged only to the first generation, the latter were the seed of the ordinary episcopal and presbyteral ministry which came to be permanent in the Church. From this passage it looks as if that distinction is too neat. It does not appear that Paul makes a rigid distinction between Timothy and Epaphroditus, though the former belongs more to the mobile missionary team and the latter is mainly a leader of the church in Philippi. Both are nevertheless members of the apostle's entourage, and Epaphroditus himself is given the title *apostolos* (translated *messenger* here); and it is going too far to say that in Paul's mind its use here was entirely non-technical whereas when he applied it to himself it always had, as it were, a capital 'A' and denoted a fully defined office which he shared with Peter and the rest (see notes below). At this time the line between the missionaries and the leaders of the local churches was probably much more blurred than the more schematized pictures of either *Acts* or later history-writing often show. The fact that Paul can call

Epaphroditus his *synergos* (*fellow worker*) probably confirms this (see below).

༺༻

19
Timothy: appears only momentarily in the *Acts of the Apostles* ($16^{1ff.}$), but is much more prominent in Paul's writings (Rom. 16^{21}; 1 Cor. 4^{17}; 16^{10}; 2 Cor. 1^1; Col. 1^1; 1 Thess. 1^1; 2 Thess. 1^1; Philem. 1). The latter picture should be firmly adopted as the more reliable guide to the actual situation. It is confirmed by the fact that he is made the recipient of two of the three almost certainly pseudonymous Pastoral Epistles, indicating that this estimate of his importance was shared by some of Paul's followers in the next generation (cf. also Heb. 13^{23}).

20
like him: the Greek adjective *isopsychos* (lit. 'equal-souled') is not adequately rendered by this expression. It probably refers to his likemindedness with Paul rather than with others, and the sense is that he is the person Paul can most completely rely on to share his own concern for the Christians in Philippi.

21
They all look after their own interests: cf. 1^{17}, though there the reference is to members of the Christian congregation in Rome, here more narrowly perhaps to members of the apostolic team.

25
I have thought: English would use the present tense here. In epistolary Greek the writer projects himself into the time of the letter's reception.

Epaphroditus: quite unknown apart from this reference, he was probably a leader of the Philippian church, and almost certainly of pagan background, to judge from the formation of his name from that of the goddess Aphrodite.

fellow worker (synergos): it looks as if Paul reserves this title for associates in active apostolic work and, probably, in consequent suffering too (see John Knox, *Philemon among the Letters of Paul*, pp. 56f.).

fellow soldier (systratiōtēs): this is a rarer title and may have a more specialized meaning. In the one or two occurrences of it in popular usage, it seems to be associated with comradeship which involves a financial element. (See Philem. 2.) So here, Epaphroditus has been the bearer of material aid to Paul (cf. 4^{18}). (See Knox, op. cit., pp. 58f.)

messenger (apostolos): the word, a noun from the verb meaning *to send out*, means in the ordinary Greek of the time 'a letter' or 'a bill of lading' or sometimes, 'a messenger'. *Messenger* or *delegate* is its basic sense in the New Testament. But also (see commentary above) it carries more and more, especially in some of the later New Testament books, the more technical sense of *Apostle* – an official missionary; and it is not easy to say when the one sense shades into the other. Here, as in 2 Cor. 8^{23}, it is more probably the former than the latter; Epaphroditus is not being seen as the Philippians' apostle or missionary in a strict sense, nevertheless he is their messenger on Christian business. As far as Paul's own usage is concerned we can sum the matter up by saying that when he applies the title to himself the technical element comes from the source of his commission – he is, in his typical expression (e.g. 1 Cor. 1^1), an apostle of Jesus Christ – rather than from the word itself.

minister (leitourgos): as in v. 17, Paul uses the image of the sacrificial cult, and he refers to it again in v. 30. Epaphroditus, like a priest, has made a sacrificial offering on behalf of the Philippians to Paul in his need (cf. 4^{18}).

27

sorrow upon sorrow: Epaphroditus' death following upon either his illness or Paul's imprisonment.

30

risking his life: suffering, for Paul, is always the mark of real Christian service; cf. his boasting of his own sufferings in passages like 3^8 and 2 Cor. 11^{23-30}. This is based on general grounds of course – readiness to suffer always shows the genuineness of a man's attachment to a cause; but also on more specific ones. Especially since the time of the Maccabean martyrs of the mid second century B.C., Judaism had given great honour to martyrs and cultivated both their memory and the kind of piety which they inspired. Paul the Pharisee was the heir of that tradition, and it was to find a continuation in the devotion to the martyrs which was so prominent in the Church from the second century onwards. But Paul also gives high value to suffering for another, more strictly Christian reason: that it is the supreme expression and outcome of identification with Christ whose death is so much the heart of his doctrine (see 1^{29}).

¹*Finally, my brethren, rejoice in the Lord. To write the same things to you is not irksome to me, and is safe for you.*

²*Look out for the dogs, look out for the evil-workers, look out for those who mutilate the flesh.* ³*For we are the true circumcision, who worship God in spirit*ᵉ*, and glory in Christ Jesus, and put no confidence in the flesh.* ⁴*Though I myself have reason for confidence in the flesh also. If any other man thinks he has reason for confidence in the flesh, I have more;* ⁵*circumcised on the eighth day, of the people of Israel, of the tribe of Benjamin, a Hebrew born of Hebrews; as to the law a Pharisee,* ⁶*as to zeal a persecutor of the Church, as to righteousness under the law, blameless.* ⁷*But whatever gain I had, I counted as loss for the sake of Christ.* ⁸*Indeed I count everything as loss because of the surpassing worth of knowing Christ Jesus my Lord. For his sake I have suffered the loss of all things, and count them as refuse, in order that I may gain Christ* ⁹*and be found in him, not having a righteousness of my own, based on law, but that which is through faith in Christ, the righteousness from God that depends on faith;* ¹⁰*that I may know him and the power of his resurrection, and may share his sufferings, becoming like him in his death,* ¹¹*that if possible I may attain the resurrection from the dead.*

¹²*Not that I have already obtained this or am already perfect; but I press on to make it my own, because Christ Jesus has made me his own.* ¹³*Brethren, I do not consider that I have made it my own; but one thing I do, forgetting what lies behind and straining forward to what lies ahead,* ¹⁴*I press on toward the goal for the prize of the upward call of God in Christ Jesus.* ¹⁵*Let those of us who are mature be thus minded; and if in anything you are otherwise minded, God will reveal that also to you.* ¹⁶*Only let us hold true to what we have attained.*

¹⁷*Brethren, join in imitating me, and mark those who so live as you have an example in us.* ¹⁸*For many, of whom I have often told you and now tell you even with tears, live as enemies of the cross of Christ.* ¹⁹*Their end is destruction, their god is the belly, and they glory in their shame, with minds set on earthly things.* ²⁰*But our commonwealth is in heaven, and from it we await a Saviour, the Lord Jesus Christ,* ²¹*who will change our lowly body to be like his glorious body, by the power which enables him even to subject all things to himself.*

4^1 *Therefore, my brethren, whom I love and long for, my joy and crown, stand firm thus in the Lord, my beloved.*

e Other ancient authorities read *worship by the Spirit of God*.

We have examined the suggestion that the last paragraphs of ch. 2 bear the marks of the ending of a letter. If *chairete* (translated, *rejoice*) be taken in its other sense as the ordinary closing greeting, *farewell*, then we can add 3^{1a} to ch. 2 and find the case for this view considerably strengthened. However, this rendering is not at all certain (see detailed notes) and the question cannot be so easily settled.

Not only 2^{19-30}, but also ch. 3 in its own right is prominent in the discussion of the integrity of *Philippians* (see Introduction, pp. 40f.). Many see it as one of the best candidates for treatment as a separate unit. But we cannot make a decision simply on literary grounds; at all points matters of content intertwine with arguments from structure.

At the beginning there has to be a decision about the degree of looseness of structure one is prepared to find credible in a single work of this character. If we regard *Philippians* as a fairly formal work, then clearly there are breaks in the structure and thought which are intolerable and are most readily explained by saying that it is a collection of fragments. But if this is an informal letter, in which the writer, while having important and definite things to say, allows his thought to hop and drift easily, we have no need to be surprised at even rather violent breaks and changes of subject. In other words if rough coherence of thought in the letter as a whole can be demonstrated, giving evidence of a mind occupied with a certain range of topics, this will weigh much more heavily in favour of its unity than disjointed literary structure will weigh against it. Therefore the thought of the passage clearly demands prior attention; only in the light of that can the question of the unity of *Philippians* – so far as this chapter is relevant to it – be rightly tackled.

The prior question is itself complex and divides into two: (i) Against whom is its vivid language directed? Is just one group of opponents in mind or more than one? (ii) Does it fit with what Paul is saying in the rest of *Philippians* or not? The answers to these questions will emerge from the exposition of the chapter, and to that we now turn.

Exposition

The first verse is on any showing abrupt and difficult, and fits equally well (or badly!) with almost any total interpretation. It is entirely unclear what *the same things* are being compared with; does Paul imply that in what follows he will repeat the message he has already just given? The evidence for this is that exhortation to internal peace and unity in the church runs like a thread through the whole epistle (1^{27}; 2^{1-3}; 3^{16-21}; 4^2). The prominence of this theme well justifies Paul's mild apology here. If this is right then verse 3^{1b} itself points to the unity of the epistle. But Paul may be referring to the teaching he has given to the Philippians in the past, either by letter or in person, and this of course fits well with the view that ch. 3 is a separate letter.

The first section, vv. 2–11, contains probably the most succinct statement we have of Paul's central doctrine of the work of Christ, formulated in some of the same terms as in *Romans* and *Galatians*, where it is treated more extensively. Here the tone is more personal and from the heart than anywhere else. Its simplicity and clarity make it a passage of great importance for understanding this doctrine. It is written not by way of exposition for its own sake but in lively response to opponents who deny it. V. 2 indicates that these opponents are not members of the church in Philippi but either Christian visitors from elsewhere or non-Christians who are engaging in controversy with them. Certainly they are Jews whose Jewish claims Paul is able to match (vv. 4–6); but whether they are *Christian* Jews or not is not immediately clear and we can attempt to decide that issue only in the light of the whole chapter. In v. 2, Paul attacks them with pure invective, and he adopts the same tone in v. 19. These sudden outbursts which contrast with the sunny atmosphere of the rest of the epistle have led some to support the view that this chapter is not of a piece with it. But other passages elsewhere show Paul to be easily capable of these alterations of mood: cf. Gal. 3^1 and perhaps 4^{21}; also Phil. 1^{17} is severe. In any case the fact that Paul speaks to his church in tones of joy and confidence does not mean that he will feel a similar quiet benevolence towards those who attempt to subvert them – quite the contrary. Further, though there is no doubt that *dog* in particular is an abusive term, we do not know how far its use indicates bad-tempered anger and how far it was an almost conventional term for those standing outside and in opposition to the true Israel (which for Christians is the Church, for Jews the strict confines of Judaism). Certainly it is common enough in the New Testament alone (Matt. 7⁶; Mark 7²⁷; Rev. 22¹⁵), to make the latter sense more likely.

It is important to grasp the precise point of Paul's difference from those aggressively Jewish opponents. He is not making a distinction between two moral standards, *righteousness under the law* (v. 6) and *the righteousness from God that depends on faith* (v.9), the second being higher than the first; the first already attained by Paul in his Jewish days (*blameless*, v. 6), the second only now possible for him. Nor is it the point that becoming a Christian has given Paul the ability actually to achieve a higher moral performance. He was already blameless by the exacting and comprehensive provisions of the Jewish Law. Though Paul brings to the fore (e.g. in Rom. 13⁹) the command to love the neighbour (cf. Lev. 19¹⁸), he nowhere hints that Christians had moral precepts unknown to Jews. In order to see his meaning the key word is *righteousness*, and the real point at issue is between two kinds of righteousness, that enjoined by the Law, and that which depends on faith in Christ. It is Christ who constitutes the point of differentiation, for he is the source or basis of the new kind of righteousness. It is then apparent that this righteousness is not wholly definable in moral terms, perhaps not primarily in moral terms, for it is at heart a question of attitude to Christ. Vv.10f. look as if it were to be defined also in terms related to man's hope of new life from God – *the resurrection from the dead*; for discussion of it leads Paul straight into the statement of that hope, and the verses that follow sustain the theme. The resurrection-hope is Paul's most natural and comprehensive way of expressing the idea of 'man's ultimate bliss'. It is therefore the fulfilment of the relationship with Christ which is based on the new kind of righteousness; to whose closer definition we must come. But first we eliminate one shallow solution.

One might be tempted to suppose that Paul had been led to use the word righteousness in this context for reasons connected with his own personal history. Surely the word is chiefly ethical in meaning, and surely what has happened is that Paul, preoccupied as a Jew above all with the problem of obedience to the Law, saw the religious task in these terms, and when he came to believe in Jesus as Israel's Messiah could most naturally express the new life in 'righteousness-language'. That this is unlikely to be the whole truth becomes plain when the antecedents of the pauline usage in the Old Testament are examined.

The English word itself is misleading, and we must clear up a lexical difficulty to which it gives rise. The trouble is that it fails to reveal the word-families (both in Greek and Hebrew) which lie behind it in the biblical text. The Greek *dikaiosynē*, translated *righteousness* or *justice*, is cognate with *dikaios* (*just* or *righteous*) and *dikaioō* (*to account just* or *righteous* or *to justify*). The advantage of the word *righteousness* as a translation is that it helps to avoid the flavour of our use of *justice* which is untrue to the biblical usage. When the Old Testament speaks of God's justice or righteousness,* it does not think, as we naturally should, of his fairness or equity, of measuring his conduct and ours by reference to abstract moral standards. Rather it is a question of God's determination to carry out his good purposes and to set affairs in the order which he desires for them. The right is wholly the expression of his will, worked out in human affairs and especially in the destiny of his people. Always the word is seen in personal terms and in terms of the claims of each specific relationship to which it is applied. To be righteous is to satisfy the claims of a relationship rather than those of an abstract ethical norm. Thus (to take a simple example from human relations) when Saul says that David is more righteous than himself, he means that David has taken the obligations of the relationship existing between the two of them more seriously than he himself has done (1 Sam. 24¹⁷).

Of chief importance are the relationship between God and Israel and the claims to which that gives rise. On God's side the relationship is directed not only towards the people's obedience but also towards their salvation. Its claims always look to that end, so that its purpose lies not only in the moral realm but also in the historical – and ultimately in that of eschatology, for the historical process is thought of in the light of its future consummation in a decisive intervention by God. This close connexion in the Old Testament between righteousness and ultimate salvation brought about in the course of history (which already adumbrates the pauline passages before us) is perhaps clearest in *Deutero-Isaiah* (40–55): see especially Isa. 45⁸, ²³ᶠ·; 46¹²ᶠ·. If this is the way *God's* righteousness is understood, then *man's* righteousness consists in his acceptance of the demands of his relationship with God, a relationship which, as we have seen, always looks to the coming consummation.

* See G. von Rad, *Old Testament Theology, Vol. I* (Edinburgh, 1962), pp. 370ff.

Quite often in the Old Testament the term also has forensic associations. In *Deutero-Isaiah* the model of the law court is plainly in mind: e.g. $43^{9, \ 26}$; and the same is true of the *Book of Job*, where Job makes his claim to be righteous (9^{15}) the ground for his seeking a favourable verdict from God (6^{29}; 13^3, $^{13-16}$).

All these elements are present in the pauline use, and it may be that the forensic element is strengthened by the translation into Greek, with the more strongly legal associations of the word in the Greek world. Bultmann describes its use as 'forensic-eschatological'*: the general imagery in mind is that of a law court in which man's relationship with God is to be determined, and this is seen as the goal of God's purpose.

Paul is convinced that the Jewish view of God's purpose and of man's best way of working towards it, that is, by obedience to the Law, is now shown to be worthless and misguided. Another way, and the only true way, is now plain; *through faith in Christ* in whom God has acted to make his righteousness known and available (Rom. $1^{16f.}$). Paul has decided that if man's object is to reach the right relationship with God, then the Law is neither relevant nor useful. Righteousness, man's right relationship with God and rightness of direction towards him, is not to be found there, but in connexion with Christ.

On the basis of this passage alone, though it is abundantly clear that Paul feels this passionately, it is not plain exactly why it should be so. The full case has to be assembled from *Romans* and *Galatians* (especially Rom. $3^{21ff.}$, $5^{1ff.}$; Gal. $2^{15ff.}$); but in order to make sense of our present passage we must give here some account of the considerations which moved him. There is, however, one most valuable point that is as clear from these verses as from any other place in Paul's writings: the vital importance for Paul of the person of Christ and of Christ's impact upon him. It is not as if consideration of the defects of the Law has prompted Paul to cast around for alternatives. *The surpassing worth of knowing Christ Jesus my Lord* (v. 8) stands in its own right.

Nevertheless the defects of the Law are real. True, Paul can say that it is good and valuable (Rom. 7^{12}) and that it stems from God (Rom. 7^{14}), even that by comparison with a worldly outlook it is a way of

* R. Bultmann, *Theology of the New Testament*, Vol. I (London, 1952), pp. 270ff.

pleasing God (Rom. $8^{7f.}$). But one of its chief values is the negative one that it makes a man conscious of sin (Rom. 7^7). Indeed, as far as positive usefulness to man is concerned, the Law is radically deficient. It is powerless to bring man to full relationship with God (Gal. 3^2, $^{21f.}$). By setting man a standard which he does not keep and seems powerless to attain by his moral effort, it shows up man's condition and aggravates it without at all relieving it.

Paul's view of the Law's origin and future is in line with this. Like other Jews of the Dispersion he was reluctant to see the whole Law as the unmediated work of God, bearing his direct authority. It was, he holds, *ordained by angels* (Gal. 3^{19}); and he (even as a Jew? – certainly as a Christian) saw the commands of the Decalogue as having in some way superior validity (Rom. $13^{9f.}$). For Paul the Law as a whole was at best a temporary guide for man, and now its day was over (Gal. 3^{19}, ^{24}).

Nevertheless the need of man which the Law failed to satisfy and the saving love of God which it failed to convey both remained. What was required was that man should be brought to share in God's righteousness, and this could best be done by some direct act of gracious generosity which would lift him into partnership with God; something much more direct and intimate than the mere placing of law before his eyes. Paul held that this was what had occurred in the life, death and resurrection of Jesus. This was the act of righteousness *par excellence*; as in the Old Testament, not a static disposition of God but a dynamic quality, bringing about what he desired.

There is one final feature of the Law to which Paul draws attention and which, psychologically speaking particularly, probably gave it the *coup de grâce* as far as he was concerned. By its provisions (Deut. 21^{23}), Christ, as an executed criminal, was subject to its curse, yet Paul knew him as the sinless one (Gal. 3^{13}; 2 Cor. 5^{21}). There must be something radically at fault in a law according to whose provisions such a thing could happen. Its day must be over, and the act itself must be a means of release from its claims for all who transgress its terms and desire the freedom it is powerless to give.

As the means to forgiveness it is replaced by *faith in Christ*, which is man's willing openness to God's gift, a total readiness to be drawn into the act of salvation and so into relationship with Christ as God's agent in that act.

If in our passage Paul simply states rather than argues the uselessness of the Law, so also he fails to say why Christ should be the one through whom righteousness is now conferred and the forgiven relationship established. The hymn in 2$^{6-11}$ is one way in which Paul would have explained it; he would have told the story of the drama of Christ, culminating in his exaltation to the position of cosmic lordship. But he would also have shown how at all points he fulfilled the promise of the Old Testament Scriptures, rightly interpreted. Both in his sufferings and in his subsequent exaltation by God he was the fulfilment of the whole saving activity of God.

What exactly had he done? He had brought it about that God's forgiveness and the full reconciliation with him which that implied were now open to man; man was 'right with God' on the basis of faith – that is, simple, trusting acceptance of God's gift. Not only in the present but also for the future, both immediate and long-term, new life was available for man, by virtue of his relationship with Christ; hence Paul's reference in this context to the resurrection from the dead (vv. 10f.; see above, p. 97). From the moment of his entering this relationship in baptism (Rom. 6$^{3\text{ff.}}$) the Christian has taken on the pattern of Christ's suffering, and in it feels the authentic seeds of the resurrection-life growing within him (vv. 10f.; cf. 2 Cor. 4$^{7-12}$).

Thus, from v. 10 to v. 16 and then again in vv. 20f., attention moves from the establishing of the new relationship (in which the key word is *righteousness*), to the future hope to which it logically gives rise. Now the key word is perhaps *perfect* (v. 12 and v. 15 = *mature*), and with this word Paul moves from Old Testament concepts into his other key, that of Hellenistic religion. It does occur in the Old Testament (e.g. Deut. 18^{13}; cf. Matt. 5^{48}), and here it is fully integrated with ideas of Jewish origin; but in its application to the future, final state it is not far from the language of the mystery cults where the initiates were often known as 'the perfect ones'. As in 1 Cor. 2^6 it is possible that Paul takes it out of the mouths of those whom he is opposing; they *think* they are mature (v. 15).

But how exactly does Paul envisage the future in store for Christians, which he has not yet attained but towards which he presses with such fervour? What is it that *lies ahead* (v. 13)? Once more this passage is brief and cryptic, and we must look elsewhere in Paul's writings in order to understand what he means. (See also above on 1$^{19-26}$.) Apart from the crucial new fact of relationship with Christ, Paul's concept of the future in this passage seems to be not dissimilar from that of Pharisaic Judaism. He looks forward to the resurrection of God's people from the dead. But Christ makes these points of difference: (*a*) he has already risen from the dead and this fact is the guarantee of the future resurrection of his people (Rom. 8²⁹; 1 Cor. 15²⁰ff.). Here this is implicit in v. 10f. (*b*) He will at his second coming transform the bodies of his followers to be like his own risen body, by the exercise of the lordship which he has received (v. 21; cf. 1 Cor. 15⁵¹f.).

But clearly this future consummation which Christ will bestow (seen in typical Jewish manner in terms of the transformation of the whole person) is of a piece with the relationship already established with him. From this point of view the vital step comes at the earliest moment, when the relationship begins. This is the step described here in terms of the acquiring of righteousness, or, more simply, *knowing Christ Jesus my Lord* (v. 8). (In *Romans* and *Galatians*, it is more characteristically spoken of as being justified by God – a word cognate in Greek, as we saw, with the word translated *righteousness*.) From the initial step to the final consummation, the Christian is most characteristically spoken of as being 'in Christ' (cf. v. 9 *be found in him*).

There is therefore in the whole process a unity – given by the person of Christ. The overwhelming importance of this for Paul, which comes out most clearly in v. 8, is a feature of his thought whose neglect quickly leads to difficulty. For in the course of his writings he can speak of different parts of the process in such a wide variety of ways that he easily appears to be inconsistent and it is hard to arrive at a coherent picture of his doctrine. Thus sometimes he uses the language of resurrection and new life for the Christian's present existence, as if he already enjoys that participation in the risen life of Christ which in our present passage is reserved for the last times: see Col. 3¹; 2 Cor. 4⁷⁻¹²; and, less unambiguously, Rom. 6³⁻¹¹. The strongest statement along these lines is in the *Colossians* passage, and there are those who take it as evidence that Paul was not the author of that work. But this is an unnecessary inference. The new relationship with God through Christ so dominates his outlook that the variety of statement simply reflects a variety of emphasis, determined by the needs of the audience or the demands of the argument in each particular case. Thus, in these verses, where Paul seems to be confronting people who are over-optimistic about the degree of perfection they have achieved, he lays stress on what still remains to be attained and on the need to strive. Elsewhere he appeals rather to the greatness of what has already been received. The fundamental outlook underlying both emphases finds perhaps its simplest and most striking expression in 1^{23} where he can speak of a Christian's death as leading to his being *with Christ*.

We are now in a position to return to the questions which we raised before we began this long exposition.

(1) *Against whom is Paul writing?*

Apart from the word *dogs* (v. 2) it would be hard to tell whether the opponents are Jews inside the church or outside it, but, as we saw earlier, this term probably signifies those not in the people of Israel, and so, from Paul's point of view, non-Christian Jews. V. 3 confirms this: the Church, not Judaism, is the true Israel. This is entirely consistent with vv. 2–11 and not inconsistent with v. 18. It might be imagined that Paul would weep for those who live *as enemies of the cross of Christ* only if he had grounds for expecting them to be friends, that is, if he was thinking of erring Christians; but Paul continued to yearn for the conversion of his people, from whom he had now to his distress been separated (cf. Rom. 9^{1-5}), and to whom the cross, which to him was the way to salvation, was merely a stumbling-block (1 Cor. 1^{23}).

It is sometimes held that though law-keeping Jews are obviously in question in vv. $2^{ff.}$, this cannot be so in v. 19. Here it looks more like libertines of the kind who became prominent in some Gnostic groups of the second century. But this really depends upon taking *belly* to imply gross self-indulgence. It is, however, not at all certain that this is right. Early Christian commentators took it as a reference to over-devotion to the Jewish food laws. But it is probable that it no more points to the precise nature of the views of the persons concerned than do the parallel words *destruction* and *shame*. In Rom. 16^{18} the same word is used in what appears to be a fairly general sense for that sphere of things which is opposed by Christ and which is passing away. This is not at all incompatible in Paul's mind with devotion to the Law; for him that certainly belongs to the sphere of the 'flesh', when regarded as sufficient in itself. Similarly it may seem hard to describe faithful Jews as men *with minds set on earthly things*. But this is not a comment on their moral performance; it simply states that for Paul 'they are concerned with values which pass away, having neither divine origin nor eternal quality'.*

Some commentators (e.g. Koester, in the article just cited) see much more evidence that Hellenism is the dominant strand in the views which Paul here attacks. The best support for their case comes from the claim of Paul's opponents to a degree of spiritual perfection (later a Gnostic technical term) which he considers dangerous and excessive (vv. 12–16). However, at least one ground for their claim, their success in keeping the Jewish Law, hardly supports this view.

The three words in v. 19 (*end, god, glory*) also come into the discussion. It is alleged that these all allude to advanced spiritual claims (signifying respectively: spiritual goal, union with the divine, participation in the divine), and so plausibly come from the same world of thought. On this view Paul is saying that what his opponents consider to be the marks of high spiritual state are in fact destructive, pernicious, and disgraceful.

Hellenism and embryonic Gnosticism there may be, but it remains impossible to eliminate the strong signs of Judaism. Indeed it was at this time by no means impossible for Hellenistic Jews to share religious ideas and aspirations of this kind with those among whom they lived (see the commentary on *Colossians*, especially on ch. 1 & 2). Even in opposing them, Paul can make use of concepts which probably owe something to the same sources (e.g. knowing Christ, vv. 8 & 10; being possessed by Christ, v. 12). The fact is that the ideas which were to flower in the Gnostic sects of the second century grew up in many different soils.

Commonwealth (v. 20) may also support the view that Jewish opponents of some kind are here in view. *Politeuma* can easily mean simply 'state', as the present translation indicates; but sometimes it has the more specialized meaning of a colony of foreigners living within a state to which they do not belong. If Paul is writing with Jews in mind this ambiguity would be peculiarly telling. All over the Roman world Jews lived in just such groups, and concern with their communal life is part of the *earthly things* to which Paul thinks they devote too much attention. Christians, by contrast (the *our* is emphatic

---

* H. Koester, *The Purpose of the Polemic of a Pauline Fragment*, N.T.S., 8 (1962), p. 328. This article is a most useful discussion of many issues raised by Phil. 3. See also A. F. J. Klijn, *Paul's Opponents in Philippians 3*, Nov. Test., 7 (1965), pp. 278ff.

in Greek) have their homeland elsewhere: in heaven where Christ reigns and whence his return in power is eagerly awaited. But again there is an alternative. Taken in its common sense of state, the word would be most apt from the point of view of the receivers of the letter, the Gentile congregation of Philippi, the Roman colony, proud of its status. Moffatt's translation boldly brings out the point: 'We are a colony of heaven', that is, 'Our Rome is heaven'.

We conclude on balance that Paul's opponents here are Hellenistic Jews, outside the church and opposed to it, perhaps people of the kind we meet again in *Colossians*. But one point must be clearly stated: in the Gentile world to which Paul was writing, there was no absolute distinction between the cultural background of Jews on the one hand and Gentile Christians on the other. To a considerable degree they are likely to have shared common culture and common ways of religious thought and speculation.

(2) *Relationship with the rest of the epistle*

We have already in the course of our discussion referred to several points which are relevant to this question, and there is no need to go over the same ground again. But a few other points remain.

There are more connexions of theme and word between ch. 3 and the earlier part of *Philippians* than has often been noticed, and they are such as may be best explained by the kind of loose mental association which takes place naturally in the course of a piece of fairly informal writing.* Perhaps these connexions constitute the strongest argument for the integrity of the epistle. In particular there are in ch. 3 several terms which are possible reminiscences of 2^{6-11}, all the more impressive because the later passage is written in a more firmly Jewish key, with more solid use of Old Testament categories of thought than the hymn of ch. 2, and more awareness of the history of Israel. Thus the odd expression *being found in human form* (2^8) is echoed in 3^9. The humbling of Jesus in 2^8 can be compared with the (lit.) *body of our humiliation* (3^{21}). And the words translated *change* and *like* in 3^{21} are closely related to the important words translated *form* in 2^{6-8}. The transposition from Christ's cosmic lordship in the hymn to his intimate lordship over the individual Christian (*my Lord*, 3^8)

---

* See T. E. Pollard, *The Integrity of Philippians*, N.T.S., 13 (1966), pp. 57ff.; and B. S. Mackay, *Further Thoughts on Philippians*, N.T.S., 7 (1961), pp. 161ff.

does not tell against this view (and note 3^{21b}). Also, *politeuma* (*common-wealth*) occurs only in 3^{20}; the corresponding verb (*politeuesthai*) only in 1^{27} (lit. *live-state-wise worthily of the gospel of Christ*). *Latreuein* (*worship*)3^3 takes up once more the liturgical image of $2^{17, 30}$. *Kerdos* (*gain*) is rare, but is found in 1^{21} and 3^7.

More broadly, it is certainly the case that the themes of humility and obedience are common to both parts of the epistle. 2^{1-11} and 3^8 make the parallel between Christ's self-abasement and Paul's own personal surrender of what was dearest to him on the worldly plane. In the Church as in his own life he desires that the pattern of Christ's experience, exaltation *via* humble suffering, should be reproduced (3^{17}). All this is the exact opposite of those vices for which he has attacked the Philippian church itself ($1^{15, 17}$).

There seems to be no sufficient argument for separating this passage from the earlier part of the epistle. In another vein, more personal to Paul and therefore more marked by his own Jewish heritage, it expresses the same doctrine and exhorts to the same quality of life.

ಬಬ

1
rejoice: this is probably the right translation and certainly so if the epistle is a unity. But it can also mean *farewell* and Paul's *finally* (cf. 4^8) supports the fragment-theory which that meaning would entail. However, Paul's usual closing greeting is *charis* (grace be with you, etc.) – though see 2 Cor. 13^{11}. And the expression rendered *finally* occurs again happily in the middle of a work at 2 Thess. 3^1; it can in any case equally well mean *furthermore,* simply marking the transition to a new section.

2
those who mutilate the flesh: this is a periphrasis for a single Greek word, *katatomē,* which Paul uses because of its similarity of sound to *peritomē* (*circumcision*) in the next verse. He stigmatizes the sacred Jewish rite as self-mutilation, which was expressly forbidden in the Law (Lev. 21^5).

3
worship God in spirit: the textual variant noted in the margin is better attested and more likely to be correct than that used in the translation.

4
in the flesh: not *in the body* but rather, in line with ordinary pauline usage, *at the level of human attainment and human values.*

5

on the eighth day: i.e. in exact conformity with the Law, cf. Gen. 17¹².

tribe of Benjamin: cf. Rom. 11¹. His Jewish name, Saul, was that of the king who sprang from that tribe.

Pharisee: this explains much about Paul's Jewish background. The Pharisees were the dominant party in Palestinian Judaism, standing for the strict observance of the Law with the scribal tradition, and filled with the hope of the coming Kingdom of God and the resurrection of his servants from the dead. But this information about Paul also tells us something about Pharisaism, in that Paul is clearly familiar with many Hellenistic religious concepts and uses them naturally. It is a warning against seeing the Pharisees in too narrowly parochial a light.

6

zeal a persecutor: cf. Gal. 1¹³ᶠ·; 1 Cor. 15⁹ᶠ·. As this last reference makes especially clear, the fact that he had been a positive persecutor of the Church made God's acceptance of him all the more a matter of sheer grace, in Paul's eyes. It was also a fact which he seems to have felt impelled to mention, whenever he was writing autobiographically, as if out of a kind of purgative honesty (cf. also Acts 8³; 9¹ᶠᶠ·).

blameless: Paul's statement here makes a difficulty for those who wish to interpret Rom. 7⁷⁻ᵉⁿᵈ as a piece of autobiography and probably renders that interpretation untenable.

8

gain Christ: a strange phrase, to be understood in terms of the image of a profit and loss account which Paul is employing in these verses.

10f.

Notice the chiastic structure *(ab ba)*: resurrection, sufferings; death, resurrection.

13

forgetting what lies behind: perhaps his life in Judaism, but more probably his attainments so far as a Christian.

20

Saviour: Paul's only use of this title for Christ. It refers to him in his role at his final return. In this it is congruous with Paul's use of the cognate words *save* and *salvation* (cf. 1¹⁹; 2¹²), which also most commonly refer to the consummation of the work already begun in the believer. As title for Yahweh in O.T., see Isa. 12²; 45¹⁵.

21

to subject all things: cf. 2⁹⁻¹¹ and 1 Cor. 15²⁸ with Ps. 8⁶.

crown: cf. 1 Thess. 2^{19}. They are an adornment to Paul's ministry. A Greek memorial of the period has a similar use of the word.

²I entreat Euodia and I entreat Syntyche to agree in the Lord. ³And I ask you also, true yokefellow, help these women, for they have laboured side by side with me in the gospel together with Clement and the rest of my fellow workers, whose names are in the book of life.

⁴Rejoice in the Lord always; again I will say, Rejoice. ⁵Let all men know your forbearance. The Lord is at hand. ⁶Have no anxiety about anything, but in everything by prayer and supplication with thanksgiving let your requests be made known to God. ⁷And the peace of God, which passes all understanding, will keep your hearts and your minds in Christ Jesus.

⁸Finally, brethren, whatever is true, whatever is honourable, whatever is just, whatever is pure, whatever is lovely, whatever is gracious, if there is any excellence, if there is anything worthy of praise, think about these things. ⁹What you have learned and received and heard and seen in me, do; and the God of peace will be with you.

Those who favour partition-theories are divided on what to do with this passage: if 3^{1}–4^{1} is taken as part of a separate letter, then 4^{2}f. certainly follows suitably after the other personal sections (2$^{19-30}$) about Timothy and Epaphroditus. But we have seen no compelling reason for supposing that this is justified; we take Paul to be simply writing first passages about particular individuals and then more general exhortations as they occur to him. If, however only 3$^{2-\text{end}}$ is extracted, 3^{1} being left as part of the main letter, then v.1a becomes the beginning of Paul's rather protracted farewells, and v.1b an apology for his return to the theme of the need for harmony in 4, where he points to one particularly serious case of friction (cf. 2^{2}f.).

We know nothing else about the two women, Euodia and Syntyche, whose dissension is singled out by Paul, presumably because it was a peculiarly strong disturbance to the unity of the church in Philippi. They are among Paul's *fellow-workers*, those actively engaged with him in the apostolate. A great many women occupy this place in Paul's entourage – Phoebe, Prisca, and Mary in Rom. 16$^{1, 3, 6}$, for example; something wholly unlikely in Judaism. On some aspects of the part they played the evidence is uncertain, in particular with regard to the gatherings of the church for worship. 1 Cor. 14$^{34-36}$ enjoins silence upon them, but in 1 Cor. 11^5 we read of women praying and preaching, presumably at meetings of the church. Perhaps some women received explicit authority for this; notice Phoebe's formal title in Rom. 16^1. But whatever the particular arrangements, Paul's underlying principle is stated in Gal. 3^{28}.

Having referred to the women's poor behaviour and then to the work to which they are called, Paul goes on to speak, by contrast, of the disposition which they, and all his readers, ought to possess. It is characterized by joy at the imminence of the Lord's return. This gives them confidence free from all anxiety. All their thinking is maintained and stabilized *in Christ Jesus*, on the basis of their secure relationship with him. Paul then goes on to describe this thinking in the most general moral terms: the virtues he mentions are those which any pagan would approve. These qualities they are to possess, imitating Paul himself (v. 9).

This uniquely detailed commendation of virtue as a Greek saw it (some of the words, those translated *lovely* and *gracious*, are found only here in the New Testament), is interesting theologically. It shows Paul unselfconsciously acting upon that positive evaluation of pagan ethics which he gives in Rom. 2^{14}. The basis for it is in Rom. 1$^{19ff.}$, where Paul says that the creation itself is sufficient evidence for the knowledge of God's being and of his moral commands. The pagan is perfectly capable of knowing the main ethical principles by which man is to live. (Paul does not formally distinguish between the moral and the ceremonial law but probably, in common with other Hellenistic Jews of his time, this is what he has in mind.) Here Paul goes one step further by actually using ordinary Greek ethical terms as the means of his exhortation and apparently as a description of his own conduct. Such behaviour brings the presence of God (v. 9). He characterizes this moral way as a whole by the central Greek term for moral *excellence (aretē)*.

ॐ

3
yokefellow: this word has been the subject of endless and often over-ingenious discussion. The difficulty is that Paul appears suddenly to

address a single individual in a letter otherwise directed to a whole church (1¹). The simplest explanation is that he sees the Philippian congregation as a unit, a body of people who share with him the burden of the apostolic work – he and they together like two oxen. But the protagonists of a fragment-theory can find here grist to their mill. Some see the word as a proper name; but there is no evidence of the word (*syzygos*) ever being used in that way.

laboured side by side: the same word as in 1²⁷. The image is that of the games, cf. 3¹⁴.

Clement: there is no reason to identify him with the Roman presbyter of the nineties of the first century who was concerned in the writing of the letter which goes by his name (*1 Clement*); but many have not been thereby prevented from making the identification. The name is common.

the book of life: the idea of a heavenly book in which God inscribes the names of his faithful servants appears already in the Old Testament, cf. Exod. 32³²; Ps. 139¹⁶; and then more strongly in apocalyptic speculation, both Jewish (Dan. 12¹) and Christian (Rev. 20¹²⁻¹⁵; Luke 10²⁰). It will be used for the Judgement at the Last Day. Cf. Col. 1⁴, p. 151.

4
Rejoice: once more this could mean *farewell* (cf. 3¹), but it makes better sense if it does not.

5
The Lord is at hand: even in this late epistle, written perhaps near the end of his life, Paul does not cease to expect the imminent return of Christ. Cf. Rom. 13¹¹; I Cor. 16²².

6
have no anxiety: cf. Matt. 6²⁵ᶠᶠ.

7
the peace of God: peace in the Bible is a much more full-blooded concept than in our modern usage. It stands for a total well-being which is commonly associated with the state of salvation. It is therefore a gift from God, cf. Eph. 2¹⁴, very close to *righteousness from God* in 3⁹. As such a comprehensive gift, it can be relied upon to protect man completely. Note the use of the reverse expression in v. 9.

8
The R.S.V. translation of this verse, though accurate, is not entirely intelligible. It is best to take the two *if* clauses as summing up the contents of the *whatever* clauses; and both together are to fill the Christians' minds and inspire their conduct.

¹⁰*I rejoice in the Lord greatly that now at length you have revived your concern for me; you were indeed concerned for me, but you had no opportunity.* ¹¹*Not that I complain of want; for I have learned, in whatever state I am, to be content.* ¹²*I know how to be abased, and I know how to abound; in any and all circumstances I have learned the secret of facing plenty and hunger, abundance and want.* ¹³*I can do all things in him who strengthens me.*

¹⁴*Yet it was kind of you to share my trouble.* ¹⁵*And you Philippians yourselves know that in the beginning of the gospel, when I left Macedonia, no church entered into partnership with me in giving and receiving, except you only;* ¹⁶*for even in Thessalonica you sent me help*ƒ *once and again.* ¹⁷*Not that I seek the gift; but I seek the fruit which increases to your credit.* ¹⁸*I have received full payment, and more; I am filled, having received from Epaphroditus the gifts you sent, a fragrant offering, a sacrifice acceptable and pleasing to God.* ¹⁹*And my God will supply every need of yours according to his riches in glory in Christ Jesus.* ²⁰*To our God and Father be glory for ever and ever. Amen.*

ƒ *Other ancient authorities read* money for my needs.

This passage gives us as good a sight of the intimacy of Paul's relationship with one of his congregations as we find anywhere in his correspondence. On the one hand he is bound to them by many valued bonds of kindness. On the other hand, as their pastor and teacher, he can never refrain from setting all their relations in the context of the gospel and the essential lines of Christian discipleship. And he is not unaware that there is a possibility of the latter looking discourteous in relation to the former. He has learned as a Christian how to glory in sufferings both for the sake of Christ and as identification with Christ's own sufferings (cf. 3¹⁰f.; 2⁵⁻¹¹); this gives him a certain detachment from the vicissitudes of his life. Yet he is not thereby aloof from human relationships and appreciates the kindness which he has recently received from Philippi (as well as earlier instances of it), knowing the love which inspires it.

From a passage like this it is evident that by comparison with the church at Corinth, seen reflected in *1 & 2 Corinthians*, the congregation at Philippi had caused Paul few problems and had been strong enough to join devotedly in his missionary work. In this it may have been the exception rather than the rule. V. 15 gives a glimpse of the massive discouragement which obviously faced Paul's apostolate at the human level.

Some argue from v. 18 that Paul is here writing what is clearly a 'thank-you' letter; so it is likely that it comes immediately upon reception of the gift; so this passage is unlikely to be part of the same letter as 2^{25ff}, which shows the bearer of the gift, Epaphroditus, as having had time to be seriously ill and to be well on the way to recovery. All this is however needless conjecture. If the section with which we are here concerned *is* part of the single letter then the sending of gratitude for the gift is only one reason for writing. Paul does it most graciously, and knows the Philippians well enough to be able to chide them a little and warn them, while at the same time being courteous. There is no real incongruity here.

Nor is the question of the amount of time involved really difficult. Lightfoot (*Commentary*, p. 38, n.1) thought that 'a month would probably be a fair allowance of time for the journey between Rome and Philippi', but Sir William Ramsay's estimate was less optimistic – at least seven weeks. Admittedly, if 2^{26} is taken to imply both that a letter has gone to Philippi reporting Epaphroditus' illness and that another letter has returned saying how sorry his friends are to hear the news, we must allow a gap of at least four months between Epaphroditus' arrival with the present and Paul's letter of thanks. And this would assume that Epaphroditus fell ill on the journey or immediately on arrival in Rome. Even assuming a delay of this length, the picture does not seem impossible. The plan was for Epaphroditus to take the letter of thanks with him when he returned. This return was delayed by his illness; so the letter was also deferred. But of course there is no certainty that the period was as long as this; 2^{26} does not actually say that letters had gone in *both* directions. Epaphroditus knows that they have heard of his sickness – that is all; he knows that information has gone to them, whether by letter or by a traveller we cannot tell. Moreover, if 4^{10-20} is part of an immediate letter of thanks, written months before the rest of *Philippians*, why was it not sent by Epaphroditus if he was well; and if he was already ill, why is the fact not mentioned in a context which surely makes it natural to do so? One suggestion, that our epistle is indeed a single whole, but that an earlier non-extant letter of thanks had been sent, making our passage a second expression of gratitude, is unevidenced and unnecessary. It tells against it that the word *apechō* (*I have received*) in v. 18 is the ordinary technical word for acknowledging receipt.

ɷ

10

The hint of reproach in the earlier part of the verse is immediately removed by what follows. Paul makes entirely legitimate excuses on their behalf: *they had no opportunity* – either because Paul's whereabouts were uncertain or not easily reached (perhaps we may think in terms of the long sea journey described in Acts 27) or because before his imprisonment he had not been in need.

11f.

Not that I complain of want: the latter suggestion for interpreting the end of v. 10 is perhaps confirmed by this. Certainly Paul made it a matter of pride that he was normally financially independent of his converts, though he recognized that he had a perfect right to be supported by them: cf. the much more querulous tone of his remarks on this matter, especially when contrasting his own behaviour with that of other apostles, in 1 Cor. 9$^{3-18}$. That passage makes plain, better than our present verses, that this was not a question of sheer awkwardness and obstinacy. It was pastoral wisdom in one who was engaged in often difficult relations with a number of different congregations composed of varied kinds of people, Jews, Greeks, etc. In such circumstances it was foolish for Paul to lay himself open to the charge of being specially beholden to any particular groups. He wanted to preserve at all costs complete freedom and immediacy for the flow of the gospel from him to his people. For this he needed to avoid all entanglement with secondary matters. (See especially 1 Cor. 9$^{12b \& 18f}$; cf. 2 Cor. 12^{14ff}.)

content: this hardly gives the full flavour of *autarkēs*. It signifies the dispassionate detachment from the vicissitudes of life which was the ideal of many in the ancient world, especially of the Stoics and those influenced by them. In expressing this ideal of self-sufficiency, Paul comes nearer than anywhere else to showing a definite relationship with the Stoicism of his times. But the sentences that follow show that this influence has not bitten very deeply into him. In particular, the acceptance of abasement (v. 12) is not something which a Stoic would applaud; the very word used by Paul is one which for them often headed the list of attitudes to be avoided (see M. S. Enslin, *The Ethics of Paul*, pp. 38f.). V. 13 sets Paul's quality firmly in the context of his Christian discipleship and so, implicitly, of his life 'in Christ', cf. 2^8. The passage should be read alongside 2 Cor. 11$^{22-28}$ & 1 Cor. 4^{11}.

15

the beginning of the gospel: the difficulty in interpreting this phrase comes from the presence of the words *when I left Macedonia.* Without them it would simply refer to the start of Paul's missionary work in the area of Philippi. It certainly cannot mean the beginning of his Christian life or of his mission as a whole. Perhaps it is best to take it as meaning the beginning of the missionary work in which the Philippians themselves had participated. Even then, the reference in the next verse to Thessalonica is not entirely clear – Thessalonica itself is in Macedonia; *and* rather than *for* at the beginning of v. 16 would have made it easier.

16

Thessalonica: Acts 17$^{1-9}$ places a brief visit (hardly long enough for the Philippians to give aid *once and again*) to this town immediately after the activity in Philippi described in ch. 16.

sent me help: they did the same during his period in Corinth, as 2 Cor. 11$^{8f.}$ shows. Perhaps it is this aid which is chiefly in mind in v. 15.

once and again: more than once is probably the sense, rather than *repeatedly.* It is a rare phrase but there are one or two instances in the Septuagint, especially Neh. 13^{20}. (*Hapax kai dis* = literally, *once and twice.*) The background is Hebrew not classical Greek.

17

fruit: this word can be used in the vocabulary of commerce to mean *profit,* and may well have this sense here, alongside other business terms which follow. Reverting to his more independent stance, Paul welcomes the gifts from Philippi less because they help him than for the sake of the increase they make to the church's stock of generous behaviour. The next verse indicates that it is God who will take note of this fact; he will regard their gift as an offering to himself.

18

a fragrant offering: liturgical imagery once more (cf. 2$^{17, 30}$). This phrase is the common technical term in the Levitical law in the Pentateuch, usually translated *a sweet savour.* It signifies the quality which a sacrificial offering should possess in order to be acceptable (e.g. Lev. 1^9); or else it refers to the sacrifice itself (e.g. Ezek. 16^{19}). See 2 Cor. 2^{14} for a not dissimilar use of the same image. In the distant background is the primitive idea of the deity taking pleasure in the smell of the sacrifices offered by man (cf. Gen. 8^{21}).

19

will supply: the verb is the same as that translated *I am filled* in v. 18. Their supplying of his needs will ensure that God himself will supply theirs. Spiritual needs are probably chiefly in mind, in view of the phrase *his riches in glory* (which probably means *his glorious or heavenly riches*, though it may be that the phrase *in glory* should be taken instead with the verb). The thought of an exchange of material for spiritual generosity recurs in Rom. 15²⁶ᶠ·.

need: the use of this word also echoes its use in v. 16 (mg.) to refer to Paul's need.

20

With this conventional ascription of praise to God, compare Rom. 11³⁶; 16²⁷; Gal. 1⁵.

4²¹⁻²³   FINAL GREETINGS

²¹*Greet every saint in Christ Jesus. The brethren who are with me greet you.* ²²*All the saints greet you, especially those of Caesar's household.* ²³*The grace of the Lord Jesus Christ be with your spirit.*

Though the expression is Christian, the pattern of these closing greetings is broadly conventional.

Apart from matters of content dealt with below, the only question of any importance which these verses raise is, yet again, that of the unity of the epistle, in the sense that each analysis of its structure places them differently. For example, if ch. 1–2 were originally a separate letter, this passage may well have been its conclusion. In this case the final editor will have given it its present position, seeing it as a suitable conclusion to the collected correspondence.

The temptation to detach these verses arises from the doxology in v. 20 which looks like a perfectly satisfactory ending. But perhaps this temptation should be resisted. F. V. Filson* has pointed out that a considerable number of the New Testament epistles (*Hebrews, 1 & 2 Thessalonians, Galatians, 2 Timothy,* as well as *Philippians*) end in a four-fold passage consisting of (*a*) personal information and instructions, (*b*) a formal benediction or doxology, (*c*) brief personal counsel, expressed less formally, and (*d*) a simple benediction as a final greeting. This structure seems almost as stereotyped as the opening pattern of greeting followed by thanksgiving. It arises from the dual purpose of nearly all the New Testament letters; they were both general communications to a congregation or group of congregations and also personal letters to friends. The first two sections of the four-fold

* *Yesterday* (London, 1967), pp. 22ff.

pattern spring from the first purpose, the last two from the second.

ראש

21

every saint: cf. 1¹. He sends greetings to each Christian individually.

brethren: if there is any distinction between these and *all the saints* in v. 22, it will be between Paul's own immediate entourage (like Timothy) and the members of the church in Rome. However, it cannot be said that Paul's very frequent use of the word suggests anything but the most general sense, so that the two expressions are probably synonymous.

22

those of Caesar's household: not members of the royal family – there is no evidence whatsoever of any such person being converted to Christianity at this early stage; nor even necessarily members of the palace staff in Rome. This is a technical term signifying the members of the imperial service who in many parts of the Empire, and especially in the provinces assigned to the emperor's direct rule, looked after imperial property and other interests. They were usually freedmen or slaves. An inscription of A.D. 55 tells of the erection of a bath for the use of Caesar's household (*familia Caesaris*) – as far away from Rome as the shores of the Black Sea. (See G. S. Duncan, *St Paul's Ephesian Ministry*, p. 110.) Why are these Christians singled out? Perhaps to demonstrate that people from such circles were now in the Church; perhaps because some of them came from Philippi.

23

The blessing which closes the letter is quite typical except for the substitution of *with your spirit* for *with you* (but see Gal. 6¹⁸ & Philem. ²⁵). The *grace* of Christ is his free, saving love. Normally, apart from his closing blessings, Paul speaks more of the grace of God or, as in 1², the grace of God the Father and of Christ. In these closing passages Paul sees Christ as performing the divine role with full authority; he is *kyrios (Lord)*, cf. p. 78.

spirit: denotes the inner self of man, but, as the usage (see above) implies, it is here virtually the equivalent of the personal pronoun. However, if it is used here at all deliberately, then the best clue to Paul's meaning is to be found in 1 Cor. 2¹⁰⁻¹⁶, where he expounds his understanding of the presence of the spirit in Christian believers; their inner selves are made to share in the divine spirit, i.e. the inner self of God. In fact it is much more likely that here we simply have an example of the ordinary Hebraic idiom, whereby 'my soul', 'my spirit', mean simply 'me'.

The Letter to
the Colossians

Introduction

COLOSSAE AND THE COLOSSIANS

The three cities mentioned in this letter, Colossae itself, Laodicea, and Hierapolis (4^{13}), lay close together in the valley of the Lycus (the modern Çürüksuçay), in south-west Phrygia, about a hundred miles east of the Asia Minor coast at Ephesus. The first two cities stood on the river itself, the last on high ground above its confluence with the Meander. In our period Laodicea was the most important of the three, economically and politically. Colossae was eleven miles to the east, Hierapolis six miles to the north.

Colossae has not been excavated, therefore less is known about its condition at this time than about, for example, Philippi. In Paul's time it was already an old city; by 480 B.C., it was, according to Herodotus, 'a great city of Phrygia', and for some time after that period it remained the chief place of the area. Its name (cf. Gk *kolossos*, giant) might be thought to bear witness to this importance, but this is unlikely; it seems to be an adaptation into intelligible Greek of a native Phrygian name (perhaps linked with a lake, Koloe, not far away), and also appears in a variant form Kolassai in some documents, including some New Testament manuscripts. From the mid third century B.C., when Laodicea was founded, Colossae was gradually eclipsed – the new city was favoured by the Antiochid rulers in whose empire the territory lay and there was not room for two major centres so close to one another on the trade route which was a chief means of prosperity. Still, it is likely that older books over-estimate the decline of Colossae.* They base themselves largely on a misreading of the Greek geographer Strabo. Such evidence as there is (an inscription and coins from the second and third centuries A.D.) shows the maintenance of respectable city-status in Imperial times, with the usual complement of officers and institutions.

* See D. Magie, *Roman Rule in Asia Minor* (Princeton, 1950), p. 985, cf. pp. 126f. This should be read by way of corrective, alongside the old standard work of W. M. Ramsay (*Cities and Bishoprics of Phrygia* (Oxford, 1895), Vol. I, pp. 208ff).

The population of Colossae was basically Phrygian, but the last three centuries before Christ had probably brought Greeks and Syrians in considerable numbers. Certainly this was true of Laodicea. In any case the old native Phrygian culture had over these years been entirely overlaid by Greek culture, the old language replaced by Greek. Economically Colossae depended on wool and was now a satellite of Laodicea, an important centre for the manufacture of clothing and carpets. Its position, in the valley and on the road from Sardis to Apameia, made distribution easy.

Laodicea was named after the wife of its founder, Antiochus II (261–46 B.C.), a member of the dynasty to whom Syria and Asia Minor had fallen on the death of Alexander the Great. This must have been before 253 B.C. because Queen Laodice was divorced by her husband in that year. It was set up as the centre of military and political power in the area, and peopled by colonists – a means of importing to the area the Greek culture of the ruling Antiochid dynasty. By the first century B.C. it was well known for its wealth, derived both from the wool and textile trades and from banking. From Rev. 3[14ff.] it is apparent that the reputation was maintained in the following century and that the church in the city was not immune from the dangers of affluence.

Hierapolis was the old religious centre of the whole area, as its Greek name (*hiera polis* = holy city) indicates. Its status depended upon the possession of hot springs and a cave, which was seen as the entrance to the lower world. It was a sanctuary, a focus of Phrygian devotion, long before it became a city (*c.* 180 B.C.); but by our period, on the strength of thermal baths and dyeing and textile industries, it was a well-established and prosperous place. It is likely that though Greco-Roman culture, and in particular the Greek language, had by this time become dominant, the power of traditional rites made the Greek veneer thinner than elsewhere. The assimilation of local cults to those of the ruling power, and so of Phrygian religion to Greek and Roman, worked powerfully as it did all over the Empire; but, under whatever names, the old habits persisted. Hierapolis was even a religious exporter. It was a home of the Phrygian mysteries, which found their way to many parts of the ancient world; people were initiated into the secrets of this cult, in a variety of adaptations, in Greece and other more distant places. It was one version of the cult of the Mother Goddess, promoter of fertility, which worked by associating the devotee with the story of the goddess, an initiation which was believed to assure his salvation.

But the cults of all these cities were many and varied, dedicated to deities from many places, with Greek and Syrian as well as Phrygian names, each easily mingled with others, each carrying its own assurances, attracting its own devotees for this purpose or that. This was the religious world which Paul addressed; or to be more precise, this was the dominant background of religious belief and practice which the Colossian Christians will have shared before they heard and accepted the message of Epaphras (1⁷), who brought the gospel to their town.

One other religious group of importance to us was represented in Colossae, in what strength and with what degree of organization we do not know, but certainly present – the Jews (see pp. 128ff.). About 200 B.C., Antiochus the Great had settled two thousand Jewish families in Lydia and Phrygia, so it may well be that the Jews of Colossae had already lived in the city for some period and had an established synagogue; about this we do not know. Long settlement would make more understandable their apparently strong syn-cretistic* tendencies and openness to unorthodox ideas of which *Colossians* gives evidence. Both before and after our period there are other signs of this in the area: fusion of Jewish worship with the native cult of Zeus Sabazios (the closeness of the name to the Jewish '*Sabaoth*', 'of hosts' – the common Old Testament epithet for God – no doubt made this easy); and Jew-Gentile marriages.† But despite this element of openness in the lives of these Jews in a Hellenistic environment, something paralleled in many parts of the Greco-Roman world, they were still in many ways a people apart, re-cognized and often resented as such.

As we shall see, it is no wonder that Gentile converts to Paul's gospel, communicated through his 'fellow-worker' Epaphras, saw in a speculative and syncretistic Judaism something which seemed to combine the benefits of their old ways and their new; with age, venerability, and a routine of well-defined observances thrown in for good measure.

We should see the foundation of the churches in this area as a fruit

---

* Syncretism: the acceptance into a single pattern of religious thought and practice of elements quite diverse in provenance.

† A. D. Nock, *Conversion* (Oxford, 1933), p. 64.

of Paul's work in the major city of Ephesus, which was the capital of the Roman province, *Asia proconsularis*. From the evidence of *Colossians*, the Letters to the Seven Churches in Rev. 2–3, and the correspondence of Ignatius of Antioch*, dating from the early years of the second century, it is clear that, so far as we can tell, the Church was at this time more firmly established in the western part of Asia Minor than in any other area. By about A.D. 110 it already existed in a dozen or so important cities. However, there is no information about the church in Colossae which will enable us to continue its story beyond the time of Paul; all we have is the glimpse into its affairs given by *Colossians* and *Philemon*. Rev. 3[14ff.] shows us Laodicea at a somewhat later date. Hierapolis comes into view again in the first half of the second century through the writings of its bishop, Papias.†

PAUL AND COLOSSAE

Apart from the letter now before us and *Philemon*, its companion-piece, we have no clear information about Paul's dealings with Colossae. The only other possible item is the pair of references in Acts 16[6] and 18[23] to Paul's passing through Phrygia and Galatia, *strengthening all the disciples*. The writer of *Acts* may well have meant Phrygia to include the churches of the Lycus valley, but how far this is one of his generalized statements about Paul's movements, based less on real knowledge than on a desire to show him incessantly engaged on his missionary and pastoral work, and serving to link together major episodes, we cannot be sure. It is even possible that it was the writer's knowledge of the existence of a letter by Paul to Colossae which made him include this glancing reference to the area in which it lay even though he had no stories to tell of Paul's doings there – presumably because the historical Paul never in fact went there (unless the hope of Philemon[22] was realized). Our most direct evidence, *Colossians* itself, points this way. But whatever the facts were, certainly the concept which lies behind the picture of Paul in *Acts* demanded that he be shown going everywhere, continually and assiduously; for, after portraying an opening 'golden age' of the

* See in *Library of Christian Classics*, Vol. I (London, 1953), *Early Christian Writings* (Penguin Classics, 1968), and numerous other editions.

† For the surviving fragments, see J. B. Lightfoot, *The Apostolic Fathers* (London, 1891), pp. 514ff.

Church, dominated by Peter and the Twelve, *Acts* goes on to present
Paul as the exemplary missionary of the second phase of the Church's
existence. It would have been unthinkable that he should never have
gone to a church which his correspondence showed him to have had
in his care; but, solid evidence being wanting, it sufficed that he be
shown going just to the area in which Colossae lay. The author
was both historian and Christian theologian and apologist, with
ideas to communicate, endeavouring to satisfy both roles (pp. 34ff.).

So, to understand Paul's dealings with this church, we turn to the
two letters, *Colossians* and *Philemon*. In many ways we are fortunate,
for between them they tell us a great deal about the people concerned,
about their circumstances, and about the way they looked at the
Christian gospel. Some of the data are much easier to interpret than
others; sometimes it is hard to exclude speculation if an intelligible
picture is to emerge.

The information which the letters provide for us is, then, of two
kinds; personal and circumstantial, and theological. At first reading,
the two kinds of material seem so disparate that it is as if, in the case of
Colossians, we were dealing with two separate pieces of writing which
have little to do with each other. The case of Onesimus, the reason
for the writing of the letter to Philemon, which appears also in the
latter part of *Colossians*, has nothing to do with the dangerous views
being propagated at Colossae which are the prime motive for the
letter. We need to remember that the same people are involved in
both matters. The same Colossian Christians, who wondered how
much they ought to speculate about the angels and were inclined to
put too much emphasis on fasting and various Jewish taboos which
had never been part of their religion, also gossiped about Onesimus
and Paul's attempt to get his way with his owner. Indeed, Paul may
well have trodden the more delicately in dealing with his personal
business in order not to jeopardize the chances of his doctrinal correction being accepted and absorbed. An outcry about the slave
would certainly divert attention from theology even if it did not
lead to positive antipathy to Paul and all his works.

We begin with the personal information, mainly the question of
Onesimus, concerning whom, in *Philemon*, Paul makes certain specific
requests (see pp. 229f.). (Other matters receive comment as they arise in
the text.) First we shall outline one of the most attractive and alluring
suggestions made in recent New Testament scholarship. Its attractive-

ness comes not only from the picture it paints but also from the fact that it offers a comprehensive solution to a great many puzzling historical questions. It is the work of E. J. Goodspeed and J. Knox, and was put forward as a complete argument in 1935 by the latter in his short work, *Philemon among the Letters of Paul.**

This suggestion arose not from any specific concern with *Colossians* and its problems but rather from two other questions. Both relate to the eventual collection of Paul's letters after his death (probably towards the end of the first century) and their acceptance as canonical (i.e. official and authoritative) literature in the Church. The questions concern the purpose of *Ephesians*† (see pp. 249ff.) and the reason for the survival of a letter as brief as *Philemon*.

Briefly, the suggestion is that *Philemon*, a short letter of no great doctrinal significance, survived, alone among letters of its kind, because it was of great importance to those responsible for collecting Paul's letters. The person most likely to have carried out this task is Onesimus himself, the slave whose life and fortunes were entirely altered by Paul, who both made him a Christian and through this letter, we may presume, won his freedom or at any rate his full acceptance by his Christian master. If Onesimus was indeed the collector of Paul's letters and preserved this one because it was of such vital importance to himself may he not be the same Onesimus who, in Ignatius' epistle to the church in Ephesus (*c.* A.D. 110), appears as the bishop of that city? The name is in fact a common one, but still the coincidence is at least interesting; and all the more so when the picture which is emerging allows a solution to the vexing problem of the nature and purpose of the *Epistle of Paul to the Ephesians*.

That work, so unlike the rest of Paul's writings, and in many ways so unlike an epistle at all (see pp. 237ff.), probably not bearing any mention of Ephesus in its original manuscript, has long been a source of difficulty. Not only its authorship but also its precise function have remained elusive. May it not be that it was written by a devoted disciple of Paul, deeply imbued with his thought and terminology, as an introduction to the collected letters? And for this office too

---

* First published in the U.S.A.; English edition, London, 1960.

† See E. J. Goodspeed, *The Key to Ephesians* (Chicago, 1956); J. Knox, *Marcion and the New Testament* (Chicago, 1942).

there is hardly a better candidate than Onesimus, the one-time slave, and later bishop of the church in Ephesus.*

But how does this affect the situation which confronts us in *Colossians* and *Philemon*? Here we come to some of the more conjectural elements in Knox's reconstruction. He focuses on two points: it looks as if Archippus were related to *the letter from Laodicea* (Col. 4¹⁶ᶠ·); and in Philem. ² the reference to *the church in your house* is singular (i.e. literally *thy house*), the singular being maintained throughout the letter, except in vv. 3, 22, and 25, so that the letter is chiefly addressed to one person. He suggests that in the greetings which head our *Philemon*, that name stands first because he is the leading Christian in the area. But the person with whom the letter is mainly concerned, the master of Onesimus, is Archippus, named last so as to lead directly into the business which affects him. Philemon resided at Laodicea and, having read the letter, was to send it on to Colossae with, as Paul no doubt hopes, his firm support for the request it contained. Col. 4¹⁶ᶠ· confirms this. *Philemon* is indeed *the letter from Laodicea*; it has come directly from that city, the capital of the area, which, if Paul's messengers came from the west (e.g. Ephesus), lay on their route. Mention of that letter naturally puts Paul in mind that Archippus should be urged not to neglect the 'piece of service' (*diakonia*) which he has been given to do, i.e. the pardoning of Onesimus, his return to Paul, and probably his manumission. On this view Philem. ² indicates that Archippus was host to the Colossian congregation, perhaps as its most prosperous member, perhaps as its leader.

* Knox thinks that one interesting difference between *Colossians* and *Ephesians* can be explained most naturally in terms of this suggestion. In Col. 3²⁵, in the overlong section on the duties of slaves, itself to be explained by Paul's preoccupation with the case of Onesimus, we read, *For the wrongdoer will be paid back for the wrong he has done, and there is no partiality.* The odd thing about this is that it is surely superfluous to make the last statement; why should a slave expect partiality? Not at all, of course, in the normal run of events; but *Philemon* might well be read as if Paul were asking for special treatment in the matter of the wrong which Onesimus has done to his owner, or at any rate being unusually indulgent (v. 18). Here Paul, in this *apparently* general statement, is affirming his good sense, his strict fairness, according to the normal canons of master-slave relations. In Eph. 6⁹ the phrase is transferred to the section on the duties of masters, where, in a general statement, it is surely more appropriate. Who but one intimately involved would have made such an alteration? And would not the ex-slave Onesimus have felt particularly keenly the need to remind slave-owners who became Christians of the demands of love which are laid upon them?

Entrancing as this theory is, there are many points at which it has to resort to conjecture. Unfortunately too, there are positive arguments against it. In the first place, in Philem. 2 it is certainly most natural to suppose that all the people there named live in the same place, i.e. Colossae, and that Philemon is the person chiefly addressed. In the second place, if Philemon is in Laodicea, what are we to make of Nympha(s) and his-her church (see p. 221), mentioned in Col. 4¹⁵? Can we suppose that there were two regular Christian congregations in Laodicea at this time? Perhaps Philemon is the leader, Nympha(s) the host(ess) of the church – we cannot say. It is just possible that Nympha(s) is the leader (or hostess) of the church in Hierapolis, which was small enough to be referred to most naturally in this way and would by this means be 'brought into the picture'. Perhaps the most formidable difficulty which this reconstruction has to face is that of attributing *Ephesians*, most deeply Jewish in background and thought, to the Gentile ex-slave, Onesimus. Only yet more speculation can make this achievement credible.

Nevertheless, despite its strongly hypothetical quality, there are many attractive features of Knox's suggestion, and without it we are forced to admit considerable gaps in our total picture of the situation before us (which is no reason for feeling compelled to fill them at any price!).

Finally in this connexion, there are two small points which are worth mentioning, both concerning *Philemon*, both puzzling. First, if this letter is destined for Colossae, it is, given its semi-public address, strange that Paul should have appended greetings substantially the same as those already included in *Colossians*. Why should he repeat himself in this way? Second, though admittedly there was no compelling reason to include doctrinal matter in this letter, it is a little surprising that given the serious situation revealed in *Colossians* he should have been able to refrain from saying something about it in a letter to one who, whether Philemon or Archippus, is probably a leader of the Colossian church. What is surely ruled out is that in a small place like Colossae, there were two congregations, of which one, that centring on Philemon and his house, has maintained itself unspotted from the teachers who are such a serious menace to the other.

We now turn to the attempt to identify the theological situation in Colossae which the letter reflects. The detailed evidence is reviewed in the course of the commentary, and here we shall simply state what are in effect conclusions from that evidence. They will serve the reader as pointers to his own consideration of the letter itself.

It is a matter of trying to place on the 'thought-map' of the first century world two groups of people in Colossae: the members of the Christian congregation and those propagandists whom Paul regards as seducing them from the true gospel. The evidence is chiefly to be found in 1^{15-34}, but there may be relevant hints in other parts of the letter too. It will appear in the commentary that one of the difficulties is to decide to what extent Paul is consciously taking up some debated word from the discussions in Colossae and quietly correcting its sense – bringing it into conformity with the pattern of his own teaching. There is another and more important reason why the evidence is not wholly clear: the background of many of the terms used is ambiguous. It could be mainly Jewish or mainly Hellenistic – though in either case we are almost certainly dealing with a situation where syncretism (the mixing of religious ideas from a variety of sources) is the order of the day. (See the commentary on 1^{15-20}, and 2^{16}ff.)

As we approach the situation in Colossae two factors come before us for our consideration. First, the members of the Colossian congregation did not, we may assume, come to their Christian faith with religiously blank minds. Indeed the very fact that they were open to the new preaching probably indicates that they were 'interested in religion', however different in certain crucial ways the gospel proved to be from anything they had previously meant by it. Their earlier religious tendencies were surely an important factor in their looking with interest (to say the least) at the doctrine now opposed by Paul.

Consideration of these tendencies makes the strongest *a priori* argument for what we may call (see p. 22) the Gnostic interpretation of the situation at Colossae, that is, the view that the discussion there was being conducted in terms of ideas and words which were characteristic of the Gnostic sects of the second century. Hitherto the Colossians' religion will have consisted of a mixture of oriental, Greco-Roman, and native Phrygian rites and ceremonies, surrounded by extravagant mythologies and speculations. We can imagine that several elements in the teaching which Paul now counteracts made a strong appeal to them: the cosmological and angelological information, seen as offering a road to salvation; also perhaps the fasting, which is well attested as part of the preparation for initiates and seekers of visions in the mystery cults of the period (2^{16-18}).

Paul's approach to this world of thought is astute. There is little doubt that some of the words he uses will immediately have brought it to the minds of his readers: *fullness* (1^{19}; 2^9); *mystery* ($1^{26f.}$; 2^2); *embateuō* (Gk 2^{18}), for all of which the commentary should be consulted. Also, his language about Christ as the new Man (2^{19}; 3^{10}) would probably remind them of oriental myths about the archetypal Man. But, while using the familiar terms, Paul always ignores their old sense and pours into them a sense of his own; and his sense owes most to other sources, more congenial to him and more serviceable for expressing the gospel: the wisdom-speculation (see p. 76) and apocalyptic thought of Judaism. Admittedly the latter was itself by no means free from debt to some of the oriental sources which had filled the Greco-Roman world, and this complicates the picture; but our main assessment stands. The thought of *Colossians* has its base in Jewish theology. Paul uses the words in a way that suits him, thus disarming them; and by refusing to accept the pagan battleground, so far as *ideas* are concerned, he appears to be flattering his Gentile Christian readers with perhaps a more thorough Christian formation than they possessed. There would be no better way of bringing this formation to perfection.

Second, the commentary will show that the false teaching (as Paul considers it to be) is in fact strongly Jewish. As we come to consider this, we need to form a picture of the relationship between the Church and Judaism in a provincial town of the Roman Empire at this time. Both were minorities, but the Jews were at least a fairly familiar group, often established in the business community of the place for some years. Their synagogue worship, consisting of the reading of the Old Testament Scriptures, contrasted with the sacrificial rites of the various pagan cults, and customs like the strict dietary laws and circumcision made them stand out from other groups. Moreover, their clannishness within the community as a whole was common knowledge and from time to time an occasion of hostility. They tended to attract to themselves a number of Gentile adherents ('god-fearers'), all the more so if (as apparently in Colossae) they were interested in amplifying their Judaism with speculative ingredients from sources which also contributed to the pagan cults. It is likely on general grounds that some of the Colossian Christians had been 'god-fearers', though the meagre appeal to the Old Testament in this Epistle indicates that Jewish influence was less thorough here than among those who joined the churches in other parts of Asia Minor (cf. *Galatians*). In relation to this group, strange but venerable, proud of its age-old heritage and its divine vocation, how will the Church have appeared? To such outsiders as noticed it at all it will have appeared, we can be sure, as simply an offshoot of the synagogue, small and domestic; 'the meeting in X's house' (Col. 4¹⁵; Philem.²). To the Jews, too, the line will have been blurred, and there must have been considerable uncertainty in these early years whether this group belonged within Judaism or had put itself beyond the pale. Were its mainly Gentile members to be entertained as somewhat eccentric god-fearers in the hope that they would become more amenable in time, or were they to be kept completely at arm's length, as claiming the Jewish inheritance while sitting light to the Law which was its essential mark? If their main distinctive tenet was the identification of Jesus as the Messiah, this was a matter for argument and for scriptural debate, not, at this date, a ground for immediate exclusion. However, when it came to an identification of this same Jesus, now exalted to God's right hand, with the eternal creative wisdom of God, and to seeing him as the Lord of a new order open to all men of whatever race (see pp. 20f.), the case must have appeared much more problematical. From the Jewish side, therefore, the relationship will have been one of debate and controversy, sometimes no doubt acrimonious but rarely at this time in an atmosphere which assumed final separation. It was not at all a matter of two distinct religious bodies facing one another across an established frontier which was clear to both.

As far as the Christians themselves were concerned, again the situation was far from clear. They knew they were the heirs of the promises cherished by the Jews. Jesus, it was true, was a figure of cosmic significance and they could speak of him in terms not uncongenial to their familiar, pagan, religious aspirations, but even these terms many Jews could share and use in discussion. Paul was no doubt known as one who had worked out a comprehensive theory about the relationship of the Church with Israel, and certainly as one who saw the distinctiveness of the Church as utterly crucial (see *Galatians*), but it was not a particularly simple theory, especially to those who lacked his Jewish education; and to many Gentile Christians it no doubt resolved itself into the attempt to decide what could and what could not be taken over by a Christian from the parent body.

The line was indefinite. To some Jews the Christians would seem an eccentric group (and as such not unique) on the fringe of Judaism, and their claims about Jesus worthy of serious discussion. To a good many Christians, Judaism, a half-abandoned parent, remained impressive; it was massively venerable, had given them much, as Paul did not deny (Rom. 9^{1-5}), and, something especially attractive to many of them, it afforded in its Law the great benefit of a comprehensive and detailed scheme for practical religious life. The Law gave a way of progress in moral life and, in the information about the universe which went with it, a sufficiently detailed Baedecker to the cosmos to enable one to feel more secure amid its numerous alarms and uncertainties. In the dialogue between the two sides some Jews may have gone further, and been glad to try and incorporate Christ into their system. If the bug of syncretism had bitten them this would not have seemed at all out of the question.

We have, in this discussion of the background, made several points which bear on the probable situation at Colossae, but now we must be more precise; and the last paragraphs may get us near to the heart of the question.

Whether or not they are members of an established Jewish community or transient visitors, we suggest that the false teachers whom Paul attacks are Jews of a strongly syncretistic and perhaps sectarian turn of mind who do not dismiss the Christians out of hand or afflict them with petty persecution (cf. 1 Thess. $2^{14\mathrm{ff.}}$; Phil. 1^{29}; John 16^2), but are probably quite prepared to add Christ to their already ample hierarchy. They find the Christians' message interesting and suggestive, and can make sense of it in their own terms. Moreover they have special gifts to offer in return, not only information about the angelic powers which fill and rule the cosmos, but also techniques for spiritual advancement (by visions, fasting, and careful observance of holy days, cf. $2^{16\mathrm{ff.}}$).

For Paul this is nothing but seduction. To give in to its wiles is to forsake the gospel itself. Man's need is not spiritual improvement or a firmer grasp of the topography of the universe, but new life with God and rescue from sin and the other evil powers which oppress him. To bring this about has been the work of Christ, in whom God was fully operative. He has re-established man's whole being on new foundations, not of 'knowledge' or supposed 'wisdom' (cf. 2²³) but of Christ himself, known in the Christian community whose Lord he is. It is a community open to all, given for all, simply because, in Christ, God has acted for man as man, renewing his life as God's creature (cf. 1¹⁵⁻²⁰; 3⁹⁻¹¹).

We have suggested that the teaching which Paul combats attracted partly because of its venerable Jewish source, as well as because of its inherent quality. It may also be that the kind of Christian statement which they had received from Epaphras made the Colossians particularly open to certain aspects of this teaching. We do not refer now to its Jewishness or its commendation of the ascetic practices of the Law, for, as far as we can tell from Paul's language in addressing them, the Colossian Christians were thought not to know much about the Old Testament. He never appeals to scriptural argument and makes hardly any scriptural allusions. Epaphras (cf. 4¹¹f.) was a Gentile Christian whose preaching will probably have included only the most essential references to Old Testament texts (cf. 3¹ and Ps. 110¹). Such Old Testament terminology as he will have absorbed and used will have been that which was most congenial to a Hellenistic mind; that is, the theology of the divine wisdom (see p. 76). It is likely that Col. 1¹⁵⁻²⁰ owes more to this idiom than to any other, and that it was a liturgical form, perhaps taught by Epaphras, appealed to by Paul precisely because it is something he and they share. To bring out the true bearing of a valued formula is a most persuasive tactic, and it looks as if he does just this, by adding a word here and there to underline its significance (see pp. 155ff.).

'Wisdom' was something which all parties could agree was desirable. It represented a religious ideal to which all could aspire; it signified genuine and deep religious knowledge, and the sense of being on the right road to salvation. It is no accident that the word occurs widely in this letter, more often than in any of Paul's writings, except *1 Corinthians*, where it is largely concentrated in the opening chapters. According to the Jewish teachers it was to be found in esoteric knowledge (mysteries? cf. 1²⁶f.) and a strict way of life. It was not hard for the devout Colossians who had joined the Church to think of it in terms of these elements, though for them the knowledge of Christ was at the heart of it. The Jews themselves, we have suggested, were probably not unwilling to find a place for him in their schemes. It might well have seemed to be a situation where mutual influence could benefit both parties. But for Paul, Christ was not to be interpreted in terms of wisdom or as one ingredient in wisdom; rather, wisdom was to be interpreted in terms of him. He was the reality of which the old attempts at wisdom were but shadows (cf. 2^{17}). He was the true secret of God, prepared from the beginning, now disclosed to the world (cf. $1^{26f.}$; $2^{2f.}$). In him alone God's purpose was made plain and carried out.

We said that sometimes Paul uses terms from the pagan background of his audience and gives them a Christian sense, thus drawing their sting (see p. 128). There are a few points where he appears to use the same tactics with reference to the ideas of the Jewish teachers. Thus *mystery* was a term in apocalyptic and speculative Judaism as well as in pagan religion (cf. $1^{26f.}$, see p. 179); Paul's anchoring it in God's action in Christ was a blow both at the false teachers and at the pre-Christian ideas to which the Colossians were tending to revert. In a word like this Jew and pagan could chime in together. Also, in $2^{11f.}$, Paul is probably reflecting the fact that the Jewish teachers advocate circumcision as necessary for membership of God's people; to them the Gentile Christians, as we have seen, probably looked like men who were 'playing at' being Jews, refusing the full yoke of the Law. Paul says they have circumcision enough – in baptism which brings full new life in Christ.

We cannot believe that the Colossians learnt much from this letter which they did not know before. Paul is careful to use language which is congenial to them and to refrain from the unfamiliar (e.g. argument from Old Testament texts, such as he uses in Gal. $4^{21ff.}$). We suggest that much of the material from 1^{21} onwards simply elaborates a formula (i.e. 1^{15-20}) well-known to them. The assumptions stated in the 'if' clauses in 2^{20} and 3^1 may well presuppose their knowledge as well as Paul's own statements earlier in the letter. He knows that they received the gospel in terms such as these. His concern is to recall them to their fundamentals and to show that certain lines of thought and action are wholly incompatible with them.

Finally, the false teachers of Colossae are often referred to as 'heretics'. This implies, in this context, both that they were Christians and that they were an aberrant group. It is true that we cannot be sure that they were not in fact Christians who had been influenced by Judaism of a speculative and probably sectarian kind, subverters within the fold, but there is nothing in *Colossians* to suggest this. The easiest hypothesis is that they were Jews, part of whose strength was that they could stand before Christians as members of the parent, majority body, and that these were days when the line between Jews and Christians was less clear to many than it was to Paul.

NOTE ON GNOSTICISM AT COLOSSAE

For definition, see p. 22.

It is so common to speak of the false teaching at Colossae as Gnostic that it is worth trying to be clear what this statement involves and how much the evidence supports it. We shall point to detailed matters as they come up in the course of the commentary, while giving here a brief guide to the state of the question.

Gnosticism, in the narrower sense (p. 22), is a phenomenon first fully evidenced in the second century A.D., in the beliefs of a large number of sects related in varying degrees of closeness to the main body of the Christian Church. They are described in the writings of Christian Fathers who opposed them and in their own writings which have come to light in some quantity in recent years.*

There are two strong arguments against believing that the false teaching at Colossae was an early manifestation of these beliefs. The first is that *Colossians* gives no evidence of certain elements which were integral to the Gnostic outlook. Thus there is no sign that these teachers took a radically dualistic view of the universe, seeing it as divided between good and evil deities or divine powers, and as the scene of their conflict; there is no evidence that the esoteric instinct, the concern for 'inner truth' revealed only to the privileged initiates, was powerful at Colossae; and the speculation does not seem to have been particularly extravagant.

The second is that the teaching is adequately explained on the basis of contemporary Judaism, and there is no need to look further afield.† As against the Gnostic explanation, this one leaves few loose ends.

The taboos about food and about the observance of special days (2^{16}), the importance attached to angels and the favourable view

---

* Ed. R. M. Grant, *Gnosticism – an Anthology* (London, 1961).

† See *Le Origini dello Gnosticismo* (*The Origins of Gnosticism*) (Leiden, 1967), especially essays by S. Lyonnet and S. Pétrement, to which these paragraphs are particularly indebted.

taken of them as agents of God (2^{18}), the unwillingness to give any unique position to Christ (1^{15-20}) – all of which Paul attacks; these are the common views of Jews for whom the Law was the key to salvation. Paul sees the angelic powers as otiose or evil rather than benevolent; in their ignorance they had been behind the crucifying of Christ (1 Cor. 2^8) and in that act he had defeated them (Col. 2^{15}). For Paul this incipient dualism is no more than a supernaturalizing of the earthly struggle of good and evil in the one universe over which God reigns; for the Gnostics it becomes a radical division of the universe between good and evil powers, with the material world being far removed from the creative or direct redemptive activity of the good deity. Paul takes this step not in the interests of mere speculation but because for him Christ is the unique mediator of God's creative and redemptive action, and needs no angelic aid, a fact rendered crystal clear by the angels' turning against him and their subsequent defeat.

Finally, Gnostics could hardly as a rule be accused of the *worship* of angels (2^{18}), which for them were inferior beings concerned in the sordid task of creating the material world. Against Jews, who gave them a much more honoured place as cooperators with and agents of God in the creation and rule of the world and in the communication of the Law, the charge was more understandable, especially from one who saw their position as rightly occupied by Christ alone, their victor. Here too the later Gnostics seem to have gone further along .lines which Paul had just begun to mark out. If for Jews angels were close agents of God, and angels were now shown to be on the evil side, then it was not an unnatural speculative development to see the Jewish deity (*Yahweh*) as himself among the inferior deities; and this step is taken in the schemes of some Gnostic sects. (On angels, see further p. 164.)

(On angels, see further p. 164.)

AUTHENTICITY AND INTEGRITY

The pauline authorship of *Colossians* is less doubtful than that of *Ephesians*, more doubtful than that of *Philippians*. The case is made difficult by the fact that almost all the causes for doubt arise in connexion with the first two chapters. This leads to the proposing of complicated solutions; in terms, for instance, of additions having been made later to a shorter original pauline letter. While some scholars make suggestions along these lines, others take the view that *Colossians* as a whole is pseudonymous.

As in the case of *Philippians* and *Ephesians*, the evidence which has the greatest *prima facie* claim to scientific objectivity, that of computer calculations of stylistic features, tells against pauline authorship though some experts dissent; but for reasons stated elsewhere (p. 39) we do not believe that this evidence can be allowed to hold the field alone. What other evidence is there?

Most of it is of a detailed kind and the reader must assess it as it comes up for consideration in the course of the commentary. He will soon discover that a decision depends upon the weight he is prepared to put upon certain features of thought and style which are allegedly unlikely to come from the mind of Paul. In fact the trouble in *Colossians* is not that these features are clearly non-pauline: we can find parallels for nearly all of them in the undoubtedly pauline writings. The difficulty is rather that certain kinds of expression (notably from Jewish wisdom-theology, see p. 76), which are present elsewhere in Paul but not prominently, here hold the centre of the stage. We can account for this in a number of ways. It might be that a post-pauline writer, a disciple of the master, found a way of thought, which only appears on the fringes of the mind of Paul himself, particularly congenial or else appropriate to his audience. Or it might be that Paul himself consciously adapted his discourse to the ways of his audience; he wrote so that they would understand. No wonder then that what makes only a brief appearance in one letter becomes the dominant idiom of another. An obvious example is the almost total absence from the Corinthian correspondence of the language of justification which is so prominent in *Romans* and *Galatians*. It might be the case that Paul also adapted his discourse to the movement of his own thought. There is no call for surprise at his ability to use an idea or image in different ways, according to context. Thus in Col. $1^{18, 24}$ *the church, ekklēsia,* is more clearly the universal, as against the local, Church than anywhere else in Paul's writings (discounting *Ephesians*), and here, by contrast with Romans 12 and 1 Corinthians 12, the idea of the body of Christ is applied to the universal and not the local Church. This is often taken as evidence of the inauthenticity of *Colossians*. But an inspection of the multiple use to which this idea is already put within the single letter *1 Corinthians* will show that here we have simply another variation on the theme, one quite capable of issuing from the same writer (cf. p. 181).

This theory of pauline adaptability finds confirmation in his own words in 1 Cor. 9$^{19-23}$.* W. L. Knox (*St Paul and the Church of the Gentiles* (Cambridge, 1939), p. 178) made this point by saying that 'any system of thought and language that expressed the position of Jesus as the Lord was equally acceptable'; Paul was essentially the apologist and evangelist, not the philosopher.

This solution is attractive. A point against it, which seems too strong to be brought within its terms, is the almost total absence from *Colossians* of reference to the expected return of Christ and the attendant events, elsewhere so prominent in Paul's writings. On the contrary we find here expressions which seem to represent a quite different way of looking at the world and at Christian life – in terms of a present enjoyment of the fruits of the coming age (see the commentary on 1^5; 3$^{1ff.}$). But, brief as they are, the words of 3$^{4, 6, 24}$ tell against this. They stand obstinately as witnesses to a temporally viewed eschatology; certain events will happen in the future to fulfil what has so far occurred. And this remains true even though the main perspective in *Colossians* is in terms of two simultaneous rather than successive spheres of life: an upper and a lower, in the former of which the Christian's place is already asssured. The fact is that these two ways of looking at God's saving activity for man and at the believer's consequent status, stressing in the one case what is still to be done and in the other what has already been accomplished, co-exist throughout Paul's writings (see p. 203). Sometimes one is uppermost, sometimes the other, as occasion and audience demand. In this matter, which is so central to Paul's whole thought, it might seem to be stretching too far the notion of his adaptability when we find one way almost excluding the other. Beyond certain limits, a man cannot adapt his thought without ceasing to be true to himself. Our own judgement is that in *Colossians* these limits are not reached and certainly not overstepped.†

We must admit, however, that the question is not an easy one. A great number of the commonest pauline theological words are lacking

* Cf. H. Chadwick, *All things to all men*, N.T.S., 1 (1955), pp. 261ff.

† For the question of Paul's adaptability in the matter of eschatology in particular, see C. F. D. Moule, *The Influence of Circumstances on the Use of Eschatological Terms*, J.T.S., 15 (1964), pp. 1ff.

in *Colossians* (e.g. righteousness, justify, believe, save) and though large tracts of assuredly pauline writing can be found which also lack a comparable collection of his central words, there is here an unparalleled 'concentration of absence' which might be thought to strain the explanation we have adopted. Perhaps more serious is the absence also of a large number of particles (words very common in Greek but generally not finding equivalents in English usage; to be rendered if at all by words such as 'then', 'for', 'so') which Paul normally uses liberally. Such words are liable to be an unconscious betrayer of authorship. The same is true of other stylistic features, like the heaping up of synonyms and of subordinate clauses, which abound in parts of *Colossians*, though they all occur, in more modest quantity, in the undoubtedly pauline epistles.

Those who feel that *Colossians* as it stands is too full of features little found in the genuine pauline letters, and too lacking in features that are common in them, to be from his hand often agree in attributing its characteristics to Hellenistic rather than Jewish influences; they see them as springing from early Gnostic speculation about the structure of the cosmos and the hierarchy of spiritual beings and compare statements here with later Gnostic literature and the beliefs of the mystery religions. But at best the evidence in *Colossians* is, as we have already seen, sparse and the connexions are tenuous. A Jewish background, even if of a heterodox kind, is at least as likely at almost every point. Paul in his other letters shows himself no stranger to this kind of thought. Also, as we have seen (p. 128), where Paul uses *words* from this background, he gives them his own, Christian, *sense*: he acts deliberately.

Where the opponents of pauline authorship do not agree is in proposing an alternative solution. Not all wholly deny Paul's hand in *Colossians*. Noting that most of the material unlikely, on grounds of style and vocabulary, to be from Paul occurs in the first two chapters, many critics, from the middle of the nineteenth century onwards, have suggested that these chapters were subject to heavy interpolation while containing a basis which is Paul's own. The various theories identifying these interpolations are often extremely intricate, and there has been little agreement among their proponents. The reader of the commentary will not find it hard to see which are the sections which come into question.

Holtzmann, who was the first to propose this type of explanation

(1872), arrived at it through studying the relationship of *Colossians* with *Ephesians*. He felt, as others have felt since, that this undoubtedly close relationship is to be explained not by the direct dependence of *Ephesians* on *Colossians* (which is the most common view, especially among those who think the latter pauline but the former not), but by the extensive insertion into an original pauline *Colossians* of quasi-quotations from *Ephesians*, probably by the latter's author.

Apart from this theory, the best support for the view that *Colossians* depends on *Ephesians* comes from a careful investigation of the movement of thought in the two letters in passages where they are using comparable language. For an example of such investigation of some of the key passages, we refer the reader to J. Coutts, *The Relationship of Ephesians and Colossians* (N.T.S., 4 (1958), pp. 201f.). He holds that the writer of *Colossians* (whether the same as the writer of *Ephesians* or an imitator) has sometimes seized upon phrases from his model and used them less convincingly in their new contexts. The flow of the argument in *Ephesians* is held to be much more coherent. But, against Coutts's view, it may simply be that we are dealing with two different kinds of writing; *Ephesians* is much more of a set-piece and we should expect its argument to be more fully worked out and internally integrated. However, if there is felt to be any strength in this case for the dependence of *Colossians* on *Ephesians* it certainly supports (for those who believe that *Ephesians* is non-pauline) the other arguments which tell in favour of either the pseudonymity of *Colossians* as a whole or the interpolation of non-pauline elements into an original shorter letter of Paul's own.

Our own view (see especially pp. 209f.) is that *Colossians* is a single, coherent piece of writing; we see no adequate reason to dismember it, just as we see no adequate reason to doubt that it was written by Paul. Perhaps the strongest argument of all in favour of authenticity is the close interlocking of *Colossians* and *Philemon* in the circumstances of their writing (see above p. 124). The pauline authorship of the latter is hardly to be doubted, and the two letters make a pair. Admittedly this argument is not foolproof against partition theories, but at least it gives Paul a foothold in *Colossians* which is hard to dislodge.

Note: We give fuller treatment to the relationship of *Ephesians* to *Colossians* when we come to deal with *Ephesians* (p. 247). And, as far as detail is concerned, in the course of our commentary on *Colossians* we make only the barest reference to the passages in *Ephesians* which are strikingly similar to *Colossians*. These parallels are noted more fully in the commentary on *Ephesians*, as they occur. The reason for this procedure is that we take *Ephesians* to be probably pseudonymous, the work of a post-pauline disciple and imitator, so that it is not of direct use in helping to elucidate the mind of Paul in writing *Colossians*. The reverse is not true. Even if the writer of *Ephesians* sometimes seems subtly to have misunderstood what he took from *Colossians*, he is deeply indebted to it and it is vital as a point of comparison with his work. The same holds true if *Ephesians* is taken as pauline, for it is still most easily read as dependent on *Colossians*.

PLACE AND TIME OF WRITING

For a treatment of the general considerations that arise in connexion with these questions we refer the reader to the General Introduction p. 23) and the Introduction to *Philippians* (p. 41).

In the setting of all we know of Paul's life, Rome remains the most obvious first candidate to consider as the place of origin for *Colossians* and *Philemon*. Those who think that the Roman imprisonment must have been the longest one that Paul suffered – the one when he had most chance to settle down and *feel* himself to be a prisoner, as he certainly seems to do in these letters – will support this view. So will those who believe that the theology of *Colossians* is so advanced that it must come from as late as possible in Paul's life. On the other hand those who (like the present writer) think that most of the ideas in *Colossians* have parallels in Paul's other writings and that he was a man who adapted himself to the needs and ways of thought of his audience, will feel free to consider other possibilities; and they will note Paul's plural references to his imprisonments in 2 Cor. 6[5] and 11[23].

But the chief difficulty about a Roman prison as the place of writing for these letters is simply the great distance of Rome from Colossae. This problem confronts us also in the case of *Philippians*, but it is a good deal more difficult here. The very fact of Onesimus' presence with Paul, the whole tone of the negotiations about him, and the travels involved (see especially Philem. [22]) give the impression that the distances are not great. As Ephesus was clearly a centre of Paul's life and work for a lengthy period this is perhaps the best suggestion that can be made. It satisfies the conditions and yields a credible picture.

Why Paul should have been put in prison there for, presumably, a lengthy period we just cannot say. The event recalled in Acts 19²¹ff., or some other incident of this kind, may have had something to do with it.

In other words, while in the case of *Philippians* the balance of probability seems to tilt just in favour of Rome, here it seems to tilt just away from it. But it is impossible to be sure.

The question of date is very closely related. The Roman theory means a date about A.D. 58–60. If Ephesus is right, then some time in the late forties is more likely. This totally dispels the idea that in this book we meet the late, mature Paul who had by this time absorbed a Hellenistic way of thought and a more advanced christology (seeing Christ as pre-existent* and his rule as cosmic in scope), both of which were not so prominent in his mind in his earlier days. The dating question apart, we believe that the christology found, especially, in Col. 1¹⁵⁻²⁰ is in fact dependent on Paul's Jewish formation, and paralleled in other letters (in particular *1 Corinthians*, e.g. 1²⁴, ³⁰; 8⁶ cf. p. 163).

We also believe, as we have already suggested, that his use of certain ideas and images in this work in senses other than those found in his other letters is not a matter of his advancing into more complex or refined thought but evidence of his ability to use them flexibly as circumstances demanded. There are plenty of instances of this feature of Paul's thought.

Those who find themselves impelled to reject the authenticity of *Colossians*, in whole or in part, usually because they see in it evidence of more strongly Hellenistic thought of a Gnostic kind than Paul elsewhere displays, naturally incline towards a later date, at least for the completed work.

There is one other question which has some bearing on the date of the letter. In the years before his last journey to Jerusalem Paul was much preoccupied with making a collection of money from his churches to take to the mother church in Jerusalem (Gal. 2¹⁰; 1 Cor. 16¹ff.; 2 Cor. 9; Rom. 15²⁶). There is no mention of this collection in *Colossians* (or *Philemon*). If it be thought that Paul's concern with this matter was so great that during this period he would be bound to mention it every time he put pen to paper, then its absence here certainly rules out that period as the date of writing. Those who ac-

* i.e. as having had an eternal heavenly life before his appearance on earth.

cept this condition will then find themselves forced to put *Colossians* into the later part of Paul's life, and assign it to either a Caesarean or a Roman imprisonment. But if the idea of the collection arose only in the last years of Paul's missionary career (cf. John Knox, *Chapters in a Life of Paul*, London, 1954), it could equally well belong to the years before the Jerusalem meeting which led to the collection (Gal. 2¹⁻¹⁰). This view allows us to set the imprisonment in Ephesus or some other city nearer to the Lycus valley than either Rome or Caesarea.

CONTENTS OF THE EPISTLE

As in the case of *Philippians* the best way to see what this letter is about is to read it through quickly in a modern translation (e.g. N.E.B., that by J. B. Phillips or the Jerusalem Bible). But – and here *Colossians* will differ from *Philippians* and *Philemon* – the modern translation is likely to deepen the obscurity in certain ways. It will become apparent that even if it is roughly clear what Paul is writing about, it is difficult to see precisely what he means. The commentary will elucidate the epistle in detail. Here, without going into much detail, we simply give an outline of the subject-matter by way of introduction.

As we have already shown (pp. 122ff.), Paul was moved to the writing of this letter by a theological question and a practical one. Roughly, the theological question dominates the first two thirds of the letter, the practical question the last third. But in the middle they overlap; and in the passage from 3¹¹ onwards, while the momentum of the theological discussion is beginning to peter out, the practical question begins to assert itself, first in cryptic references, then more overtly.

This procedure of cryptic reference followed by explicit statement is adhered to also in the first part of the letter, that mainly devoted to the theological problem. Even in the at first sight formal and standard greetings and thanksgiving which come at the beginning, there are hints of what is to come. They are in Paul's usual manner in these openings – serene, positive, non-polemical. In 1⁹ *wisdom* is presented and acknowledged as an ideal; in 1¹³ Christ is proclaimed as the unique one into whose kingdom God has transferred his people, having rescued them from the power of darkness. At these words no Colossian Christians could cavil. Before the letter is ended they will have been taught how to accept their implications. The hope is that they will have swallowed the bait.

But we are still at the beginning. In the verses that follow, 1^{15-20}, the bait is presented in full – a splendid hymn to Christ, again giving no offence to any Christian in the Colossian congregation, but on the contrary accepted as an edifying and deeply significant statement of the Lord's role in God's work in creation and redemption. Then Paul goes on to lead his readers still further down the gentle path that will lead to their safe return to the truth of his gospel. 1^{21-27} shows how they themselves are the product of this saving work done in Christ, and how their Christian life, and also Paul's apostolate, have no standing-ground apart from it.

It is now time for Paul to come into the open, and having coaxed the Colossians into sympathy by statements of the Christian facts, and the facts of their own situation, with which they could hardly disagree, he unveils more and more completely the full seriousness of the gap between these facts, which constitute the Christian faith, the mystery of Christ ($1^{26f.}$; 2^3), and the teaching with which they are dallying. From 2^{16} onwards there is no mistaking his meaning. And virtually everything that Paul has to say here may be read as an exposition of 1^{15-20} which (he hopes) they will have swallowed without a qualm (cf. especially 1^{19} and 2^9; 1^{16} and 2^{15}; 1^{18} and 2^{18}).

The most important point of the contrast is between Christ as the all-sufficient mediator of God's being and of his saving gift to man, and the angels as a graded hierarchy of communication and revelation; to this Paul repeatedly returns (2^8; 2^{15}; 2^{18}; 2^{20}). Because the angels whom Christ has defeated and superseded were also the mediators of the Law to the Jews (cf. Gal. 3^{19}; 4^3), the issue of obedience to the Law arises as a practical question. Paul is at pains to show that the Law is not the way of obedience to God, but is pure sham; it is not of divine origin (2^{22}) and it does not even achieve its object (2^{23}). Paul regards it as obsolete ($2^{16f.}$, $2^{0f.}$) and nullified by Christ ($2^{14f.}$).

The true way of obedience to God has now to be outlined, and Paul does it in $3^{1ff.}$, first by stating once more, succinctly, the Christian's status (3^1), then by describing the way of life now put behind (3^{5-8}), and finally by painting glowingly the glory of the new life available in Christ and the virtues which flow from it (3^{9-17}).

Christians live out this life in defined human circumstances; that is, families and households, with wives, children, and slaves. So Paul turns from his lofty statement of the nature of Christian love and goodness to the practical implications (3^{18}–4^1), and rounds off this section (all of it, be it noted, a roughly logical sequence) with a few items of homely counsel (4^{2-6}).

Paul now goes on to personal matters, greetings from this colleague and that, commendations of his messengers, kind thoughts for beloved friends – and above all, a firm hint or two (4^9 and perhaps 4^{17}, see p. 125) which *Philemon* will make clear. In the light of these hints, which we may regard as backing up the shorter letter, we are able to look back over the earlier part of *Colossians* with a fresh eye; in the reference to the unity of slaves and free men in Christ (3^{11}), and the commendation of compassion and forgiveness ($3^{12f.}$), we see Paul doing again what he did in the first part of the letter in connexion with the theological question, that is, quietly winning his readers to agreement before they can see exactly where he is leading them. Here it is towards support for his requests concerning Onesimus.

Further Reading

Books and articles on particular questions are referred to in the appropriate place in the introduction or commentary, and we now mention some of the general works which will be found useful.

The classical English commentary is that of J. B. Lightfoot, published in his series of commentaries on the pauline epistles in 1875 (in one volume with *Philemon*). More recent commentaries in English include those by C. H. Dodd (London, 1929), L. B. Radford (London, 1931) and C. F. D. Moule (Cambridge, 1962). The latter is the most easily accessible and generally useful commentary on the Greek text. It deals with *Philemon* as well as *Colossians*. See also G. B. Caird's *Paul's Letters from Prison* (Oxford, 1976).

For the setting and background of the epistle, W. L. Knox, *St Paul and the Church of the Gentiles* (Cambridge, 1939) is essential, and ch. 7 deals especially with Colossae. The most important work of E. Percy – *Die Probleme der Kolosser- und Epheserbriefe* (Lund, 1946) – has not been translated; it lies behind all the more recent discussions of the thought of the two epistles with which it deals, even though its case for the authenticity of both as works of Paul has by no means won general acceptance. On the more general background of ideas, there are many books, in particular F. C. Grant, *Roman Hellenism and the New Testament* (Edinburgh and London, 1962), and R. Bultmann, *Primitive Christianity in its Contemporary Setting* (London, 1956). E. Käsemann's important but somewhat speculative essay on Col. 1^{15-20} is easily available in his *Essays on New Testament Themes* (London, 1964). On that passage, see also the valuable treatment in Jack T. Sanders, *The New Testament Christological Hymns* (Cambridge, 1971). John Knox, *Philemon among the Letters of Paul* (London, 1960) is to be read for its stimulating suggestions for the understanding of both *Colossians* and *Philemon*.

The Letter of Paul to the Colossians

¹Paul, an apostle of Christ Jesus by the will of God, and Timothy our brother, ²to the saints and faithful brethren in Christ at Colossae: grace to you and peace from God our Father.

The general structure of the greeting with which Paul opens this letter is much like that to be found in his other letters, and for a discussion of that structure we refer the reader to the parallel passage in the commentary on *Philippians* (pp. 47f.). He will also find there a treatment of the significance of these pauline greetings and of such terms in the verses now before us as are also to be found in Phil. 1,$^{1f.}$. These include the reference to Timothy, the description of the recipients as *saints ... in Christ*, and Paul's salutation to them in the form *grace to you and peace from God our Father*.

But the greeting here does not only have things in common with those which head other epistles; it also has its own distinctive features, and given Paul's careful avoidance of the ordinary conventional greetings used in letters at the time (see p. 47), these are not likely to be without significance. Even in passages like this, where the use of contemporary conventions might be expected, Paul, so it seems, chooses his words deliberately.

The most important feature is Paul's description of himself as *an apostle of Christ Jesus*. It stands out particularly in contrast to the term *servant* which he uses in Phil. 1^1. It looks as if, in relation to the church at Colossae but not to that at Philippi, Paul felt it appropriate to use the title which states his authority – to display his badge of office. It is worth trying to be a little more precise about the way he does it, and comparison with the parallel passages in other letters will help us. The title appears in all the undoubted pauline epistles which are addressed to churches, apart from *Philippians* and *1 & 2 Thessalonians*. It also appears in *Ephesians* and *1 & 2 Timothy*, though not in *Titus*. It is not in *Philemon*, but one would hardly expect it in a letter such as this, primarily addressed (though the distinction may be a fine one) to a small group of individuals rather than a congregation. However, it does not always appear in exactly the same form, and it looks as if the choice of form might be related to the nature of Paul's relationship with the church concerned; in other words, he uses the greeting to help convey the tone of his message. Thus it occurs in both *1 & 2 Corinthians*, letters written at a stage in Paul's dealings with this congregation which certainly warranted a firm reference to his authority. In *Galatians* it becomes a banner which Paul is waving in the face of his readers right through the first two chapters. The title itself is defiantly announced and elaborated in 1$^{1f.}$, and though Paul does not explicitly refer to it again (but cf. 1^{17}) the authenticity of Paul's apostleship and of the gospel which he preaches is what is in question throughout. In *Romans*, written to a church still unknown to Paul and not founded by him, the title is introduced more delicately, and put second to the more humble name *servant*. Paul is, after all, not *their* apostle, they are not within his jurisdiction in any sense; so he here describes his apostleship in more general, though decidedly didactic terms. Finally, in *Colossians*, Paul uses the title as straightforwardly as possible. There is no need in this case for either elaboration or justification, for this is a congregation within Paul's undoubted sphere of influence, of whose allegiance he seems to feel reasonably assured. Certainly they include Christians who are misled both in doctrine and in observances, but they do not appear to be factious or rebellious. On the other hand they need to be reminded of his position, for Paul did not found the church in Colossae (Epaphras was his agent, 1^7), nor does he know them personally (2^1). His way of describing himself here is therefore entirely appropriate.

The full title is *apostle of Christ Jesus*, a phrase which Paul seems to have practically made into a technical term. In Gal. 1^1 he takes it to pieces, exposes what really lies behind it. It is essentially assertive, polemical – and pauline; for it arises straight from Paul's nagging awareness that his claim to the title of apostle was contested by Christians influential enough to be worth refuting. 1 Cor. 9$^{1f.}$, 2 Cor. 10–12 and Gal. 1–2 are the most notable passages where Paul makes this refutation. It is not entirely clear who exactly were the Christians who denied Paul's apostleship; much controversy has raged over the question whether they included the leaders of the mother church in Jerusalem, James the Lord's brother in particular (Gal. 2^{12} may imply hostility on a particular issue, but 2^9 gives a happier impression of the over-all situation), or whether it was a matter of Jewish Christians acting without that authority, or even of Gentile Christians who were ill-disposed towards Paul. The refutation is always sharply made, for two reasons. First, there were certain plausible grounds for the charge. Paul was certainly not either in the original group of disciples of Jesus or among the early missionaries working out from the Jerusalem church. 'Apostle' in the earliest days is perhaps more likely to have carried the second of these senses than the first (in 1 Cor. 15$^{5, 7}$ *the twelve* are distinguished from *all the apostles*), and the identification of the two groups found at the beginning of *Acts* (e.g. 1$^{2, 21-26}$) is probably later schematizing. Nor had Paul had the privilege of seeing the risen Christ in the earliest days. From 1 Cor. 9^1 (cf. Acts 1^{22}) it looks as if this was regarded as an essential qualification; and it was Paul's boast and claim that, even if the event had occurred some time later, he had indeed seen the risen Christ: 1 Cor. 15^8; Gal. 1$^{12, 16}$; cf. Acts 9. Moreover this experience was the occasion of his receiving the commission for the Gentile mission (Gal. 1^{16}); he became an apostle as he became a Christian. So the second ground for the sharpness of his refutation of slurs on his right to the title 'apostle' is quite simply that this was to deny the whole basis of his Christian life and work. Paul was an apostle through and through (1 Cor. 9^{16}).

Paul asserts his claim to the title the more effectively by calling himself not simply an apostle but, as in our present passage, *an apostle of Christ Jesus*. In itself *apostolos* quite simply means one sent out, *a messenger*, and Paul himself can use it in that ordinary sense, for example in Phil. 2^{25}. But even in this case it carries the slightly more formal sense of *emissary*; and clearly in Paul's time it was current in the Church, originally in Palestine (Gal. 1^{17}) but then more widely (Rom. 16^7), as the normal term for missionaries. But who would such men say they represented? Perhaps they would often think of themselves as the emissaries of a Christian congregation, that in Jerusalem or elsewhere. Paul was clear that his own apostleship neither did nor could rest on such a foundation; he was the *emissary of Jesus Christ*, and nothing less than the whole phrase would adequately support either the claim which he needed to make against opponents or indeed the reality of his position. Here the addition of the phrase *by the will of God* should probably be taken as strengthening a little more Paul's claim to the apostolic title. The formula used here to state Paul's style is identical only with that in 2 Cor. 1¹ (which also has the same mention of Timothy).

Two difficulties arise in connexion with v. 2, neither of them serious and neither of them admitting a firm solution. The first is one of translation. The word rendered above *saints* (*holy ones: hagioi*) could equally well be an adjective qualifying *brethren*, like *faithful* (*pistos*). In fact the two words would support one another in sense: each carries the idea of dedication to God (for *hagios*, see p. 48). The sense would then be *to the holy and faithful brethren in Christ at Colossae*. The Greek word order tells against this, yielding *to the saints at Colossae and faithful brethren in Christ*. But in English this almost reads as if two categories of people are in mind, which is most unlikely. The R.S.V. rendering is as good as any; the uncertainty is simply in knowing how seriously to take the word order.

The other difficulty is one of emphasis; is there any special stress on *faithful*, differentiating those who hold the true gospel at Colossae from those who purvey false teaching? The countering of the latter occupies so much of the first two chapters of the letter that this may well be so, but it is quite impossible to be sure.

THANKSGIVING AND PRAYER

³*We always thank God, the Father of our Lord Jesus Christ, when we pray for you, ⁴because we have heard of your faith in Christ Jesus and of the love which you have for all the saints, ⁵because of the hope laid up for you in heaven. Of this you have heard before in the word of the truth, the gospel ⁶which has come to you, as indeed in the whole world it is bearing fruit and growing – so among yourselves, from the day you heard and understood the grace of God in truth, ⁷as you learned it from Epaphras our beloved fellow servant. He is a faithful minister of Christ on our^a behalf ⁸and has made known to us your love in the Spirit.*

⁹*And so, from the day we heard of it, we have not ceased to pray for you, asking that you may be filled with the knowledge of his will in all spiritual wisdom and understanding, ¹⁰to lead a life worthy of the Lord, fully pleasing to him, bearing fruit in every good work and increasing in the knowledge of God. ¹¹May you be strengthened with all power, according to his glorious might, for all endurance and patience with joy, ¹²giving thanks to*

the Father, who has qualified us[b] to share in the inheritance of the saints in light. [13]*He has delivered us from the dominion of darkness and transferred us to the kingdom of his beloved Son,* [14]*in whom we have redemption, the forgiveness of sins.*

a Other ancient authorities read *your.*
b Other ancient authorities read *you.*

All Paul's genuine letters (we exclude the Pastoral Epistles) except *Galatians* go on from the opening greeting to thanksgiving and intercession. We discuss the structure and general significance of these passages on p. 52. As we have already seen in the case of the greeting, Paul does not content himself with standardized phrases. He speaks to a particular audience and he speaks as pastor and apostle. His language is such, here and in other comparable passages, that he might well be reproducing the kind of utterance he was accustomed to make in solemn liturgical gatherings of his churches. We have no means of knowing for certain, but these passages could easily be *eucharistia* (thanksgiving) in more senses than one: the literal and, perhaps more loosely, the liturgical. Their tone is sonorous, they are full of abstractions and rolling participial phrases. The example now before us is particularly rich in these features. In Greek, the whole of vv. 3–8 is a single sentence, vv. 9–20 virtually another (though, as we shall see, within this vv. 15–20 are such a distinct entity that despite their grammatical connexion with what precedes they are best taken separately).

They are the liturgical (or quasi-liturgical) utterances of a practical pastor and apostle. That is, they show concern for the actual circumstances of the particular church (e.g. v. 7) and for the spread of the gospel (v. 6, 10).

The ground of Paul's pastorate and apostolate is God's action in Christ for the salvation of man, and this is the content of his thanksgiving: vv. 12–14. Here is the *logical* beginning of this passage; in fact, however, Paul starts one step further on, or appears to do so. In vv. 3–5 we also have thanksgiving, but the subject here is the faith of the Colossian Christians, i.e. that which has resulted from God's act in Christ and the preaching of it (v. 5b). Nevertheless their faith and love, for which he thanks God, are the direct result of *the hope laid up in heaven,* that is, the assured consummation of God's saving acts. This means the same as *the inheritance of the saints in light* (v. 12);

and just as the 'qualification' for that has already been received by the believer, so the hope is already *laid up*. Christ *has* been exalted, Christians by baptism participate already in his life (3¹), and so the future consummation is one with the present possession. It is not therefore surprising that in Paul's use *hope* sometimes has (as here and in 1²³, ²⁷) a more clearly present than future reference. There is no adequate reason for counting the use of this word in *Colossians* as an argument against pauline authorship, as some have suggested (any more than the small degree of stress on the action expected of God at the Last Day: see the Introduction, p. 136).

The form of the passage seems, then, to be somewhat circular. It begins with thanksgiving (vv. 3–5a) for the Colossian Christians' faith, notes how they came to receive it, and includes within that a reference to the gospel's universal spread (vv. 5b–8). It then continues with prayer that this faith may flourish and develop, both in terms of their relationship with God and in practical living (vv. 9–11). This growth for which Paul prays will itself be a fruit of that same divine power which brought about, through Christ, their entry into the new life. If therefore (to repeat) the two sections of thanksgiving seem to take a slightly different approach, the first thinking of the Colossians' present Christian life, the second of their initial entry into it through God's work in Christ, they share an assured faith in the effectiveness of that work and of the status to which it has led the believers.

ಣ

3
We: it is impossible to say whether this is an epistolary plural, quite appropriate especially in a rather formal section like this, or whether Paul is consciously associating Timothy with himself. In 1²³ he moves to the singular and, apart from 1²⁸ (where the plural may signify something or nothing), maintains it for the rest of the letter.

4f.
in Christ Jesus: probably the sphere of faith's exercise rather than its object.

faith … love … hope: cf. Eph. 1¹⁵. This triad of virtues occurs not only here and in the well-known 1 Cor. 13¹³, but also in an exactly parallel setting, 1 Thess. 1³, and in Gal. 5⁵ᶠ. (though here the connexion is less close and it is improbable that *faith* is used in the sense of the virtue of trust or faithfulness, but means rather self-commitment to God). Only here is there an attempt to relate them logically rather than simply to list them. Notice that *love* (*agapē*) is here seen as a quality exercised not generally but within the Christian community – like the conventional Jewish interpretation of Lev. 19¹⁸, which confined its application to fellow Jews and which Matt. 5⁴⁴ and Luke 10²⁹ᶠᶠ· revolutionize. Whenever Paul names a sphere for its exercise it is always, apparently, the Christian circle.

laid up: cf. 2 Macc. 12⁴⁵ for the same idea in Judaism. It is suggested that the idiom reflects the manner at the Persian court of recording the names of notable persons in the state archives. In this case it has come by way of the apocalyptic idea of the 'book of life' in which the believer trusts his name will be recorded, assuring his safety on the Day of Judgement (cf. Dan. 12¹; Phil. 4³; Rev. 5¹; 20¹⁵). Much of Jewish apocalyptic language was Persian in origin. (Cf. Eph. 1¹².)

heard before: this might mean that they have heard of the hope's content before its still-awaited realization. But this is unlikely because the whole stress in the use of the word *hope* here is on its present possession in the mind of the believer rather than on its future consummation; and that present possession comes in the very reception of the gospel, not at any later stage. The force of the *before* is rather to direct attention to the fact that their assured possession of the Christian inheritance is something that belongs to the basic content of the preaching they received, i.e. before any of the erroneous notions which Paul would correct came on the scene.

word of the truth: this phrase, equivalent to *the gospel*, is a Hebrew way of saying what would be put more naturally in Greek and English as '(God's) true word'. The phrase occurs, without the article, in Ps. 119⁴³, in Paul's Alexandrian Jewish contemporary, Philo, and in other writings. Here its content is defined by the word *gospel* which follows.

the gospel: lit. *the good news*. For the most succinct statement of what in Paul's view constituted the gospel see 1 Cor. 15³ᶠᶠ·, a formula which in essence was not his own invention but inherited by him. It consists of the facts of Jesus' death, burial, and resurrection, seen as God's action for saving man from sin and as the culmination of the Old Testament revelation. And indeed the verb related to *gospel* (*euaggelizomai* = to announce good news) is already found in the LXX in passages which prophesy God's coming act of deliverance: e.g. Isa. 40⁹; 52⁷; 61¹. For the primitive church, exemplified in Paul, this good news has now been both defined and actualized in the death and resurrection of Jesus, to which they bear witness.

6

in the whole world: this looks like pardonable exuberant exaggeration (cf. Rom. 1^8; 2 Cor. 2^{14}); but it may be explained by Paul's theories about what constituted the adequate saturation of an area with the proclaiming of the gospel. Thus in Rom. 15^{23} he can soberly state that in the whole area *from Jerusalem and as far round as Illyricum* (v. 19) he *no longer (has) any room for work* and so proposes to press on *via* Rome to Spain. His sense of the imminence of Christ's return, before which it is necessary to preach the gospel on as wide a scale as possible (cf. the universal scale of Paul's missionary outlook revealed in Rom. 11), may account for this, but it also throws light on his strategy; he seems to have thought, at least partly, in terms of simply planting the Church in certain representative centres from which it was to grow, receiving from him such help as could come from letters and visits (either personal or by delegates).

bearing fruit and growing: if the missionary method just mentioned really was what Paul had in mind, it bears a resemblance to one passage in the Gospels, perhaps already current in oral tradition and so known to Paul; that is, the parable of the sower (Mark 4$^{1ff.}$). In this there is the sowing of the seed broadcast and indiscriminately; we also find both the terms which occur here, in Mark 4^{8,20}, but they do not appear elsewhere in Paul. Some (e.g. W. L. Knox, *St Paul and the Church of the Gentiles* (Cambridge, 1939), p. 149, n. 5) suggest, in view of later Gnostic use of the parable in connexion with advance in esoteric knowledge, that he is using the language of people at Colossae in order to correct them.

7

from Epaphras: Epaphras is a member of the Colossian congregation, at present with Paul. He is also probably one of its leaders, for he was certainly its founder. How this came about, that is, how he came to act as Paul's agent in founding a church in a place which Paul himself had never visited, we do not know. Nor is it possible to glean much information about the organization of the group around Paul, his missionary staff; either Epaphras' main place is with Paul but he occasionally goes on journeys to churches on Paul's behalf; or else he is a (even *the*) leader of the Colossian church, honoured as its founder (would he ever have been called its apostle?) and just temporarily visiting Paul, perhaps because of his imprisonment. Like Paul he is a *servant* (better, 'slave') of Christ (see on Phil. 1^1, p. 47).

our: cf. *us* (v. 12). The uncertainty in the text at these two points arises from the same cause and is repeated a great many times elsewhere.

Over the many centuries of manuscript tradition before the invention of printing, copies of New Testament books were commonly made by dictation, often to a group of scribes simultaneously in a scriptorium. In ordinary Greek a number of vowels, including *u* and long *e*, came to be pronounced alike (namely as *ee* in 'meet') so that, especially if the sense allowed it, words spelt differently but sounding alike could easily be mistaken for one another. One of the commonest cases of this is the confusion between *hēmeis* (we) and *hymeis* (you), which is the case here. The R.S.V. readings make the better sense, but it is not crystal clear, especially in v. 7.

8

in the spirit: Rom. 5^5 is the best exposition of this verse.

9

with the knowledge: this word (*epignōsis*) is the noun corresponding to the verb rendered *understood* in v. 6, and it refers back to it. They are to develop in the process begun when they first received the gospel (= *the grace of God in truth*, v. 6). The noun occurs again in v. 10. It is a compound of the commoner *gnōsis* and carries basically the same meaning. Not common in the LXX (though Prov. 2^5 and Hosea 4^1 are useful parallels to New Testament usage), it becomes in the New Testament (and all the uses are in fact in Paul, or letters attributed to him, apart from a few in *2 Peter*) 'almost a technical term for the decisive knowledge of God which is implied in conversion to the Christian faith'.* The frequency of its use by Paul means that there is no need to see its sense here as determined by supposed Hellenistic or Gnostic traits in teaching at Colossae which regarded the knowledge of spiritual powers as the key to salvation; it is more likely to be one of those cases (see p. 128) where Paul uses a word which would immediately echo in the ears of his Gentile, ex-pagan, now Christian readers, only to give it a quite different sense. That sense is most adequately explained on the background of Old Testament ideas of the knowledge of God: it is obedient awareness of his demands in response to his saving action, a response made by man as a whole person. Its sense is therefore moral as much as intellectual. Paul's view that man's knowledge of God is essentially dependent upon God's knowledge of man is made clear neatly in Gal. 4^9 and 1 Cor. 13^{12} (cf. also on 2^2).

spiritual wisdom: while there is no necessary reference to esoteric speculation, regarded as special 'wisdom', in Colossae, the force of *spiritual*

* R. Bultmann in *Theological Dictionary of the New Testament* (E.T.) (Grand Rapids, 1964), Vol. I, p. 707.

(= *coming from God*, and, almost, simply *Christian*) may be to distinguish true wisdom from false, cf. 1 Cor. 1$^{20ff.}$, and once more Paul may be taking over his readers' vocabulary.

11

strengthened with all power: in Greek, an elegant alliteration: *dynamei dynamoumenoi*.

his glorious might: the English conceals another Hebraism (cf. *word of the truth*, v. 5), literally 'the might of his glory'. 'Glory' carries the sense of God's almost physical majesty and splendour.

endurance and patience: both largely pauline virtues in the New Testament, though the former word is also important in Luke.

12

inheritance: this word indicates that Paul has in mind the idea of the Church as the true Israel of God: the people in, by, and for whom God's saving purpose is worked out. The *klēros* (e.g. Exod. 6^8) is the Land of Promise, now paralleled and realized in the life of the Christian community (*the saints*). Here the primary stress seems to be on the inheritance as already received; in 3^{24} on what is still to be conferred. For the use of the image of light for the Christian life, cf. 2 Cor. 4^6: an image probably not seen by Paul as simply metaphorical, but as in some way literal, linked with 'glory' in v. 11. Cf. *the dominion of darkness*, v. 13; and for the whole set of ideas cf. Acts 26^{18}.

13

the dominion of darkness: given the contemporary mythological view of the universe, whereby spiritual forces represented actual beings and realms, Paul probably saw this phrase in a literal way, though it would also bear the developed metaphorical sense that it has for us.

kingdom of his beloved Son: the idea of the kingdom *of Christ* rather than *of God* is not very common in the New Testament (cf. Matt. 25$^{31ff.}$). Paul's view of the matter is best seen in 1 Cor. 15$^{24-28}$, where it appears that Christ will hand over his kingdom to the Father when all his enemies have been finally subjected to him. This is consistent with the passage here, in which the reference is to the present, and with pauline references to the kingdom *of God*, which look to the future. *His beloved Son* is yet another Semitism (lit. 'the Son of his love'). It may contain a reminiscence of the formula in the stories of the baptism and transfiguration of Jesus (Mark 1^{11} and 9^7).

14

redemption: this word (*apolytrōsis*) is related to *delivered* (v. 13) and also to *inheritance* (v. 12). All probably indicate that Paul has in mind the exodus of the tribes of Israel from Egypt, seen as a divine act of rescue and salvation, and as the great parallel to God's act in Christ. The word carries the sense of setting free (prisoners, slaves), and normally involves the idea of a ransom – but not always, the only LXX use, Dan. 4³⁴, being a case in point. Certainly in the pauline usage the idea of release is uppermost, with the matter of a ransom-price being hardly explicit, perhaps not even implicit. Here redemption is equated, as the effect and purpose of God's work in Christ, with *the forgiveness of sins*. The equation is surprising since this phrase, chiefly found in *Luke-Acts*, has no parallel in the rest of Paul, except in the doubtfully authentic Eph. 1⁷. For Paul, sin (singular) is usually seen as an almost personified force, from whose rule Christ has brought deliverance. Only in 1 Cor. 15³, which is probably a pre-pauline formula, does Paul come near to the idea in our present passage. In so far as it shows a shift away from a dramatic view of Christ's death as effecting release of man from the power of evil to the less vivid idea of the forgiveness of our sins as a gift which follows upon his work, some see in this expression evidence of the non-pauline authorship of *Colossians*. But the dramatic imagery dominates the immediately preceding verse (cf. 2¹⁵), and the point here may be to stress the essentially moral content of *redemption*, as against any quasi-Gnostic view of it as initiation into a higher spiritual state. As usual Paul suits his expression to the needs of his readers.

I¹⁵⁻²⁰   THE HYMN FOR CHRIST

¹⁵*He is the image of the invisible God, the first-born of all creation;* ¹⁶*for in him all things were created, in heaven and on earth, visible and invisible, whether thrones or dominions or principalities or authorities – all things were created through him and for him.* ¹⁷*He is before all things, and in him all things hold together.* ¹⁸*He is the head of the body, the church; he is the beginning, the first-born from the dead, that in everything he might be pre-eminent.* ¹⁹*For in him all the fullness of God was pleased to dwell,* ²⁰*and through him to reconcile to himself all things, whether on earth or in heaven, making peace by the blood of his cross.*

We now come to one of the most difficult passages in the New Testament, certainly the most difficult in this epistle. The difficulty lies not in making rough general sense of it – it is by no means unintelligible, not even obscure – nor does it lie in ascertaining the original text as there is only one variant of any importance and that does not affect the sense. The difficulty lies in giving anything like precise answers to a series of related questions. Before we list them, there is one feature of the passage worth noting at the outset, which may well strike even a person reading it in English for the first time: namely that it has certain rhythmic patterns – repetition of words like *first-born*, a number of clauses all beginning with *he is*, and the reiteration in numerous forms of the idea of Christ's pre-eminence in the universe. This impression of definite patterns, hazy as it may be, is in fact confirmed by further study, especially after comparison with other biblical and non-biblical texts, and it is most plausibly suggested that we are here dealing with a liturgical text of some kind, which may have had an existence independent of the letter in which we find it. Whether or not it was written by Paul – and that is one of the questions which must be asked – it was inserted by him in his letter because it well, and perhaps acceptably, expressed the message which he wished his letter to convey – a message which turns out to be a corrective to unorthodox thinking in the Colossian church; it will have been the more impressive if it was a formula already valued by both Paul and his readers.

The important suggestion about the passage was first worked out in detail by Norden (*Agnostos Theos*) in 1913, and many successors have elaborated his work; but the wide agreement on the *fact* of form and pattern has certainly not led to agreement on their exact nature. There are many suggestions, and their assessment is the second question which faces us. Thirdly, there is the meaning of the hymn (as we shall call it, for convenience*) – we must try to decide on the background of the terms used; are they Jewish or Hellenistic? What sort of people are likely to have composed this work? Supposing it not to be his own composition, is Paul's understanding of it (even his wording) exactly the same as theirs? While the hymn is clearly Christian as it stands, was it necessarily an original Christian composition or does there perhaps lie behind it a pre-Christian pagan (or Jewish) text of some kind? Finally, in its independent form, what use did Christians make of the hymn? Did they chant it on any sort of occasion or only on special occasions – solemnly at the Eucharist

---

* It may be that to call it a creed would give a better impression of its nature, but 'hymn' is a more general term, and we cannot suppose that different types of text used in the Church's worship were very carefully differentiated at this early stage.

or at Baptism, or as they went about their work? All these questions arise; perhaps none can find a definite answer.

Let us first try to identify the nature of this text a little more closely. R. P. Martin in his book *Carmen Christi* (Cambridge, 1967), which is a study of Phil. 2⁵⁻¹¹ (see p. 46), has drawn attention once more to the significance for New Testament studies of the words of Pliny, Roman governor of Bithynia (northern part of Asia Minor) in A.D. 112, in a letter to the Emperor Trajan.* Describing the habits of a Christian group which he has been investigating, he speaks of their meeting 'regularly before dawn on a fixed day to chant verses alternately amongst themselves in honour of Christ as if to a god'. There would be no reason to expect Pliny to be particularly accurate in his knowledge of the private liturgical customs of a minority religious group, obtrusive and puzzling though they seem to have been to some Roman authorities at this time, if his evidence did not tally so well with other pieces of information that lie before us. 'Verses . . . in honour of Christ as if to a god': this is a perfect description, from a pagan point of view, of several passages in the New Testament which bear signs of rhythmical construction. Prominent among them are Phil. 2⁶⁻¹¹ (see pp. 70ff.) and, in less mythological and dramatic and more philosophical vein, these verses in *Colossians*.

In neither case is it a question of obvious Greek poetic form; the rhythm and pattern come, as in the Psalms which were also no doubt in the liturgical stock of Paul's churches, from verbal repetition and the reiteration of ideas in regular order. We shall now try and see what pattern really does lie in this hymn, so that we can be as clear as possible about the shape of the work we are to interpret. Indeed, to understand the shape will no doubt help us to follow the flow of ideas and perhaps throw light on their likely source. So though we shall now examine the structure of the passage, we shall not be able to separate this entirely from questions of sense and origin.

Structure

We have already pointed out that scholars have come to no final agreement on this question, and a number of good suggestions are in the field. In the first place, there is what may be called the traditional

---

* Ed. Betty Radice, *The Letters of the Younger Pliny* (Penguin, 1963), p. 294.

view, in that it goes back to Norden's pioneer work. Others have refined and elaborated it since his time, and we give here the arrangement set out and cogently advocated by J. M. Robinson.* He divides the hymn into two parallel verses, or strophes.

I

He is the image of the invisible God,
The first-born of all creation;
For in him all things were created, in heaven and on earth.
All things were created through him and for him.
He is before all things,
And in him all things hold together.

II

He is the beginning,
The first-born from the dead.
For in him all the fullness of God was pleased to dwell†
And through him to reconcile to himself all things;
And he is the head of the body,
That in everything he might be pre-eminent.

This gives us a pair of strophes, each of six lines, and it takes full account of those elements of repetition whether of word or idea which we noted at the beginning. The two strophes are to a large extent in parallel, line by line. But this reconstruction is made at the cost of some re-arrangement of the hymn as Paul presents it to us and of some omissions. Thus, the last clause of v. 18 has been moved to the end of the second strophe, while the first clause of that verse takes its place just before it and loses its reference to the Church. Also the list of heavenly powers in v. 16 is dropped. These are regarded as spoiling the pattern and so to be unlikely to belong to the original hymn, which either Paul or some other person has felt free to adapt and to

* In J.B.L. (1957), pp. 270ff. This important article contains a comparison of a number of the main theories about the form of the hymn. An exhaustive comparison of even more of them is to be found in Gabathuler, *Jesus Christus, Haupt der Kirche, Haupt der Welt*, Col. 1¹⁵⁻²⁰ (*Abhandlungen zur Theologie des A. und N. Testaments no. 45*), (Zürich, 1965) – not translated into English. For a simpler scheme than Robinson's, along not dissimilar lines, see E. Schweizer, *The Church as the Missionary Body of Christ*, N.T.S., 8, pp. 6ff.

† Robinson believes that the original wording of this line and the next was a little different from this.

amplify for his own purposes. Some of the additions necessary to bring the hymn laid out above to what we find in *Colossians* are indeed words representing strong pauline themes, only too likely to have been introduced by him to make his favourite points, e.g. *the church* (v. 18), and the reference to *the blood of the cross* in v. 20. The neatness of this reconstruction is further seen in the fact that the two strophes deal with the two great 'moments' of the Christian gospel, Creation and Redemption; Christ is proclaimed as supreme in both spheres, both acts.

Lines in the two strophes correspond. While in the first strophe a given line uses a particular word or idea in connexion with creation, in the second strophe the same word or idea relates to redemption. This is clearest in the second lines, with the repetition of the word *first-born* (*prōtotokos*), but is not difficult to discern in most of the others. In the first lines, it is not immediately obvious; here and in some other cases, it becomes clearer when the background and meaning of some of the words is examined (see pp. 163ff.).

Much of the passage remains to be accounted for, and Robinson sees this as mainly a pair of pauline insertions (not all but most of the expressions are found elsewhere in his writings) placed asymmetrically in the two strophes, and simply filling out the meaning in a way relevant to the false teaching at Colossae. These additions aim to make clear Christ's unique role in creation and redemption, unrivalled by all angelic powers.

The two insertions are: (i) (*things*) *visible and invisible, whether thrones or dominions or principalities or authorities*, v. 16 (we examine the sense of these solemn titles later); (ii) *whether on earth or in heaven*, v. 20. Two other, again very plausibly pauline, insertions complete the passage as it now stands, and as Paul finally used it. We have mentioned them already: the addition of *the church* to line 5 of the second strophe, and *making peace by the blood of his cross* at the end. It is a further point in support of the view that these passages are pauline insertions that either the actual words or the gist of them reappear in 2$^{9-19}$, where Paul is directly concerned with the aberrant views which are favoured by some of the Colossian Christians; here too he has them in mind as he underlines the message of his text.

Of course an account of this kind, involving considerable manipulation by Paul of an already existing piece, may strain common sense (especially where it is a question of actually rearranging lines), and it certainly makes it rather more likely than not that the original hymn was written by someone other than Paul; to make it say fully pauline things, so it appears, he had to add to it. He may have done the same in Phil. 2^{6-11} (v. 8 *even death on a cross*, cf. 1^{20} here; see p. 71). The argument which best commends such a view is that he wants the climax to be a statement of the significance of the Cross of Jesus, which the original, with its mainly philosophical and abstract tone, did not have; the stress on the same point in $2^{14f.}$ gives support to this.

On a purely formal analysis, then, feeling that, as we shall see, linguistic and grammatical arguments are not decisive, Robinson believes that the original hymn was not by Paul. On general grounds it is not-at-all unlikely that he chose a neutral formula, well-known to his audience, perhaps indeed their own composition, perhaps given to them by Epaphras, and set out to say through it something that would impress them: that its true import is against the views to which some of them are tending and in favour of the doctrine which he will fully explain in the first half of his letter.

Other critics, adopting a similar analysis, have also come to the conclusion that a non-pauline hymn has been taken over and adapted by him. Käsemann,* for example, thinks that the basis of the passage is a Gnostic hymn which has been taken over and chris-tianized. He sees the liturgical text as beginning with v. 12 (with the formal words *Giving thanks to the Father*) and the actual hymn with v. 13. We feel, however, that vv. 12–14 are of a piece with the section which begins in v. 3, all of which bears a strongly liturgical stamp, as do the parallel passages in other epistles (e.g. Phil. 1^{3ff}): see p. 149.

This type of analysis, of which we have used J. M. Robinson's as an example, is, as we have shown, based upon the criterion of the re-petition of words and ideas discernible in the passage. We now turn to another analysis, based upon another stylistic and formal feature. This analysis has the advantage of dispensing with the assumption that Paul has re-arranged an earlier text in order to produce Col. 1^{15-20}. It is the work of E. Bammel,† who presents an elaborate chiastic structure as the key to our passage (i.e. the repetition of words and ideas but in reverse order: *ab ba*, a well-known stylistic device, not

* *Essays on New Testament Themes* (London, 1964), pp. 149ff.
† *Versuch zu Kol.* 1^{15-20}, Z.N.W. (1961), pp. 88ff.

at all surprising in literature of this kind at this period and common in the New Testament as in the Old Testament★). Again, we have to assume one or two insertions, but these are small and not disruptive. As in the earlier example, the hymn divides into two strophes, largely parallel, line for line, and concerned with the two themes – Creation and Redemption, each seen as the work of Christ, the cosmic Lord. The complication comes mainly in the first strophe and concerns, largely, the passage which Robinson was forced to put down to pauline insertion. The main weakness is that in each strophe three lines are left over at the end, which are not part of the pattern; and however convincingly they can be shown to develop what goes before, they still mar the neatness of the scheme.

I

a He is the image of the invisible God,
b The first-born of all creation;
b For in him all things were created,
         α in heaven
         β and on earth,
         β visible
         α and invisible
         β′ whether thrones (visible)
         α′ or dominions (invisible)
         α′ or principalities (invisible)
         β′ or authorities (visible)
a All things were created through him and for him:
     He is before all things,
     And in him all things hold together.
     He is the head of the body (the church).

II

a′ He is the beginning,
b′ The first-born from the dead (that in everything he might be preeminent).

★ See, for example, Prov. 10¹⁻⁵, where statements about the wise/good man alternate in this pattern with statements about the foolish/wicked man. And 1 Tim. 3¹⁶, perhaps another liturgical text of the early Church, where, in the same pattern, statements about Christ's victory in the earthly and heavenly realms alternate.

b' For in him all the fullness of God was pleased to dwell,
a' And through him to reconcile to himself all things,
                    Making peace by the blood of his cross,
                    Whether on earth,
                    Or in heaven.*

Once more, unfortunately, some elements in the alleged pattern
are more striking than others. The chiasmus which is most im-
mediately clear is that labelled $\alpha\beta$ $\beta\alpha$. Most of the others require explanation and depend upon an understanding – and indeed a
particular view – of the terms employed. We deal with this in detail
below; briefly, the parallels make sense once it is understood that
many of the words are the common currency of Jewish speculation
about cosmic spiritual powers and wisdom-theology.†

The clause bracketed in b' is thought not to be part of the original
hymn, simply on the grounds that a purpose-clause is not, in Bammel's view, likely in a liturgical text of this style (but cf. Phil. 2^{10}).

On this view of its structure, the hymn was already as it stood
much more immediately appropriate for Paul's purpose than in
Robinson's view. Also, simply because it is all a single piece, its
background is more probably Jewish‡, and its sense closer to the mind
of the Paul we know from the undoubtedly authentic epistles. Even
if it is not his own composition (which is not excluded), it accords
easily with the teaching he puts forward in 2$^{9ff.}$, which at almost
all points has parallels elsewhere in his works (see below).

If we are forced to decide between the two types of analysis outlined above, we incline to the latter, partly because it is the simpler
hypothesis, involving less dislocation of the text which lies before us,
and partly because, accepting pauline authorship of the epistle, we
believe that the text would be more likely to be used by Paul if he
had the longer form.

* The minor change in the final triplet is suggested by Bammel on the
grounds that an insertion is most likely to have begun with the participle.

† This, a continuous intellectual tradition in Israel from early times, finds
some of its first expressions in Prov. 1–9 and in Psalms like 1, 111, 119. It is
developed in *Ecclesiasticus* and the *Wisdom of Solomon*. See von Rad, *Old
Testament Theology*, Vol. I (Edinburgh and London, 1962), pp. 418ff.

‡ Robinson's pauline insertions are here part of the text, and are largely
Jewish in character.

Background and Meaning

In theory these are distinguishable, in practice so closely related that it is better to deal with them together. They have already intruded into our examination of the structure of the passage, and there we found hints of complexities ahead. Broadly, there are two possible lines of argument. If we believe that the hymn was composed in roughly the form used by Paul, then we can assume that its background is compatible with Paul's own and that its idiom is not far removed from that in which the gospel has been taught to the Colossian Christians. If, however, we believe that Paul has taken over a Gnostic or strongly Hellenistic hymn which needed to be supplemented for Christian use, we shall be led to think that the people at Colossae (whether the Christians or the subverters or both) were of a more Greek and pagan cast of mind and that Paul takes over their words only to adapt and so to correct them. Our last section led us to favour the former view. Let us see where it leads us in this new connexion.

We begin with an element which is secondary by comparison with the great christological assertions which are the main point of the hymn – the solemn and grandiose terms which appear in pairs in v. 16. What do these refer to, and what can they tell us about the thought-world to which the hymn belongs? Often all the last four words (*thrones, dominions, principalities, authorities*) have been taken to refer to angelic powers, of the kind venerated by the Colossian subverters (cf. 2[10, 18]). But two things cast doubt on this.* First, there are no really convincing parallels, in Jewish lists of classes of angels, to the use of the term *thrones* in this sense; and *authorities* (*exousiai*) though possible, is also unlikely to bear this sense. Second, the earlier pairs of words in the verse (*things in heaven and on earth*; *visible and invisible*) make it look as if the writer deliberately means to comprehend both angelic and human powers in his scope; all powers, of whatever kind, are subject to Christ's creative and saving lordship. If this is right then *dominions* (admittedly a rare term) and *principalities* will refer to the angelic powers who are so important in the religious outlook of the Colossians, and *thrones* and *authorities* will refer to human powers. (For *principalities* (*archai*), which is the commonest word of all for angelic rulers, cf. Rom. 8[38] and 1 Cor. 15[24].) This accords perfectly with the chiasmic structure, see pp. 160f.

* cf. Bammel, op. cit.

This concern to make clear Christ's position over against the angels, and to prevent his being classed as one of them (even if the chief one), was of great importance in the early Church. For Jewish Christians particularly, but also for Gentile Christians who easily found equivalents in their own background to the detailed Jewish speculation about angels at this time, the angels were forces to be reckoned with.* They acted as a kind of buffer between God and the world, swaying the fortunes of nations, responsible for all sorts of natural happenings, even, for some among the Jews,† including Paul, the channel through which God had given the Law to Israel in the time of Moses (Gal. 3^{19}; cf. Heb. 2^2; Acts 7^{53}). Feelings were mixed about them – sometimes they were seen as a tyranny under which man laboured, uncertain, capricious, and largely hostile; sometimes as gentle and beneficent. The universe abounded with angels of both kinds. In effect, they enabled men to objectify life as they found it, to give an account of the forces to which they felt exposed.

They also became important as man sought, not only to observe the world, but to come to terms with it, to reconcile himself to it when it seemed threatening, and to appreciate it joyfully when it treated him well. So, for those who had been used to seeing the angels in these roles and who had now come to see Christ as the key to their relationship with God, it was vital to define the link between him and them. For certainly, at this time, putting right one's relationship with God involved not just coming to terms with oneself, by finding forgiveness of sin, but also coming to terms with a universe felt to be alive with personal spiritual forces, who were in some rather ill-defined sense God's subordinates but often apparently closer than he to the immediate concerns of life.

The most clear-sighted early Christian writers for whom this was a natural idiom of thought were not slow to go to the heart of this problem. They held that Christ had defeated these angelic powers so far as they were evil and hostile to man and had superseded them so far as they were beneficent. In other words he was the amply sufficient, unique mediator between God and man, rendering all

* See the *Book of Jubilees*, 2^2 (Charles, II, p. 14) which dates from the second century B.C., and here gives a full list of the categories of angels, including those who control the material elements of the universe (cf. *stoicheia*, Col. 2^8).

† For references see E. W. Burton, *The Epistle to the Galatians* (Edinburgh, 1921), p. 189.

others powerless and superfluous. What was more, whereas they in effect separated man from God, he brought them together, by fully representing God to man. Man 'in Christ' need no longer feel timorous about the universe he lived in, no longer threatened by it, whatever the appearances; for not only man but the very angelic powers themselves were now reconciled (v. 20) to God or defeated by him through Christ (2^{15}).

Christians had to find terms to describe all this. This hymn is one such attempt, and we shall find that it makes use of ideas already well-developed in Judaism, intelligible to men of pagan upbringing, and capable of expressing the gospel. Another attempt, along different lines, is found in Heb. 1. There the writer's very first concern is to make quite clear the distinction between Jesus and the angels with whom he might so easily be confused. He sets out to show that Jesus is not to be classed with them but is in a category of his own. He finds a solution by discovering a series of Old Testament texts which can be read as contrasting the position of angels with that of the Son and as subordinating them firmly to him.

That the problem of the angels persisted, and that sometimes even main-stream Christian writers could be off their guard in speaking of them can be illustrated from the second-century writer, Justin Martyr (*First Apology*, 6★), who can describe the object of Christians' worship and adoration as 'the Father of righteousness ... and the Son who came from him ... and the army of the other good angels who follow him and are made like him, and the prophetic Spirit'. (Cf. 1 Tim. 5^{21}.) Those Christians at Colossae who provoked the writing of 2^{18} would have understood what this meant.

It appears that for Paul the contrast between Christ and the angels could scarcely be over-emphasized. He seems to have believed that those angelic powers who had control over the world had actually been behind the crucifixion of Jesus, presumably inspiring the human perpetrators of that act (1 Cor. 2^8). Because that event was the means of his triumph and vindication by God, it brought about their defeat (Col. 2^{15}). Paul nowhere writes out in full the story he would have to tell in order to make his meaning wholly intelligible, but it seems to be connected with two elements in the role of the angels, according to Jewish belief.

First, they were the assistants of God in creation: for example it was

★ L.C.C., I, p. 245.

to them that God was speaking when he said, in Gen. 1^{26}, 'Let *us* make man in *our* image'. According to Philo, they were especially responsible for the creating of the irrational part of man's soul, that part of him in which sin had arisen. Second, they were closely associated with the Law. For some Jews of the Dispersion they appear to have been the channel through which God gave to Israel the greater part of the Law, and for many more they were the guardians of those who set out to keep it faithfully. In Jubilees 4$^{15ff.}$,* angels give instruction on earth in 'knowledge and wisdom' and in the proper ordering of the calendar. And in the War Rule of the Qumran Sect (Vermes, p. 136), the people of Israel are described as 'the saints of the Covenant, instructed in the laws and learned in wisdom . . . who have heard the voice of Majesty and have seen the Angels of Holiness (cf. Col. 2^{18}), whose ear has been unstopped, and who have heard profound things'. In effect, then, the angels are God's agents in both Creation and Redemption, the Law being in Judaism the prime instrument of God's saving purpose.

We are not far here, especially in the last quotation, from the outlook which Paul has to contend with in Colossae (and elsewhere, cf. Gal. 3^{19}; 4$^{3, 9f.}$). It helps us to explain the intimate link which Paul sees between the Law and the angelic powers in Christ's victory (Col. 2$^{14f.}$), and the absolute necessity for him to find terms to describe Christ which will show that he alone plays the part in Creation and Redemption which for Jews belonged to the angels and to the Law. Concepts lay to hand in the Jewish theological tradition itself.

We now turn to the idiom which he uses to state his positive case. Much of the language used here recurs in 2$^{9ff.}$, where the tone is much more polemical: our present passage acts as a curtain-raiser. What is the source of its language?

We have already had occasion to say that it has close affinities with that Jewish theological tradition which centred on the figure of Wisdom. This is clear if we look at some leading examples of that very long tradition:

(1) Prov. 8$^{22-36}$. Here we find 'wisdom' seen as the first of God's works and can compare the words *beginning* in Col. 1^{18} and *first-born* in 1$^{15, 18}$. Wisdom is also God's agent in creation, Prov. 8$^{30f.}$, cf. Col. 1^{16}. And there is a strong hint of Wisdom's role in salvation – 'He who finds me finds life and obtains favour from the Lord' (v. 35, cf. Col. 1^{20}).

* Charles, II, p. 18.

(2) Wisdom of Solomon 7$^{21f.}$; 8^6; 9^1. These are much later examples (first century B.C.) of similar teaching. The first passage has the term *all things* (*ta panta*), so frequent in our passage, and, as we shall see, to some degree a technical term.

(3) Ecclesiasticus 24. In this chapter, Wisdom and the Law of Israel are almost identified as the great means of blessing to God's people. If we add an extension of this idea, found in rabbinic thought, that the Law was the instrument through which God created the world, we can see that here, as in 2$^{14ff.}$ more explicitly, Christ occupies the place of the Law as well as of Wisdom in the work of God.

To see Jesus in these terms is fairly common in the New Testament. Given the available categories, it was one of the best ways of making clear his unique mediatorial position, and as we have seen, Judaism had already done much preparatory work by fusing and identifying terms. Besides our present passage, good examples are 1 Cor. 8^6, which is a close parallel, 1 Cor. 1^{30}, Luke 11^{49}; and very closely related, though using other words, are John 1$^{1-3}$ (see below) and Heb. 1$^{3f.}$.

The fact that it was the man Jesus whose significance came to be seen in this way meant that another strand of thought was easily associated with this pattern; that is the thinking, common in Judaism at this time, on the subject of Adam, seen as not only the first but also the archetypal man, symbol of the whole human race (see in relation to Phil. 2$^{6-11}$, p. 73). In Wis. 9^2 Wisdom is the maker of Man and she is the instructor of the good man (Wis. 1$^{1-4}$). In the setting of the Church's teaching about Jesus, it was an easy step to identify the one with the other. Thus, in Col. 1^{15}, Christ is the image of God (cf. Gen. 1^{26}).

In John 1$^{1-14}$, instead of wisdom we find the term *word* (*logos*), used in much the same range of senses; it can be seen from Wis. 9$^{1f.}$ that by this time the two were very close in meaning, as agents of God in his creative work. Already in the work of Philo of Alexandria, the Wisdom-theology had been able to absorb a certain amount of philosophically more sophisticated material by fixing on *logos* as the term for the creative agent or principle, a term with an established and sufficiently similar use in the Platonism then fashionable in Alexandria. Philo the Jew also has passages which compare with our hymn, and he indeed anticipates the identification, particularly natural for Christians endeavouring to interpret the figure of Jesus, between the archetypal Man, Wisdom, and Word; in one passage he heaps the titles together: 'For he is called Beginning (*archē*) and Name of God and Word and Man-according-to-the-image (cf. Gen. 1²⁶) and the Seeing One, even Israel.' This passage helps to show how Jewish speculation could already set side by side the terms which occur in the first lines of our two strophes: *image of God* (v. 15) and *beginning* (v. 18). (For *image*, cf. 1 Cor. 11⁷; 2 Cor. 4⁴.)

If there is perhaps an indirect influence from the common Platonism of the day, there are also likely to be in our passage traces of the elementary Stoicism which was in practice often mingled with it. Thus the term *ta panta* (*all things*), which occurs four times, is the common term for the totality of things – the All; and the idea that the All 'holds together' *in him* (v. 17) and *was created for him* also has a Stoic ring. This does not necessarily betoken a pre-Christian or Hellenistic origin for the hymn; passages like 1 Cor. 8⁶ show that Paul, who certainly thought of his upbringing as thoroughly Jewish (Phil. 3⁵), was quite capable of this kind of statement. Such language had been absorbed by Judaism, and it is a Church which is predominantly Jewish in mental formation if not necessarily in membership that has produced the Colossian hymn. Nevertheless, it was language which could be understood, in varying ways, by each element in Paul's audience – the Jewish teachers whose doctrine it rebuffed, the ex-pagan Christians who were bemused by them, and those Christians who had absorbed Paul's gospel well enough to see with his eyes.

This judgement is confirmed by an important suggestion made by C. F. Burney* and supported by many scholars since his time. This has the effect of stressing the influence of Jewish wisdom-speculation to the minimizing of Stoicism and perhaps even of the platonized Judaism seen in Philo of Alexandria. According to this suggestion the passage is an early example of a development which went far among Jewish rabbis as well as the early Christian fathers.† Its

---

* *Christ as the ARXH of the Creation*, J.T.S., 27, pp. 160ff.; or, for convenience, see in W. D. Davies, *Paul and Rabbinic Judaism* (London, 1948), pp. 150ff.

† For a later example, cf. Origen: 'In the beginning, God made heaven and earth. What is the beginning of all things, if not our saviour and Lord Jesus Christ, first-born of all creation? Now it is in this beginning, that is in his Word, that God made heaven and earth' (*Homily on Genesis* 1¹; third century A.D.).

starting point was a painstaking investigation of the story of the
Creation in Gen. 1 for deeper theological insight about the structure
of the universe than it presented on the surface. This investigation,
weighing the account word by word, found a clue to the meaning
latent in its first words (*In the beginning*) in Prov. 8²² (another passage
concerned with creation), taken to mean, as in the LXX, 'The Lord
created me (i.e. Wisdom) as the beginning of his way.' This meant
that the terms 'wisdom' and 'beginning' could be identified, and
the opening words of Gen. 1¹ could be interpreted instrumentally:
'Through the Beginning (= Wisdom) God created.' Application to
Christ followed easily. Working along these lines, Burney held that
Col. 1¹⁵⁻²⁰ is in fact 'an elaborate exposition of *Běrêshîth* (= *in the
beginning*, Heb.) in Gen. 1¹, in the Rabbinic manner'. He goes on to
lay out the way this is done: 'Three explanations are given of the
preposition *bě*: then four explanations of the substantive *rêshîth*; and,
the conclusion is that in every possible sense of the expression, Christ
is its fulfiller.' Thus:

Běrêshîth	in reshith	in him all things were created (1¹⁵).
„	by „	all things were created through him (1¹⁶).
„	into „	all things were created for him (1¹⁶).
Rêshîth	Beginning	he is before all things (1¹⁷).
„	Sum-total	in him all things hold together (1¹⁷).
„	Head	he is the head of the body (1¹⁸).
„	Firstfruits	he is the beginning, the first-born from the dead (1¹⁸).

An objection often raised to this interpretation, which so depends
upon a Jewish background, is that the hymn is too Christ-centred to
have come from any mind (even Paul's) formed in Judaism. The
parallels which are cited from other parts of Paul, like 1 Cor. 8⁶ and
15²⁴⁻²⁸ are careful to put the ultimate weight on the Father: he, not
the Son, is the one *for whom we exist* (1 Cor. 8⁶ contrast Col. 1¹⁶), the
goal of creation. We do not believe that this objection carries weight.
That Christ had already in Paul's time begun to attract to himself,
perhaps half-consciously, the language normally appropriate to God,
is amply evidenced, particularly the use of the title Lord (*kyrios*),
even in quotations from the Old Testament where it certainly refers
to God (e.g. Rom. 10¹³, cf. Phil. 2¹¹). Our passage goes no further in
principle, and it may be correct to interpret it as speaking of God as

the object of the act of reconciliation which Christ performs (see below).

That belief in the effectiveness of Christ's saving work should so early have developed theologically to the extent that he was identified with the agents of God's work 'from the beginning' (Word and Wisdom) is a remarkable testimony to the intellectual vitality of the early Christian communities. It was a natural and necessary step if the unity and continuity of God's activity in the world were to be asserted. This hymn, with its two strophes – the one showing the creative work of God as wholly subject to Christ, the other showing the redemption of the world as centring upon him – is one of the great examples of it in the New Testament. If the hymn is not of Paul's composition, it is evidence that this doctrine was understood and could be creatively handled by Christians other than him in the first decades of the Church's life.*

We now sum up our case. Starting from our conclusion (tentative as it was) about the structure of the passage and so taking it as the work either of Paul himself or of someone close to his mind, we have stated evidence about its meaning and background which is entirely in accord with this. Further evidence for the same view comes from the fact that Paul's method here is at one with that which he employs in the whole of this letter. The detailed notes on particular words will show Paul using terms which would indeed find an echo in the minds of his Hellenistic readers at Colossae, but filling them with a Christian sense. They were terms which would also make immediate sense to the Jewish teachers, for most of them came from Jewish theology (where indeed Paul had no doubt first met them): but again, the application was new, and firmly Christian. Paul writes so that *all* at Colossae who read or hear of him will receive something salutary from his words. At this stage in his letter he is not being overtly polemical. He is probably quoting a formula which he knew the Colossians valued and used. Shortly, in 2$^{9ff.}$, Paul will go further in making clear its true implications, about which they are perilously uncertain.

* Käsemann (op. cit.) feels able to root the passage more precisely in early Christian life, holding that it is a baptismal liturgy. Some of its language, especially vv. 12ff. which he includes in the unit, and references to baptism later in the epistle (2^{12}) could point to this, but it is hard to be so definite.

15

first-born of all creation: later controversy about the exact nature of Christ, especially that raised by Arians in the fourth century, seized upon this phrase to show that he belonged to the creaturely rather than the divine sphere. But of course this was to force into the words a precision which they do not contain and to make them pronounce on issues which their author never had in mind. If we are right in seeing the clue to this passage in the wisdom-literature, then this must mean that Christ came into being before all creation, and was God's agent in the creative work (cf. vv. 16f.). It also includes the idea of headship and supremacy (cf. v. 18; Rev. 1⁵).

18

head: Cf. 1 Cor. 11³. There Christ is described as *the head of every man,* here, as befits the context, of *the body,* meaning orginally perhaps the entire universe. Though this idea probably represents one of the Stoic elements in the passage (the *logos* seen as the soul indwelling the cosmos), it is not too far from the Adam of Genesis 1 who was given dominion over all creatures. Christ as the new Adam or archetypal Man has this dominion on an even wider scale.

the church: cf. 1²⁴. This is almost certainly, as we have seen, an addition, for it spoils the parallelism of the lines of the hymn and the universal scale of the vision which it otherwise presents. But the fact that the idea of the body of Christ is used in the hymn to refer to the universe and not, as in the rest of Paul, to the Church, need not make us think that the hymn must have a pagan base, nor even that the hymn could not have been composed by Paul himself. In his undoubted works, even in the course of a single writing, *1 Corinthians,* Paul uses this image in so many different senses that further adaptations of it are not at all surprising. It is always used to make thoroughly pauline points. Even the change from one sense to another (by adding *the church*) is by no means violent: the Church can be seen as the first-fruits of redeemed creation (cf. Rom. 8¹⁹).

19

The grammatical sense of this verse is not easy, especially if it is thought that it must fit smoothly with the first phrase of v. 20. The Greek does not make it unambiguously clear that the translation given here is the right one. Some suggest that the subject of the verb *was pleased* must be 'God' (unexpressed) – 'God was well-pleased that all the fullness should dwell in him and through him to reconcile all things to him (self?).' This does help to knit the sentence together; but it is not easy to see what 'him' refers to in each case, and it involves a most abrupt introduction of 'God' as the subject. If 'Christ' is the subject, the sense is still awkward. So the common view is that *all the fullness* is the subject, as in our translation (the words *of God* do not appear in the Greek). What then does this phrase mean?

The word *fullness* (*plērōma*) occurs eight times in Paul's undoubted writings, often in a sense quite foreign to ordinary English usage. But it is not always in quite the same sense and each case has to be examined separately. Those who interpret the whole passage as coming from quasi-Gnostic circles see this as an early example of its common and technical sense in the Gnosticism of the second century: it refers to the whole body of heavenly angelic powers and spiritual emanations, or the sphere which they inhabit. If the hymn were written to 'take off' such views, it might – with good effect – use the word with that sense in mind; what the subverters saw in their speculations as diffused through a whole series of spiritual entities is all to be found in the unique person of Christ, the sole mediator between God and the world. Paul uses the word again in 2⁹ and once more this could be the point. The Jewish angelological doctrines which were one element behind second-century Gnostic schemes are certainly present at Colossae (cf. 2¹⁸). But it may nevertheless be anachronistic to see this technical sense already present in a document as early as this, even if the probability of a Jewish background of a more orthodox kind were not as strong as we have shown it to be. It is more likely to mean 'the whole being and power of God'. Philo spoke of the *logos* as 'most full' of God, a usage not unlike that found in Paul. (For the use of the word in the second century sects, see R. M. Grant, *Gnosticism – an Anthology* (London, 1961) pp. 160, 170f.)

An ingenious suggestion* starts from the observation that the words *was well-pleased in him* have parallels in the New Testament – in the story of the baptism of Jesus, Mark 1¹¹. If this Semitic turn of phrase is rightly discerned in our passage, then it means that the words *in him* do not follow *dwell* but go with *was well-pleased*, as indeed their position in the Greek text indicates. If the comparison with the Baptism-story is to be followed up, then *all the fullness* may be seen as an equivalent for what is there expressed in terms of the Spirit. Thus alongside the reference in the second strophe to the resurrection and the cross of Jesus, we have also a mention of another crucial moment in his earthly life, his commissioning. There are, however, difficulties with this suggestion, not least the absence of other uses of *plērōma* in quite this sense and the relationship with 2⁹, where *in him* certainly goes with *dwell*. The probability is that the meaning of the two verses is much the same.

* See G. Münderlein, *Die Erwählung durch das Pleroma*, N.T.S., 8, pp. 264ff.

20

reconcile: cf. 2 Cor. 5¹⁹ᶠ·; Rom. 5¹⁰ᶠ·; Eph. 1¹⁰. Here alone, apart from
Eph. 1¹⁰, do we find the idea of the *reconciling* of the cosmic powers. A
little later, in 2¹⁵, there is the quite different and more typically pauline
idea of their being disarmed by Christ. Some take this as confirming the
view that Paul is here using a formula which is not his own composition.

to himself: the R.S.V. makes this refer most clearly to God, and 2 Cor.
5¹⁹ supports this interpretation. But it may refer to Christ; the hymn
as a whole is christocentric; and the Greek is identical with *for him* in
v. 16 (*eis auton*), which on both Robinson's and Bammel's analyses (see
pp. 158 and 160) comes in the parallel line in the first strophe. V. 21
fails to settle the issue.

I²¹⁻²³   PAUL DRIVES HOME THE MESSAGE
                 OF THE HYMN

²¹*And you, who once were estranged and hostile in mind, doing evil deeds,*
²²*he has now reconciled in his body of flesh by his death, in order to present*
you holy and blameless and irreproachable before him, ²³*provided that you*
continue in the faith, stable and steadfast, not shifting from the hope of the
gospel which you heard, which has been preached to every creature under
heaven, and of which I, Paul, became a minister.

These verses simply go on from the second strophe of the hymn and
begin to apply it to the audience in Colossae; here for the first time
those holding aberrant views in that congregation begin to come
directly into view (v. 23). This occurs in the most general way: Paul
says that there is a danger that the effects of the reconciliation with
God proclaimed in the hymn and enjoyed by the believers may be
threatened by *shifting from the hope of the gospel which you heard.*
    The fundamental idiom in vv. 21f. is sacrificial. It is a succinct
statement of a way of regarding Christ's work which is frequently
alluded to by Paul. It starts from man's estranged condition – a
condition shared (cf. Rom. 1–2) by Jews and Gentiles alike. In the
sacrificial system of Israel, atonement for sin was effected by the
offering of unblemished animals in the Temple. The release and offering of their life, in the shape of the blood, carried with it the offering

of the offender's life and rendered him once more acceptable to God (cf. Lev. 9²ᶠᶠ·; 17¹⁴). This provides a telling image for the action of Christ and its saving effects for man; an image which is poignant and striking, particularly for Jews. It soon came to carry with it the idea of a contrast between the ineffective or only partially effective repeated sacrifices of Judaism and the one sacrifice of Christ, effective for all; this development was thoroughly worked out in *Hebrews*.

All essential parts of this picture are present: the sinner's estrangement from God, the victim with whom the sinner identifies himself, the resulting reconciled condition of the offerer. But the Christian data produce modifications. The victim, Christ, actively identifies himself with man, the sinner, and by this action associates man with his own status as a blameless offering. So man is joined with Christ in the perfect relationship with the Father. For the idea of Christ's identification of himself with man in order to restore man to relationship with God, cf. 2 Cor. 5²¹; 8⁹; Gal. 3¹³ – each in a different idiom. For the use of the sacrificial image, sometimes in a more fragmentary way than here, cf. Rom 3²⁴ᶠ·; 12¹ᶠ·.

It might be thought that the use of the term *body* here bore little relation to its use in v. 18 or v. 24: it looks as if it simply emphasizes the fact of Christ's physical death, taking up v. 20 (cf. *reconcile* in v. 22). But the corporate significance attaching so constantly to Paul's use of the word is not wholly lacking here. The community Paul has in mind is not always the same. Here it is the believers who are reconciled as a community *in his body of flesh*. For a passage working the idea out more fully in death-life terms, cf. Rom. 6³ᶠᶠ·. The death of Christ, an act of God performed in the one of whom the affirmations of 1¹⁵⁻²⁰ are true, is of universal significance and validity, both in time and space. If any particular moment in the Christian life is here in mind, then (as our comparison with Rom. 6³ᶠᶠ· suggests) it is baptism, cf. 2¹⁰⁻¹². This rather than the Last Judgement is in that case the moment of the believer's presentation before God.

So strong is Paul's emphasis on the believer's appropriation of the work of Christ that it is often forgotten how much he talks of the need for perseverance and the danger of losing the gifts and promises of God: with v. 23 should be compared 1 Cor. 1⁸; 9²⁴⁻²⁷.

చ౪

22

body of flesh: this phrase, found in the New Testament only here and, in a slightly different, pejorative sense, in 2¹¹, turns up in the *Commentary on Habakkuk* discovered among the Dead Sea Scrolls at Qumran. There it bears its simple sense, the physical body: 'And they inflicted horrors of evil diseases and took vengeance upon his body of flesh' (Vermes, p. 238).

23

the faith: this use of the word, meaning in effect 'the Christian religion', becomes much commoner in the later writings of the New Testament, a sign of an increasing fixity in the Church's view of herself, but is found elsewhere in Paul, e.g. Rom. 1⁵; Gal. 1²³.

the hope: as in v. 5, the stress is probably more on the Christian hope as a present assurance in the believer than on the content of it which looks to future fulfilment. But the Christian gospel is seen so much in terms of the continuity between what God has already given to the believer and its future consummation that the distinction is not easy to draw.

to every creature: see on v. 6. It may be once more the exaggeration of fervour. But the idea in Paul's mind may be what we should see as more mythological; the phrase is in Greek exactly the same as that translated *all creation* in v. 15. The whole creation *under heaven* may signify not only the material world but the spiritual beings believed to inhabit the air. Many early Christians saw Christ's saving work as having been proclaimed also to them, and so to the whole creation: cf. for example the statements of the creed-like formula in 1 Tim. 3¹⁶, in many ways similar in thought to Col. 1¹⁵⁻²⁰; also from the second century the idea that at his ascension, Christ was publicly acclaimed by the heavenly powers now subject to him (see Justin, *First Apology*, 51*).

minister: the word here may be quite non-technical, simply 'servant', but see on Phil. 1¹, p. 47.

I²⁴–2⁷   HOW PAUL SEES HIS MINISTRY

²⁴*Now I rejoice in my sufferings for your sake, and in my flesh I complete what is lacking in Christ's afflictions for the sake of his body, that is, the church,* ²⁵*of which I became a minister according to the divine office which was given to me for you, to make the word of God fully known,* ²⁶*the mystery hidden for ages and generations*ᶜ *but now made manifest to his*

* L.C.C., I, p. 275.

saints. ²⁷*To them God chose to make known how great among the Gentiles are the riches of the glory of this mystery, which is Christ in you, the hope of glory.* ²⁸*Him we proclaim, warning every man and teaching every man in all wisdom, that we may present every man mature in Christ.* ²⁹*For this I toil, striving with all the energy which he mightily inspires within me.*

2¹*For I want you to know how greatly I strive for you, and for those at Laodicea, and for all who have not seen my face,* ²*that their hearts may be encouraged as they are knit together in love, to have all the riches of assured understanding and the knowledge of God's mystery, of Christ,* ³*in whom are hid all the treasures of wisdom and knowledge.* ⁴*I say this in order that no one may delude you with beguiling speech. For though I am absent in body, yet I am with you in spirit, rejoicing to see your good order and the firmness of your faith in Christ.*

⁶*As therefore you received Christ Jesus the Lord, so live in him,* ⁷*rooted and built up in him and established in the faith, just as you were taught, abounding in thanksgiving.*

> c Or *from angels and men.*

This passage raises two crucial matters: first, the way Paul understands his sufferings in relation to Christ and the life of the Church; and second, the way he understands the gospel whose proclamation is entrusted to him. In each case, hints already given are now developed.

We deal first with Paul's statement about his sufferings in v. 24. It is a difficult verse, and we shall expound it first by showing how it relates to its context in the letter, so that we can be clear about the flow of Paul's own mind, then by examining the background of the terms he employs. We shall find that in some degree the latter did not make it easy to express his intended meaning.

At first sight the passage looks like a fresh departure. In fact it is closely related to what goes before. Most obviously, it takes up (v. 25) the mention of Paul's own function as a servant of the gospel from the end of v. 23. It also takes up (v. 24) the sacrificial ideas of vv. 21f. If the believer is one who has come to participate in Christ's death (v. 22, cf. Gal. 2²⁰; Rom. 6³ᶠᶠ·; 2 Cor. 5²¹), so certainly is Paul the apostle. But in the apostle's participation in Christ's passion, which is externalized for him as for all Christians in the actual sufferings which come his way (Phil. 3¹⁰; 2 Cor. 11³⁰; 12⁷⁻¹⁰*), there is an extra

---

* Here there is also a polemical factor: sufferings and not the conventional marks of authority are the authentic signs of apostleship because they are the means of identification with Christ.

dimension: they are *for your sake*. In this they are like Christ's sufferings (cf. *for our sins*, 1 Cor. 15³), though of course wholly secondary to his and dependent upon his, for the apostle is his servant and delegate. So the apostle looks not only towards Christ but also towards those Christians for whom he is reponsible, and he looks towards them not only as pastoral leader but also as one whose sufferings are on their behalf (cf. 2 Cor. 11²⁸ᶠ·).

Col. 1²⁴ often strikes people as a rather extreme way of formulating this idea; partly because it is hard to avoid reading it with the theological sensitivities of more recent times in mind. It is easy to see Paul as here exposing himself to the charge that he regards Christ's sufferings as somehow an insufficient sacrifice for human sin, and then to rush to his defence against it. But this procedure is anachronistic. Paul is not addressing himself to the problem whether Christ's suffering and death made a perfect atonement for the sins of the whole world and emerging with a dangerously loose answer. His words must be read in their context. Having made plain the complete centrality and universally efficacious nature of Christ's act, he explains how first all believers and then he himself, the apostle, participate in the fruit of that act. In the setting of the life 'in Christ', his sufferings have a vital place: not as making up any deficiency in Christ's self-offering as a reconciling act, but as displaying and building up the authentic pattern of Christian life in the Church (*for the sake of his body*). This pattern consists of 'life-through-death', 'glory-in-weakness' (cf. 1 Cor. 1²⁵⁻²⁷; 2 Cor. 4¹¹ᶠ·; 12⁹ᶠ·; 13⁴). It is the pattern of Christ's own saving work, into which the believer has been incorporated, and the apostle leads the way in reproducing it, by virtue of the office he has received from God.

Along such lines as these we are to find the main sense of the verse, but we must now turn to the background of the ideas which Paul uses. In particular there is the belief, common in the schemes of Jewish apocalyptic speculation which outline the events ushering in the Last Day, that the final intervention of God would be preceded by a time of intense sufferings of all kinds, afflicting God's faithful servants as well as sinners. This remained as an element in Christian apocalyptic patterns: cf. Mark 13⁹⁻²⁷, with parallels in Matt. 24 and Luke 21; 2 Thess. 2. Though the believer is assured of salvation at the Lord's return, he has no immunity from sufferings, especially in the shape of persecution which will grow to new intensity as the Day approaches. Also there is the notion of a quota of sufferings which is to be completed before the End will come (cf. I Thess. 2¹⁶; Rev. 6¹¹), and this no doubt marks Paul's expression here.

A further strand of contemporary Jewish religious thought which may play a part here is the belief that the suffering and especially the death of a righteous man can atone for his own sins and for those of others: cf. 2 Macc. 7³⁷ᶠ·; Isa 53¹². Christians familiar with this belief, such as (almost certainly) Paul, were faced with the problem of expressing satisfactorily their conviction about the uniqueness and all-embracing quality of Christ's suffering and death. They began by showing that *his* death was 'according to the scriptures' (I Cor. 15³), i.e. fulfilled a unique place in the saving action of God in Israel's – and the world's – history. It was moreover the death of God's Son – his unique agent (Rom. 8³²). But in *Colossians* another approach predominates: Christ's death is unique in that he is identified with the pre-existent wisdom of God (see pp. 166f.): in and through him the whole divine life and work are expressed. Nevertheless something of the belief in the value of *any* good man's sufferings for God remains, and in this verse Paul endeavours, in a way not entirely free from ambiguity, to express it in association with the overriding belief in the universal effectiveness of Christ's work, and in the light of the believer's life 'in Christ'.

If v. 24 took up from v. 22 the idea of Christ's reconciling death and united it with the role of Paul, already introduced in v. 23, the passage goes on to pick up and develop *the gospel* (also from v. 23). The concern is less with the content than with the movement of the gospel, which Paul, as an apostle of Jesus Christ and a servant of the Church (v. 25), conveys and proclaims (v. 28). As far as content is concerned Paul expresses it in one word – *Christ: him we proclaim* (v. 28). Passages like I Cor. 15³⁻⁵ and I Cor. 2² show what he means by this and illustrate again the fact that 'suffering' and 'gospel' are inseparable ideas for Paul. But if *Christ* can be said to be the content of the gospel, it can also be expressed as *Christ in you*; that is, the believers are living statements of the message, by virtue of the fact that Christ dwells in them.

In fact in these verses the actual word *gospel* is not repeated from v. 23, but two synonymous expressions are used instead: *the word of God* (v. 25), and *the mystery (mystērion)* (vv. 26f.). Both of them serve to anchor the work of Christ in God's eternal purposes. For *the word*

is the most general Old Testament term for God's message (fundamentally, of judgement and salvation) to Israel, constantly conveyed
through prophets (e.g. Isa. 55$^{10f.}$; Jer. 42^7). That *word of God* is now,
in the proclamation of the work of God in Christ, *fully known* (lit.
'fulfilled').

Mystery (see detailed note below, p. 182) would be an evocative
word to all whom Paul has in mind in writing to Colossae. To the
Christians, once pagans, it would be a reminder of the cults familiar
all around them ('the mysteries') in which prescribed rites brought
the devotees into a relationship with the deity which assured salvation. To the Jewish teachers its associations would be with the
apocalyptic literature with which no doubt they were familiar.
There it expresses the belief that the plan of God, long concealed by
him, would speedily be disclosed to all in the universe. The second of
these two traditions is that out of which Paul's own understanding of
the word comes, but to both groups Paul says that God's plan has now
been revealed and carried out by Christ. Typically he uses their word
and gives it fresh meaning, in the light of the Christian facts. In 1^{26}
and 2^2 it receives content from Christ's death and resurrection, and in
1^{27} from the believer's participation in those saving acts (cf. Rom.
6$^{3ff.}$; Col. 3$^{1ff.}$). For Paul the second flows naturally from the first.

Yet the reality of the mystery's embodiment in the believer is not
free from ambiguity. On the one hand it is a fact (*Christ in you*), on
the other it is something for which Paul still labours (1^{28}-2^3). At first
sight (*every man*, v. 28), it looks as if those in whom Paul toils to
bring about Christian maturity here are people at present unbelieving,
but 2^1 makes plain that it includes the believers too. The point has
already been made in an easier way in 1$^{22f.}$; the believers have been
reconciled by Christ so that he may present them before God, yet
they must be warned of the dangers of slipping away from that status
which they have received. In v. 28 it is now not Christ but the apostle,
his delegate and deputy, who presents the believer to God – or desires
to do so – in a state of full Christian maturity.

A glance ahead to 3$^{1-5}$ will reveal the same duality of view. The
Christian has risen with Christ to the new life, but still has to *put to
death* the symptoms of the old, pre-Christian life. It is customary to
describe this common phenomenon in Paul's theology in terms of on
the one hand, the conferring by God of Christian status, and on the
other, the working out by the Christian of the moral implications of

that status. This handy rationalization has much to be said for it. Nevertheless, it is worth remembering that Paul nowhere makes it, but rather leaves statements, which seem to be formally inconsistent, side by side, as if their inconsistency needed no explaining and involved no problem for him. Gal. 5^{25} is perhaps the neatest example of it: the assertion of status, in the indicative verb (*we live*), followed by exhortation to its moral expression in the imperative (*let us walk*) – for Paul the receiving of the divine gift brings no magical immunity from moral struggle and no charter to disregard moral demands. On the other hand the status (seen in Gal. 5^{25} in terms of the Spirit) precedes and is not the reward of virtue (cf. Col. $2^{6f.}$). In principle, perhaps, the idea is not difficult; it becomes difficult when, as especially in $3^{1\ \&\ 5}$, Paul uses identical language of the status already possessed and that which still has to be striven for. This work of building up the believers for the future consummation is the essence of the apostle's pastoral oversight. Paul exercises this care even over those whom he has not visited. The apostolate to the Gentiles which Christ has entrusted to him gives him an assured position from which to address them.

ಞ

24
Now: in Greek this word must be temporal and not simply conjunctive. What is its force? Is Paul contrasting his present attitude towards his sufferings with earlier chafing at them? This is not very likely, unless *Colossians* is an earlier letter than has generally been supposed; for the same doctrine is found (see above p. 176) in *2 Corinthians* and *Galatians*, as well as *Philippians*. More likely the word refers to his imprisonment which, precluding active work entirely, demands a positive interpretation. Paul has just referred in v. 23 to his preaching work, now he has another, equally apostolic, task.

complete what is lacking: the two Greek words (verb and then a noun, 'the lacking-things') make a neater pair than the R.S.V. shows: 'fill up the empty space'.

Christ's afflictions: the view we have taken of this verse in the exposition would be supported if it were right to translate, as the Greek word-order makes possible and even probable, 'I complete what is lacking of the afflictions of Christ-in-my-flesh'. Paul's relationship with Christ determines his attitude to his sufferings (cf. 2 Cor. 1^5). It is not Christ's sufferings which are being completed but Christ's sufferings-*in-Paul*.

his body, that is, the church: see on v. 18. This image is used by Paul in a series of related but distinct ways (see p. 135). In 1 Cor. 12 and Rom. 12, where it is also applied to the church, it seems, given the context, that the local congregation is primarily in mind. Here there is a further variety of application: to the universal Church (a use which *Ephesians* takes up, 1^{23} and 5^{23}). The origin of the idea in Paul's mind is much disputed (see J. A. T. Robinson, *The Body* (London, 1952); E. Best, *One Body in Christ* (London, 1955), pp. 203–25): it may depend directly on the Hebrew assumption of the corporate solidarity of human groups like clans, tribes, and peoples, though Judaism did not use this particular image to express it; it may show the influence of the Stoics, for whom this image illuminated the unity of the diverse elements in the universe – but if so, it has undergone radical adaptation in being applied to the person of Christ and his relationship with the Christians. Paul's own statement in 1 Cor. 10^{17} is perhaps sufficient indication that its immediate source is Christ's words about the eucharistic bread at the Last Supper (cf. 1 Cor. 11^{24}): the oneness of the loaf, called Christ's body and shared by the members of the congregation, leads naturally to the application of the title to them.

church: the use of this word, *ekklēsia*, for the Christian community was well-established by Paul's time, and is employed by him already in almost as wide a variety of senses as 'church' receives today. It means, most simply, a meeting or assembly, and we have examples of this sense in 4^{15} and Philem.². Usually in Paul it refers to the local church (e.g. 4^{16}; Gal. 1^{22}; 1 Cor. 1^2), but here, perhaps more clearly than anywhere else in his writings (though cf. 1 Cor. 10^{32}; 12^{28}, and Eph. 1^{22}), it is used for the universal Church (as in v. 18). The use of the word probably goes back to the first Hellenistic Jewish Christian groups: cf. Gal. 1^{22} and 1 Thess. 2^{14}. Though a natural term for the Christian body to have selected, it may have been chosen in conscious distinction from *synagōgē*, which the Jews used as the name for their congregations. The two words carry the same basic sense. It is hard to know how far it also expressed the Church's claim to be the true people of God – the new Israel, the heir of God's promises; in the LXX the word very often has a purely secular sense, but is also used for the assembly or congregation of Israel. For a semantic discussion see J. Barr, *The Semantics of Biblical Language* (Oxford, 1961), pp. 119–29; and for a full treatment of Paul's usage, see L. Cerfaux, *La Théologie de l'Église suivant S. Paul* (Paris, 1948) (also in English translation).

25

divine office: this term, Gk *oikonomia*, literally means the management of a household (*oikos* = house). Here it refers to settled administrative office, perhaps in a general sense, but cf. Gal. 6¹⁰, where Paul makes use of this image for the Church.

26

mystery: see above p. 179. In the Greek world, *mystērion* (usually in the plural) referred to esoteric cults and the rites by which worshippers were initiated into them. In the LXX, the word occurs first in Dan. 2²⁸ᶠ·, then in later books, e.g. Wis. 2²². It signifies God's secret purpose for Israel's future destiny, a purpose which the writer claims to reveal (cf. Tobit 12⁷). The use of the word to refer to the Christian gospel is in line with this usage, and that is its sense here. In other places (e.g. v. 27), it refers to particular aspects or implications of the gospel, or even apparently to doctrinal formulations peculiar to Paul (e.g. 1 Cor. 15⁵¹, concerning the future of those Christians who are alive on earth at the time of Christ's return in glory).

Besides the use of the *word* in Jewish literature there are many parallels to the *idea* which Paul has here of the revealing of divine truth hitherto concealed. In the books of the Apocrypha and in the other Jewish writings of the period, including the Dead Sea Scrolls, we commonly find the idea applied to much the same range of subjects as in Paul: God's dealings with the universe as a whole, and with men and angels within it; the future destiny of man and the world. For example, in the *Book of Hymns* from Qumran, 7²⁷: 'Thou hast given me insight into thy truth and knowledge of thy wondrous secrets': and in 2 Esdras 7²⁸, where we find the idea of the concealment of the Messiah until the moment destined for his revelation (cf. John 1²⁶). Cf. also Eccles. 48²⁴ᶠ·; 2 Esd. 14⁵ᶠ·. Some of these passages speak of special servants of God to whom the revelation is entrusted (cf. Col. 1²⁶ᶠᶠ·).

All this serves to show that, in a concept such as this, Judaism and certain aspects of pagan religion were speaking a common language, though the eschatological preoccupation of the former and its strong communal aspect (i.e. its concern with the Jews as a people) constituted important points of difference. It is not hard to see why the Jewish teachers at Colossae found it easy to communicate with the members of the Gentile Christian congregation there.

hidden for ages and generations: 1 Cor. 2⁷ᶠ· is the passage where Paul most fully states what he has in mind in using the word *mystery* to refer to the gospel; and there it is said that the angelic powers were ignorant of the saving action of God through Christ's death, and indeed were themselves the unwitting agents of that act (cf. Col. 2¹⁵). Here we may have a similar idea; for *aiōnes* (translated *ages*) could be a term for angelic powers ruling the world of time and space. *Generations* would then mean the inhabitants of the earth and, taking the preposition which

begins the phrase in its meaning 'from', we get the sense 'hidden from
those in heaven and earth', giving a reminder of the repeated mention
of earthly and heavenly powers in 1¹⁶ (see p. 163). The difficulty is that
this use of the word *aiōnes*, which becomes a technical term in this sense
in second-century Gnosticism, is not found in Jewish literature and is
only paralleled in the New Testament in Eph. 2² (R.S.V. *course*, wrongly;
see p. 281). However Ignatius' letter Eph. 19² (*c.* A.D. 110) certainly
uses it in our sense in a passage similar in many ways to 1 Cor. 2⁷ᶠ.*
Paul may once more be taking up a technical word whose true bearing
he wishes to demonstrate.

27
The expression of this verse is harder than its meaning. The Christians,
specifically those of Colossae, are a living presence of the gospel in the
Gentile world; they are so by virtue of Christ's indwelling, which
carries with it the assurance of the future bliss which God promises
to his own (*hope of glory*).

glory: the word *doxa* which occurs twice in this verse has a basic meaning
of 'weight' or 'reputation', then 'that which makes reputation visible',
and so 'majesty', 'splendour'. Thus it was used in the LXX to translate
the Hebrew word signifying the splendour of God, often seen in
terms of the visible light and brilliance which characterized his presence
(e.g. Isa. 6¹ᶠᶠ.). This is close to its second use in this verse – referring to
the future consummation. The first use is an example of its common
application in a less precise sense to any of the attributes or works of
God, here the gospel of Christ as made known in the Gentile world.

29
striving with all the energy which he mightily inspires: see on Phil. 2¹²,
p. 87.

2¹
those at Laodicea: see Introduction, p. 125.

who have not seen my face: probably, in view of 1⁷, the congregations of
both Laodicea and Colossae are included.

3
in whom are hid: cf. 1¹⁹. Whatever the false teachers at Colossae think
can be found in other beings than Christ or other doctrines than that
which proclaims Christ, Paul asserts, at every opportunity, to be present in him alone: whether it be the life and power of God (1¹⁹; 2⁹) or,
as here, *wisdom and knowledge*. Both these terms look as if they belong
to that dual-purpose vocabulary so useful to Paul in this letter. They

* L.C.C., I, p. 93; E.C.W., p. 81.

would find answering echoes in the religious aspirations of the Gentile converts, and be part of the Old Testament-based language of the Jews. For *wisdom:* see Prov. 1; Wis. of Solomon, *passim:* Ecclus. 24; Ps. 111. For *knowledge:* see p. 153. For the force of *hid,* see on 3^3: Christ alone has – and is – the key to God's secret purposes; cf. Rev. 5$^{1-9}$.

5
in spirit: it is possible to see this as being simply a parallel to *in body* (lit. 'in the flesh'), so that the two together signify the physical and non-physical in man. Paul while not actually present with them has them very much in his thoughts. But it would be characteristic if he had in mind that Spirit of God which he and they share by their common faith and baptism: cf. 1 Cor. 2$^{10ff.}$; 12^{13}.

6f.
Several words in these verses give the impression that Paul is recalling the basic Christian instruction which the Colossians had received. (i) *Received:* this is the technical word used for the taking over of formal tradition, cf. 1 Cor. 11^{23}; 15^3. (ii) *The Lord:* the addition of this title to the name Christ Jesus in a single expression is unusual in Paul and may be a reminiscence of its use in catechetical instruction and credal formulae (2 Cor. 4^5; 1 Cor. 12^3; Rom. 10^9); as may also the use of *Christ* with the definite article. This usage sometimes indicates that its original meaning, 'the Messiah', is in mind (in Paul the title has already generally become simply a proper name). Even if this term, unlike *lord* (*kyrios,* see p. 78), would mean little to a Gentile audience, it would surely have been part of that basic Old Testament knowledge which must have been in their Christian training. (iii) *The faith:* see on 1^{23}. (iv) *You were taught:* cf. 1^7.

abounding in thanksgiving: just as the first part of v. 7 looks back to their reception of the gospel mentioned in the first half of v. 6, so these last words take up the second half of v. 6 (*so live in him*), referring to the present Christian life, now by reference to the gratitude to God, evoked by the gospel.

2$^{8-15}$ CHRIST'S REDEMPTION OF MAN

^{8}*See to it that no one makes a prey of you by philosophy and empty deceit, according to human tradition, according to the elemental spirits of the universe, and not according to Christ.* ^{9}*For in him the whole fullness of deity dwells bodily,* ^{10}*and you have come to fullness of life in him, who is the head*

of all rule and authority. ¹¹In him also you were circumcised with a circum-
cision made without hands, by putting off the body of flesh in the circumcision
of Christ; ¹²and you were buried with him in baptism, in which you were
also raised with him through faith in the working of God, who raised him
from the dead. ¹³And you, who were dead in trespasses and the uncir-
cumcision of your flesh, God made alive together with him, having forgiven
us all our trespasses, ¹⁴having cancelled the bond which stood against us with
its legal demands; this he set aside, nailing it to the cross. ¹⁵He disarmed the
principalities and powers and made a public example of them, triumphing
over them in him.ᵈ

d Or *in it* (that is, the cross).

Two general comments are in place now that we have reached this
stage in the epistle. We shall find that both are confirmed by much
of what is still to come. The first is that the main doctrinal teaching
of this epistle consists of a small number of themes, to which it
returns time and again. Each new statement of a theme – whether it
be the all-sufficiency of Christ as the mediator of God or the futility of
attention to the angels – of course has its own features, but there is
sufficient echoing of earlier language to give us a familiar landmark.
More significant is the fact that for the most part the basic statement
of these themes is in the liturgical text, 1^{15-20}. We have already suggested that this is a text which Paul and his audience had in common,
something they were accustomed to use, and so a neutral formula to
which Paul could appeal. If this is so it is no wonder that he repeatedly
harks back to it: 2^9 takes up 1^{19}; 2^{15} echoes $1^{16, 20}$ – to give only two
of the more obvious examples.

Paul makes his appeal skilfully and delicately, as we can see from his
increasingly obvious use of a tactic which we have already suspected at
several points. It now becomes clearer that he is employing some of
the favourite terms of the false teachers, terms which made them
attractive to the Colossian Christians, and which Paul turns deftly
to his own advantage: *fullness* (1^{19}; 2^9) is one example of this; *wisdom*
($2^{3, 23}$) is another.

Our second general comment concerns another aspect of Paul's
delicacy of approach. So far in this letter we get the impression that
he is indulging in a kind of shadow-boxing with his opponents.
From $1^{23, 28}$ and 2^4 it begins to look as if such opponents exist, but
they are still nebulous. Obviously Paul feels that this is not a situation

to be dealt with by frontal attack, especially when those whom he opposes are on the spot, able to defend themselves. Perhaps he knows that they have already won considerable favour among the Gentile Christians of Colossae. So he treads warily, and for the most part simply expounds the true doctrine which will show their teaching up as vain nonsense. (For another reason for this caution, see Introduction pp. 124f.). In the passage now before us he begins to come out more plainly into the open, and finally in 2$^{16ff.}$ we discover exactly what he thinks. But before he fully declares himself, he states firmly and impressively what for him is the heart of the gospel from which the Colossians are in danger of being seduced. It is the act of redemption done by Christ and the believer's association with it and enjoyment of its fruits by baptism. This is the final brick in the structure of true faith which he has been erecting, and with that before his readers he can explicitly state the subverters' tenets in a context which will make clear both their hollowness and their incompatibility with the gospel. It may be that Paul is mocking when he dignifies this teaching by the name of *philosophy* (2^8): this no doubt is what its serious purveyors and those whom they impress consider it to be. In fact it is nothing but ordinary Jewish ascetic observances (2^{16}) combined with a great deal of futile attention to the angelic powers of the universe.

The passage begins by pointing to the contrast between the doctrine the Colossians had received (v. 7) and that which is now being pressed upon them (v. 8). The authorities which lie behind the two kinds of teaching are, in the first case Christ, in the second case the *stoicheia*, the angelic powers with whom so much of it is concerned. From vv. 14f. we discover how it is that the angelic powers are connected with a body of teaching whose main practical concern turns out to be with ascetic observances (vv. 16ff.). The clue is to be found in Gal. 3^{19} and 4^3; it was Paul's belief that God had given the Law to Moses, and so to the people of Israel, not directly but through angelic mediators, so that Christ's death, in bringing to an end the dominance of the Law over man (see p. 164), meant also the defeat of the angelic powers and the end of their authority. That authority now belongs to Christ alone (v. 10). As we have seen, the subverters may also have seen the angels as God's agents in creation (1$^{15f.}$ – though this point does not reappear outside the hymn). It is clear that the angels are the centre of the web of false teaching with which Paul is concerned: all aspects of it meet in them. It is, then, a question of two rival personal mediators of salvation – Christ and the angels. At first sight they have much in common: both are agents of God, both exercise authority over man (or claim to do so), both express their authority in rules for conduct ($2^{16, 21}$ & 3^{5-4^6}). Wherein then lies Christ's superiority? First, in the fact that he is no inferior spiritual being in the hierarchy of God's creation, but is the embodiment and expression of divinity (1^{15-20}; 2^9), God's *beloved Son* (1^{13}). Second, in the fact that he has offered himself as a sacrificial victim (*in his body of flesh by his death*, 1^{22}), thus reconciling man to God and enabling man to be presented as a perfect offering before God. Thirdly, in the fact that his death meant the defeat and supersession of the angelic powers, which spelled the end of the Jewish Law which they sponsored. Finally, in the fact that through his death he brought specific gifts to man: forgiveness, the need for which was piled up by the Law's demands ($2^{13f.}$; 3^{13}); and participation in his risen life (2^{12}; 3^{11}). The moral conduct which is required of a Christian (3^{5-4^6}) is the direct expression of this life 'in Christ'. (On the angels, see also pp. 164f.)

For Paul, no doubt all these elements formed a coherent whole. For us it is not so easy. It is hard, for example, to see how the sacrificial element, which we know could exist independently in Judaism (see on $1^{21f.}$, p. 173) really fits in with the angelology. It is also hard for us to see how any of it 'works': see General Introduction, pp. 18f., 25. Part of the reason for this is of course the enormous gap between Paul's thought-world and ours, especially in the matter of the nature and importance of invisible spiritual powers and agencies; but part of it is simply the fact that Paul himself nowhere states in full the picture which is in his mind. In particular we do not know quite what story he would have told if he had been asked to explain v. 15. We know well that soon after this time (see Ign. Eph. 19^2; Justin, Apol. 51; and later, in the fourth century, Athanasius, *De Incarnatione* 25*) an elaborate tale was told about Christ's death as a hoodwinking of the Devil and his angels. Christ gave himself into their hands in order to trick them into acting beyond their proper sphere, for they had no right to authority over the sinless Son of God. Their crucifying of him was thus their ruin and led to his victory over them. How far Paul already saw the crucifixion of Christ in these mythological terms we do not know, but 1 Cor. $2^{7f.}$ gives a hint that he did so.

* *Library of Christian Classics*, Vol. III (London, 1954), pp. 79f.

Fortunately this way of regarding Christ's death was not the only idiom that he used, and others provide us who live in different times with more congenial imagery; but it is important to remember that for Paul it was all part of his natural outlook and he made no distinction between that which the twentieth century would find easy and that which it would find difficult. In trying to understand him, we need to begin by taking him as a whole, on his own terms.

The thought of this passage swings back and forth between the work of Christ (vv. 9, 13–15) and its fruits for the believer (vv. 10–13). While the imagery of v. 15 is, as we have seen, for Paul no doubt a 'literal' account of what happened at Christ's death, the counterpart 'behind the scenes' of what was visible on Calvary, in vv. 11–13 he is using metaphorical language. He speaks of Christian baptism, and uses two different kinds of image to illuminate its meaning.

First, baptism is the Christian equivalent of circumcision in Judaism. This is true in a quite straightforward sense: each is the rite which brings admission to the religious body in question. But there is more to it than that. It is not that circumcision is just a useful illustration and the nearest one to hand, so that Paul, if his knowledge had been wider, could equally well have used the initiatory rites of a Germanic tribe to make the same point. Circumcision was the rite of admission *to Israel*, the vital symbol and sacrament of membership of God's people, the sign given to Abraham and all his progeny in Israel of the assurance of God's blessing (Gen. 17$^{1-14}$). The Church as the authentic Israel, the true heir of God's promises (Rom. 9–11; Gal. 6^{16}), must therefore admit members by a circumcision – of some sort; she must show her continuity with Israel of old. But at this point Paul's argument becomes double; for the Church is not only in continuity with the old Israel but also in discontinuity. She is not simply a prolongation of the old story, but also a fresh start. Nowhere does Paul explicitly reconcile these two aspects of his outlook, but implicitly they are reconciled in the central role of Christ. He, who springs from Israel (Rom. 1$^{3f.}$), and is also the sole head and fount of the Church, acts as the control; the aspirations, tenets, and institutions of the old Israel are to be seen wholly with reference to him and are subordinated to him. His revelation of God and his saving acts provide the yardstick by which they are to be measured. All of them therefore acquire new meaning, and some of them take on a quasi-metaphorical sense. Circumcision is one

example. We say '*quasi*-metaphorical' because the Church in fact
has a corresponding rite – baptism; but this is, Paul says, a circumcision *made without hands* – that is, not effective by the mere doing of
it, but depending on its spiritual significance, and this comes from
Christ. Its essence is the *putting off the body of flesh in the circumcision of
Christ*. (The last words probably mean simply 'Christian circumcision', i.e. baptism.) The point of baptism is the renunciation of the
sinful nature; and this is effective because it is done *with Christ* and
carries with it (as similar renunciations not made *with him* do not)
entry into his risen life. 3$^{5ff.}$ makes clear that this is the sense of these
words.

Apart from the appropriateness of his language to the rite of
circumcision in itself, there is a second level of imagery here which
helps to reinforce the centrality of Christ for the right formulation
of the relationship between the old Israel and the Church. Once more
it expresses the solidarity of the believer with Christ or, in 'Israel'
terms, his total dependence upon his relationship with Christ for his
membership of the people of God. He sees baptism as burial with
Christ (v. 12) and resurrection to new life. It may also be that the
words *the circumcision of Christ* are not just a way of saying 'Christian
circumcision', as suggested above, but refer to the death of Christ, the
putting off of *his* flesh in literal act, thus completing the mention of
the gospel facts: cf. 1 Cor. 15$^{3-5}$. For this way of understanding
baptism, cf. Rom. 6$^{3ff.}$.

Finally, we may have here yet another reference to the injunctions
of the Jewish teachers. There seems to be little point in mentioning
the rite of circumcision when addressing an audience of Gentile
Christians unless pressure is being put upon them to adopt it as
religiously desirable. It looks as if the situation at Colossae was not
very different from that in the Galatian churches (cf. Gal. 5$^{2ff.}$),
though the tone of this letter is a good deal less violent and, for that
matter, less explicit. In answer to such pressure Paul adopts his customary manner: he takes the word but gives it its true Christian
sense: for a believer in Christ, circumcision means baptism.

ಠಜ

8
philosophy: this term would often cover religious and mystical ideas.
Both Jews and Greeks would be sensitive to Paul's gibing use of it.

human traditions: cf. Mark 7[8] for the same expression. It is applied in both cases to the supplementary, non-biblical Law of Judaism, the elaboration constructed, on a biblical base, by the scribes. Palestinian Jews would have accorded it full divine authority, but many Hellenistic Jews, though unlikely to be as disparaging as Paul, would not have given it such a lofty place. Paul lowers it further, or rather, in view of the following phrase, in effect says that the authority of the angelic powers is no greater than that of mere human traditions. Christ stands in all the clearer contrast.

elemental spirits: in commenting on the passage we have accepted this translation of *stoicheia* without question, signifying by it the angelic powers; nor do we wish to cast serious doubt on it. But it is fair to say that many scholars take it in a sense closer to its basic meaning: the elements which make up a composite whole, e.g. the letters of the alphabet, or the material elements which make up the world. So here it could signify elementary forms of religious doctrine found in the world. That the R.S.V. translation should stand is indicated by a careful comparison with v. 20 (where the word recurs), in the light of v. 15 and 18, and demonstrated still more clearly by the comparison of Gal. 3[19]; 4[3] & 4[9]. The link between this extended sense of the word and its more straightforward meaning lies in the fact that the elements or parts of the universe, especially the heavenly bodies, were commonly seen as either themselves personal beings or the instruments of angelic or semi-divine powers.

9
the whole fullness of deity: see on 1[19]. If the later Gnostic sense of *fullness* (signifying the whole angelic hierarchy) was already current, then Paul uses the word only to make sure that it receives a fully Christian sense. Christ is the sole repository of all divine power and functions. For the use of the Hellenistic abstract noun *deity*, cf. Rom. 1[20], where a closely related word occurs (*theiotēs*, compared with *theotēs* here); in each case, the only reference in the New Testament.

bodily: the most obvious sense is 'in incarnate form', which means that this verse reproduces the sense given by the past tense of the verb (*was pleased*) in 1[19] – both refer to Christ's earthly life. But here the verb, *dwells*, is in the present tense, and this inclines many to look for a more general sense for *bodily*, such as 'in concrete reality' or 'in actual fact'. But we must take the verse in its context. Paul goes on, in v. 10, to speak of the Christians' *fullness of life in him*, and this introduction of the believers gives us the clue to the sense of v. 9. The reference is indeed first to Christ's incarnate life, but is extended in Paul's mind to his union with the Church – cf. *the body = the church*, in 1¹⁸, ²⁴. In Paul's theology, the one sense leads on to the other, and the double reference explains the present tense of the verb. The present Christ, raised bodily, bridges the two aspects, cf. 1 Cor. 15¹²ᶠᶠ.

10

head of all rule and authority: cf. 1¹⁸. In the earlier verse it looked as if the original reference in the hymn had been to Christ's supremacy over the whole universe and that the words *the church* were an addition or an afterthought in the light of Paul's ordinary use of the idea of *the body* (cf. 1²⁴) – even perhaps a copyist's addition, though there is no evidence of early manuscripts which lacked the words. Our present verse confirms this original sense of 1¹⁸, for here Christ's supremacy over all things is asserted, especially if the two words *rule* and *authority* represent invisible and visible powers respectively: see on 1¹⁶, p. 163. V. 11: cf. Eph. 2¹¹.

12

God, who raised him: as generally in the New Testament, the resurrection of Christ is not seen as a self-generated miraculous deed, but as an act of God. The pattern of New Testament thought is more fundamentally God-centred than Christ-centred.

13

dead . . . forgiven: cf. 1 Cor. 15¹⁷; Rom. 5¹², ¹⁸. The phrase *and the uncircumcision of your flesh,* added in view of the Gentile audience, is an extra factor making for 'death' in their case (Jews often describe the Gentile's spiritual state in terms of death). For though Paul sees Jew and Gentile as on an equal footing in relation to Christ (3¹¹), nevertheless to have been a Gentile in one's pre-Christian days still meant that one was in certain ways further away from God: cf. Rom. 9⁴ᶠ·. Most simply, one lacked background. In Rom. 1-2 the stress is different; there, Paul is saying that the Jew is in exactly the same sorry plight as the Gentile, despite all his pride in his special relationship with God. There is no ultimate inconsistency here, simply the giving of attention to different aspects of a situation, of whose ambiguity Paul the Jew is acutely aware. For his chief attempt to work out a reconciliation between the divine vocation of Israel and her constant failure to respond to its demands, see Rom. 9-11.

14

cancelled the bond: the word *cheirographon* means any handwritten document, and, more technically, a bond of indebtedness, a formal IOU. The following phrase (*with its legal demands*) uses a word commonly employed (e.g. in Philo and Josephus) to refer to the Law (*dogmata*).

The literal sense is then 'the bond . . . in the decrees'. The Law, disobeyed by man, stands as his accuser to God, and Christ has paid the debt.

nailing it to the cross: did Paul know of the notice put on Jesus' Cross, proclaiming him as 'King of the Jews' (cf. e.g. Mark 15^{26})? If so, did he see this as the cancellation of the rule of the Law over man by the rule of Christ?

15

disarmed the principalities and powers: see above pp. 186f. The words for the two authorities are the same as those in 1^{16} (there translated *principalities and authorities*) and in 2^{10} (*rule and authority*, here in the singular). It is meant in all three cases to be a comprehensive expression, including all powers in heaven and on earth, good and evil alike; all are subject to Christ.

a public example: see on 1^{26}, pp. 182f. In the mythological way of describing Christ's progress through birth, death, and exaltation, in relation to the cosmic powers, his earlier incognito is broken at his death, when his victory is won. Cf. 2 Cor. 2^{14}, for the idea of Christians sharing in the triumph. The translation in the margin (*in it*, i.e. the cross) is almost certainly to be preferred, for though 'God' remains *formally* the subject, Paul is by v. 15 really thinking more in terms of Christ as the agent. However, if the passage is read strictly, with 'God' as the subject of all the verbs in vv. 13–15, then we must translate *in him* (i.e. 'in Christ').

2$^{16-23}$ THE FALSE TEACHING
AT COLOSSAE

^{16}*Therefore let no one pass judgement on you in questions of food and drink or with regard to a festival or a new moon or a sabbath.* ^{17}*These are only a shadow of what is to come: but the substance belongs to Christ.* ^{18}*Let no one disqualify you, insisting on self-abasement and worship of angels, taking his stand on visions, puffed up without reason by his sensuous mind,* ^{19}*and not holding fast to the Head, from whom the whole body, nourished and knit together through its joints and ligaments, grows with a growth that is from God.*

^{20}*If with Christ you died to the elemental spirits of the universe, why do you live as if you still belonged to the world? Why do you submit to regulations,* ^{21}'*Do not handle, Do not taste, Do not touch*' ^{22}(*referring to things which all perish as they are used), according to human precepts and doctrines? ²³These have indeed an appearance of wisdom in promoting rigour of devotion and self-abasement and severity to the body, but they are of no value in checking the indulgence of the flesh.ᵉ*

e Or *are of no value, serving only to indulge the flesh.*

We are now left in no further doubt either about the doctrines and precepts of the false teachers or about Paul's attitude to them. But though we welcome this sharper focus on both these matters – we no longer have to pick up what we can from hints and oblique statements – we do not learn much that is new to us; with one important exception. So far the information we have gained about the people from whom Paul wishes to rescue the Colossian church has been in the sphere of their doctrines – especially their fondness for cosmological speculation and their view of Christ as one among a whole hierarchy of angelic powers. We have supported the opinion that the background of these people, so far as it can be discerned from the language Paul uses in controverting them (and how far it is legitimate to do that is, as we have seen, more debatable), is likely to be essentially Jewish rather than Hellenistic. The ideas and language are those found in the wisdom-writings and in Jewish speculation of the time, such as we meet in the Dead Sea Scrolls and in the apocalyptic literature. From the very fact that a Gentile Christian congregation was so open to it, it is apparent that this thought and some of the words used were not alien to men whose native religious idiom was Hellenistic.

What our present passage reveals for the first time is that the information about the *practice* enjoined by the Colossian heretics entirely confirms this judgement. These are Jews teaching strict obedience to the Jewish Law (vv. 16, 21, 23). Their veneration of the angelic powers is closely linked to this, for they no doubt see them as the immediate givers of the Law (cf. p. 164). The angels are the key element in the whole matter, at the level of religious practice as well as at the level of doctrine. One of Paul's complaints about the strictness which is demanded is that, paradoxically, in practice it lowers the whole level of religious aspiration. Instead of being concerned with the service of God, it becomes a means of bodily and spiritual discipline for its own sake. And even then it fails to achieve its object (v. 23). Aims of this kind, and reliance on such means as these to achieve them, have been superseded by Christ and they no longer have any purpose – both absolutely (v. 17), and certainly for the believers (v. 20). It is not merely immoral, but senseless and futile to take notice of these Jewish would-be philosophers who think they can simply absorb Christ into their system.

The general sense of the passage, given all that has gone before, is not difficult, and it brings further into the open much that has so far been unclear; but many details remain problematical and call for treatment in the notes below.

But first we shall present some contemporary or almost contemporary parallels, allowing the Jews of Colossae to speak for themselves through the words of people who seem to have held much the same ideas.

First, the Essenes, whom we take to be identified with the Dead Sea sect of Qumran. According to Josephus the Jew, writing near the end of the first century A.D., the novices of that brotherhood were taught to 'preserve alike the books of the sect and the names of the angels'. And the writings of the Qumran sect also give ample evidence of the importance of good and evil angels in their theology: e.g. 'All the children of righteousness are ruled by the Prince of Light and walk in the ways of light; but the children of falsehood are ruled by the Angel of darkness and walk in the ways of darkness. . . . But the God of Israel and His Angel of Truth will succour all the sons of light. For it is He who created the spirits of Light and Darkness.'*

Regulations about clean and unclean foods, about the observance of festivals and sabbaths, were of course no peculiarity of this sect among the Jews, but they were certainly prominent in its discipline: 'They shall not depart from any command of God concerning their times.'† The matter of regulations concerning drink (Col. 2¹⁶) is of more particular interest. Philo tells that the Therapeutae (a Jewish sect in Egypt, related to the Essenes) denied themselves wine, and it is possible that the Qumran sect did the same, though the evidence is not entirely clear. There was certainly a Christian tradition that John Baptist observed this discipline (Luke 1¹⁵), which belonged to the centuries-old tradition in Israel of the Nazirite vow (cf. Num. 6); and there are several points of contact between the Qumran sect

* Vermes, pp. 75f.
† Vermes, p. 72.

and the work of John Baptist. Like Paul, Jesus himself repudiated that regimen: Mark 2^{19}; Matt. 11^{19}.

Finally, the esoteric atmosphere doubtless associated with the Colossian teachers, and perhaps reflected in Paul's repeated use of the word *mystery* to describe the central affirmations of the gospel, is echoed in *the War Rule* of Qumran: 'the people of the saints of the Covenant (who are) instructed in the laws and learned in wisdom . . . who have heard the voice of Majesty and have seen the Angels of Holiness, whose ear has been unstopped and who have heard profound things'.*

From a little later, probably the first years of the second century, come the writings of Elchasai, a seer who had numerous followers and whose book enjoyed wide dissemination.† Fragments of it are preserved in the anti-heretical work of Hippolytus (early third century), and other Christian writers. This writer seems to be even closer to the Colossian teachers, and it is significant that teaching like his appears to have survived in their part of Asia Minor well into the fourth century.

Elchasai was a Jew, probably from the region east of Jordan, but his visions include Christian elements, such as perhaps the Colossian teachers were not unwilling to incorporate into their doctrinal system. But these Christian elements themselves look as if they have absorbed oriental ingredients which later blossomed more fully in the Gnostic sects. Thus, the Son of God is said to be of enormous dimensions and was probably thought to include his believers within himself in some 'literal' sense. (It is of course possible that Paul's idea of the cosmic Christ, whose followers can be spoken of as his 'body', was not wholly alien to Elchasai's much more crudely formed conceptions.) While rejecting the sacrificial cult of Judaism (in any case abolished by his time, by the destruction of the Temple in A.D. 70), he held to circumcision and Sabbath observance, and regarded the movements of the moon as important in determining the right days for administering baptism. He also saw the stars as personal powers (cf. the *stoicheia* of *Colossians*), and told of angelic warfare.

The syncretistic and speculative Judaism here represented in a much milder form than that of Elchasai, often hovered in an uncertain

* Vermes, pp. 136f.
† Hennecke, II, pp. 745ff.

relationship with Christianity in the second century and even after-wards. It was by no means clear at all times to all concerned, whether Jews or Christians, what were the bounds of orthodoxy, where exactly Judaism began and Christianity ended. The anti-heretical fathers of the late second and early third centuries wrote precisely to try and define the permissible lines. In *Colossians* we face one of the first evidences of this situation. Paul however sees the issues at stake with full clarity, and states them in terms which could both suitably convey his own teaching and at the same time be understood by his audience.

∞

16

food and drink: cf. Rom. 14, especially vv. 17 & 21, where Paul in con-trast to his attitude here displays indulgence towards Christians who have scruples about dietary matters. If that chapter is about Gentile Christians who are unwilling to eat meat from the pagan butchers (which had been formally offered to the idols of the gods, cf. 1 Cor. 8), then Paul can be absolved of the charge of inconsistency; he is being gentle with perhaps inexperienced Christians who at least are erring on the right side, and certainly there is no question of their straying into obedience to the Jewish Law, with all its implications. Here, however, this is precisely the point at issue. The abrogation of the Law, including the food regulations, was central to Paul's whole theology of the work of Christ (cf. v. 14), and observance of its rules by Gentile Christians can only show their failure to comprehend the heart of the gospel. (Cf. Heb. 9$^{9f.}$; 13^{9}.)

17

a shadow: the fact that these ascetic practices can be seen as 'fore-shadowing' the Christian dispensation confirms the view that the re-ference is to the Jewish Law (as indeed *sabbath* in v. 16 already indicates). Like Heb. 10^{1} Paul contrasts the *past* validity of the Law, within certain limits, with its present supersession (cf. Gal. 3^{24}): see also next note.

the substance: the word is *sōma = body*. The contrast *skia – sōma (=* shadow – reality) is found also in Philo and Josephus, Jewish writers of roughly this period, and there may be no more in Paul's mind than this simple contrast. But his words (lit. 'but the body (is) of Christ') must surely have carried special significance for him. He contrasts the old régime of the Law with the Church, the body of Christ (cf. 1^{24}).

In that 'body' were to be found the realities of which the old Law provided only shadows – forgiveness, reconciliation to God, new life.

18

disqualify: cf. v. 16, *pass judgement.* This is only one of the possible meanings of the word *katabrabeuō*, but it makes good sense in view of the competitive approach to religious observances which probably characterized Paul's opponents. The meaning, 'to deprive of a rightful prize', can be supported by the occurrence of the noun *brabeion* (= prize), related to our verb, in Phil. 3^{14}, which may have been written at roughly the same period. We find the simple form of the verb, *brabeuō*, in Col. 3^{15}: R.S.V. translates *rule*, but the sense is closely related to that in our present verse – it means to umpire or to judge.

insisting on: lit. 'willing'. The R.S.V. unfortunately conceals a forward-looking reference to v. 23, where *rigour of devotion* is literally 'will-worship' (see below). The religion being advocated in Colossae is man-made, generated by his own will-power, cf. 2$^{8, 22}$.

self-abasement: cf. v. 23. Literally, 'humility'. The best clue to the sense here is to be found in Isa. 58^5; the word is used in the technical sense of 'fasting' in the second century Christian writing, *The Shepherd of Hermas*.* Given our present context which is concerned with ascetic practices, this is almost certainly the right way to understand it. The use of the word in a list of Christian virtues in 3^{12} may well be a conscious contrasting of inner disposition with mere outward acts. Cf. *severity to the body*, v. 23.

worship of angels: *thrēskeia* means the devotion paid to deity. Can it then be that Jews, of all people, were urging idolatry? Almost certainly not. Paul uses the word to shock his readers into realizing what the part of the angels in the religion of the false teachers virtually amounts to. They are seen in roles (e.g. ruling the creation, guiding the destinies of nations and individuals) which rightly belong only to God or to Christ, his *image* (1^{15}). This charge might be levelled at a passage like Jubilees 2^2 (see p. 164), and, with even more justice, both Jewish and Christian writings like Tobit 11^{14} and Justin, Apology 6 (see p. 165).

It is interesting in this connexion that for Paul the position of Christ does not appear as even a theoretical difficulty for monotheism: it was to become the major problem of theological formulation of the Church's first four centuries (see M. Wiles, *The Making of Christian Doctrine* (Cambridge, 1967)). On the contrary, Christ removes what was certainly to him a major threat to the plenitude of God's authority, the attribution of parts of it to the angels.

* cf. J. B. Lightfoot, *The Apostolic Fathers* (London, 1891), Visions 3, x, 6.

visions: cf. on Elchasai, p. 195; and the whole apocalyptic tradition which was important in the background of Judaism and Christianity alike (e.g. *Daniel* and *The Revelation to John*). The verb here may well reflect the language of the pagan mystery cults and refer to the initiate's penetration into the inmost sanctuary (*taking his stand on* is an unlikely translation). If this is right, the phrase may have the sarcastic note which we have found before. The Jews appeal to nothing higher than the crude religious instincts gratified by the mysteries of Eleusis and Delphi. Such a charge would catch Gentiles on the raw and be hotly repudiated by the Jews themselves.

It might be thought that in view of his own experience on the Damascus road Paul was hardly the man to disparage visionary experiences. But though Acts (especially 26^{19}) looks on this episode in such terms, for Paul it is on a par with the Lord's initial resurrection appearances and as such validates his claim to apostleship alongside the other apostles (1 Cor. 9^1; 15$^{5ff.}$). As for his own gifts as a visionary, he is both reticent about them and reluctant to give them the high esteem which such experiences no doubt received from the Colossians (1 Cor. 13^2; 2 Cor. 12$^{1ff.}$).

19
the Head: cf. 1^{18}.

the whole body: the image of this verse is a perfectly natural extension of the idea of the Church as the body of Christ (cf. 1^{24}), whose background we have already discussed (p. 181). Many scholars see here the influence of oriental notions of the archetypal Man, the central figure of myths purporting to explain human life and fate. These ideas were at this period entering both Greek and Jewish religious speculation, and though we do not think they determine the structure of Paul's thought, this kind of thinking has probably influenced him. He uses it to re-state his central theme, the all-sufficiency of Christ as the mediator between God and man and the relationship of the believers with him in their growth towards final salvation (cf. 3^4). See also on 3$^{9f.}$; and cf. Eph. 4^{16}.

20
died to the elemental spirits: this verse can best be read as a compressed version of Paul's main argument in vv. 11–15, though here the idea of death is applied not to the pre-Christian state, as in v. 13, but the act of baptism (cf. Rom. 6), an inconsistency which some take as evidence of the composite character of *Colossians*.

submit to regulations: the verb (*dogmatizō*) is related to the noun, *dogmata*, used in v. 14 (R.S.V., *legal demands*).

16–23

21

Here again Paul is mocking the false teachers, this time for their pernickety scrupulosity.

22

cf. Mark 7[7]: both passages use Isa. 29[13] to give scriptural support to a liberal approach to the Jewish Law.

23

appearance of wisdom: like the Gentile Christians of Corinth, those of Colossae valued wisdom highly (cf. 1 Cor. 1[20]–2[16], where Paul's argument on this matter is fully worked out). So of course did Jews (cf. p. 166). Paul holds that the teaching at Colossae is illusory wisdom. The true divine wisdom is embodied in Christ, as the language of 1[15–20] particularly makes clear (see p. 167, and cf. 1 Cor. 1[24, 30]). *Logos* is better translated *name, reputation,* than *appearance* (cf. Acts 11[22]; Mark 1[45]).

rigour of devotion: see on v. 18, p. 197. This translation is not satisfactory. It means either voluntary, self-willed devotion, or quasi-, supposed devotion, both possible senses of the prefix *ethelo-,* from the root *thel-* = *to will.* If 'quasi-worship', then cf. *worship of angels,* v. 18.

in checking the indulgence of the flesh: this verse is difficult. Three main problems of interpretation arise, the first being the construction of the sentence as a whole, the second the translation of the preposition *pros* which precedes the noun *plēsmonē,* and the third the understanding of that noun itself. The R.S.V. involves (i) adding *but,* which does not appear in the Greek, before the final phrase, (ii) taking *pros* (normal meaning: *towards, with a view to*) in the slightly unusual sense of *against* (R.S.V. *in checking*) and *plēsmonē* in its bad sense of *indulgence* (usual meaning: *satisfaction, gratification*). All this is in fact perfectly possible, though it involves taking two words in uncommon senses and at one point forcing the construction of the sentence.

Another view (see Bo Reicke, *Studia Theologica,* 6, pp. 39ff.) is that the last words (*pros plēsmonēn of the flesh*) are the predicate of the opening verb (lit. *these are*), and that the whole of the intervening words (participle, *having,* etc.) is in parenthesis. The idea is then that the ascetic practices simply gratify and build up 'the flesh' (i.e. the lower, anti-God self, cf. 2[11]); that is, they accomplish the opposite of what, presumably, they set out to do. This accords with Paul's general view of the Law as associated with the realm of 'the flesh' (cf. Rom. 8[18]). The intervening expressions then all show how false the claims of the ascetic practices are: they have only a *name* for wisdom (but not the reality of it), their piety is only a *quasi*-piety, and their ascetic exercises have no value at all. (It may be that *timē,* here taken as *value,* has its other sense, *honour*, and that Paul is castigating the self-centred nature of the Jews' religion; it lacks that esteem and concern for the brethren which is so often a mark of Paul's teaching on acts of piety, cf. Rom. 14^{21}; 12^{10}. But if so, the point is made only very allusively.) The version in the margin simply assumes a break after *value* and in effect another *but* at this point – just possible.

3 $^{1-17}$ THE RISEN LIFE AND ITS MORAL
IMPLICATIONS

¹If then you have been raised with Christ, seek the things that are above, where Christ is, seated at the right hand of God. ² Set your minds on things that are above, not on things that are on earth. ³ For you have died, and your life is hid with Christ in God. ⁴When Christ who is our life appears, then you also will appear with him in glory.

⁵Put to death therefore what is earthly in you: immorality, impurity, passion, evil desire, and covetousness, which is idolatry. ⁶On account of these the wrath of God is coming^f. ⁷In these you once walked, when you lived in them. ⁸But now put them all away: anger, wrath, malice, slander, and foul talk from your mouth. ⁹Do not lie to one another, seeing that you have put off the old nature with its practices ¹⁰and have put on the new nature, which is being renewed in knowledge after the image of its creator. ¹¹Here there cannot be Greek and Jew, circumcised and uncircumcised, barbarian, Scythian, slave, free man, but Christ is all, and in all.

¹²Put on then, as God's chosen ones, holy and beloved, compassion, kindness, lowliness, meekness, and patience, ¹³forbearing one another and, if one has a complaint against another, forgiving each other; as the Lord has forgiven you, so you also must forgive. ¹⁴And above all these put on love, which binds everything together in perfect harmony. ¹⁵And let the peace of Christ rule in your hearts, to which indeed you were called in the one body. And be thankful. ¹⁶Let the word of Christ dwell in you richly, as you teach and admonish one another in all wisdom, and as you sing psalms and hymns and spiritual songs with thankfulness in your hearts to God. ¹⁷And whatever you do, in word or deed, do everything in the name of the Lord Jesus, giving thanks to God the Father through him.

f Other ancient authorities add upon the sons of disobedience.

In the preceding section, Paul has in effect dealt with the implications of the false teachers' doctrine for practical living, and has found much to oppose. To all that, Christians have died (2^{20}). He now turns to the corresponding implications of authentic Christian doctrine. (Note how 3^1 corresponds in form to 2^{20}.) His account of Christian morals therefore presupposes the truth about Christ which he has put forward in numerous ways in the first two chapters. In 3^{1a} he resumes it all in a clause which expresses the result of Christ's work (cf. 2^{12}).

The structure of the passage seems to be as follows. Assuming this result of the work of Christ and the promise of its future consummation (v. 4), he lists the vices which Christians are to shun, and sums them up by speaking of the *old nature*, which the Christian has discarded. It is replaced by the *new nature*, which restores man's original Adamic state (v. 10); and this leads naturally into a discussion of the virtues which characterize the new life (vv. 12–17).

But notice, the ethic which he enjoins is not autonomous. It is not as if it were simply a new set of commands, parallel to the old Law, but issued now on the authority of Christ. The link with Paul's doctrinal tenets is more intimate than that.

This is so in two ways, which seem to us to differ in their idiom, though Paul does not appear to have been conscious of this difference at all, and indeed relates them to one another. In the first place, the Christian has his whole sphere of existence in relation to Christ (v. 3); the new life is his (v. 1), and his future salvation is assured (v. 4). The moral qualities he is to exhibit are simply the characteristics of that new life. Logically, it is a matter of describing that life rather than urging its attainment, for it is the Christian's present possession. In the light of this, it might be supposed that there was no room left for that expectation of a final intervention of God, which filled contemporary Judaism. The notion of the virtuous life as a preparation for that Last Day would seem to be by-passed.

But in fact, alongside this stress on the believer's present and permanently assured status, the temporal perspective remains. As we saw (p. 136) it is rare in *Colossians*, but here (vv. 4 & 6) it is unmistakable (cf. 3^{24}). This is christianized but otherwise conventional Jewish apocalyptic language. So the moral behaviour here described and urged is in the context of an imminent End. The believer must behave in such a way that on that day Christ will know him as his own and keep him safe from *the wrath of God* which will be directed against all evil in that ultimate conflict and judgement.

In v. 3f. we see how Paul connects the two aspects which we have distinguished. The same Christ who is *now* the sphere of the believer's life *will* appear, as God's agent of judgement and salvation – and so of course will have his own people in company with him (cf. I Cor. 15$^{21-28}$; I Thess. 4$^{13-18}$, which show in more detail what Paul has in mind). There is no doubt that the modern reader will generally find the second kind of language less easy to interpret in his own terms than the first kind. But for Paul they go together, and the question arises whether we are justified in abandoning the one (explicitly or for all practical purposes) while retaining the other, or in re-expressing the one much more radically than the other. We do well to realize that Paul's 'future' language is assertion about God rather than mere prediction.

There is one other feature of these verses to which attention should be paid, because it illustrates a feature of Paul's pastoral persuading which some regard as sensitivity to those in his care, some as delicate tact, and some as opportunism bordering on duplicity. Having diverted his readers' minds from the heavenly hierarchies (2$^{8-23}$) and from bodily mortification (2$^{16, 21}$), he promptly goes on to urge them to *seek the things that are above* and to *put to death* their earthly selves (3$^{1, 5}$), i.e. exactly what they had been only too prone to do. Professor Chadwick comments: 'What we have here is one more instance of the typically pauline method of outclassing his opponents on their own ground.'* What he has withdrawn with one hand, he gives back with the other: but of course it is reformed in the process. The *things above* add up to – what? Simply to Christ. Mortification is concerned with deeper matters than food and drink – the deep roots of evil desires and impulses in man's heart. Once more Paul adapts himself to his audience, speaks as they are able to hear, and turns their aims to Christian account, as befits their apostle and pastor.

ಬಬ

I

have been raised: some hold that this statement that the Christian already shares in the resurrection of Christ is so much at variance with statements elsewhere which place this in the future (e.g. Rom. 6$^{5, 8}$; I Cor. 15^{23}), that they find here an argument against the pauline authorship of

* H. Chadwick, *All things to all men* (I Cor. 9^{22}), N.T.S., I, pp. 261ff.

this letter. But as we have seen (p. 136) Paul continually oscillates between the two ways of regarding the Christian life: what has been done, what is still to come. He sees each in its place and describes it vividly. Even in one short passage he can move rapidly from one aspect to the other; cf. Rom. 6^{4-11}. What will be consummated has already begun. For the combination of indicative and imperative here, cf. Gal. 5^{25} and see pp. 179f.

where Christ is seated: again, there is duality in Paul's thought. Statements like 1^{27} show that Paul by no means confined himself to – or even chiefly held – a view of the universe which saw heaven as physically placed above the earth, where God, and Christ reigning by his side, were actually located. We do not know how exactly he would have reconciled this mythological idiom (seeing the 'other world' as physically continuous with this one) with his language about the presence of Christ or of the Spirit of God (cf. Rom. $8^{1ff.}$; I Cor. 2^{10}) in the believers or about their life 'in Christ'; but clearly for Paul they were not at all incompatible. We have no reason to suppose that one aspect was more 'real' for him than the other, and we do not know how far he would have recognized words like these, about Christ's heavenly session, as metaphorical. Their source in Christian parlance is Ps. 110^1 which was perhaps the earliest proof-text from the Old Testament used to demonstrate and support the exaltation and rule of Christ: it occurs more widely in the New Testament than any other Old Testament text, being either quoted or alluded to by almost all the major writers (e.g. Mark 12^{36}; 14^{62}; Acts 2^{34}; Heb. 1^{13}; Eph. 1^{20}; I Pet. 3^{22}).

3
you have died: cf. 2^{20}. The verb indicates a single past action, i.e. baptism.

hid: cf. 2^3. We have discussed (see in connexion with *mystery*, 1^{26}) the idea, common in Jewish apocalyptic books, that the events of the Last Days, which it is given to the seer to expound, are kept secret by God from most men, and will only become public when the events themselves begin to occur. Paul sees God's essential secret, which concerns man's salvation, as revealed in Christ; and from this point of view Paul is a seer-after-the-event. Part of the same set of ideas is that the identity of those whom God will save is one element in the secret; who they are will only at the Last Day become apparent to all. God's major secret $1^{26f.}$; 2^2 has been disclosed, but this part of it remains: the life of the believers is *hid with Christ in God* until the final consummation (v. 4).

4
Christ … our life: cf. Gal. 2^{20}; Phil. 1^{21}; also John 14^6; Ign. Eph. 3 ('Christ, the life from which we cannot be torn').

5

put to death: together with *you have died* (v. 3) this makes yet another of Paul's indicative/imperative pairs, this time in terms of death rather than resurrection, cf. v. 1. The believer's baptism is for Paul a quasi-physical ground for the mortifying of vice within him.

immorality, etc.: this is the first of Paul's lists of vices in this epistle; another follows in v. 8, to be followed again by a list of virtues in v. 12. We find similar lists in Rom. 1$^{29ff.}$; Gal. 5$^{19ff.}$; 1 Cor. 6$^{9f.}$; cf. Eph. 4^{31}; 5$^{3-5}$; and, outside Paul, in 1 Pet. 4^3; Rev. 21^8. Two questions arise: about their origin and their contents. As to the first, they are typical neither of the Old Testament nor of rabbinic Judaism. Their most likely source is the ethical analysis of the Stoics, as that had passed into common currency and been adopted by Hellenistic Judaism. Paul will have received it by this route: cf., for example, Wisd. 14$^{25ff.}$. As to the contents, the list in v. 5 is typically Jewish in making *idolatry* its climax and in seeing sexual sin as related to idol-worship (cf. Deut. 31^{16}; Hos. 4^{12}); and the orgiastic nature of much Hellenistic religion would certainly add point to the association. This list is all concerned with one form or another of inordinate desire, which effectively sets its object in God's rightful place. It is therefore directly related to the false teaching at Colossae which centres on the angels who usurp God's position (see on 2^{18}, p. 197). The list in v. 8 on the other hand is concerned with sins which disrupt the harmony of the Christian community, and it looks on to v. 12–15 where the congregation is exhorted to the corresponding virtues.

G. Bornkamm* has noted that all three lists in these verses consist of five items (something not true of the other lists) and sees in this the influence of Persian religion; it is a feature shortly to be found in Gnosticism, and in Bornkamm's view such teaching is already an element in the outlook of the writer – whom he believes not to have been Paul. He notes that 2^{23} can also be seen as reporting a list of five features, probably taken from the teaching of the false teachers. The writer is then setting *his* lists, which are more concerned with dispositions than acts, in contrast to theirs.

The presence of similar lists in so many different Christian writings probably points to the existence in the early Church of a pattern of moral teaching, used perhaps especially in teaching for baptism, which had a fair degree of uniformity in a variety of places. On this see P. Carrington, *The Primitive Christian Catechism* (Cambridge, 1940) and E. G. Selwyn, *1 Peter* (London, 1946), Essay II.

* *Das Ende des Gesetzes* (Munich, 1952), p. 151.

6

the wrath of God: cf., though without *of God*, Rom. 2^5; also Rom. 1^{18}; 5^9. The use of the term without *of God* points to the fact that it was at this time a conventional term in eschatology. It stood less for a coming emotional outburst on God's part than for the certainty of his judgement and destruction of evil. It was a terrifying prospect, one of the chief prompters of the anxiety of the period and of the consequent intense longing for salvation or safety, both in the present and especially on the Last Day.

The addition in the margin has good support in old manuscripts but is probably not original; rather, it has been copied from Eph. 5^6, a verse very close to this one.

9ff.

you have put off: the same verb as in 2^{11}, a reference to baptism, the moment when the old life was abandoned and the new assumed. Cf. *put on*, vv. 10 & 12: there may be an allusion to a custom of donning new clothes on emerging from the water of baptism: cf. the image in Gal. 3^{27}. Certainly this was the custom later, but we do not know whether it had already been adopted. (Cf. Eph. 4^{22-24}).

old nature: cf. *new nature*, v. 10. This translation eases, but also fails to show the true bearing of, the original. The Greek is 'old man ... new man'. The new man is Christ and the reason why lying is forbidden is that there cannot be contradiction and tension within the one body (cf. 1^{24}; 3^{14}). Christ is the *image* of God (cf. 1^{15}), as the personified Wisdom of God and as the second Adam (see pp. 166f.; cf. Rom. $5^{12ff.}$; I Cor. $15^{22, 45ff.}$). But man, the first Adam, was made in God's image, and the Christian is enabled to reproduce it now in the new creation (cf. 2 Cor. 5^{17}). 'In Christ', the new humanity is formed. By seeing Christ in Adamic terms, Paul is enabled and indeed compelled to think in terms of the whole human race, and not merely in terms of Israel. If Christ is God's agent in creation, his Wisdom, and if he is the Second Adam, then there cannot possibly be any limitation of the new humanity which comes into existence in relation to him, by race or status (v. 11).

This imagery is intelligible if not easy. It is difficult at two points, both of them by now familiar. First, it is impossible to say how far Paul saw it as metaphorical and how far as, in some way, literal statement. Distinctions of this kind, attractive to us, would probably not have meant much to him. Second, it is also impossible to say how far this language is explicable as derived from wisdom-theology together with consideration of the place of Adam, once the two are brought to bear on the person and work of Christ. Many see it as either tinged or wholly formed by Persian mythology concerning the primeval or archetypal man (cf. the thought of the Jew Elchasai on the vast Son of God, p. 195), who includes those dependent upon him within himself. This kind of thinking, soon to develop in the Greek world in Gnostic and other groups, found easy alliance with the already existing mystery cults; and the language of 'putting on' the deity in initiation is commonplace in them. It remains uncertain which way the limited evidence points. It is perhaps fair to say that if Paul is, as we believe, the writer of this epistle, any influence from the Oriental world of syncretism is likely to be smaller rather than greater, and the strong moral content of this whole passage points strongly in the same direction. This is the work of a man whose fundamental formation is Jewish. (See also on 2^{19}, p. 198.)

new nature . . . being renewed: again, the tension between status already conferred and process still being accomplished. It is hard to say whether the new humanity which is being made new is seen in terms of the life of the individual or in its gradual working out in the spreading Church. The parallel in 2 Cor. 4^{16} and the fact that the context is moral point to the former view, though of course all believers share in the 'new man'.

in knowledge: lit. 'into' – it looks to the culmination of the process in perfect acknowledgement and awareness of God: cf. 1 Cor. 13^{12}, where the corresponding verb to our noun (*epignōsis*, cf. on 1^9) is used.

after the image: cf. Gen. 1^{27}, which is exactly quoted.

Scythian: a native of the land on the eastern shores of the Black Sea. But probably the sense is more general: it represents the most uncivilized type of barbarian, perhaps in contrast to *barbaros* itself. Who were designated by this latter term depended entirely on the speaker's point of view; to Philo, it included Romans. It could mean simply native inhabitants of a region, even within the Empire, e.g. Acts 28^2. It might virtually mean the uneducated. Here it is probably meant to cover Gentiles of non-Greek culture. It may be Paul's intention to give a comprehensive description of the composition of the Colossian church.

God's chosen ones, holy and beloved: these are all titles which belong to Israel as God's people, in the Old Testament. Now transferred to the Church, they show her as the heir of Israel. For *chosen ones (eklektoi)*, cf. Rom. 8^{33}. On *holy* see p. 48. All three terms speak of God's free and gracious choice. As his people owe their life wholly to his initiative, so also they are to look to him for the moral character which expresses it; he offers it to them like a garment ready for wearing. The virtues listed here are the opposites of the vices in v. 8; they are the qualities making for harmony in the community and so lead naturally to the mention of *love* (*agapē*) in v. 14, which sums them all up (see below). As God loves his people, so they are to love one another (cf. John 13$^{10-12}$).

13

forgiving: cf. Matt. 6$^{12f.}$; Mark 11^{25}; Eph. 4^{32}.

14

love: Paul regards this quality as more than just synonymous with the qualities which he has just mentioned. By comparison with the everyday virtues listed in v. 12, it has already acquired an almost technical Christian usage. In the background is its use in the Old Testament to describe God's choice of Israel and his attachment to her by his covenant (e.g. Deut. 23^5; Hos. 3^1). Now it expresses the concentrated and devoted desire of God for man's salvation, shown in the work of Christ; and, in consequence of this, it is to be the special mark of Christian life, which is to display a self-giving similar to that of Christ (cf. 1 Cor. 13$^{1ff.}$; Rom. 5$^{5, 8}$; Gal. 5$^{6, 22}$). The relation between Christ's work and Christian life is more fully developed in terms of this word in the Fourth Gospel (especially ch. 13) and *1 John*.

which binds everything together in perfect harmony: the Greek is simpler and means: 'which is the bond of perfectness'. Pagan moral thinkers could use the same word (*syndesmos* = *bond*) to express the idea of a principle of unity and coherence in ethics. 'Perfectness' recalls *teleios* in 1^{28} (*mature*), which is the corresponding adjective; the idea will then be that *love* is the chief characteristic of fully developed Christian life.

15

the peace of Christ: cf. Phil. 4^7. *Peace* is a richer word in the Bible than often appears on the surface. In a phrase like this it is equivalent to 'reconciliation with God', brought by Christ: cf. Rom. 5^1. The Christian's status determines his behaviour.

to which: i.e. to *the peace of Christ*.

be thankful: thanksgiving is mentioned three times in these verses. It is the central feature of the believer's response to God for his gift conferred through Christ (cf. v. 17). And when that response becomes articulate in worship, thanksgiving is the dominant note (v. 16).

16

the word of Christ: we cannot be certain whether this means, or at least includes, the tradition of Christ's own teaching, handed down in the Church, or refers rather to the teaching, the gospel, *about* Christ. The use of *word* in the singular points towards the second interpretation, in conformity with Paul's common usage.

in all wisdom: no polemic lurks in the use of this word here, as it does in 2²³ and, much more, in 1 Cor. 1^{18ff.}. Among Christians, as among both pagans and Jews, it is a proper term for religious doctrine. Or the phrase may simply mean 'wisely'.

sing psalms, etc.: it is hard to know how much we can really learn about early Christian worship from this verse. Without the article, there is no reason why *psalms* should be confined to the Old Testament psalter: it will include Christian songs of praise to God or to Christ. How far *hymns* represent a different category it is also hard to know; probably not, cf. the use of this word for the Hallel psalms in Mark 14²⁶. *Spiritual songs:* probably the kind of ecstatic or elevated utterance, felt to be inspired by the Holy Spirit who indwells the believer (1 Cor. 2^{10ff.}; 3¹⁶), of which 1 Cor. 14 describes the context; see especially 1 Cor.14²⁶.

Many scholars believe (and we have accepted this judgement) that passages like Col. 1¹⁵⁻²⁰, Phil. 2⁶⁻¹¹, 1 Tim. 3¹⁶ are themselves, or are based upon, early Christian hymns of the kind mentioned here. If so it is easy to see how they are vehicles of teaching and admonition (probably used in its sense of instruction rather than moral reproof), for they are all passages celebrating the central Christian assertions about God's work in Christ. It may seem odd to think, as Paul seems to do, of teaching being the purpose of their recitation rather than worship, but there is no hard and fast line between these two activities. Even much later in the Church's history, there is close correspondence between the form of creeds and liturgies; they spring from a common stock of formulations.

None of the passages just mentioned contains thanksgiving, and Paul does not say that this is actually expressed in the hymns of which he speaks. Perhaps it is more associated with the prayers, especially the blessing-cum-thanksgiving over the bread and wine of the eucharist, than with the songs of the early congregations. V. 17 may allude to this prayer, and the forms of thanksgiving found just after the opening greetings in Paul's letters may well be related to such early liturgical usage (see on Ephesians 1^{3ff.}, p. 259, and Phil. 1^{3ff.}, p. 52). It is worth noting that the word translated *thankfulness* in v. 16 is not the unambiguous one of v. 15 and v. 17, but can also mean *grace:* hymns are sung by Christians by virtue of the grace of God which is theirs. (Cf. Eph. 5¹⁸⁻²⁰).

[18]*Wives, be subject to your husbands, as is fitting in the Lord.* [19]*Husbands, love your wives, and do not be harsh with them.* [20]*Children, obey your parents in everything, for this pleases the Lord.* [21]*Fathers, do not provoke your children, lest they become discouraged.* [22]*Slaves, obey in everything those who are your earthly masters, not with eye-service, as men-pleasers, but in singleness of heart, fearing the Lord.* [23]*Whatever your task, work heartily, as serving the Lord and not men,* [24]*knowing that from the Lord you will receive the inheritance as your reward; you are serving the Lord Christ.* [25]*For the wrongdoer will be paid back for the wrong he has done, and there is no partiality.* [4][1]*Masters, treat your slaves justly and fairly, knowing that you also have a Master in heaven.*

The first question raised by this passage is simply that of its function here in this epistle. There is no doubt that the letter's point lies in the doctrinal message which dominates it down to 3^4; moreover, the ethical material which follows in 3^{5-17} flows straight from that doctrinal teaching and is wholly intelligible in relation to it. What we now have before us is quite different. Though it is formally christianized by the insertion of phrases like *in the Lord* (v. 18) and by other significant features, it is for the most part run-of-the-mill ethical teaching taken straight from the Jewish (or pagan) tradition. It is on a quite different level from the moral doctrine which immediately precedes it, and which, as we saw, is closely integrated with the central tenets of Paul's theology. Further, the reference to *thanksgiving* in 4^2 which takes up the topic of 3^{15-17} could even lead one to suspect that this whole passage is a piece of purely conventional Christian instruction inserted after the letter was completed. It seems to have no adequate *raison d'être* in a work such as *Colossians*. Take it out, and we are left with a skilful piece of pauline writing, motivated by his intense concern for the truth of the gospel and the well-being of those in his care; together with personal greetings which are again an entirely natural expression of his pastoral oversight of the congregation.

The suggestion that we should read *Colossians* without this section, if we wish to know the letter as Paul (at any rate initially) left it, is perhaps too drastic. The difficulty is that part of this passage is intimately related to the situation out of which the letter springs. This is the section about slavery (vv. 22ff.). In fact these verses may contain some of the most precious clues to the personal circumstances which helped to prompt the letter. We discuss this whole question elsewhere (see p. 125); let it be said now that it is evident from the reference to Onesimus in 4⁹ that this letter was written at much the same time as *Philemon* and that the same delicate negotiations there evidenced were much in Paul's mind. It may be that the insertion of this apparently ill-fitting list of household duties is another blow in the campaign of which *Philemon* is the main attack. Typically (compare Paul's attitude to presents in Phil. 4¹⁰ff.), the blow is administered obliquely. From this unexceptionable and conventional statement, perhaps close to what they had been told in the course of their instruction for baptism, the Colossians are to pick up the point which he really wishes to make: slaves and masters have duties – and at this very moment there is a fine opportunity for exercising them (p. 125). And, to show that he is no subverter of the established order, in particular of the rights of slave-owners, Paul stresses the duties of slaves.

Quite apart from the close relation of this passage with what follows, it is wrong to exaggerate the break which 3¹⁸ brings. It can be argued that general moral teaching such as that contained in 3⁵⁻¹⁷ leads naturally to certain detailed examples. The same thing occurs in Rom. 12ff., where there seems to be even less specific reason to discuss the ethical questions there dealt with. However, we are inclined to think that it was the specific case of Onesimus which led Paul to introduce the material about slaves and masters in a context which gave him barely sufficient justification, and that he added the whole formula of instruction which usually went with it, partly in order to disguise it – thinly.

As far as its general form is concerned, this list of the responsibilities of the various elements in a well-established household is not a Christian invention. There are both pagan and Jewish parallels. The former are chiefly of Stoic origin and the ones that are extant are mostly later in date than *Colossians*. The Jewish parallels often appear as commentaries on the Ten Commandments, e.g. Philo, *On the*

Decalogue, 165–7*; and the same is true of a later Christian example, *The Epistle of Barnabas* 19⁵⁻⁷,† and cf. Eph. 6². Our present passage is the earliest Christian formula of this kind which we possess, but others, not all of them necessarily dependent upon this letter, were soon to follow: Eph. 5²²ᶠᶠ·; 1 Pet. 2¹³ᶠᶠ·; Titus 2¹ᶠᶠ·; Didache 4⁹ᶠᶠ·‡ They do not all include the same items. Thus, *the Didache*, like the Philo passage mentioned above, has nothing about husbands and wives, and *I Peter* adds a section on the duties of a good subject to the emperor (cf. Rom. 13¹ᶠᶠ·).

If the form and subject-matter of this passage simply show a Christian writer taking over the conventional schemes of ethical instruction current in his time in the Mediterranean world, is the same to be said of the actual teaching which he gives, or has this been christianized either by Paul or by Christians teaching before him? We have already said that the moral teaching in these verses is much less integrated with fundamental doctrine than that in the earlier part of the chapter. It is true that each instruction in turn is related in some way to *the Lord* (i.e. to Christ) and in vv. 24f. there is a reference to the future reward or punishment which Christ will administer (cf. 3⁴, ⁶). But apart from this, there is nothing very distinctive in these admonitions.

It is sometimes alleged that the reciprocal nature of the duties outlined (i.e. the suggestion that parents have duties as well as children, masters as well as servants) is a Christian innovation: but Philo says the same,§ and so, on the matter of master-slave relations, does Paul's contemporary, the Stoic Seneca. It is true that the latter is an aristocratic intellectual and that the sector of society which he chiefly has in mind is far removed from that of a provincial town like Colossae. Still, his ideas were becoming increasingly typical of cultivated Roman opinion, and it is worth quoting him at some length.

---

* Loeb edition, ed. Colson & Whitaker (Cambridge, Mass. and London, 1929), Vol. VII, p. 89.

† See in Lightfoot, *The Apostolic Fathers* (London, 1891); E.C.W., pp. 189ff.

‡ E.C.W., pp. 225ff.

§ loc. cit. 'There are many other instructions given, to the young on courtesy to the old, to the old on taking care of the young . . . to servants on rendering an affectionate loyalty to their master, to masters on showing the gentleness and kindness by which inequality is equalized.'

His teaching is based on the Stoic tenet of the unity and brotherhood of all mankind.

I'm glad to learn, through those who come from you, that you live on friendly terms with your slaves. This befits a sensible and well-educated man like yourself. 'They are slaves,' people declare. Nay, rather they are men. 'Slaves!' No, comrades. 'Slaves!' No, they are unpretentious friends. 'Slaves!' No, they are our fellow-slaves, if one reflects that Fortune has equal rights over slaves and free men alike. That is why I smile at those who think it degrading for a man to dine with his slave. . . . [Seneca describes the brutal and humiliating treatment often meted out to slaves, thus vividly showing the contrast between common custom and what he is now urging.] Show me a man who is not a slave; one is a slave to lust, another to greed, another to ambition, and all men are slaves to fear. I will name you an ex-consul who is slave to an old hag, a millionaire who is slave to a serving-maid.*

It is also sometimes said that the position accorded to wives here ($3^{18f.}$) represents an advance on contemporary ideas. But Josephus the Jew,† a little later in the century, says much the same, and in fact in our passage wives are kept in a strictly subordinate position; there is nothing the slightest bit revolutionary here. The fact is that the passage is often read in the light of the clear importance of women in the life of the early Church, as hostesses to congregations (e.g. Col. 4^{15}) and in active apostolic work alongside Paul (Rom. 16^{1-6}), and of the doctrinal statement in Gal. 3^{28} (*there is neither male nor female; for you are all one in Christ Jesus*).

This raises sharply the decisive point which we have to decide as we try to interpret this passage; are we to treat it as a piece of rather humdrum teaching, or to read it against the background of Paul's whole doctrine, which is not very explicit here? If the former, then it is arguable that these pieces of conventional morality have been adapted for Christian use in a purely formal and not very profound way. They show the Church well up to the level of the best Hellenistic Jewish and Stoic thought of the time, but not at all in advance of it. On the other hand if we read the passage in the context of Paul's whole mind, so far as we know it, then, though the practical implications are still not particularly striking and not different from what a thoughtful Jew or pagan would say, the setting is transformed.

* See *Ad Lucilium Epistulae Morales 47*, Loeb edition, ed. R. M. Gummer (Cambridge, Mass. and London, 1953).
† *Contra Apionem II*, 199–210, Loeb edition, pp. 373ff.

In the first place the fundamental relationship of the Christian to Christ embraces all other relationships and provides the context in which they are experienced. And in practical terms the actual meetings of the congregation for the eucharist (cf. Seneca's words above about the unlikelihood of masters and slaves eating together) and for prayer, and the mutual care which characterized the tight-knit Christian congregations gave expression to this faith. There were perhaps few other groupings in the society of the time which so thoroughly transcended conventional barriers, above all that between masters and slaves.

But it may well be asked, is it not surprising that the powerful impetus towards self-sacrificing love (*agapē*) among Christians and the fact that Christ himself was regarded as having accepted slave-like-status (Phil. 2^7; Mark 10^{45}; John 13^1) did not impel Christians, especially a clear-sighted man like Paul, to go beyond even his best contemporaries? In the solidarity of mankind in Adam, renewed in Christ (cf. 3^{10}), he had a doctrine quite as powerful as the Stoic belief in the common humanity of all men. And it was already quite common for pagans to free their slaves, especially those of 'free-man type' by culture and education; the Jewish Law also enjoined the liberation of at least Jewish slaves, and Philo says that the Essenes denounced slavery on principle. But Paul does not take this step. There are two answers to this. The first is the obvious one; the Church was but two decades old, she was small and socially powerless. Her main concern at this period was to establish a footing, and to root her own life securely. This is precisely what Paul is trying to do here; Christians live 'in the Lord' – let them then work out the implications of this in their relationships with those around them, beginning with those of their own households. It is noticeable that in fact in Paul's apostolic entourage a new hierarchy, alongside that of society in general, *is* already beginning to emerge, one in which women and a slave like Onesimus can have a place of responsibility and authority which they might not otherwise have had. It was hardly to be expected that full-scale 'Christian social doctrine' should have been elaborated by this early stage.

On the other hand (and this is the second answer) in one way the Church's perspective was as wide as the universe itself. She was in no position to overturn the social structure of the Roman Empire, not even of the *petit-bourgeois* households which probably formed most of her membership; but very soon God himself would take this step. The Last Days were near, and Christians were to be ready for that time, living the life which would assure salvation when it came (v. $^{24f.}$): cf. I Cor. 7^{20-24}. In fact the need to be ready accounts for this early formulation of ethical rules. In the light of this expectation, for a slave to share his master's faith was far more important than to acquire his freedom; the freedom that mattered was his already, cf. Philem $^{16ff.}$. When the expectation of the end of the world wanes, then this attitude looks all too easily like mere social conservatism, cf. I Tim. $6^{1f.}$ (taking this as a considerably later, non-pauline work). It is worth noting that this was in an age of considerable social ferment, especially in the eastern half of the Empire, with strikes, food riots, cornering of corn by the rich, and repressive government action. Like Methodism in England in the early nineteenth century, early Christianity did not align itself with revolutionary elements in the lower orders of society.

But, finally, whatever may be alleged about the social conservatism of the teaching contained in this passage, it is worth remembering that both in matters of marriage and in the treatment of slaves, ordinary practice at the time was often far behind the level of a Seneca; this was the time when more and more slaves were being massacred in the gladiatorial games and when this practice was spreading from the west to the eastern part of the Empire. Not everyone in Colossae was in a position to dispense with Paul's instruction.

ৡৡ

18

as is fitting: the same word as that translated *what is required* in Philem.^{8}. It is close to the vocabulary of Stoic ethics. 18f.: cf. Eph. 5^{22-33}.

22ff.

The parallel sections in *1 Peter* and *Titus* (though not Eph. $6^{5ff.}$) entirely omit any reference to the duties of masters; and here too it is clear that Paul is more sensitive to the failings in slaves which affect their masters than those in masters which seem important to slaves. Paul and (if this piece of catechism is not his invention) perhaps the leadership of the early Church generally was not as proletarian as is sometimes suggested. But see on v. 25.

eye-service: i.e. giving the appearance of service but without the heart in it.

the Lord: this title for Christ (see p. 78) is the same word as that used for the slaves' *masters.* So the idea in vv. 23f. is that Christ is their *real* master, who will indeed reward them for their work – or punish them, according to the case. Similarly, *masters (lords, kyrioi)* have a *kyrios* over them, Christ himself, cf. 4¹.

25

partiality: the word *prosōpolēmpsia* is a New Testament invention, on the basis of the Hebrew idiom, reproduced in the LXX sometimes by literal translation, 'accepting-the-face'. Cf. Rom. 2¹¹; Eph. 6⁹; Jas. 2¹. Is Onesimus' offence in mind? cf. Philem. ¹⁸. If so, then Paul is trying no doubt to offset his apparent softness in *Philemon* – and at the same time to condition Onesimus' master to do what Paul wants, that is, to let the slave return to Paul to work for him. The inclusion of *slave* and *free man* in 3¹¹ (though they are also in Gal. 3²⁸ and obvious candidates) may also be part of this process of forming the master's mind. See further, p. 125.

4²⁻⁶   FINAL INSTRUCTIONS FOR
                   CHRISTIAN LIFE

²*Continue steadfastly in prayer, being watchful in it with thanksgiving;* ³*and pray for us also, that God may open to us a door for the word, to declare the mystery of Christ, on account of which I am in prison,* ⁴*that I may make it clear, as I ought to speak.*
     ⁵*Conduct yourselves wisely toward outsiders, making the most of the time.* ⁶*Let your speech always be gracious, seasoned with salt, so that you may know how you ought to answer everyone.*

Apart from his final greetings, these simple exhortations conclude Paul's letter. Their very brevity and simplicity mean that they give a useful glimpse of some of his basic attitudes. The most important is the distinction he makes between the role of the Christian congregation and that of the apostle. It is the latter's job to make the gospel known, and even in prison Paul is determined to continue with this work by all possible means (cf. 1 Cor. 9¹⁶). But for the church it is different: the apostolic vocation is a special one and they do not share it (cf. 1 Cor. 12²⁹). Their task is to 'watch', that is, to await, devoutly and fervently, the return of Christ to judge and save: cf. Mark 13³²⁻³⁷; Matt. 25¹⁻¹³. As they do so, their relation to outsiders is to be, it appears, rather a defensive one. Certainly they are in no sense to disguise their faith (v. 6), but neither are they to propagate it forcefully. They are to give an impression of sober and intelligent courtesy to those around them (cf. 1 Thess. 4^{12}; Rom. 12^{18}). Modern readers, used to thinking of the early Church as humming throughout with evangelistic activity, may be surprised to find that Paul neither found nor, it seems, advised that it should be so. The proclamation of the gospel was in Paul's view chiefly the task of the accredited apostle (the delegate of Jesus Christ) together with his team of fellow-workers (e.g. Timothy and Epaphras). The task of the Christian community was to live as befitted those who were 'in Christ', awaiting his return; of course receiving outsiders when they came (1 Cor. 14^{16}), but concentrating on the building up of a rich and intense life of worship, with the exercise of charismatic gifts (cf. 1 Cor. 12 & 14), all marked by sacrificial love like Christ's.

☦

2

being watchful in it: there may be a reminiscence of the incident in Gethsemane (Mark 14^{37}), when the three disciples slept as the Lord was about to be arrested, for the story will no doubt have been used to point the necessity of Christian vigilance; but the main reference is to the expected Last Day, desire for which was a major theme of early Christian prayer: 1 Cor. 16^{22}; Rev. 22$^{17-20}$; cf. 1 Thess. 5$^{23f.}$. Also cf. Phil. 4^6. With vv. 2–4, cf. Eph. 6$^{18-20}$.

3

a door for the word: i.e. a chance to spread the gospel. Cf. 1 Cor. 16^9; 2 Cor. 2^{12}.

to declare the mystery of Christ: see on 1$^{26f.}$, p. 182. As in 1^{26}, we have the idea, inherent in the word *mystērion*, of hidden, or esoteric truth. In Christ, God's 'truth' has now been made public (cf. Mark 4^{22}).

on account of which I am in prison: does this mean that Paul is imprisoned on a charge arising out of his apostolic work? If so, it is not easy to imagine how an imprisonment of any duration could have arisen, except through incidents in Palestine where the Jewish authorities would be influential enough to bring it about; this points to the last period of Paul's life and to Roman or Caesarean imprisonment, though 2 Cor. 11^{26} & 1 Thess. 2^{14} perhaps show the possibility of serious threats from Gentile authorities. But Paul may be speaking of the purpose of his imprisonment rather than the cause; he sees his time in prison as given to him for the very purpose of preaching the gospel, cf. Phil. 1 12ff.. This is a less likely sense of the preposition *dia* but both the parallel in *Philippians* (especially 1 16) and the earlier part of this verse suggest it.

5

wisely: lit. 'in wisdom', cf. 3 16 for this ideal. Here the reference is to practical Christian wisdom in everyday life.

making the most of the time: the verb used here (*exagorazō*) is obscure. The image is from commerce, and means to 'buy up'. So the idea is probably that of taking all opportunities. But what is *the time?* The word is *kairos* which usually carries the idea of special or significant time – *the* time for some specific use – rather than mere lapse or duration of time (more commonly *chronos*). What Paul probably has in mind here is the time which remains before Christ's return. In this period, highly charged with fervent devotion, Christians are to take care that all their dealings reflect its special character and demands. (For this perspective, cf. v. 2.) Cf. Eph. 5 15f..

6

gracious: lit. 'in grace'. Their speech, not just on their faith, but on any matter, is, like their general conduct, to reflect *the time* in which they live; for the believer, this is the time of God's grace – his gift of new life conferred through the work of Christ. Alternatively, the term may have its ordinary non-religious sense: as R.S.V. indicates. Cf. Eph. 4 29.

seasoned with salt: 'lively', 'interesting'.

PERSONAL GREETINGS

7 *Tychicus will tell you all about my affairs; he is a beloved brother and faithful minister and fellow servant in the Lord.* 8 *I have sent him to you for this very purpose, that you may know how we are and that he may encourage your hearts,* 9 *and with him Onesimus, the faithful and beloved brother, who is one of yourselves. They will tell you of everything that has taken place here.*

10 *Aristarchus my fellow prisoner greets you, and Mark the cousin of Barnabas (concerning whom you have received instructions – if he comes to you, receive him),* 11 *and Jesus who is called Justus. These are the only men of the circumcision among my fellow workers for the kingdom of God, and they*

have been a comfort to me. ¹²*Epaphras, who is one of yourselves, a servant*ᵍ
*of Christ Jesus, greets you, always remembering you earnestly in his
prayers, that you may stand mature and fully assured in all the will of God.*
¹³*For I bear him witness that he has worked hard for you and for those in
Laodicea and in Hierapolis.* ¹⁴*Luke the beloved physician and Demas greet
you.* ¹⁵*Give my greetings to the brethren at Laodicea, and to Nympha and
the church in her house.* ¹⁶*And when this letter has been read among you,
have it read also in the church of the Laodiceans; and see that you read also
the letter from Laodicea.* ¹⁷*And say to Archippus, 'See that you fulfil the
ministry which you have received in the Lord.'*

¹⁸*I, Paul, write this greeting with my own hand. Remember my fetters.
Grace be with you.*

g Or *slave.*

It is easy to read Paul's letters as if they were theological treatises, so
that passages like this, which so often conclude them, seem to be
unimportant appendices, not worth detaining the reader for more
than a moment. Some of the earliest handlers of Paul's correspondence probably had the same feeling. Many critics, supported by
evidence in the manuscript tradition, believe that Rom. 16 did not
originally occupy its present place, but came to it in the course of
the collection of Paul's letters; a list of greetings, it seems, could be
treated somewhat cavalierly.

But if we are interested in Paul's mind at the time of writing, then
these greetings are very far from being mere addenda. They are an
integral part of what Paul has to say. For instance, in the case now
before us, Paul writes to a church in a specific situation so far as its
faith is concerned – that is clear from the main bulk of the letter. But
this faith is held by individuals known to Paul either in person or by
repute. All through the letter these people are in mind; and Paul's
relationship with them is the factor which determines the idiom and
the tone which he adopts. Many of the subtler points which depend
upon this relationship are no doubt lost to us, and in other cases we
cannot be sure of their exact reference; but we can be sure that we
are right to approach the letter along these lines. There was in particular the matter of Onesimus, much clearer to us than anything
else, through the survival of *Philemon.*

A passage like this is important not only because it is as much an
expression of the writer's mind as the rest, but also because it is at

least a potential source of historical information about Paul and the early Church – information whose scarcity value is enormous. Such as it is, it can help to amplify and correct the second-hand picture provided by *Acts*, in which theological and compositional motives decrease its worth as a purely historical source.*

ဘ္ဘ

7f.

These verses are reproduced (v. 8 verbatim, v. 7 in paraphrase) in Eph. 6²¹ᶠ·; in that work they are the only reference to specific circumstances or persons (see p. 340).

Tychicus: apart from the reference in *Ephesians*, dependent upon this passage, he reappears in 2 Tim. 4¹² and Titus 3¹²; and from Acts 20⁴ it seems that he was one of the delegates of the churches in Asia (probably from Ephesus) who accompanied Paul when he took the collection from all his churches to the church in Jerusalem (cf. Gal. 2¹⁰; 1 Cor. 16¹; Acts 24¹⁷). If *Colossians* comes from the imprisonments which followed that visit, then his presence with Paul is explained. He was apparently free to act as Paul's messenger to Colossae.

minister and fellow servant: better, 'servant' and 'slave', cf. pp. 47 & 152.

8

this very purpose: as far as non-doctrinal matters are concerned, Paul confines himself in his letter to greetings and to a reference to the special matter of Onesimus – the rest of his news can be reported verbally. In other words his written communication is exclusively what he *needs* to say, as apostle and pastor.

9

Onesimus: cf. Philem. 10ᶠᶠ·. See p. 124.

10

Aristarchus: he appears as one of the delegates of the pauline churches to Jerusalem in Acts 20⁴ (cf. above on Tychicus), representing the church of Thessalonica. Is he literally Paul's *fellow prisoner*? It is true that Acts 27² shows him accompanying Paul in custody to Rome. It is also true that Epaphras, who receives this description in Philem. 23, is here shown as staying with Paul (v. 12) and not acting as one of his envoys to Colossae. But *Acts* says nothing of charges against anybody apart from Paul, and though that evidence is by no means decisive it is not easy to see why Paul's assistants (and indeed Paul himself) should be in prolonged Roman custody. Could the rumour referred to in Acts 21²⁸ of

* See pp. 35f.

defilement of the Temple by Paul's Gentile companions have led to such serious and far-reaching consequences? Rom. 16⁷ uses the same word for two more of Paul's helpers, Andronicus and Junias – in still more unlikely circumstances. Perhaps then the term is used metaphorically. Paul, in his imprisonment, thinks of Christians in general as those who have been taken captive by Christ: cf. Philem. ¹ & ⁹; also probably 2 Cor. 2¹⁴, which helps to explain the rather odd use here of a word which strictly means a prisoner *of war*. Christians are Christ's prisoners in the victorious war which he has waged with the powers of evil (cf. 1 Cor. 7²² for a parallel play with the idea of the Christian as Christ's slave). The only difficulty with this view is its presence, in a list of greetings, without any justification in the particular context (contrast Philem. ¹ & ⁹ where the whole letter is about slavery and these references are part of Paul's delicate campaign of persuasion). Also its application is strangely selective.

Mark: cf. Acts 12²⁵; 15³⁷ff.; also Philem. ²⁴. Otherwise unknown but, probably through 1 Pet. 5¹³ (whether it refers to the same Mark or not, we cannot say), his name became attached to the traditionally petrine gospel. (See D. E. Nineham, *Saint Mark* (Pelican, 1963), pp. 26f.) It was a very common name.

you have received instructions: probably a reference to a letter of Paul's now lost.

11

Jesus ... Justus: otherwise totally unknown. The Greek-cum-Latin name of a Jewish Christian. *Jesus* is simply the Greek equivalent of Joshua; Justus (righteous) implies devotion to the Jewish Law, and is not uncommon among Jews living in the Greco-Roman world.

the only men of the circumcision: i.e. the only Jewish Christians of Paul's entourage. Who are included among *these* is not clear. Does he mean Aristarchus as well as Barnabas, Mark, and Jesus Justus?

the kingdom of God: this, the key phrase of the preaching of Jesus, according to the first three gospels (cf. Mark 1¹⁴f. *et passim*), occurs relatively rarely in Paul. Jesus himself is the centre of the message of Paul. Where it does occur, it generally carries the sense of the expected consummation which God will bring and the new order of things under his rule. This is particularly clear here where the Greek means literally: *fellow workers into* (i.e. with a view to, moving towards) *the kingdom of God.* (Contrast certain references in the gospels, where the kingdom or rule of God is seen as already present in the ministry of Jesus: e.g. Matt. 12²⁸.) See Rev. 21f. for the kind of imagery with which the term would probably be associated in Paul's mind. Cf. 1 Cor. 6⁹; Gal. 5²¹.

12

Epaphras: unless he is literally a prisoner (Philem. ²³), why is he not with his church at this time of crisis? There is no way of answering detailed questions of this sort, but it may illustrate something of Paul's methods. The man responsible for setting up a particular church does not remain with it if he once joins Paul's team of workers, even when, as apparently in this case, he is a native of the place concerned. Once more (see pp. 145f.) we may have evidence of a fairly elaborate strategy in Paul's work, involving a distinction between apostles-missionaries and local churches and their leaders. In any case, as v. 13 shows, Epaphras had worked on a wider scale in the Lycus valley than simply in Colossae.

13

Laodicea and Hierapolis: see p. 120.

14

Luke ... and Demas: cf. Philem.²⁴. Luke reappears in 2 Tim. 4¹⁰ (perhaps an authentic fragment in an otherwise non-pauline letter?) together with Mark and Tychicus.

15

Nympha and the church in her house: the ancient manuscripts support this translation for the most part, but some read *his* house; and the name (in the accusative in the text, *Nymphan*) could be either male, Nymphas, or female, Nympha. If the latter, then she was probably the most affluent of the congregation at Laodicea, or possibly Hierapolis, who was able most easily to let her house be used for the meetings of the church. If the former, then we are likely to have a reference to the leader (we cannot tell what his title will have been: elder, overseer/bishop?) of the church there, as well as its host. How far leadership in the church tended to be associated with social position at this time, and with practical matters like possession of a house big enough to act as meeting-place and headquarters for the congregation, we do not know. *Church:* see on 1²⁴ p. 181.

16

the letter from Laodicea: perhaps *Philemon,* see p. 125. Marcion, using a collection of Paul's letters in the first half of the second century, calls our *Ephesians* by this title, but there is no necessary reason why he should have been right. The fact that Paul includes greetings to the church of Laodicea in *this* letter argues slightly in favour of the view that the Letter to Laodicea had been sent at some earlier time. If so, it is now lost.

17

Archippus: cf. Philem.². A (or the) leader of the Colossian church, perhaps in the 'headquarters household'. His *ministry* (*diakonia*) may be this leadership; is he reminded of it pointedly because he has shown signs of dabbling in the views of the Jewish teachers? It is hardly likely to refer to technical diaconate at this early date, though that was soon to be the sense of the word (cf. 1 Tim. 3⁸ᶠᶠ·). But it may well concern a specific piece of service for Paul, cf. the theory of J. Knox, p. 125.

18

my own hand: perhaps only this last verse, perhaps all the greetings, were written by Paul's own hand rather than through a secretary, cf. Gal. 6¹¹; 1 Cor. 16²¹; and Philem. ¹⁹ where there is the same uncertainty as here.

grace: Paul ends as he begins, cf. Col. 1².

The Letter to Philemon

Introduction

Much of the Introduction to *Colossians* also applies to this brief letter especially pp. 123ff. The two works belong together. They were addressed to the same church or to neighbouring churches, and no doubt they were collected as making up a single correspondence when the letters of Paul were first brought together, about the end of the first century. It is a pity that in the course of time *Philemon* came to be separated from *Colossians* in its position in the New Testament.

The question arises why so brief and non-doctrinal a letter as this was accepted into the collection at all. It is unlikely that it was simply its pauline authorship which was responsible, for Paul must surely have written a great many notes and even longer epistles (e.g. *Laodiceans,* Col. 4[16], unless *the letter from Laodicea* is in fact *Philemon,* cf. p. 125), which were still extant at the end of the century in his churches. We cannot be sure, but probably it was a need to appeal to the doctrinal authority rather than veneration for the *person* of Paul (after the manner of the later veneration of martyrs) which inspired the collecting of his letters. If this is so, then only some strong personal factor, such as that suggested by J. Knox (see p. 125) can explain the inclusion of *Philemon.*

We have, then, already said enough about the general setting which may lie behind the writing of this letter, but we must now see whether it is possible to be more precise. The very fact that this letter is so non-doctrinal and so concerned with personal matters, about which it is nevertheless not quite explicit enough, has led both popular piety and New Testament scholarship into speculative paths. Many reconstructions have been offered of the way in which Onesimus came to be with Paul, of the wrong he had done his master (v. 18), and of the subsequent events. We must try, however, to confine ourselves to expounding what the letter itself tells us.

There is no great difficulty in that. Somehow or other, Onesimus a slave has come to be a most useful (this happens also to be the meaning of his name, v. 11) servant for Paul, the prisoner (v. 13). Paul is clearly being held in the liberal conditions of custody known as *custodia libra.* That he was a runaway slave and that this is why Paul is so delicate and charming in this letter aimed at assuaging his master's wrath is a legend without foundation. We just do not know how he came to be with Paul; probably he had been lent to Paul to be of service to him over a difficult period. And the reason for Paul's delicacy is simply that he wishes to retain his services longer.

There are two other factors. One is that while he has been with Paul, Onesimus has become, like his master, a Christian. The fact that all three parties now share the faith means that Paul is able to insert an appeal to the master on grounds which would not have been available to him before. Paul uses this advantage to the full (vv. 15–17).

The other factor is that in some way Onesimus *has wronged* his master, vv. 18f. (cf. on Col. 3²²⁻⁵). We do not know at all what this refers to, but it sounds like one of those minor domestic transactions which lie somewhere between borrowing and stealing. All in all, the master seems to be a rather fiery character who needs careful handling but usually comes to heel when a firm line is taken. He is also a man whose Christian allegiance can be relied upon and appealed to, and v. 19 (a piece of sheer arm-twisting) gives the impression that he has once been with Paul, perhaps in Ephesus. This may explain how his slave came to be lent out.

Paul's final pressure comes in the promise – or threat – of a visit. He does not expect his imprisonment to be prolonged.

The Letter of Paul to Philemon

[1]*Paul, a prisoner for Christ Jesus, and Timothy our brother, to Philemon our beloved fellow-worker* [2]*and Apphia our sister and Archippus our fellow soldier, and the church in your house:* [3]*grace to you and peace from God our Father and the Lord Jesus Christ.*

[4]*I thank my God always when I remember you in my prayers,* [5]*because I hear of your love and of the faith which you have toward the Lord Jesus and all the saints,* [6]*and I pray that the sharing of your faith may promote the knowledge of all the good that is ours in Christ.* [7]*For I have derived much joy and comfort from your love, my brother, because the hearts of the saints have been refreshed through you.*

[8]*Accordingly, though I am bold enough in Christ to command you to do what is required,* [9]*yet for love's sake I prefer to appeal to you – I, Paul, an ambassador[a] and now a prisoner also for Christ Jesus –* [10]*I appeal to you for my child, Onesimus, whose father I have become in my imprisonment.* [11]*(Formerly he was useless to you, but now he is indeed useful to you and to me.)* [12]*I am sending him back to you, sending my very heart.* [13]*I would have been glad to keep him with me, in order that he might serve me on your behalf during my imprisonment for the gospel;* [14]*but I preferred to do nothing without your consent in order that your goodness might not be by compulsion but of your own free will.*

[15]*Perhaps this is why he was parted from you for a while, that you might have him back for ever,* [16]*no longer as a slave but more than a slave, as a beloved brother, especially to me but how much more to you, both in the flesh and in the Lord.* [17]*So if you consider me your partner, receive him as you would receive me.* [18]*If he has wronged you at all, or owes you anything, charge that to my account.* [19]*I, Paul, write this with my own hand, I will repay it – to say nothing of your owing me even your own self.* [20]*Yes, brother, I want some benefit from you in the Lord. Refresh my heart in Christ.*

[21]*Confident of your obedience, I write to you, knowing that you will do even more than I say.* [22]*At the same time, prepare a guest room for me, for I am hoping through your prayers to be granted to you.*

[23]*Epaphras, my fellow prisoner in Christ Jesus, sends greetings to you,*

²⁴*and so do Mark, Aristarchus, Demas, and Luke, my fellow workers.*
²⁵*The grace of the Lord Jesus Christ be with your spirit.*

a Or *an old man.*

For the form of the greeting, see p. 47, and for its contents, pp. 123ff.
The idea that Philemon, Apphia, and Archippus were husband, wife,
and son is an instance of legend active when history fails. *Your house*
is in fact singular – '*thy house*', but we cannot be sure who is meant;
see p. 125. Certainly it does not necessarily imply that the three constitute a single household.

prisoner for Christ Jesus: cf. Col. 4²; Phil. 1¹⁶. This translation no doubt
reflects one element in the meaning of this phrase, but the more literal
rendering is 'Christ Jesus' prisoner'; he thinks of his conversion as his
being made captive by Christ; cf. on Col. 4¹⁰, pp. 219f. The same phrase
occurs in v. 9.

sister: i.e. fellow-Christian, cf. *brother* in v. 16 – and frequently.

fellow soldier: the only other use of this word in the New Testament is
in Phil. 2²⁵, of Epaphroditus (see p. 92). It is an example of Paul's not
infrequent military metaphor for the service of a Christian: cf. the
extended working-out of it by the author of *Ephesians* (6¹⁰); 2 Cor.
10³ᶠ·; Rom. 6¹³ (R.S.V. *instruments*; lit. 'weapons'); 13¹². The word
itself is one of those compound-words, using the preposition *syn-*(lit.
'with'; translated *fellow-*), which are very common in Paul's writings.
   It is a rare word, and there is some indication from contemporary
usage that it may imply a financial or business relationship between
the persons concerned. This suggestion, from John Knox (*Philemon*, p.
58), supports his view that Archippus and not Philemon is the owner
of Onesimus and therefore the man with whom Paul is trying to reach
agreement (p. 125). He points out that Epaphroditus, the only other
Christian of whom Paul uses this term, also has financial dealings with
him; he is the bearer of gifts from the church of Philippi (Phil. 4¹⁸).
Knox also distinguishes this title from that of 'fellow-worker', which
he takes to imply that a man is a member of Paul's apostolic team.
However, it is worth noting that in Phil. 2²⁵ Epaphroditus is called by
both titles, which is perhaps evidence that the military title is no more
than a reference to one of Paul's metaphors for the Christian life.

church in your house: cf. on Col. 1²⁴ and 4¹⁵, p. 221. This is not as purely
private a letter as is often supposed. Its customary title misleads. Lit.

'thy house'. The singular is kept up throughout, except in v.22. See p. 125.

For the form of the thanksgiving, here as in Paul's other letters, see p. 52. As always, the thanksgiving is not made up of formal or conventional phrases, but carefully prepares the ground for what is to come. Given the particularly practical purpose of the letter, this is not as striking here as might be expected, but it is nevertheless quite clearly the case. A man whose Christian faith and love have been so much stressed, and whose importance to Paul as a source of strength and encouragement has been so appreciatively praised, could hardly refuse the request which Paul goes on to make.

remember: cf. Rom. 1⁹; Phil. 1³.

your love . . . all the saints: either the *love* and the *faith* are directed both towards Christ and towards the Christians, in which case *pistis* (*faith*) must be in the general sense of 'loyalty', 'faithfulness'; or this is an example of chiasmus, the literary form in which terms or ideas are arranged in the pattern *ab ba*. Thus, *love* is seen as directed towards *the saints*, and *faith* towards Christ. But there is no strong reason to reject the first way of interpreting the passage.

saints: cf. p. 48.

in Christ: lit. 'into Christ'; so *the knowledge* or *the good* are regarded as leading their possessors towards Christ. On *knowledge* (*epignōsis*), see p. 153.

comfort: for Paul's sense of the importance of encouragement as a fruit of shared Christian life, see his use of the term (*paraclēsis*) in 2 Cor. 1³⁻⁸.

heart: this word, lit. 'entrails', recurs in vv. 12 & 20. It sees this part of the body as the seat and source of the emotions, especially love, mercy, and pity. 'Inmost self' gives the sense in all three uses in this letter. (The usage has both Greek and Old Testament background.)

bold enough to command: even though in his opening greeting Paul does not use his apostolic title (contrast Col. 1¹), he does not hesitate to assume the role of one in authority. This is not a letter between equals.

Paul had many claims upon the recipient, and he will mention them all. Among them is his status as pastoral overseer of his churches.

what is required: to anēkon = 'the decent thing'.

9

for love's sake . . .: cf. 1 Cor. 13[5].

ambassador: two words differ by only a vowel – *presbutēs* (old man) and *presbeutēs*. The manuscript evidence favours the former here; nevertheless many scholars think that the second is the word intended. There are many examples of scribes confusing the spelling of the two words. If the writer of *Ephesians* knew and used the letter, he understood it in this sense, cf. 6[20]: but this is not decisive. More important, 'old man' and 'prisoner' hardly make a mounting pair of words to describe Paul's status; they are in different categories, the one relating to his person, the other to his role. *Ambassador* and *prisoner* fit together well. The implication is that his having become a *prisoner* has not put a stop to his activities as Christ's *ambassador*, cf. Phil. 1[12ff.]; Col. 4[3].

10

appeal . . . for: either 'concerning' or 'in order to have' Onesimus. (Knox, *Philemon*, p. 20, suggests the latter.)

father: Paul uses this image for his relationship to his converts in 1 Cor. 4[14] and 2 Cor. 11[2] (cf. Phil. 2[22]). R.S.V. conceals the Greek, which goes, literally: 'whom I begat in my bonds (as) Onesimus'. The idea may be that now he has really begun to live up to his name; or else that this name was given to him when he became a Christian (Knox's suggestion).

11

useless . . . useful: Onesimus' name simply means *useful* or *beneficial* (cf. related verb in v. 20). But here Paul in fact uses another adjective, *euchrēstos*, and its negative. The implication is perhaps that the master lent to Paul a slave of poor quality (cf. v. 18). His new usefulness is a little vague, perhaps intentionally so. Is the slave now reformed into conscientiousness? Or is his usefulness simply as now a fellow-Christian alongside his master (v. 16)? Or is Paul saying that he himself finds him adequate (at least) as a servant, while his master ought to find his new-found Christian life ample commendation?

12

I am sending him back: this verb, lit. 'to send up', is usually used of the referring of cases to a higher court. Its four other occurrences in the New Testament, all in *Luke-Acts*, have this judicial sense. So here Paul is asking for the master to judge on Onesimus' case. It reads as if there had been pressure on him to return the slave, though cf. v. 14. (See Knox, op. cit., p. 21.)

13
imprisonment for the gospel: cf. Phil. 1¹³, ¹⁶; Col. 4³.

14
consent: in view of v. 12, the word, *gnōmē*, probably also contains its sense of 'opinion', 'judgement'.

15
for ever: again, Paul uses deliberate ambiguity. Onesimus is to return to his master's charge – at least for the moment; though, if the latter is at all sensitive to Paul's expressed needs, he will soon send him back to Paul for as long as he needs him. But in another sense, whether Onesimus stays with his master or goes back to Paul, he will be eternally bound with his master – in their common Christian discipleship.

16
There is a tendency to read a verse like Col. 3¹¹ as if it represented a glorious assertion of new values which all early Christians accepted. This part of *Philemon* shows that it is more likely to be an example of Paul's special clarity than a commonplace of early Church opinion. He cannot take for granted any reversal of ordinary social ethics, in the shape of the immediate emancipation of the slave (cf. pp. 212ff.).

17
partner: koinōnos, related to the word which is translated *sharing* in v. 6, and more commonly *fellowship*. It is an important pauline word for expressing the new common life into which Christians come and which outweighs all differences among them.

This relationship, which already exists between Paul and the master, now also embraces the slave. But, as v. 19 shows, the master and the slave also have in common another aspect of their relationship with Paul: both are his converts.

19
with my own hand: we cannot tell whether this refers to the whole letter or just to this concluding passage. Cf. p. 222.

20
I want some benefit: i.e. 'I want to get something out of you in return for all I have done for you – especially as I offer to repay any sum which Onesimus owes.' The verb is related to the adjective which is the name of the slave, and there may be an intentional pun: what he wants to

get out of the master is Onesimus himself; he wishes to be able to use the Useful One.

21

obedience: cf. v. 8. Paul returns firmly to the apostle's role. As in *Colossians* there comes a moment when delicate phrases, with their double reference, are replaced by frank speaking.

do even more than I say: Paul must be hinting that in addition to the reception of Onesimus in Christian love and then his return to Paul for further service to him, he would like his master to grant him his freedom. It is true that Col. $3^{22}-4^1$ (see pp. 213f.) makes no such recommendation as a general rule, nor does any other New Testament passage. This is surprising from many points of view, at first sight, and we have discussed the question in the pages referred to above. It might have been expected that the fact that the Jewish Law requires the release of a Jew's slaves of his own race after six years' service (Deut. 15^{12-18}) would have found some echo in the teaching given to the *new* Israel, the Church, even at this early date. But this is not so. Apparently, in the tight-knit Christian communities it was felt that shared Christian status made it unnecessary to take steps to remove social distinctions; one wonders whether Christian slaves would have agreed. See on v. 16.

23ff.   CLOSING GREETINGS

All these persons are mentioned also in the greetings at the end of *Colossians.*

25

For the concluding greeting, see on Phil. 4^{23}, p. 116.

The Letter to
the Ephesians

Introduction

We come to *Ephesians* last in this volume, out of its biblical order. We have left it to the last because it is in every way a special case. It has the general appearance of a letter, but most of its material is more suitable to a sermon or treatise. It claims pauline authorship, but there are many grounds for thinking that it comes neither from his hand nor even from his life-time. It is headed 'To the Ephesians', and has been so from the days of our oldest manuscripts, yet its destination is far from certain; Marcion in the second century knew it as 'To the Laodiceans', and the best ancient copies omit the word *in Ephesus* in the first verse. It is, for the most part, pauline in vocabulary (though with qualifications), yet often oddly unpauline (or, better, 'off-pauline') in teaching. Speaking Paul's language, it lacks all his passion and irony. Yet it shows closer dependence upon the letters of Paul, above all *Colossians*, then Paul ever does himself. The study of *Ephesians* therefore bristles with problems, every one of them formidable. For that reason we have isolated it from the other epistles for separate treatment.

There is one question which, if it could find an answer, would immediately help to solve most of our problems. That is, did Paul write this book or not? Does it bear the marks of his style and thought? If the answer is Yes, then we can try and see how his ideas have arrived at the shape they bear in *Ephesians*. We can recognize that in this work we possess an example of formal and rhetorical writing by Paul to put alongside his other more occasional works. We are in a position to know the approximate date and narrow down the circumstances of composition. If the answer is No, then we turn to a different range of considerations. We know that in *Ephesians* we have the work of an inspired and able pauline disciple. We can see how far he has maintained, how far developed, how far misunderstood, the thought of his master. We can try and fit him into what we know from other sources (little enough, it is true) about the life and thought of the post-pauline years. We can imagine circumstances which may have led to the composing of the work in this form. The question of authorship then seems to be the key. It is not surprising that it has received more attention than any other.* Unfortunately, it has led to no consensus of expert opinion. Argument answers argument without clear outcome.

Where direct assault fails, indirect attack may succeed. Investigation of style, vocabulary, and thought proves inconclusive; but it may be possible to find enough hints in the epistle itself to enable us to form some idea of its purpose and its setting in the life of the early Church. What situation does it presuppose? What questions is it concerned to answer? Then: do these belong to the life-time of Paul or could they only have arisen in later times? In recent years attention has concentrated on this approach, and a number of works, mostly brief articles, have appeared.† So far they have pointed to more of a common mind than the former inquiry. On the whole they tell in favour of a late first-century date and so against the authorship of Paul.

Notice that the two methods of approach are quite different. In the first case, an already known pauline yardstick is used for the measuring of *Ephesians*. That is, work begins from the undoubted epistles, from which we can tell what Paul thinks and how he writes. *Ephesians* must then fit the pattern – or not. In the second case, however, *Ephesians* is, at least initially, allowed to speak for itself. Then, when it comes to be compared with other works, we place it alongside not only the undoubted letters of Paul, but the whole of early Christian literature, in the New Testament and outside it. And not only Christian literature, but also the Jewish and pagan writings of the time which contain comparable ideas and forms.

Ephesians is different – in its contents, in the degree of uncertainty about its origin and purpose, and in the approach which it demands. We recognize that none of the questions raised by this writing can

* See especially the two major works, E. Percy, *Die Probleme der Kolosser- und Epheserbriefe* (Lund, 1946), and C. L. Mitton, *The Epistle to the Ephesians* (Oxford, 1951), the former affirming, the latter denying pauline authorship. See also Mitton in Ex.T., (1956), pp. 195ff.

† See especially: H. Chadwick, *Die Absicht des Epheserbriefes*, in Z.N.W. (1960), pp. 145ff.; E. Käsemann on 'Ephesians and Acts' in ed. Keck and Martyn, *Studies in Luke-Acts* (London, 1968); J. C. Kirby, *Ephesians, Baptism and Pentecost* (London, 1968); R. P. Martin, 'An Epistle in Search of a Life-Setting' (which contains a most useful survey of recent research), in Ex.T., 79 (1968), pp. 296ff.

be regarded as settled. Nevertheless it is impossible not to adopt a position, even if only for the sake of argument. We speak in this commentary, therefore, without too much prejudice, not of Paul, but of 'the writer'; and we try to see how the interpretation of his work goes if he is taken to be a Christian leader of something between thirty and fifty years after Paul's death in the sixties of the first century. Much of *Ephesians* makes good sense in the light of what little we know of the circumstances of those years, and it is often better sense than the assumption of pauline authorship will allow.

But we must show how such a stance is reached, and so turn to particular questions.

THE CONTENTS OF EPHESIANS

We ought first to provide a guide to the contents of the work and discuss some of the uncertainties which arise even in dealing with this seemingly straightforward matter.

At first sight *Ephesians* is a letter just as Paul's other writings are letters. It has roughly the same sort of opening and closing greetings. It follows the opening with a thanksgiving to God. It devotes the first part of the work to mainly doctrinal material and goes on to mainly ethical and hortatory material. Like the other letters dealt with in this volume, it mentions Paul's imprisonment (3^1; 4^1; 6^{20}). It says something about the way the letter is to reach its destination and shows personal concern with its readers ($6^{21f.}$). In all these ways it is at one with Paul's other works. Is there any more to be said?

As we describe the contents in more detail, it will soon be evident that there is. *Ephesians* divides into two; three chapters in each half. The first half is more doctrinal, the second more concerned with questions of morals. But the division is far from absolute. More than in the other epistles, doctrinal teaching is thoroughly mingled with ethical, so that the second half (with the exception of 6^{1-9}) is less distinctive than the rough division implies. To put the same point in other terms, *Ephesians* is much more homogeneous than perhaps any of Paul's writings. This homogeneity applies not only to the form of the material, but also to the theme. A single motif embraces almost the whole of *Ephesians* – the unity which Christ has brought about: between heaven and earth, Jew and Gentile, man and woman, and above all, mankind and God, a unity made visible in Christ's union with his Church.

In the first half the greeting is immediately followed by a passage corresponding to the Thanksgiving in other epistles. It has two notable features. First, like only *2 Corinthians* among the undoubted pauline works, it is cast in the shape of a Jewish Blessing or *berakah*, opening with the form 'Blessed be God who . . .' (see p. 259); unlike *2 Corinthians*, however, *Ephesians* has a thanksgiving passage in addition (1[16ff.]), though, despite its form, its content is largely intercession (vv. 17[ff.]). Second, it is very hard in the case of *Ephesians* to tell where the *berakah* ends. Perhaps it can most naturally be taken as running from v. 3 to v. 14, but its solemn rhetorical style is maintained at least up to the end of chapter 3 and in several parts of the second half. Some scholars therefore consider that the writer thought of this form continuing to the end of chapter 3.

Those who think this (notably J. C. Kirby, op. cit.) generally believe, however, that the writer was using a *berakah* which already existed (as a sermon or a form of prayer, perhaps for use in baptism) and was adapting it for a work which bore the shape of a letter. Thus Kirby believes that the more personal (using 'I') parts of these chapters (1[15-23]; 3[1-13]) were inserted at this stage. This view is not easy to verify. But if there is anything in it, it helps to give substance to the feeling that this work is essentially different from the other works ascribed to Paul, in that the solemn opening thanksgiving is not, as it usually is, simply an introductory paragraph. Others prefer to see in ch. 1–3 a series of liturgical units which the writer has woven into epistolary form – a view which again takes account of the 'sameness' of these chapters.* (In this matter, *Ephesians* merits comparison with *1 Peter*, see J. Coutts, N.T.S., 3, pp. 115ff.)

Whatever weight we give to these suggestions, in describing *Ephesians* as it stands, it is fair to see the Blessing in 1[3-14] as praise of God for his whole redeeming act done through Christ, in its past, present and future aspects. In the rest of the chapter the writer prays for the full realization by the believers of the greatness of this work. In chapter 2 he describes its fruits, first in terms of the salvation of man from sin into his new relationship with God (vv. 1–10), then in terms of the bringing together of Jew and Gentile in the Church which centres on Christ (vv. 11–22). This aspect of Christ's uniting

* cf. G. Schille in T.L.Z. (1957), pp. 326ff.

work continues to hold the stage in ch. 3. For this writer it is the heart of the gospel message. In vv. 1–13, Paul's own share in it is outlined: he was the agent and servant of this new harmony. The chapter ends with another prayer for the realization of the universal blessing and a doxology.

In ch. 4, the tone turns to one of exhortation, but the theme is still unity. God has established unity in every aspect of the Christians' life, and has provided the Church's ministry to establish and guard it; then let the work be continued and full Christian maturity, 'growing up into Christ', be worked for and achieved. For this to be so, the moral rigour of the Christian life has to be accepted. The old pagan ways and the new life, characterized by truth and love, are utterly incompatible (4^{17}–5^2). Then there are more particular moral matters to be taken care of; sexual licence of all kinds and degrees is to be shunned – that is the special weakness of the Gentile way of life. Avoiding such dangers, Christians are to be heartened by the fellow-ship of their meetings together (5^{3-20}).

The Christian household too is to reflect the central facts of the gospel, especially the union (again that theme) between Christ and his Church. The relationship between husband and wife is the earthly mirror of that union. This is no mere analogy, but a profound truth, somehow bound up with the whole fabric of things (5^{21-33}). Other aspects of family life must also be conducted in a fitting manner; the behaviour of children and parents, slaves and masters.

Finally, the Christian is urged to see his life as a constant battle against the evil powers of the universe. In the heavens they are now under Christ's lordship, but they are still most active in wickedness in this world. In practical terms this means the bold proclamation of the gospel to all men, in reliance upon the all-sufficient gifts of God (6^{10-20}).

The letter concludes with a brief note about the despatch of the letter, and a farewell.

The brief note ($6^{21f.}$) raises a question, simply because it is (unlike most other reflections of *Colossians* in this writing) an almost word for word reproduction of its parallel, Col. $4^{7f.}$, and because, with its circumstantial detail, it stands in such sharp contrast to the rest of *Ephesians*. If *Ephesians* is pauline it causes little difficulty; Tychicus was the deliverer of this general letter to (probably) a group of churches in Asia Minor, and he also carried a special letter to Colossae which lay on his route. But if *Ephesians* is not pauline, then these verses may be explained in a variety of ways, and a decision (if decision be possible) will not depend on them alone but on the view taken of the work as a whole. The simplest explanation is that they were inserted by a later scribe, who wanted to add to the 'paulineness' of the work, presumably to increase its authority. But no manuscript supports such a view. If it happened, it happened early. If the writer himself included these verses, our difficulty is to know what was in his mind. Was it, to be blunt, an attempt to deceive his readers into thinking this was a work of Paul's? Like the writer of the Pastoral Epistles in his similar personal passages, he is in that case claiming not merely Paul's mantle but his flesh and bones. We need to remember that if this were so, we should be wrong to judge him by our conceptions of fraudulence. It may be that he felt such a crisis of authority to be facing the Church that desperate measures (and this measure probably seemed less desperate than it would to us) were justified to keep the ship afloat; only the voice of Paul sufficed. Let it then ring out in tones as authentic as could be contrived. (On this, see section below.)

Or do we have here simply a piece of verisimilitude, inserted in no spirit of deception, but only to add to the likeness of *Ephesians* to the works of the Paul of history? Nobody was taken in; nobody was meant to be taken in. A respected successor of Paul spoke with his master's voice and that voice was heard. Between these possibilities there is now no chance of making a final choice; the evidence is quite insufficient.

THE DECEPTIVENESS OF EPHESIANS

That a deeply Christian work should be issued (and then canonized) as the work of Paul the apostle, when it may well not be his composition at all, seems at first sight incongruous and even shocking. This hurdle, however, is more easily jumped than most. In the ancient world, among Jews, Greeks, Romans, and Christians, the practice of pseudonymous writing was both common and acceptable. It was a way of claiming the patronage of a departed leader, of assuming his mantle. This is not to say that it was always done with what we should call 'honesty'. Often indeed it was a weapon in the 'power game'. But it was a weapon whose use was not questioned in principle, though particular instances of it might be attacked. We ought not to assume that commonly accepted definitions of honesty remain unchanging through the centuries.

In early Christian circles there was one factor which even intensi-fied the tendency to write under the name of others. This was the well-attested claim to be inspired by the Holy Spirit, cf. I Cor. 2$^{10\mathrm{ff.}}$; Rev. 1^{10}; John 14^{26}; 16^{13}. To look no further, the whole vast apocry-phal literature (see Hennecke, I-II), mainly from Gnostic sects of the second century and later, shows that just off the main stream of Christ-ianity there was a plethora of writing put out under the name of one of the apostles or other early leaders. It was not necessarily just a calculated way of asserting authority and so winning a hearing. It could also be a perfectly sincere product of 'inspiration' – with all the dangers of that notoriously subjective quality, best tested against other criteria.* Feeling himself assured by the Spirit, the writer had no need to hesitate in producing 'apostolic' words to the churches of his time.

Within the New Testament a number of books are either certainly or probably pseudonymous, including some or all of the Gospels and the Pastoral Epistles. Many would say that all were, apart from the central epistles of Paul. There is then nothing outlandish or out-rageous in suggesting that *Ephesians* may come into this category.

But why should we suppose that it does? The features which point in this direction do so with varying degrees of assurance.

SIGNS OF POST-PAULINE DATE

The most positive indications that *Ephesians* comes from the Church of the later rather than the mid-first century are its attitude to Judaism and its picture of the Church's leaders.

It is clear from 2$^{11-22}$ that the work is addressed to Gentile Christ-ians. But it is also clear that their membership of the Church, alongside Jewish Christians, is no longer something to be aggressively asserted; it is rather serenely and thankfully accepted. We have no evidence that this state of affairs had been reached in the lifetime of Paul. The evidence points the other way. The matter is, it is true, complicated

* K. Aland in *The Authorship and Integrity of the New Testament* (London, 1965), also published in J.T.S., 12 (1961); and J. C. Fenton, *Theology*, 58 (1955), pp. 51ff.

by our estimate of the *Acts of the Apostles*. Opinions differ whether that book overdraws its picture of the Church's harmony in the fifties of the first century. If so, then it does nothing to support a pauline date for *Ephesians*.

For this work the Church is a firmly established community, and can look back to founding fathers – the *apostles and prophets* (2^{20}; 3^4). This implies consciousness of a history. The first generation can already be seen as venerable; and Paul himself, in whose name the author writes, appears in this light. Moreover, the organized structure of the Church has a primacy of value in the eyes of the writer of *Ephesians* which again looks as if it belongs to a period later than Paul's. Thus the Church's ministers are the chief fruit of the Lord's exaltation (4^{8-12}). No longer, as in 1 Corinthians 12, is it a question of a whole rich flowering of spiritual gifts in the Church, such that, so it seems, everybody had an active role. Now there are set orders, almost a clergy, who can hardly include the whole body of the faithful. The laity seem to have subsided a little into passivity.

None of these features demands the view we have taken. It is possible to argue that in a work which is apparently addressed in a general way to a number of congregations Paul would naturally emphasize the official elements in the Church; possibly to argue also that he would detach himself from the hurly-burly of fending off Jewish Christians (and Jews) who resented the free influx of Gentiles; possible finally that he would calmly regard the apostles and inspired preachers as fundamental to the Church's life and the key figures in the possession of the Church's revelation. But it is hard to deny that all these features fit more appropriately into the circumstances of a later time.

SIGNS OF UN-PAULINE TEACHING

Because *Ephesians* is so chock-a-block with echoes of the undoubted writings of Paul, it is easy to suppose that not only the words but also the ideas are in line with them. Whatever the writer's intention this is so far from being the case, sometimes at quite crucial points, that it seems to many impossible that Paul and this writer are one. This is not an easy matter because in the undoubtedly authentic epistles, Paul does not always sing the same tune. It is not so much that he is inconsistent with himself as that he adopts varied approaches and postures, giving a central place in one work to ideas which find no place at all in another. But the variations in *Ephesians* are not of this kind. It is a matter of the writer's seizing upon pauline words and phrases, then moving them, often ever so slightly, in such a way as to make them mean quite unpauline things. The commentary constantly refers to cases of this. We mention now only a few of the more striking examples. Here again it is a matter of 'hunch' or fine judgement rather than proof.

One of Paul's central tenets is the believer's *incorporation* into Christ. It is not our concern here to say what this idea means or where it originated. What is undeniable is that it is one of Paul's chief ways of thinking of the Christian's relationship with his Lord. It is expressed most commonly by the phrase *in Christ*, also by more extended images like the body of Christ (Rom. 12 & 1 Cor. 12) or the temple (1 Cor. 3[16]). It is what Albert Schweitzer called Paul's 'Christ mysticism'. Though this language cannot be pressed to signify a total identification of Christ and the believer in all ways, yet it tends strongly in this direction. For example, the idea of being a member of the body of Christ is usually put in such a way that Christ is seen as the whole organism and his people as incorporated into him. Precisely this feature gives the language its intensity and power. It is true that in 1 Cor. 11[1ff.], for the purposes of his argument there, Paul uses a different image: Christ is the 'head' of the individual (male) believer. (But the image is not pressed – the believer is not compared to Christ's torso, for example – and indeed 'head' may be closer to our ordinary usage, as when we speak of the head of a school or firm without any vivid sense of the 'body image' in mind.) In *Ephesians*, however, we find a high degree of spiritual intensity in the use of this language combined with the preserving of a clear distinction between Christ and his people. Christ's headship is referred to several times (1[22]; 4[15]; 5[23]), but it expresses not only his intimacy with his people and his role as source of their life, but also his distinctness from them. Other passages share this tendency and are noted in the commentary. In other words, the 'mysticism' is, in this respect, less thorough-going, the tendency to identification is carried less far. Moreover, the phrases *in Christ*, or *in the Lord*, generally used elsewhere in an intensive sense, are here both unusually common and yet much weakened in sense; *in Christ* mostly means little more than 'through Christ's agency'. (See J. A. Allan, N.T.S., 5, pp. 54ff.) However, important as this contrast is, it should not be treated as absolute; examples can be quoted against it, e.g. Eph. 3¹⁷ in one direction, 1 Cor. 15²³ in the other.

Not unrelated to this sense of the distinctness of the Christian body from Christ the head, is our writer's way of speaking of the Church – the *ekklēsia*. Always he sees it as a whole, a universal society, with an eternal and cosmic destiny (1²²f.; 5²⁷). Only here in the works ascribed to Paul is the Church seen as corporately playing such a lofty role – as the body for which Christ has received universal lordship (1²²), as the channel for conveying God's wisdom to the cosmic powers (3¹⁰), as the place where perpetual glory is given to God (3²¹). Only here in the pauline epistles is the word used exclusively for the universal as against the local Church. All this goes beyond the usage of *Colossians* (cf. Col. 4¹⁵f. as against 1¹⁸, ²⁴). There the universal Church is recognized but is not the subject of any developed doctrine. It is of course possible to argue that in a work which like *Ephesians* is general in its matter and its address such development is natural. Neither view positively imposes itself.

We have already said that the softening in *Ephesians* of the pauline doctrine of incorporation into Christ does not in the least mean a slackening of spiritual intensity – quite the contrary. If that quality is to be measured by awareness of the transcendent majesty of God and sense of the 'other world' (however envisaged), then *Ephesians* is unsurpassed in the whole of the New Testament. Time and again it speaks of the cosmic scale of God's power and of his saving work through Christ, so often indeed that to give full references would be to list almost every section (but see especially 1¹⁸ff.; 3⁹f.; 3²⁰f.). Paul himself does not in the least lack this outlook, but it is so much more strongly evident here that it gives a different cast to the whole work. It is easy to put this down to the fact that this is not really a letter but a work written in the idiom of liturgy or of preaching (much less distinct in the early Church than later). Nevertheless it is a difference from Paul which needs to be noted and explained.

For this writing, the union of Gentiles with Jews in the Church is the heart of the gospel (2¹¹–3⁶). This is seen neither as their entry into Israel (after the manner of proselytes in Judaism) nor as the discarding of Israel's age-long heritage, but as the creation in Christ of a new people of God – a third entity, resting however on the promises to Israel, whose place she has inherited. In two respects this differs from the characteristic viewpoint of Paul. First, Paul did not look at Jew-Gentile relations from this angle. For him the situation chiefly presented itself as posing an agonizing question: how Israel's rejection of Jesus, her Messiah, was to be reconciled with God's promises to her (cf. p. 286). Second, in Paul's view, the heart of Christ's reconciling work was not the breaking of barriers between Jew and Gentile as in *Ephesians*, but the breaking of the barriers between man (Jew and Gentile alike) and God. It is true that *Ephesians* does not lack this aspect ($2^{1-10,16}$), and also mentions other results of Christ's work; for example, the subjection of the cosmic powers to his control ($1^{21ff.}$), and the provision of the Church's ministry (4^{11}). But it is hard to imagine Paul's ever writing a deeply considered utterance such as this, which proportioned things in this way.

Other matters are more debatable. *Ephesians* (if G. B. Caird's view of 4^9, see page 310, is correct) has no doctrine of the pre-existence of Christ, except perhaps in 1^4; yet this is a doctrine prominent in the closely related *Colossians*, as well as elsewhere in Paul's writings. If *Ephesians* were by Paul, it is at least worth remarking that in a work that must have been written at the same time as *Colossians*, dependence upon this aspect of the Jewish tradition of teaching about Wisdom (see p. 166) is so meagre.

Similarly, though the Christian's future hope is lively enough here ($1^{13f.}$, $18f.$), it does seem to have lost the freshness which it has in Paul. The End has receded a little from view. Events hitherto seen as imminent have turned into a magnificent backcloth before which the Church on earth conducts her existence. Christian parents can be counselled to settle down to the education of their children (6^4). Christian marriage has lost that transience (in view of an End expected speedily) which led Paul to such carefully balanced advice in 1 Cor. 7. It has become a settled institution and the subject of profound theological reflexion ($5^{22ff.}$). Most important of all, the Church is already united to Christ, as wife to husband, and lives to grow towards him (4^{15}) rather than to await his return with longing (contrast Phil. 3^{20}; Rev. 22^{17}).

Finally, certain important pauline words are either missing or used differently. There is no reference at all to justification, though if Paul had written 2^{1-10} he would hardly have avoided it. Instead the verb *to save* receives an uncharacteristic use (see p. 283). The Jewish Law, as a principle of life, hardly comes on the scene, except in 2^{15}

INTRODUCTION

(which is very close to Col. 2¹⁴). The words *mystērion* and *oikonomia*
seem to be used in senses other than those found in authentic Paul.
The difficulty is that authentic Paul himself uses his key words (e.g.
faith, law) in quite different senses within a few verses.

SIGNS OF PAULINE CONNEXIONS

Almost every verse in *Ephesians* has a parallel – sometimes close,
sometimes tenuous – at some point in the undoubted writings of
Paul. Only very occasionally does it amount to reproduction (e.g.
5¹⁹; 6²¹f.). By far the largest number of correspondences, including
the cases of virtual identity, is with *Colossians*, in which nearly half the
verses of *Ephesians* find a verbal parallel. But there are links with every
one of the authentic epistles, though in the case of *2 Thessalonians* it is
hard to claim more than echoes.

In many cases the relationship between the passage in *Ephesians* and
its parallel elsewhere is intriguing. Actual quotation runs for a mere
word or two, yet the similarity between the passages as a whole is too
close to be ascribed to the freely evolving mind of Paul. Whether
the writer was Paul or not, it looks as if he either had copies of the
other epistles before him, or had soaked himself in them. He has not
been a slavish imitator – or a careless one, for though his adaptations
are often slight (the shifting or inserting of a word or two), they
nearly always suffice to move a pauline statement into line with the
distinctive viewpoint of *Ephesians*. (See, e.g. Col. 3¹⁸ in relation to
Eph. 5²¹f., to take a simple instance, p. 332.) It is impossible to say
how conscious such adapting was. That it was both thorough and
on the whole consistent is clear.

To account for these phenomena, we must regard the writer as
having thought in terms of a 'pauline corpus' of letters, and even in
terms of 'paulinism', both notions which it is hard to believe Paul
himself ever entertained. He wrote to those to whom he had something to say, and that, as far as we know, was that. The bringing
together of his letters, and the process which led to their acceptance
as authoritative documents belongs to the time after his death,
probably towards the end of the first century.

The only views which succeed in making pauline authorship
credible, while taking account of this 'super-paulinity' of *Ephesians*,
are those which regard it as a conscious attempt by Paul either to

sum up the quintessence of his faith, or (better) to gather together some of his prayers and other liturgical compositions made over a long period of years. Both however founder on the fact (see the section above) that some of the teaching and attitudes seem positively un-pauline; the second, also, on the work's closeness of texture.

We have so far done no more than mention the special relationship of *Ephesians* with *Colossians*. In the introduction to the commentary on *Colossians*, we have already discussed its nature and implications, and given an account of some of the theories propounded to explain it (pp. 124ff., 138). Here we mention other aspects. In the first place, apart from the small number of virtually identical passages, the way in which *Ephesians* uses *Colossians* is not greatly different from the way in which it uses the other epistles – except in sheer quantity. There is the same failure to quote more than a few words at a time, the same tendency to make minor changes, the same adaptation to the viewpoint of *Ephesians*. The quantity of similarity constitutes the special point of interest and demands explanation. Why the writer of *Ephesians* (supposing him not to be Paul) found *Colossians* of particular value, we have no means of knowing. But we may suspect that his reasons were circumstantial rather than doctrinal, for despite similarities the focus of interest in the two writings is not the same. *Colossians* is primarily concerned to establish the true doctrine of Christ's person and his lordship over the cosmic powers, *Ephesians* with the Church, his body. (For a possible situation which made *Colossians* precious to this writer, see p. 124.)

Other features of this relationship call for attention. Though there is much to be said for the view that our writer had the epistles actually before him, *Colossians* in particular, and was not merely working from memory, it has to be said that there is nothing systematic about his procedure. He uses a considerable proportion of *Colossians* (about a third) at some point in his work, but nowhere does he follow it in order for very long. For example, in the opening Blessing the following verses of *Colossians* come into comparison: 3^{12}; 1^{22}; $1^{13f.}$; 1^{20}; 1^{14}; 1^{9}; 1^{27}; 1^{25}; 1^{20}; 1^{12}; 1^{5}; 1^{12}; 1^{14}. (For a complete table of all the pauline parallels and allusions, see E. J. Goodspeed, *The Key to Ephesians* (Chicago, 1956).) His desire to use *Colossians* is subordinated strictly to his own plan. *Colossians* may give him words and phrases, but it does not give him his sequence of ideas (just as it does not give him, to any great degree, the ideas themselves). On the other hand there is no part of *Ephesians* which lacks the influence of *Colossians*. In Goodspeed's lay-out, only about thirty verses fail to yield at least an allusion to *Colossians*, and the only substantial passages without parallels are 4^{4-12} & 5^{26-32} (plus perhaps 2^{6-9}). As might be expected it is often hard to distinguish between plausibly deliberate parallels and fortuitous echoes.

In attempting an evaluation of the relationship of *Ephesians* and *Colossians*, it is hard to avoid the conclusion that they cannot be from the same pen. One of them may be pauline (we believe that *Colossians* is); neither of them may be pauline; that both are pauline is scarcely credible. If Paul wrote either of them, he could hardly have written the other as soon afterwards as the close relationship makes most likely (especially in view of $6^{2\,\mathrm{of.}}$), using almost identical phrases and words to express significantly different ideas. It is most unlikely that Paul kept copies of his letters, so that the view that he was referring to his own work written some time in the past has little to commend it. And even then the shifts in meaning, understandable in an imitator, are improbable in the same author.

Finally, under the heading of 'pauline connexions', there are considerations of style. It is on these questions that the massive works of Percy and Mitton (see above, p. 236) chiefly dwelt. The most striking stylistic features of *Ephesians* are the use of pairs (or trios) of synonyms (e.g. 1^{19}; 2^{14}; 6^{18}); of genitival phrases (*passim*, but e.g. I, $5, 6, 9, 10$); of very long sentences, especially 1^{3-14}; of cognate verb and noun (e.g. 1^{23}; 3^{19} *plērōma-plēroō*; 1^{21} *onoma-onomazō*; 2^4 *agapē-agapaō*). In none of these matters can it be said that parallels are lacking in genuine Paul (Percy's case largely rests on producing them) but always they are more numerous in *Ephesians*. That being admitted the discussion shifts. Does the elevated style of *Ephesians* adequately account for their increased use, with Paul as the author, or must it be taken as itself evidence of a different author? Stalemate on this question has been avoided through work such as that of K. G. Kuhn (see N.T.S., 7, pp. 334ff., on 'Ephesians in the light of the Qumran texts'). He points out that the increased quantity of the features to which we have referred can be seen as marking not merely a more elevated style (which a special purpose might adequately explain) but also a more Semitic style; Semitic syntactical features are four times as prominent here as in the rest of the pauline corpus of letters. For example, the long sentences are not nicely constructed Greek periods but loosely linked series of clauses and phrases such as are found in Jewish literature. Clearly this raises more acutely the question of authorship, and if it is decided that the writer is other than Paul, provides a useful datum for the search for his identity.

On the question of vocabulary: not only are certain important pauline words rare or lacking (see above p. 245), but sometimes a non-pauline alternative is preferred to Paul's usual word (e.g. the word for 'heaven' is *epourania* not the usual *ouranoi*). Also, *Ephesians* has the unusually high number, among 'pauline' epistles, of about ninety words not used in undoubted Paul. Some of these words are characteristic of Christian literature at the end of the first century (e.g. 'the beloved' as a title for Christ, 1[6]). This criterion, however, is a tool of most uncertain accuracy, especially in view of the distinctive nature of *Ephesians*. More objectively, computer tests are generally held to tell against pauline authorship (see p. 39).

THE WRITER AND HIS AIM

We turn to a constructive statement of the nature and purpose of *Ephesians* – and therefore, inevitably, to a degree of speculation. On the question of authorship, while we have discovered little in the way of decisive argument, we have found ourselves more and more taking the position that the writer is unlikely to have been Paul. The strongest arguments which point in this direction are not concerned with style or vocabulary but with various features of thought and content, which are most appropriate to the last years of the first century, when the pauline corpus had been collected and Paul's name was already, in certain churches at least, authoritative. *1 Clement* (*c.* A.D. 96) shows something of this feeling in existence in Rome (E.C.W., p. 25). (Alleged allusion to *Ephesians* in that writing is confined to a passage, ch. 46, whose parallel, Eph. 4[4–6], may well depend on an older liturgical formula.)

Such a sense of Paul's authority would most naturally be expected in the churches of Asia Minor, where he had laid deep foundations, where, by the early years of the second century, there were more churches than anywhere else, and where there was so much ferment of speculative religion that an appeal to authority in the cause of unity may already have been necessary. Both Marcion's description of

Ephesians as 'To the Laodiceans' and its customary title connect it with that area and we have no reason to doubt that this is correct – as far as it goes.

Further precision is more problematical. As we have seen (above p. 235) and as the detailed commentary will show (p. 257), the address in 1^1 (to the church *in Ephesus*) is unlikely to be original. The best solution to the problem of that verse, with its awkward Greek, may well be one that goes back to Archbishop Ussher, 1654, viz. that the letter was an encyclical, addressed to a number of the churches of the province of Asia, in whose copies, therefore, a blank was left for the insertion of the names. The material in the epistle agrees well with such a suggestion. (See G. Zuntz, *The Text of the Epistles* (London, 1953), pp. 228, 276f.) That a copy remained, without any insertion, at the place of writing, is not surprising. Nor is it surprising that the place of writing was such an important centre of paulinism that the collection of Paul's letters was maintained (perhaps made) there, so that our epistle became attached to it. That the place was Ephesus is at least likely, and is one reasonable explanation for the eventual insertion of *in Ephesus*. The collection contained no letter by Paul to his pre-eminent foundation, the church in Ephesus, and to add this name must have seemed a natural procedure. Though this version came to dominate the manuscript tradition, Marcion may have possessed a copy deriving from the copy originally sent to Laodicea. On the other hand he may simply have made an inference from Col. 4^{16}. It is worth noting that the omission in old manuscripts (pre-fifth century) of *Ephesians* is paralleled in Rom. 1^7 (*in Rome*) – another epistle which seems to have had a complicated history, existing in different versions in different places. (For the suggestion that the influential second century heretic, Marcion, whose devotion to Paul was complete and utter, was responsible for the cutting out of the name from the letters to the two churches which had specially rebuffed him, see T. W. Manson in *the Bulletin of John Rylands Library*, 31, p. 229.)

Whatever the reasons for the confused state of the opening verse, we must now take a wider look at the whole question of the situation from which this work came and which it was designed to meet. It is a question which has not failed to arouse the imagination as well as the learning of biblical scholars.

By far the most influential, thoroughgoing, and attractive solution

is that proposed by E. J. Goodspeed and John Knox, which we outlined in introducing *Colossians* and *Philemon* (see pp. 124ff.). The suggestion is that *Ephesians* was written to be the preface to the pauline
corpus, collected at Ephesus in the later years of the first century.
Hence its generalized character and hence its nature as the quintessence of paulinism. It is a work of *pietas* and of introduction. The
chief objection to this suggestion is that it is not altogether easy to see
why a pseudo-pauline letter should be a suitable means for carrying
out this task. Moreover, it is not clear that such a definition adequately
describes, let alone exhausts, the apparent purpose of *Ephesians*.
And none of the early manuscripts places *Ephesians* first in its pauline
collection, even though they all vary a certain amount in their order.
Knox finds a way of explaining this, but it has been by no means
universally accepted (see J. Knox, *Philemon Among the Letters of Paul*
(London, 1960), pp. 63ff. and C. H. Buck, 'The Early Order of the
Pauline Corpus', in J.B.L., 58, pp. 351ff.).

The further suggestion that the writer of *Ephesians* was Onesimus,
the ex-slave, identified with Onesimus, bishop of Ephesus in the time
of Ignatius (see p. 124), meets the great hazard that *Ephesians* is the
work of a strongly Semitic as well as a strongly pauline mind. Kuhn
(op. cit.) has shown how close are the similarities of *Ephesians* both
in language and in thought with the writings found at Qumran.
Ephesians is more, not less, Jewish than Paul. The twin facts (*a*) that
our writer was of profoundly Jewish mentality and (*b*) that he so
entirely welcomed the Gentiles' acceptance into the Church are
not easy to hold together. At this point perhaps the hesitant inquirer
comes nearest to plumping for pauline authorship, whatever the
difficulties. Certainly, if the writer was a Jewish Christian, he had
courageously accepted the pauline width of mind and was ready to
apply it in the altered circumstances of the post-pauline generation.
Onesimus is not entirely ruled out; we do not know for certain that
he was a Gentile not a Jewish slave, nor is it impossible that he schooled
himself in the language and traditions of Israel.

Though the Goodspeed–Knox theories have been more influential
than others (they have been in circulation for over thirty years), they
do not stand alone. J. C. Kirby, for example, taking account of the
strong liturgical tone of *Ephesians* and its very possible baptismal
associations (cf. 2^1; 5$^{8, 14}$), sees it as constructed on the basis of the
prayer-tradition of the church in Ephesus, which regarded itself as a

headquarters of the pauline tradition (op. cit., pp. 165ff.). R. P. Martin emphasizes its affinities with the viewpoint of *Acts* – concern for the unity of the Church as a Jew-Gentile community, stress on the apostolate as the centre of authority, and 'awareness that the Church has a future on earth *sine die*' (op. cit., p. 300). See also Käsemann (op. cit., see above p. 236).

One further factor remains to be noted. *Ephesians* shares with *Colossians* (and, to a degree, with *1 Corinthians* and *Galatians*) an outlook on the world which is best described as mythological. The writer sees the centre of gravity of the universe as being *in the heavenly places*, which are filled with a population of good and evil angelic powers, who sway the affairs of men (1^{21}; 6^{12}). He sees Christ as a cosmic figure, related in a mysterious union with those who adhere to him so that their life and his interpenetrate ($1^{22f.}$; $4^{15f.}$; 5^{23-32}). This outlook is not assumed by the writer as a gesture of sympathy towards those he addresses; it is natural to him – for him, it is 'the way things are'. Yet he christianizes it resolutely. His non-Christian contemporaries, for whom also this was normal religious thinking, delighted in the complexities of their systems. The more mystery was piled upon mystery, the more luxuriant the speculation, the more widely diffused the divine essence, and the more windows they opened upon 'cosmic truth', the more deeply satisfied they felt. But for our writer, as for Paul in *Colossians*, the pull is in the opposite direction. All centres on Christ. He alone holds the authority of God and exercises true lordship. So far *Colossians* and *Ephesians* are at one. But now they divide. In the former, the emphasis is all on Christ's significance in relation to the cosmic powers and their work; Paul is meeting threats to the Christian message at that central point. In *Ephesians*, the pressure-point is different. It is the universal Church whose title-deeds must be exposed and defended, whose indissoluble unity with Christ must be established, and whose place in God's cosmic scheme must be made clear.

As we have had occasion to say elsewhere in this work, there is no incompatibility at this period between the Jewishness we find in *Ephesians* and this Gnostic thought, which circulated so widely in the Mediterranean world. The Dead Sea Scrolls are evidence enough for that.

Who then was the writer of *Ephesians*? He was first of all a typical religious man of his time, most probably a Jew by upbringing, for he was at home with the Old Testament and with contemporary ways of handling it (see on 4^8, p. 310); at home too in the current religious philosophy, with its passion for speculation, its love of celestial rhetoric, its obsession about salvation. But he was now a Christian who had found in Christ and in the life of the Church a realization of his dreams. They had been transformed partly, and sufficiently, from future hope to present reality ($1^{13f.,\ 18f.}$). Christ's death and triumph had been a new beginning for all men (2^{17}; $3^{9,\ 21}$), opening the way to salvation here and now (2^{4-9}).

He was also a paulinist. Not simply a man who shared his doctrine, but also one conscious of inheriting his authority, and needing to exercise it. He writes indeed as one deeply aware of the venerability of the apostolic office (2^{20}; 4^{11}). And in writing in the name of Paul alone, without mentioning the names of any associates, as was the custom of the Paul of history, he assumes an almost papal eminence on behalf of his master.

What circumstances brought about his work? For we must not commit the error of supposing that he wrote 'in the void'. Even if his times were uneventful, there was still an actual situation from which and to which he spoke. We may assume that he laid special emphasis where others, in his view, laid too little. So we rephrase our question: what tendencies does our writer take pains to counteract? First, he is an *assertive* paulinist. He is therefore opposed to those who underplay Paul's importance. Specifically, he places Paul at the hub of the whole enterprise of uniting Gentiles with Jews in the Church (3^{1-13}). There were, then, others who resented the claim of Paul (now mediated through his heirs) to authority in the Gentile congregations. The *sedes Pauli*, in whatever form, is, for this writer, the focus of authority to which those churches ought to look, regardless, perhaps, of whether they owed their foundation to him or not.

Second, he is a strenuous defender of unity in the Church. There were, therefore, those who were threatening it. To judge from 2^{11-22}, a few of them may have been Jewish Christians reluctant to accept Gentiles into full partnership (if so, they are no longer a serious threat), but many more were Gentile Christians tending to discard their Jewish heritage or ignoring its richness. Both must realize that they are one, on a new basis – Christ himself, who is their *peace*.

Third, he asserts the cosmic dimensions of Christ's power (4^{13-16}) and of the Church's destiny (1^{19-23}; $3^{20f.}$). There were, therefore, those whose horizons were too narrow, who saw Christ as one force among others and the Church as a local, sectarian affair; or who were discouraged by the failure of the Church's mission to match the largeness of her claims.

Finally, he stresses not only the role of Paul, but also of the Church's original and present ministers as a body (2^{20}; 3^5; $4^{11f.}$). There were, therefore, those who resented the authority of their founders and leaders. To our writer, these great ones were a prime guarantee of the Church's identity in time and space and so of her faithfulness to Christ. Without them there was danger of shipwreck.

To make his case it is not unlikely that he relied upon the most solemn elements in the traditions of his church – the words used when it met for worship (cf. 5^{19}). That these words bore a deeply pauline imprint is not surprising in a pauline church, which may have read at least some of his works for years; *Colossians*, for a reason beyond recovery, seems to have been specially treasured by this author. If we are right to see baptismal associations in these words, that too need occasion no surprise, for in the first centuries, baptism, the great sacrament of redemption, had a place in Christian esteem not in the least commensurate with its smallness as a mere event in a person's life. It was an act of once-for-all significance. It was the moment of total transition from darkness to light, death to life; continually recalled, appealed to, and valued.

We cannot here go into full comparisons, but it is evident that in putting the weight on these matters, *Ephesians* shares the world in which *Acts* and the Pastoral Epistles were written. In all these writings we find the same threats being met by the same conservative and protective reactions. They were the Church's chosen way of dealing with her first crisis of authority, when she was called upon to say how truth was to be distinguished from falsehood, authentic Church from breakaway group. Her answer was that Christ himself was her sole basis and that he was truly encountered in the life of the Church in each generation, a life empowered by the Holy Spirit and articulated through the apostles and pastors of whom Paul was the great authentic voice. These works are the first self-conscious utterances of the historic Church.

It is easy in reading the New Testament to be preoccupied with the very earliest days; in reading the Gospels to think of the times of Jesus and ignore the Church of a few decades later which wrote them;

INTRODUCTION

in reading the *Acts of the Apostles* to have in mind the thirties to fifties and forget the circumstances of its composition; easy also in reading Paul to consider only the apostle's lifetime and not the period when the letters were edited, collected, and first valued as a corpus. In other words, for the understanding of the New Testament, we need to have our eyes at least as much on the end of the first century as on its second quarter, at least as much on the second as on the first Christian generation. Once we begin to think in this way, we can see where *Ephesians* fits, and see that it came to birth at a moment crucial both for the formation of the New Testament and for the Church's whole future history.

NOTE ON EPHESUS

Because the connexion of this work with Ephesus is possibly tenuous and at any rate unlikely to be what it appears to be, we say little about the city. It was the capital of the Roman province of Asia, which covered the western part of modern Turkey. It was an important port, a great centre of commerce. It was the home of the cult of Artemis (or Diana), glimpsed in the story told in Acts 19, and her temple was one of the Seven Wonders of the World. The church in this great city was a chief centre of Paul's work and was later the home of the apostle John.

Further Reading

We have referred to the chief books and articles as they were relevant to our discussion, and others are mentioned in the course of the commentary on the text.

The old standard English commentary is that by J. Armitage Robinson, published first in 1903. Others are by E. F. Scott (London, 1930), F. C. Synge (London, 1941), F. W. Beare, in *The Interpreter's Bible*, Vol. 10 (New York, 1953) and G. B. Caird, in the *New Clarendon Bible* (Oxford, 1976). Important foreign language commentaries are those by C. Masson, in French (Neuchatel & Paris, 1953), and, in German, by Martin Dibelius (as revised by D. H. Greeven (Tübingen, 1953)), and, on a much larger scale, by Heinrich Schlier (Düsseldorf, 1963).

On the question of authorship, we have already referred to the two works by Percy and Mitton (see p. 236). A briefer survey of the question will be found in the contributions by D. E. Nineham and J. N. Sanders to *Studies in Ephesians*, ed. F. L. Cross (London, 1956).

On the background and composition of *Ephesians*, the two books by E. J. Goodspeed – *The Meaning of Ephesians* (Chicago, 1933) and *The Key to Ephesians* (Chicago, 1956) – should be read first, as among the earliest attempts to make a new approach to the problem, by way of the circumstances from which the epistle arises. The later work almost duplicates (and abbreviates) the earlier. Both contain a full table of the parallels to *Ephesians* in the other epistles, the former in Greek, the latter in English.

On p. 236 we give a list of the more important recent works which have taken this approach further, with not inconsiderable results.

The Letter of Paul to the Ephesians

1–3   The Thanksgiving

1¹⁻²   THE OPENING GREETING

¹*Paul, an apostle of Christ Jesus by the will of God, to the saints who are also faithful[a] in Christ Jesus:* ²*grace to you and peace from God our Father and the Lord Jesus Christ.*

a Other ancient authorities read *who are at Ephesus and faithful.*

These opening verses play an important part in the attempt to detect the nature and origin of *Ephesians*. So the chief questions which they raise have been discussed in the Introduction (p. 250). Here we comment mainly on matters of detail.

At a casual glance we seem to have before us a typical pauline opening; but a closer look raises doubts. In the first place, the R.S.V. rightly follows the best manuscripts in relegating the address to Ephesus to the margin – it was no part of the original text – and thereby shows *Ephesians* up as an oddity. For no other work of Paul is addressed to Christians in general rather than to a specific congregation. (How and why an address to Ephesus in particular came to stand in the text is a matter for speculation: cf. Introduction, pp. 250ff.)

However, the straightforward impression given by R.S.V. is misleading. Though it renders the best Greek text available, it fails to make clear its strangeness. In Greek, *saints* (='holy(ones)' = *hagiois*) is an adjective used as a noun. It is parallel to *faithful* (= 'faithful (ones)' = *pistois*) and we should expect the two words to be joined simply by 'and'. In fact there also comes between them a participle (translated *who are*), which leads most naturally not merely to another adjective but to something more substantial – for example, 'in such and such a place'. This gives a series of possibilities. Either the original mentioned a place; or, if it was a circular, it left a gap for the insertion of names in the several copies; or simply the Greek was awkward. In the first case, it is hard to see why the name ever dropped out; and this must have happened early for it to be lacking in the oldest manuscripts. In the second case, it is possible to imagine how eventually some copies bore a name, while others lacked one; though we then need to explain why only Ephesus appears in the extant tradition. In the third case, and perhaps in the second, the work of an improving scribe may explain the development.

Another special feature of this greeting is that it comes from Paul alone. In all his genuine letters, except *Romans*, even in the highly personal *Philemon*, Paul associates his friends with himself. In the case of *Romans* he is writing to a church which knows neither him nor, probably, the members of his entourage. If he were writing to Ephesus, a church as well known to him as any, it would be extraordinary for Paul not to mention those with him, unless of course he had been left alone since the writing of *Colossians* (1^1). (Col. 4$^{7f.}$ is duplicated in Eph. 6$^{21f.}$, so that the two writings have the appearance of being written within days of each other). On the assumption of pauline authorship and Ephesian destination, then, the use of Paul's name alone is unexpected. As we have seen, on other assumptions it is much more understandable (p. 253).

The form in v. 2 has no special features. On the pauline greetings see p. 47. They are a Christian adaptation of current formulae, owing something to both Greek and Jewish practice.

אאא

1

apostle: see, for general sense, pp. 145ff., and for possible overtones here, p. 240.

the saints: most naturally, it means Christians in general, as usually in the New Testament. They are God's people, consecrated to his service. But some (e.g. Kirby, op. cit., pp. 168, 170) see here a narrower application of the word – to Jewish Christians. One or two pauline passages (e.g. 2 Cor. 9^1; Rom. 15^{26}) have this sense, so it is not impossible even in an imitator of Paul. It has the advantage of giving a point to the somewhat laboured (cf. the use of the participle) distinction between the 'holy ones' and the 'faithful ones'; they are Jewish and Gentile Christians respectively. Eph. 2^{19} is cited in support; there *the saints* may well be Jewish Christians, especially those of the first years. The word may then have three distinct meanings in this one short work, for in 1^{18} (and possibly elsewhere too) it almost certainly refers to the angels (cf. p. 275).

2

grace and peace: see on Phil. 1^2, p. 51. Cf. Eph. 6$^{23f.}$ where both wishes are repeated, as the writer concludes his work.

PRAISE OF GOD FOR HIS GREAT ACTS
IN CHRIST

^{3}*Blessed be the God and Father of our Lord Jesus Christ, who has blessed us in Christ with every spiritual blessing in the heavenly places, ^{4}even as he chose us in him before the foundation of the world, that we should be holy and blameless before him. ^{5}He destined us in love^b to be his sons through Jesus Christ, according to the purpose of his will, ^{6}to the praise of his glorious grace which he freely bestowed on us in the Beloved. ^{7}In him we have redemption through his blood, the forgiveness of our trespasses, according to the riches of his grace ^{8}which he lavished upon us. ^{9}For he has made known to us in all wisdom and insight the mystery of his will, according to his purpose which he set forth in Christ ^{10}as a plan for the fullness of time, to unite all things in him, things in heaven and things on earth.*

^{11}*In him, according to the purpose of him who accomplished all things according to the counsel of his will, ^{12}we who first hoped in Christ have been destined and appointed to live for the praise of his glory. ^{13}In him you also, who have heard the word of truth, the gospel of your salvation, and have believed in him, were sealed with the promised Holy Spirit, ^{14}which is the guarantee of our inheritance until we acquire possession of it, to the praise of his glory.*

    b Or *before him in love, having destined us.*

In most of Paul's letters, including the other three included in this volume, the opening greeting is followed by a thanksgiving, an extended and christianized version of ordinary Hellenistic practice. But here and in *2 Corinthians* another form occurs, though in the case of *Ephesians* the thanksgiving is merely deferred to 1$^{16ff.}$. This form, 'Blessed be God, who has ...', is perhaps the commonest of the expressions of Jewish piety, the *berakah*, or 'blessing'.* This is not a blessing imparted from God to man, but an act of praise expressed by man before God for some action on his part, already performed (such as creation or redemption) or now desired (such as the provision of food or the coming of his kingdom).

    * On this form, see J. C. Kirby, *Ephesians, Baptism and Pentecost* (London, 1968), pp. 84ff.

This kind of prayer was used by Jews on all imaginable occasions. To take an example from everyday domestic usage, the blessing recited over bread at a meal (cf. Mark 6⁴¹; 14²²) ran: 'Blessed art thou, O Lord our God, King eternal, who bringest forth bread from the earth.'

Its roots lay deep in Old Testament piety. There is, for example, the utterance of Abraham's servant when his search for a wife for Isaac, his master's son, was quickly rewarded: 'Blessed be the Lord, the God of my master Abraham, who has not forsaken his steadfast love and his faithfulness toward my master Abraham.' Many examples are occasioned by some piece of good fortune of this kind; but others are much grander and belong to the realm of solemn liturgy. Solomon's long prayer at the inauguration of the Temple in Jerusalem opens and closes with the *berakah*-formula (1 Kings 8¹⁵ & ⁵⁶). Psalms like 105, 106, 148, and 150 are expressed in this form, some more, some less elaborately. 1 Macc. 4³⁰f. is an instance which is historical in tone.

In the synagogues of the New Testament period, many new examples of this pattern of worship were arising. This one is typical:

Blessed art thou, O Lord our God, King of the Universe,
who formest light and createst darkness;
who makest peace and createst all things;
who givest light in mercy to the earth and to those who live thereon,
and in goodness renewest every day continually to the work of
   creation.
Be thou blessed, O Lord our God, for the excellency of the work of
   thy hands,
and for the bright luminaries which thou hast made;
let them glorify thee.
Blessed art thou, O Lord, who formest the luminaries.

Another looks more to the coming fulfilment of God's promises than to his great past blessings in creation and in his saving acts in the history of Israel:

Magnified and hallowed be his great Name in the world which he
   created.
May he establish his Kingdom in your lifetime, and in your days,
and in the lifetime of all the house of Israel speedily and in a near time.
And say ye Amen.

May his great Name be blessed for ever and to the ages of ages.
(Quoted in Kirby, op. cit., pp. 87f.)

As we should expect, the Dead Sea Scrolls show the formula in use
in the worship of the community at Qumran (e.g. Vermes, p. 183). No
form was more characteristic of the prayer of Judaism.

The passage before us gives us a fine early Christian example of this
form, rivalled in the New Testament only by 1 Peter 1$^{3-12}$. It bears
all the marks of careful formulation, with the high solemn tone of
the language of worship. In Greek it is a single sentence, which
enhances its hieratic quality. To a considerable degree, this exalted
tone is sustained throughout at any rate the first half of *Ephesians*, but
as we shall discover when we come to look more closely at the structure of I$^{3-14}$, there are reasons for thinking that this may be a piece
with its own independent life and history. That is, it may be a
Christian liturgical formula, a counterpart of the examples we have
given from the worship of the synagogue. This does not necessarily
mean that it comes from an earlier writer than the rest of *Ephesians*;
it does mean that it may be a distinct unit with a purpose of its own.

What that purpose was we have insufficient evidence to say with
certainty. But as we have seen in the Introduction (p. 251), there are
hints scattered through *Ephesians* which make it likely that either the
idea of baptism, or even the occasion of a particular baptism colours
the work. Certainly it is not difficult to read this *berakah* as a
thanksgiving for being accepted by God into the new relationship
which he has established with man through Christ.

We have set this *berakah* against the background of Old Testament
and contemporary Jewish parallels. The general similarity is clear
but there are also points of distinction. A glance at the examples
quoted above will show that in one way our formula is closer to
those of the Old Testament than of the first-century synagogue or
Qumran. Whereas the former almost always (but see 1 Chron. 29^{10})
use the third person form, 'Blessed be God who ...', the latter had
moved to the second person, 'Blessed art thou, O God, who. ...'
But our present passage and the parallel in 1 Peter 1 (as well as the
much less formal passage in 2 Cor. 1$^{3ff.}$) use the older form. It is
impossible to build much on this; *Ephesians* may be here simply
modelled on *2 Corinthians*. But if it is an independent piece of Christian liturgy, it shows that same reliance on the Old Testament text

rather than the customs of the contemporary synagogue which we find, for example, in the *Epistle to the Hebrews*, and which may disclose the activity of scripture-soaked Gentile converts rather than Christians of Jewish race. But there may be nothing significant here; Paul the ex-Jew does the same in 2 Cor. 1³.

Much more important, the centrality of the work of Christ distinguishes this passage from the comparable *berakah* of Judaism. There is no longer the rather sharp division between thanksgiving for God's past blessings (the gifts of life and of the natural world, and great acts like the Exodus from Egypt or the return from the captivity in Babylon) and praise for the assurance of future blessings (such as the coming of the age of bliss and the fulfilment of God's promises to Israel). Christ occupies the central place and spans the gap between past and future. In him the promises of God have already been realized on the universal scale. Those who accept him share a life whose content has been transformed and to which a wholly new impetus has been given. The past act sustains the believers in the present and carries them forward into an assured future as on the crest of a powerful wave.

An examination of the structure of the passage will bring this out still more. At first sight the language is so opaque that the discerning of any pattern seems unlikely. But on closer examination, a few repeated phrases emerge, such as *to the praise of* (vv. 6, 12, 14), and *according to his purpose* (vv. 5, 9, 11). Can we go any further and see these as symptoms of a more comprehensive structure? Some scholars think that we can.

Ernst Lohmeyer, a distinguished German scholar of the last generation, who was inclined to perceive poetic structure in implausible as well as more plausible passages (cf. p. 70 for an example of the latter), felt able to demonstrate a full verse pattern; the passage was a piece of poetic hymnody. But most are agreed that it will not bear such rigid treatment. If this is in any sense poetry, then it is because of a certain regularity of phrase and theme and a division into roughly equal sections, not because of any fixed metrical or rhythmical pattern.

Any division of the passage is disguised by the fact that grammatically it is a single sentence. Nevertheless, the repeated phrases referred to above are a good starting-point. If, using them as a clue, we treat the passage as made up of three admittedly unequal sections, roughly vv. 3-6, 7-12, 13-14, we can go on to say that in the main the first section centres on the work of the Father, the second on the Son, and the third on the Holy Spirit. Suggestions have been made that a more regular liturgical form may lie behind our present piece, which will then have been expanded by the writer to fit more suitably the homiletic character of his work as a whole (cf. J. Coutts, N.T.S.,3 (1956-7) pp. 115ff.). But these demand an excessive ingenuity and assume perhaps over-confidently that a poetically more satisfactory piece is there waiting to be discovered at the heart of our present passage.

J. Cambier, for example, has recognized this (Z.N.W., 54 (1963) pp. 58ff.), and regards the Blessing as belonging as it stands to the work as a whole. It proclaims the central facts of salvation, with which *Ephesians* is concerned throughout, moving in orderly progression from God's choosing of his people through Christ (vv. 4-6), to an account of the benefits thereby conferred (vv. 7-12), and finally an assurance of the present possession of the Holy Spirit which guarantees the benefits. V. 3 introduces the whole passage with the declaration that God is the source of salvation and of all that it brings. Within each section the phrase *to the praise of his glory* acts as a refrain which reiterates this centrality of the Father.

That the passage was not conceived as a clear-cut composition is indicated by the fact that another basis of division is equally striking. Even if formally it is a single sentence, the R.S.V. has not done violence in splitting it up, for the connexions between clauses are often very loose. This is especially true of the sections beginning *in him*, at vv. 7, 11 & 13 (Gk 'in whom'). The division at these points is made even more evident by the conclusion of the preceding unit in each case with a loosely appended phrase. Recognition of this feature helps to lighten the apparent density both of the syntax and of the sense. In particular it brings out the prominence of Christ in initiating and sustaining the new life given to the believer.

The basis of this passage in Jewish blessings, as far as its form is concerned, supports the view that it is a mistake to expect a more rigid structure than this. The fact that they have no greater rigidity means that it is also unprofitable to seek it in this passage, either in its present form or in some hypothetical earlier version which the writer has taken out of the liturgical stock known to him. Other arguments tell against the attempt to isolate this passage too much from its context. Whatever links it may have with early Christian forms, perhaps baptismal in character, this *berakah* is closely integrated with the rest of *Ephesians* (especially ch. 1–3), so much so that some critics hold that the earlier liturgical matter stretches through the whole of these first chapters (cf. Kirby, op. cit. p. 129). Moreover it has exactly the same kind of links with the genuine pauline epistles as the rest of the book.

We turn now from the structure to the content of our passage. We have mentioned the strong emphasis on the work of Christ. This emphasis – he is mentioned thirteen times – overlays the roughly trinitarian pattern to which we have referred. Yet it is thoroughly in line with pauline thought that Christ, however crucial, is but the means of man's return to God the Father. The Father is the source of Christ's work (v. 3), that work is the product of his eternal purpose (vv. 4, 5, 9, 11), and its object is to bring him honour (*to the praise of his glory*, vv. 6, 14). (In the other occurrence of the phrase, v. 12, the reference is perhaps more likely to be to Christ's rather than the Father's glory.)

God's purpose is not only eternal but also cosmic in scope (vv. 3, 10). On the grandest possible scale, therefore, it fulfils man's hopes and satisfies his aspirations. The temporal references (vv. 4, 10, 14) show that the main framework of thought derives from the Jewish expectation of God's decisive intervention in history, bringing salvation. The writer sees this intervention as initiated by Christ, and the believers as already well on the way to the perfect attainment of its fruits (v. 14).

The intervention is seen first in terms of revelation. It is the making known of a mystery hitherto concealed, the disclosure of the eternal purpose (v. 9). It is then something which man apprehends with his mind and does not simply undergo passively. Moreover it is something to which he personally responds, seeing it as a gift (v. 6); and its chief effect is the renewal of his moral life on the basis of the gift (vv. 4, 7). Confidence in God's active favour is indeed one of the most constant notes of the whole passage (cf. also vv. 13f.).

Yet neither the knowledge nor the moral restoration results from the purely spiritual fulfilment of divine promises. They have their roots in the physical fact of the Cross – *through his blood* (v. 7). This is one of the few references to the historical Christ in *Ephesians* (cf. 2¹³), though even here there is no dwelling upon it as an event. All the stress is on its significance. His death was redemptive; perhaps like the Passover lambs whose blood was daubed on the Jewish homes in Egypt and safeguarded Israel's departure from the land of bondage; perhaps like the sin-offering in the Temple whose sacrifice brought the reconciliation of the sinner with God. *Blameless* (*amōmos*), v. 4, is a word often used in sacrificial contexts to describe the *unblemished* animal whose offering brings about the purification of the offerer; the Christians are raised to share Christ's own purity (cf. 5^{27}).

In setting out so comprehensively the Christian gospel of salvation, this passage acts as a basis for the rest of *Ephesians*, which goes on to develop its ideas.

ɪɕɹ

3

God and Father: takes up v. 2 and looks on to v. 5. God can now be called *our Father* because the sonship of Jesus has been extended to us. The idea implicit here is worked out in Gal. 4$^{6f.}$ and Rom. 8$^{14-17}$. I Pet. 1^3 repeats the formula exactly.

has blessed us: the verb is in the aorist, i.e. represents a single action in the past. It refers either to the saving action of Christ, in particular the Cross, cf. v. 7, or to baptism in which this is appropriated by the believer. The latter suggestion is supported by the presence of numerous other possible references to baptism; the same is true of the similar passage in I Pet. 1$^{3ff.}$.

us: to whom does the 'we' of this passage refer? The natural meaning is 'Christians in general'. Yet this view has the difficulty that in v. 13 'we' can be contrasted with 'you'. The usual explanation is that here the writer turns to Gentile Christians in particular; in relation to them, he stands either for the Church as a whole, Jew and Gentile alike, or for the first generation of Christians. Sometimes it is suggested that in v. 13 the writer begins to add his own words to the *berakah* which he had taken over.

But another view should be considered. If *Ephesians* is rightly described as a post-pauline, and perhaps ultra-pauline, manifesto, then in this opening passage we should see the presentation of the credentials of Paul in whose name the writer speaks. The 'we' is the apostle. (Note: the plural *sons* in v. 5 does not count against this, for the Gk is literally 'for adoption'.) Later (v. 15) he turns to the singular 'I', but here we have the plural appropriate to solemn statement. We should read the passage in the light of Paul's account of his conversion and call to his apostolate in Gal. 1: there the historical Paul presented his credentials more passionately. It is a passage also referred to in 3$^{3-6}$, which should be read in conjunction with 1$^{3-14}$. Gal. 1^{15} like Eph. 1^4 speaks of the apostle's choice by God for his work. Eph. 1^9 reflects Gal. 1^{12}: cf. Eph. 3$^{3-6}$. Eph. 1^{12} asserts 'Paul's' seniority as a Christian: is it a pauline propagandist studiously avoiding mention of others still more senior whose claims (or those of *their* successors) were being urged in his day? Then in 1^{13} 'Paul' turns to his flock, Gentile Christendom, who have been brought into the faith which the Paul of history first conveyed to them. Such a view, of course hypothetical, illustrates the range of possibilities when we try to determine the background of this passage, and counsels caution in seeing it as exhaustively accounted for by describing it as a baptismal *berakah*, adapted for its epistolary setting. The historical setting of the writer may also make its contribution.

spiritual blessing: the adjective carries its full meaning – blessings are conveyed by and lead to participation in the Holy Spirit, cf. v. 13 and Rom. 8$^{1ff.}$; 1 Cor. 12$^{1-13}$. *Blessing* too is a rich word. As a glance at the story of Isaac's blessing in Gen. 27 will show, the Jewish tradition used the word to signify very definite, concrete, and assured benefits. Here too there is nothing vague or uncertain about it. It stands for the sum total of the promised and expected gifts of God to man. Note the play on three different words from the same root: *eulogētos ... eulogēsas ... eulogia.*

in Christ: this phrase is about twice as common in *Ephesians* as it is in genuinely pauline usage. Generally, its use in this work lacks the more profound sense which Paul often gave to it (e.g. expressing a doctrine of the Christians' identification with Christ and with one another), and it has become something of a commonplace, most often, as here, carrying an instrumental sense, *through* or *by means of Christ.*

in the heavenly places: the blessing which Christ's work confers upon the believer is operative above all where his triumph has been realized, cf. 2^6; 4^{10}: that is, in the upper realms above the earth, where angelic powers formerly reigned and whence Christ has now deposed them, as vv. 20–23 describe (cf. Phil. 2$^{10f.}$ and Col. 1$^{15ff.}$). The word signifies less the place than the powers which had ruled there. Despite all that the thought of this passage owes to the purest Jewish concepts and attitudes, the concern here with heavenly security, mentioned before all else (before forgiveness and goodness of life), breathes the same atmosphere as the mystery cults and Gnostic groups (see p. 22). This perspective finds little echo in the tradition of Old Testament religion though by this time it had found its way into Judaism, both in the Dispersion in the cities of the eastern Mediterranean and in Palestine itself (cf. p. 268). Vv. 13f. show the same view. To be secure in a world of uncertainty, suffering, and disaster, it was essential to be at one with the controller of the *heavenly places*, whose power transcended all earthly authorities. The Christian knew that this meant living *in Christ Jesus* (v. 2), whom God had exalted above all things. This precise expression is not found outside *Ephesians*, where it occurs five times.

4

he chose us: this is the first verb in the indicative mood in the passage. Like the others that lie ahead (*he bestowed*, v. 6, and *he lavished*, v. 8), it tells us the content of the blessing which occasions the praise offered to God. The word is *eklegō*, the common LXX word to express the choosing of Israel by God as the instrument of his purpose, cf. e.g. Isa. 41^8; 43^{10}; 49^7. Now the object of this choice (or election, as the terminology of theology has it) is *us*, that is, the Church (though see on v. 3, above), made up jointly of Jews and Gentiles, based on Christ (cf. 2$^{11\mathrm{ff.}}$). But the choice was made *before the foundation of the world* (cf. 2 Thess. 2^{13}). Contemporary Judaism commonly asserted the importance of vital elements in religion by speaking of their existence from all eternity (e.g. the Law, God's glorious throne, the name of the Messiah*): they had been made before the world itself. Included now in their number is not only Christ, who had been seen as pre-existent from the Church's early days (cf. 1 Cor. 8^6; Phil. 2^6; and later, Heb. 1$^{1f.}$ and John 1^1), but also the identity of the Church's members. They, as a community, are one with Christ and equally part of God's eternal purpose for the world. (John 15^{27} may be making the same point, as at any rate one element in its meaning.)

holy and blameless: cf. Col. 1^{22}. For *holy*, see p. 48. The two words are virtually synonymous. The image is that of sacrificial victims, cf. Rom. 12^1.

5

This verse virtually duplicates v. 4, though the life that results from the realizing of God's purpose is now described in terms of sonship rather than blamelessness, but in both cases the emphasis is on status conferred rather than on the moral performance, which is to flow naturally from it. (There is little to choose between the arrangements in text and margin, though the first creates a nice balance between *in love* and *the Beloved* at the end of the next verse.)

purpose: Gk *eudokia*, which is better rendered 'favour', or 'good pleasure'.

* G. F. Moore, *Judaism* (Cambridge, Mass., 1958) Vol. 1, p. 526.

6

to the praise of his glorious grace: lit. 'of the glory of his grace'. Rich
pleonastic genitival phrases of this kind are one of the most striking
features of the style of *Ephesians*; though they can be paralleled in
Paul's genuine writings (e.g. 2 Cor. 4⁶), they occur here in much greater
quantity, and are one of the strongest signs that we are dealing with a
document designed for solemn use, probably in worship, and based on
liturgical models. (Cf. already in v. 5, also vv. 9, 11, 12, 14.) The form
is thoroughly Jewish: cf. e.g. Vermes, p. 100, line 7f.

grace . . . freely bestowed: noun and verb are from the same root – 'grace
with which he graced us'. It is the emphasis, so common in genuine
Paul, on the unconditioned nature of God's saving act, cf. 2⁵, ⁸.

the Beloved: i.e. Christ. If this is a conscious reference to the story of
the baptism of Jesus, cf. Mark 1¹¹, this may be further evidence of the
baptismal function of this *berakah*. But it may simply reflect Col. 1¹³ᶠ·,
as the next verse continues to do.

7
Cf. Col. 1¹⁴, ²⁰; Rom. 3²⁵ᶠ·; 5⁹.

redemption: see p. 154.

forgiveness: aphesis is a favourite word of Luke rather than Paul among
the New Testament writers. See p. 155.

riches of his grace: cf. 1¹⁸; 2⁷; 3⁸, ¹⁶; Rom. 2⁴; 9²³.

9
in all wisdom and insight: in the Greek these words precede the verb and
could easily be attached to the end of v. 8. Such an arrangement is
favoured so far as the *form* of the sentence is concerned, by comparison
with Col. 1⁹ ⁽ᵃⁿᵈ ²⁸⁾ which these words recall, but a comparison of
sense favours our text as it stands. As in v. 5, we then have in the Greek
a clause opening with a participle (cf. *destined*), preceded by a phrase
starting with *in* (cf. *in love*).

For *wisdom,* see p. 76.

mystery: cf. p. 182. As commonly in *Ephesians*, overlapping words are
piled up (*mystery, will, purpose, plan*). This word contributes the point
that God's purpose has been hitherto concealed, but now declared in
Christ. Jewish apocalyptic literature and the writings of Qumran are
full of the word and the idea of the eventual revelation of God's long-
laid secret plans. Thus we find in one of the Qumran hymns: 'For thou
hast given me knowledge through thy marvellous mysteries, and hast
shown thyself mighty within me in the midst of thy marvellous

council' (Vermes, p. 163). Even the phrase 'conformable to the secrets of his will' occurs. The same kind of thinking is to be found in the Greek world in the mystery cults and Gnostic sects.

The content of the divine secret denoted by *mystērion* varies from one occurrence of the word to another. Even in Paul's undoubted writings it is by no means always the same, though most commonly it refers to the incarnation of Christ and the redemptive work which he accomplished (so, for example, in Col. 1²⁷). But in *Ephesians* it usually refers to the reconciliation into unity by Christ of hitherto discordant elements – Jews and Gentiles (cf. 3⁴⁻⁶), heaven and earth (v. 10). In 5³² it describes the profoundly significant analogy between the unity of husband and wife on the one hand, and Christ and the Church on the other. Always it carries the flavour of truth too deep for the human mind to fathom, but now open to at least a degree of privileged apprehension on man's part. Because its already existing Jewish use commonly concerned the awaited intervention of God at the Last Day, its application by the first Christian writers to Christ and his work is one of the signs of the thoroughness with which they saw him as the fulfilment of the whole eschatological hope of Judaism. The distinctive application as well as frequent use of the word in *Ephesians* strikes some scholars as an important sign of non-pauline authorship (Mitton, pp. 86ff.), but it is doubtful whether it takes us very far in establishing this case; Paul's key words can differ in sense within a few verses in his undoubted writings and his use of *mystērion* elsewhere already covers a wide range.

10
plan: Gk *oikonomia.* See on 3², p. 297.

fullness of time: cf. Gal. 4⁴.

to unite all things: cf. Col. 1²⁰. See p. 173.

11f.
The writer goes back once more over the point made in vv. 5 & 9, largely taking up the actual words of the earlier verses.

first hoped: the verb is *pro-elpizō,* which means 'hope before'. The exact force of the prefix *pro-* is not clear. In view of the contrast with *you* in v. 13, it could draw a distinction between the first Jewish Christians and the Gentiles who have now entered the Church. But it is hard to believe that the first person plural in the earlier part of the passage carried an exclusive reference to Jewish Christians. To distinguish the Gentile Christians in v. 13 implies no exclusion of them from the first person plural of vv. 3ff. (cf. 1 Pet. 1³ᶠ·). Perhaps it is better to take this one case at least as an apostolic *we*, which is all the more plausible if the writer addresses his audience in the name of a Paul endowed with lofty and venerable authority (see on v. 3 above). But even the genuine Paul might have spoken of himself as having come to hope in Christ before his converts. Alternatively, the *pro* simply means that the writer looks forward to the future fulfilment of the hope.

13

you: i.e. Gentile Christians, cf. 2^{19}.

the word of truth: cf. Col. 1^5.

salvation: used only here in *Ephesians*. See p. 64.

sealed with the Holy Spirit: the image in mind here is not entirely clear. Paul had used it already, again with reference to the gift of the Spirit, in 2 Cor. 1^{22}. There is a full discussion in Lampe, *The Seal of the Spirit* (London, 1951), pp. 3ff. It is almost certainly an image for the rite of baptism, which follows the hearing, i.e. accepting, of *the word*, or *the gospel*, cf. Acts 2$^{37f.}$. The general background seems to be the practice of marking cattle or slaves as a sign of ownership: cf. 1 Cor. 7^{22}. There was already a long tradition of its religious application in both paganism and Judaism. Perhaps a more specific clue is to be found in Ezek. 9$^{4ff.}$, where those faithful to the Lord are to be marked on their foreheads. This was frequently taken up in eschatological writing. God would recognize those faithful to him on the Last Day by their bearing of the mark, cf. e.g. 2 Esdras 6^5 for the use of sealing in this connexion. The most vivid New Testament instance is Rev. 7$^{4ff.}$ and 9^4. Eph. 4^{30} (which again makes the link with the Spirit, like our present passage and 2 Cor. 1^{22}) confirms that the context of thought here is thoroughly eschatological. The present possession of the Spirit guarantees full possession when God brings about the consummation of all things. Whether there was already any actual rite linked with baptism which was seen as the *act* of sealing (like the later signing with the cross), it is impossible to say.

This is the first mention in this writing of the Holy Spirit. With the striking exception of *Colossians*, the Spirit is prominent both in the undoubtedly pauline epistles and in *Ephesians*. The thirteen references here are scattered through the six chapters. The thought scarcely goes outside lines already established in the Old Testament and Judaism. At its simplest level, the Spirit (lit. breath or wind) is a way of speaking of God's powerful activity, and the image is thoroughly anthropomorphic. While this flavour does not disappear, other more sophisticated associations are added. The Spirit comes to be associated with certain divine gifts – inspiration of various kinds: 1^{17}; 5^{18}; 6^{18}. It is also seen (and here there is an infiltration of Stoic notions) as a unitive agent or principle on God's behalf: 2^{18} and $4^{3f.}$ And it is associated with the plenary revelation of God's power awaited at the End of the World and now anticipated in the Church: 1^{13}; 3^5. In the period between God's decisive action in Christ and its coming consummation, the Spirit acts in Christians to lead them to the full realization of God's work in them: 3^{16}; 4^{23}. In 4^{30} the Spirit comes near to being personified, as for example in Wisdom of Solomon $7^{22ff.}$, which is one instance among many, especially in later Judaism, of treating attributes of God as semi-independent agents.

promised: cf. note above. The outpouring of the Spirit upon God's people was an important element in the expectation for the Last Days: see Joel $2^{28ff.}$; Isa. 32^{15}; Acts $2^{14ff.}$.

14
guarantee: this word, found also in 2 Cor. 1^{22}, is taken from the language of commerce, where it means a deposit or down-payment, securing an article by the handing over of a first instalment (*arrabōn*).

inheritance: a word of the utmost richness in the Old Testament for the fulfilment of the promises to the people of God, above all for the gift of the Promised Land to Israel after the Exodus wanderings. The longing and expectation which it evokes aptly express the ardent desire of the Church for the heavenly consummation. (Cf. Num. 34^2.)

until we acquire possession of it: this is a loose and tendentious translation. Literally it means *with a view to the redemption of the possession.* How is the genitive *of the possession* to be understood? It would not be uncharacteristic of *Ephesians* if it were just loosely explicatory of the word that precedes it; the redemption consists in taking possession of the inheritance whose first instalment has already been paid. This leads to the R.S.V. understanding of the phrase, with *we* as the agents. But it is not an accurate rendering and it fails to give value to *apolytrōsis* (*redemption*). God is the most likely agent in redemption. N.E.B. translates accordingly: 'that Spirit is the pledge that we shall enter upon our heritage, when God has redeemed what is his own.' Both here and in 4^{30}, as in Rom. 8^{23} (though not in v. 7), *redemption* is placed at the Last Day rather than seen as already given. There is no real contradiction here, for the present gift leads on to the consummation.

THE FRUIT OF CHRIST'S
TRIUMPH

^{15}*For this reason, because I have heard of your faith in the Lord Jesus and your love^c toward all the saints, ^{16}I do not cease to give thanks for you, remembering you in my prayers, ^{17}that the God of our Lord Jesus Christ, the Father of glory, may give you a spirit of wisdom and of revelation in the knowledge of him, ^{18}having the eyes of your hearts enlightened, that you may know what is the hope to which he has called you, what are the riches of his glorious inheritance in the saints, ^{19}and what is the immeasurable greatness of his power in us who believe, according to the working of his great might ^{20}which he accomplished in Christ when he raised him from the dead and made him sit at his right hand in the heavenly places, ^{21}far above all rule and authority and power and dominion, and above every name that is named, not only in this age but also in that which is to come; ^{22}and he has put all things under his feet and has made him the head over all things for the church, ^{23}which is his body, the fullness of him who fills all in all.*

c Other ancient authorities omit *your love.*

The blessing is followed by a Thanksgiving such as we usually find in Paul's letters immediately after the opening greeting, as in ordinary epistolary practice (see p. 52). This passage is particularly close to the corresponding section in *Colossians*. However, it is hard to avoid the impression that the statement of thanksgiving is purely formal; the writer knew that Paul always included such a statement – even though he has already provided an equivalent in the *berakah* of vv. 3–14 (though see Dan. 2$^{20 \& 23}$ for an example of Blessing followed by Thanksgiving). For the point of this passage, at any rate up to v. 20, is rather to pray that the blessings referred to in the *berakah* may be fully accepted by the Gentile Christians who are being addressed. There is thus much harking back to the Blessing which goes before. In v. 9 God is praised for giving spiritual insight to his people; now in v. 17 the writer prays that this wisdom may be communicated to his people. V. 18 combines the *riches* of v. 8 with the *inheritance* of v. 14, now by way of prayer for the readers' understanding of what they have received, rather than of praise for the assured gift.

So the passage makes no wholly new points, except that in the last few verses (20–23) it brings out much more fully Christ's universal dominion and the role of the Church, in which that cosmic rule is embodied. These four verses express this lordship with such a majestic sweep of language that some see here too evidence of a liturgical piece.

One of the most notable features of these last verses is the distinction drawn (v. 20) between the resurrection and ascension of Christ. In genuine Paul this distinction is not found; he prefers to think in terms of a single-act exaltation of Christ, and makes no division into two episodes. This does appear however in Acts 1, and is one of a number of features which *Luke-Acts* and *Ephesians* have in common. These shared features are one piece of evidence pointing to a post-pauline date for *Ephesians* (see p. 241).

We said that the note of thanksgiving is scarcely more than formal, perhaps a gesture to the conventions of correct pauline letter-writing, for despite the non-epistolary nature of his material, the writer does cast his work in the shape of an epistle. Another such gesture is the reference to hearing of the audience's faith (v. 15). The genuine thanksgivings often contain some allusion to the circumstances of either writer or readers (e.g. Phil. 1^7; Col. 1^7), and here the writer comes as close as anywhere to personal statement about his audience. But the impression is transient. There is no significant departure from the elevated theological style. The rather distant tone of this verse makes it hard to believe that the writer, whether Paul or an alert pseudo-Paul, had Ephesus in mind as his audience, for Paul knew no congregation better than that one and scarcely needed informing of their faith by hearsay.

ॐ

15

For this reason: typical linking-phrase, having no very precise reference, cf. 3^1, ^{14}, though the Greek differs. Cf. Col. 1^4. The words *your love* (no *your* in the Greek) are omitted by the best and oldest manuscripts. It is easy to see how both the desire to distinguish between what was directed to *the Lord Jesus* and to *all the saints*, and the influence of Col. 1^4 would press them into the text. On the other hand the Greek has a repeated definite article on either side of *love* and a scribe's eye could easily skip from the one to the other. If the words really were not there originally then the writer betrays a sub-pauline view of faith as a loyalty that could be directed towards Christ and one's fellow-Christians alike. For Paul, in a context like this, faith in Christ was *sui generis*.

the saints: see p. 258.

16

I . . . give thanks: Paul's Thanksgivings are divided between the singular and plural form. Where the plural occurs, it may be an apostolic 'we' or simply reflect the fact that Paul has associated friends with himself and his writing. Here (1^1) he is alone; contrast Col. $1^{1\ \&\ 3}$. The Blessing used the plural; that was a solemn prayer in the name of the whole Christian community, or perhaps a 'we' of more formal apostolic pronouncement.

17

Father of glory: a Hebrew turn of phrase, referring to glory both as the mode and 'place' of God's being (cf. 1 Cor. 2^8; Acts 7^2) and also perhaps as that which issues powerfully from him (cf. the analagous expressions in 2 Cor. 1^3 and Heb. 12^9). Schlier (p. 77), pointing to a comparison of Rom. 6^4 and 1 Cor. 6^{14}, notes that *glory* (*doxa*) and *power* (*dynamis*) are virtually synonymous. *Glory* is a visual image, *power* a mechanical one for the same divine activity. The rest of the verse tells what the power of God bestows.

spirit of wisdom: cf. Col. 1^9. 1 Cor. $12^{7f.}$ and $2^{6ff.}$ give the background in pauline thought, but the tradition reaches back in Jewish thought to Isa. 11^2. *Spirit* is again a word which carries the idea of God's power; at root, it is the image of breath or wind. As in most of these Semitic genitival phrases, the second noun has adjectival force: 'wise spirit'.

knowledge (*epignōsis*): see p. 153. This *knowledge* stems from God's inspiration not man's intellectual energy.

18

Cf. Col. $1^{12,\ 26f.}$; 2 Cor. 4^4. Though the language of this and the preceding verse would be entirely congenial to a member of one of the Gnostic groups in the Hellenistic world, with their concern for the communication of esoteric spiritual knowledge, nevertheless it is wholly explicable on the basis of Jewish tradition, both in the Old Testament (both prophetic and 'wisdom' writings) and in the Judaism of the first century. Apocalyptic literature was full of the idea of the revealing of heavenly secrets to the chosen messenger. Thus, it is said of the expected priestly Messiah of the House of Levi: 'And the glory of the Most High shall be uttered over him, and the spirit of understanding and sanctification shall rest upon him' (Test. Levi, 17^7, Charles, II, p. 314).

eyes of your hearts enlightened: the participle is in the perfect tense, implying a completed action. The reference is probably to baptism. The choice of the image of light leads to the mention of the eyes. The heart is, in Jewish tradition, the seat of thought, where *wisdom* and *knowledge* would be apprehended. The expression has Hellenistic parallels. Cf. also 1 Clem. 36² & 59³ (E.C.W., p. 42 and 54).

hope to which he has called you: in Greek this is yet another genitival phrase – 'hope of his calling'. Despite the closeness of this verse to Col. 1²⁶ᶠ·, the content of the *hope* is quite different. In *Colossians* it is simply Christ himself; here it is the future perfection of the divine endowment which the Last Day will bring (cf. v. 14). It is closer to the use of the word in Col. 1⁵, but even there the hope is already 'laid up in heaven' rather than a gift to be realized in the future: in both cases the word signifies *that which is hoped for* rather than the attitude of hopefulness.

called: a common and important pauline word, signifying deliberate choice by God, bringing both individuals and the Church as his new people into relationship with him; cf. the idea of God's choice in 1⁴. Cf. too Rom. 9¹¹; 1 Cor. 1¹; Phil. 3¹⁴.

riches of his glorious inheritance: Cf. 1⁷ᶠ· & ¹⁴. This clause expounds the *hope* to which God has called his people. In Greek the connexion is helped by the similarity between *call* (*klēsis*) and *inheritance* (*klēronomia*). Lit: *riches of the glory of his inheritance.*

inheritance in the saints: cf. Col. 1¹². God will fulfil this inheritance, which is Heaven, among the *saints*, the believers, at the Last Day, as he gave the promised land to Israel of old as *her* inheritance. Cf. Wis. of Solomon 5⁵; Acts 20³². It is possible that here, and in 2¹⁹ & 3¹⁸, as in 1 Thess. 3¹³ (though not in Eph. 1¹), the *saints*, or 'holy ones' refers to the angels, rather than the Christians, for in all these contexts they are part of the heavenly realm which will be manifested at the End. Many Jewish writings describe angelic beings by this term: e.g. Job 15¹⁵; Ps. 89⁵ᶠ·; and from the Qumran War Rule (Vermes, p. 139), 'For thou wilt fight with them from heaven ... for the multitude of the Holy Ones (is with Thee) in heaven ... Thou wilt muster the (hosts of) thine elect ... with thy Holy Ones (and with all) thine Angels.' This sense which is certainly possible here is at variance with the normal pauline usage, and with that of the rest of the New Testament, which by the *hagioi* means simply the Christians, as the people consecrated to God, just as Israel had been under the former dispensation.

19f.

power ... might: cf. Col. 1¹¹. In commenting on v. 17, we noted the close relation of *glory* and *power*; vv. 18b–19 make this connexion explicit. *In us:* 'we' may equally well be synonymous with *the saints* of the previous clause or distinguished from them, according to the meaning given to *saints*. The writer wishes to stress the unimaginable immensity of divine power manifested in the resurrection and exaltation of Christ; it has meant the total subjection to him of all authorities throughout the cosmos, and now operates also in those who believe in him (cf. 3^{20}). Stylistically, v. 19b and 20a is typical of this writer; a genitival phrase, lit. 'according to the working of the strength of his might' (three virtually synonymous words, frequent in liturgical language, sonorously heaped up); and the use of like-sounding and related words, which is brought out if we replace the R.S.V. *accomplished* by 'worked'. Multiple expressions for God's strength are common in the Qumran literature.

20

Note that the resurrection is seen, as virtually always in the New Testament, as an act of God, rather than as a self-generated deed of Christ. Jesus did not rise from the dead, but was raised by the Father. For this writer the resurrection is but the preliminary to the exaltation. It is the latter, here expressed in language drawn from Ps. 110^{1} and Ps. 8^{6}, which is the core of the Christian gospel in our writer's conception.

sit at his right hand: Ps. 110^{1}, which is quoted by almost all New Testament writers, the most universal early Christian proof-text (cf. e.g. Mark 12^{36}; Acts 2^{34}; Heb. 1^{13}).

21

rule ... authority ... power ... dominion: cf. p. 163. These are the titles of various degrees of angelic beings in Jewish terminology, seen as ruling the various heavenly spheres. Often, as in 4^{10}, the place of their rule was referred to rather than their titles. Cf. Col. 2^{10}; and 1^{16}, where the subject is Christ's role in their creation, a matter nowhere mentioned in *Ephesians*.

name: cf. Phil. 2^{9}, p. 84.

this age ... that which is to come: the conventional Jewish division of time into *ages*, sometimes seen as a series of eras, sometimes more simply, as here, as two ages, the present and that which will be inaugurated by God's cataclysmic intervention at the Last Day. Many Christians, including Paul, saw the age to come as already inaugurated at the coming of Christ and thought of the Church as living in the last days, with one foot in the new age (cf. 1 Cor. 10^{11}). The resurrection of Christ was the authentic sign that this was so, for resurrection was one of the sure marks of that age. Here the formulation is conventionally Jewish, though the writer certainly sees many of the expected features of the new age as already granted to the Christians (e.g. redemption and the Holy Spirit, 1⁷, ¹⁴), even if the fullness of the gifts still awaits them.

22

under his feet: Ps. 8⁶. This was a text of supreme importance in the early Church, as its frequent use in quite different New Testament authors testifies: e.g. 1 Cor. 15²⁷; Heb. 2⁸; cf. also Matt. 28¹⁸. The closest parallel to our present passage is that in 1 Cor. 15, which describes the triumph of Christ, the Second Adam.

head: cf. 1 Cor. 11³. See on Col. 1¹⁸, p. 171, and on 5²³, p. 332.

23

the fullness of him who fills all in all: this phrase presents several problems. *Fullness (plērōma)* is the first difficulty. It means either 'that which fills up' or 'that which is filled up', i.e. either the complement or the completed whole. Thus, taking the word to refer to the Church, the writer says either that the Church in some way completes Christ (and Col. 1²⁴, which uses a related verb, see p. 180, shows how this can be understood), or that the Church is filled by Christ, as well as being under his headship. On the latter view – and 3¹⁹ supports it – it is neater to take the participle translated *who fills* as passive (in Greek the same form is used for the passive and for the middle voice, which may bear an active sense, as R.S.V. takes it), so that Christ is in turn filled by God (cf. 1 Cor. 11³): 'the fullness of him who is filled'. The consequence of *this* is that *all in all* (= 'all things in all men'? cf. 1 Cor. 15²⁸) has to be taken as adverbial (= 'altogether', 'completely'). Alternatively it is possible that the whole phrase refers not to the Church at all, but to Christ, so that the passage corresponds exactly to Col. 1¹⁹; Christ is the plenary expression and embodiment of God (rather than the Church the plenary expression of Christ, as on the first view).

Dr H. Chadwick (Z.N.W., 51, pp. 145ff.) suggests that the phrase should be taken as in apposition to the whole preceding clause: *He has put . . . his body.* God has set Christ as both transcendent over the Church and immanent within it. The words then become a balanced statement of Christ's role, in a form which would give heart to the small, perhaps despairing Church; weak as she is, she is organically united to Christ, the Lord of the universe.

A further, attractive suggestion is to see Christ and Church, head and body, as a unity, cf. 5²³ᶠᶠ·: together they are filled by him (i.e. God) who is supreme, *fills all* (cf. 1 Cor. 15²⁸). This accords with 3¹⁹, where it is the believers who are to be *filled with the fullness of God.*

Plērōma requires three further comments: (i) it is a word which possessed a vague but impressive religious sonority and it may be unwise to seek too precise a meaning for it. Our writer is fond of such words, and also enjoys putting related pairs of them together. He does it again with the same pair in 3^{19}. (ii) Despite its vagueness, one of the word's associations is with the hierarchy of heavenly powers in Gnostic thought. As in Col. 1^{19} (see p. 172) there may be a deliberate taking over and decontaminating (to use Dr Chadwick's word) of the Gnostic word, by applying it to Christ. He contains and represents the fullness of being, which Gnosticism saw as diffused through the powers, and the Church, as his body, shares in this great status. If however the word refers only to the Church, this is its sole occurrence in this sense. (iii) The term is not without Old Testament background, cf. Jer. 23^{24}.

Uncertain as the exact sense of this verse may be, it reinforces the message of 1^{10} – that Christ with his Church lays claim to authority over the whole world; and though he is said to be *head* of *the Church*, yet the associations of that title in Hellenistic thought imply easy extension to lordship on the cosmic scale.

body: see on Col. 1^{24}. Only in these two writings is the term used for the universal, as distinct from local, Church (cf. Rom. 12; 1 Cor. 12). When the word has this cosmic flavour, it is hard to avoid the impression of links with Gnostic speculation about the nature of the universe – though it is an easy extension from Paul's simpler uses of the idea whose main source seems to be the language of the eucharist (cf. 1 Cor. 10$^{16f.}$).

2$^{1-10}$ FROM DEATH TO LIFE

^{1}*And you he made alive, when you were dead through the trespasses and* *sins* ^{2}*in which you once walked, following the course of this world, following* *the prince of the power of the air, the spirit that is now at work in the sons of* *disobedience.* ^{3}*Among these we all once lived in the passions of our flesh,* *following the desires of body and mind, and so we were by nature children of* *wrath, like the rest of mankind.* ^{4}*But God, who is rich in mercy, out of* *the great love with which he loved us,* ^{5}*even when we were dead through our* *trespasses, made us alive together with Christ (by grace you have been* *saved),* ^{6}*and raised us up with him, and made us sit with him in the heavenly* *places in Christ Jesus,* ^{7}*that in the coming ages he might show the im-* *measurable riches of his grace in kindness towards us in Christ Jesus.* ^{8}*For* *by grace you have been saved through faith; and this is not your own doing,*

*it is the gift of God – ⁹not because of works, lest any man should boast. ¹⁰For
we are his workmanship, created in Christ Jesus for good works, which God
prepared beforehand, that we should walk in them.*

It was easy to see that 1$^{15-23}$ was both verbally and thematically dependent upon the Blessing which comes before it. The same is true
of ch. 2. The two sections which make up this chapter (vv. 1–10 &
11–end), develop in turn two aspects of God's act in Christ for which
the Blessing gives praise: (i) redemption or forgiveness of sins (1^7);
(ii) the uniting of what has been estranged (1^{10}), the general principle
being now applied specifically to the union of Jews and Gentiles
in the Church. In other words the chapter deals with the reconciliation
first of sinful man to God, and then of alienated Gentiles to the true
people of God. Man's separation from God has been overcome both
in terms of moral life and of the social setting in which that life is to be
found. At both levels God has brought about reconciliation, and he is
both its source (2^8) and its goal (2^{16}).

In a sense the splendid picture of Christ's cosmic rule painted in the
final verses of ch. 1 was a climax in its own right, after which ch. 2
is at a lower level, taking up the themes first sounded in the earlier
passage. Kirby (op. cit. pp. 126ff.) has suggested that 1$^{15-23}$ is not only
an interruption in the working out of these themes but even an intrusion into a Blessing which develops naturally from 1^4 through
ch. 2, and ends with 3^{14-end} (3$^{1-13}$ being another intrusion). There
is much to be said for this view: 3^{14} follows awkwardly from 3^{13}, better from 2^{22}; 3$^{20f.}$ undoubtedly makes a good ending to a Jewish-
type *berakah*; and it is certainly possible that the more personal
passages (1$^{1ff.}$ and 3$^{1ff.}$) were inserted into an originally liturgical
piece when it was put into an epistolary shape. But it is also possible
to take 1$^{3-14}$ as the core from which the rest develops – admittedly
with a certain amount of jerkiness and going back over already
trodden tracks. There is no part of these three chapters which does
not relate closely to the first proclamation of the writer's message in
that opening section.

In order to see the bearing of our passage we have had to place it
in the wider context of the first three chapters. Turning now to vv.
1–10 in themselves, we find a summary of the central pauline gospel.
Through Christ, God has brought to man his gracious love and
forgiveness, replacing a dark life of sinful hostility to God with new

life in his ways. It is the gospel expounded at length in *Romans* and *Galatians*, more briefly in Phil. 3, in less typically pauline terms in *Colossians*.

In some ways the statement of the gospel here *is* typically pauline: most of the expressions can be paralleled somewhere in the undoubted writings, and the general meaning accords wholly with Paul's teaching. But there are certain features of the passage which make it somewhat out of tune with the genuine Paul. Like the whole of this work (and in this respect these verses follow quite naturally from 1²³), the atmosphere of the teaching is more thoroughly cosmic and mythological than genuine Paul. This is not a question of difference of outlook, only of emphasis; Paul is more deeply interested in the conflicts of the human personality and the inner workings of the heart. Here the cosmic backcloth, the universal scale of the action, is constantly before the eye. It is of course not at all impossible that a liturgical purpose would account for this emphasis.

Again, though the language is pauline, some of the terms which the theme would lead us to expect are absent. There is no use here (any more than there is in *Colossians*) of the language of justification, though 2⁵ and 2⁸ almost demand it (cf. Rom. 3²⁴). Instead, men are spoken of as having been *saved* – in a quite uncharacteristic use of that term (cf. detailed notes). For the rest the passage is virtually a highly concentrated catena of pauline expressions, so concentrated that some find it too artificial to be Paul's own, others too pauline to be the work of anybody else.

The Greek syntax of the first seven verses, which form a single sentence, is highly complex, with the main verb (*he made alive*) not appearing till v. 5.

∞

1

you: takes up the second person of 1¹³, ¹⁸. No doubt the audience are Gentile Christians, as 2¹¹ explicitly says, but at this point there is nothing specific to Gentiles in the description of the former sinful state. This is made plain in v. 3, and the point of the dual statement (*you* & *we*) is to show that, whatever the heritage of Jews, both they and Gentiles start in the same position of estrangement from God and equally need the reconciliation which he has effected through Christ. Paul makes the same point in Rom. 2. In our present passage there is no statement of the Jews' privileges, as in Rom. 3¹ᶠ·; 9⁴. Paul could not forbear to mention them and they contributed an element of agony to his position which finds no echo here. Our writer is content to state without comment the parity between Jews and Gentiles. It is possible that as in 1$^{3-14}$, *we* refers to 'Paul'.

alive . . . dead: this is the dominant image used in these verses to speak of the new dispensation brought by Christ. Note that the reference is more strongly to morals than merely to existence or status; man is *dead through trespasses and sins*, then alive for *good works* (v. 10). Cf. 5$^{14f.}$. We are far removed then from the Gnostic idea of death as a way of describing bodily existence in itself. The image is natural enough for a Christian whose faith depends upon the resurrection of Christ, and the connexion is made explicit in vv. 5f. Cf. Rom. 6^{11} and Col. 2^{13}. The idea of sinfulness as death also occurs in Jewish writings, where it is part of a wider application of the language of death to any weakness or sickness or sorrow (e.g. Ps. 13$^{1-3}$; Hos. 13^{14}). See, for example, Ps. of Solomon, 16$^{1-8}$ (Charles, II, pp. 646f.); and from a Qumran hymn (Vermes, p. 158): 'I thank thee, O Lord, for thou hast redeemed my soul from the Pit . . . Thou hast cleansed a perverse spirit of great sin that it may stand with the host of the Holy Ones.' (Notice there the same community aspect as in our passage; it is a question of leaving the *sons of disobedience* (v. 2) or *children of wrath* (v. 3) and becoming joined to *the saints*, whether of earth (1^{1}) or heaven (1^{18}).)

2

walked: the common LXX term for conduct of life, especially in the Psalms (e.g. 119$^{3, 45}$); cf. v. 10.

course of this world: the word translated *course* is *aiōn*, lit. 'age', 'span of time', 'eternity'. In the last sense it had from the second century B.C. come to be deified – *Aiōn*, the god of eternity. The cult of this deity and philosophico-religious speculation connected with it had developed in Alexandria, where its penetration into Judaism was easy. Already the word was important in Judaism for the ages into which history was divided, especially, in apocalyptic thought, 'this age' and 'the age to come' (cf. 1^{21}). But in its syncretistic (i.e. using elements from other religions) sense it signifies for Jews the Devil who is the ruler of this age, cf. 1 Cor. 2^{8}. Sometimes it occurs in the plural with what may well be this meaning, e.g. Col. 1^{26}, see pp. 182f., and possibly Eph. 2^{7} and 3^{9}, see p. 284; certainly it occurs with this sense in Ignatius' *Epistle to the Ephesians* 19$^{1f.}$ (E.C.W., p. 81). The expression is thus parallel to that which follows it; the first uses a word with temporal roots, the second (*prince of the power of the air*) thinks in terms of the sphere in which the angelic authority operates in opposition to God. This parallelism, which extends to the third phrase, completing the verse, should probably determine the meaning we give to *aiōn*. The three titles are synonymous. The R.S.V. rendering is satisfactory as a rule (= 'the course of time during which the world continues'), but not in this context. (For a similar title, cf. John 12^{31}: 'ruler of this world'.)

the air: in the current picture of the cosmos, the atmosphere was the lowest of the successive layers which stretched outwards from the earth to the uppermost heaven. In it dwelt the demons who were the agents of the evils oppressing man, and over it ruled the Devil or Satan. It is in effect the immediate spiritual 'atmosphere' in which man's life is set, and from which he desires salvation.

sons of disobedience: a common Hebraism: = 'disobedient ones'; cf. 5^6.

3

we: i.e. 'we Jewish Christians too', or perhaps especially Paul. However great the authority with which he speaks, Paul, or pseudo-Paul, owes all to Christ.

flesh: not so much the body as the whole man orientated away from God and towards its own selfish concerns; so the next phrase expounds correctly. Cf. Gal. 5$^{19f.}$, where the works of the flesh include purely mental sins like enmity and jealousy.

by nature: i.e. as far as our own power to help the matter was concerned. The sinful manner of life was ingrained in man to the deepest level. The word is not used in any refined philosophical sense. There may well be a deliberate contrast with *by grace* in vv. 5 & 8.

children of wrath: another Hebraism (cf. *sons of disobedience*, v. 2). Radically and thoroughly, man is surrounded by God's implacable hatred of evil, and, apart from God's own spontaneous act of grace, there is no alleviation of this predicament. Of himself, he can no more remove himself from it than a child can escape from its parentage. Cf. Rom. 1^{18}; Col. 3^6.

4–10

The rest of the section shows the other side of the picture: the new life into which God has brought us through Christ. Schille (T.L.Z. (1957), pp. 326ff.), who has gone further than other scholars in seeing a series of early Christian liturgical units, all linked with the rite of baptism, as the basis of the first part of *Ephesians*, regards these verses as the response of the person being baptized. The main verbs are all aorist (single past action) and easily refer to baptism. But this view remains hypothetical.

4

mercy ... love: cf. Rom. 11^{32}; 5^8.

5

dead through our trespasses: exactly the phrase applied to *you* in v. 1.

by grace: i.e. by God's unmerited favour, as v. 10 makes clear. In this sense the word (*charis*) has developed beyond both its classical (usually it means 'graciousness') and LXX background, where it is most commonly used to mean 'favour', especially in the translating of the Hebrew expression 'to find favour in the eyes of X'. The New Testament writers, especially Paul, use it where the LXX more naturally uses *eleos* (*mercy*).

been saved: the writer uses here and in v. 8 the perfect participle of the verb *sōzō*; that is, he is speaking of an act which is past and completed. There are two points to note about this, one linguistic, the other theological.

(i) Linguistic: nowhere else does Paul use this verb in this tense. Normally it is used either in the present or the future, and the same applies to the reference of the corresponding noun *salvation* (*sōtēria*). In Paul's terminology this word refers to a process of bringing about man's assured security with God which will only be concluded at the Last Day. Thus the believers are now in the course of being saved (1 Cor. 1^{18}), and salvation, though nearer than it was, is still to come (Rom. 13^{11}). It is true that in Rom. 8^{24}, Paul uses the aorist (simple past tense) of the verb, but by adding the words *in this hope*, he shows that the realization remains incomplete.* The uncompromisingly past reference of the word here is then quite unlike Paul's usage and one of the best indications that the writer is not Paul; he would normally use the verb *justify* to denote that which God has already done for his people.

(ii) Theological: this strong past tense is in line with a very strong note of realized eschatology in these verses; that is, the benefits associated in Judaism with the Last Day and in varying words and to different degrees seen by the first Christians as brought by Christ to the world, are here seen as already fully enjoyed by his followers: *you have been saved, he raised us up and made us sit.* There is, apart from the reference to *the coming ages* in v. 7, none of the expectation of what is still to come that we find in 1^{14}. This gives some support to those who see here a separate unit coming from Hellenistic Christian circles which were sometimes inclined to over-stress the extent to which they had already been brought to perfection of life with God, cf. 2 Tim. 2^{18}; and it is even suggested that 1^{14} was introduced to modify a prayer which also took this view. Paul himself rarely makes statements which fall wholly

* 2 Cor. 6^{2} affords an exception in using the noun with reference to the present.

on one side or the other: God has acted and still will act, until the End. See, for example, the balance of tenses in Rom. 6^{1-11} and Col. 3^{1-4}.

6f.
raised us ... and made us sit: see this in the light of $1^{20, 23}$. What God did for Christ is passed on to the Church which wholly depends on him and is organically one with him. (The same point is made in other terms in John 16^{15}.) The words used are typically pauline verbs compounded with the prefix *syn* (= with): 'he has co-made-us-alive, co-raised us, co-made-us-sit' (cf. Col. 2^{12}). However, the concept here is less thoroughgoing than in the *Colossians* parallel (cf. also Rom. 6^{1-11}); it is more a doctrine of companionship with Christ, less one of incorporation. Note the absence of the idea of *union* with his death or burial.

The force of these words is that already the Christians, while continuing in this world, share Christ's authority over the angels who have hitherto had the *heavenly places* as their domain. Paul saw this rather as their future destiny: 1 Cor. 6^3.

the coming ages: the use of these words may simply be general, or it may reflect the view that the history of the world is divided into a set of pre-ordained eras, a current Jewish alternative to the notion of two ages, the present and the coming ones, which appears in 1^{21}. A comparison with 3^{9-11} shows that this may be an instance of the idea of the *aiōnes* as personified powers (cf. p. 182); these are now subordinate to the Church (cf. 2^2). (In this case translate: 'among the Aeons'.)

riches of his grace: cf. 1^7.

8
Cf. Rom. $3^{24, 28}$. The initiative and energy operating in man's salvation are God's. They flow wholly from his spontaneous mercy and love.

9
lest any man should boast: Cf. Phil. 3^3; Rom. 4^2; 1 Cor. 1^{28ff}. It is vital to Paul's teaching on salvation that man should not be in a position to claim credit in the least degree for his new-found relationship with God. To make such claims is both to misunderstand to the point of blasphemy the all-embracing power and utter holiness of God and to underestimate the abjectness of man's condition before a God such as this. Man must receive, as a beggar receives alms; only then can he receive in full measure the gifts which he so badly needs. The vessel must first be empty. It is not that man is to be crushed; quite the contrary – God re-creates him.

9f.

These two verses make a succinct commentary on the familiar grace *versus* works debate. That salvation is not to be earned by virtuous actions is no reason for underplaying their importance. Conversely, good works are to be the fruit of God's action within us, not a means of stimulating it. But to what moment does v. 10 refer, when it speaks of our being *his workmanship* (or 'product') *created in Christ Jesus*? It may refer to our physical beginning, seeing Christ as God's intermediary in this as in redemption; cf. 1 Cor. 8^6; Col. 1^{16}. Christ is presented in the role of wisdom in traditional Jewish thought (cf. Wis. 9$^{1f.}$; Prov. 8$^{22ff.}$). Or it may refer to redemption and its application to the individual in baptism, under the image of creation, cf. 2^{15}; 2 Cor. 5^{17}; Gal. 6^{15}; also the related image of new birth, John 3$^{1ff.}$. In either case the new life, with its practical moral expression, is part of God's plan, *prepared beforehand*, cf. 1$^{4f.}$, ^{11}.

2$^{11-22}$ JEWS AND GENTILES RECONCILED
                  IN THE CHURCH

^{11}*Therefore remember that at one time you Gentiles in the flesh, called the uncircumcision by what is called the circumcision, which is made in the flesh by hands –* ^{12}*remember that you were at that time separated from Christ, alienated from the commonwealth of Israel, and strangers to the covenants of promise, having no hope and without God in the world.* ^{13}*But now in Christ Jesus you who once were far off have been brought near in the blood of Christ.* ^{14}*For he is our peace, who has made us both one, and has broken down the dividing-wall of hostility,* ^{15}*by abolishing in his flesh the law of commandments and ordinances, that he might create in himself one new man in place of the two, so making peace,* ^{16}*and might reconcile us both to God in one body through the cross, thereby bringing the hostility to an end.* ^{17}*And he came and preached peace to you who were far off and peace to those who were near;* ^{18}*for through him we both have access in one Spirit to the Father.* ^{19}*So then you are no longer strangers and sojourners, but you are fellow citizens with the saints and members of the household of God,* ^{20} *built upon the foundation of the apostles and prophets, Christ Jesus himself being the cornerstone,* ^{21}*in whom the whole structure is joined together and grows into a holy temple in the Lord;* ^{22} *in whom you also are built into it for a dwelling-place of God in the Spirit.*

See the general comments on 2¹⁻¹⁰, p. 279. The subject is now the bringing together of Jews and Gentiles in the Church, the people of God. As the detailed notes show, the fact is presented in a mosaic of Old Testament allusions (above all Isa. 57¹⁹) and pauline phrases. There are also images which have a much wider currency in the New Testament world, like the new temple (vv. 21f.) and the cornerstone (v. 20).

Yet, as in the preceding passage, the pauline appearance is not wholly convincing. The tone here is one of thanksgiving for a work achieved. The reconciliation of Jew and Gentile is an accomplished fact, the Church as a joint Jew-Gentile enterprise is a going concern. It was no longer a novelty which had to be argued for and defended. If a dual character of the Church needs emphasizing by our writer, it is less to mollify Jewish Christians who resent the influx of Gentiles than to instruct Gentile Christians whose memory of the Church's Jewish roots is fading. In other words the situation is that of a generation later than Paul's own, when the whole weight of the Church had shifted, after the fall of Jerusalem in A.D. 70. It was now becoming necessary to show cause why the Old Testament heritage remained vital for the understanding of the Gospel. It was the question which the heretic Marcion was soon to ask more sharply than any, providing one of the most acute challenges to the Church's self-understanding and to her handling of the Old Testament Scriptures. So the present writer's readers are to *remember* that they were once *alienated from the commonwealth of Israel* (v. 12) and that one way of stating what has happened to them *in Christ Jesus* (i.e. by his agency) is that they are now part of that commonwealth (v. 19).

This view is supported by a comparison with other passages in Paul which deal with the same question, in particular Rom. 9–11. There, in a work also addressed to a largely Gentile audience, Paul faces the question of the place of the Gentiles in the people of God. The problem is one which involves him, as a Jew, emotionally, to a degree that makes his handling of the theology both tortuous and in certain ways less satisfactory than in *Ephesians* where it receives a 'cooler look'. Paul, utterly convinced though he is of the centrality of Christ and of the newness of what God has done through him, cannot emancipate himself from the conviction that Israel too is at the heart of God's action. He has, in a sense, two theological 'ultimates', which can scarcely be held together. Thus, in Rom. 9–11, he sets out to examine the implications of the faithlessness (i.e. by re-jecting Christ) of the people of Israel, who are, as a *datum* of his theology, the repository of God's revelation and the inheritors of his promises. Come what may, there is no escaping the fact that they are the primary sphere of God's redeeming activity. Yet they have rejected Christ, and Gentiles have accepted him – which Paul, the apostle to the Gentiles, wholeheartedly welcomes. While he is thinking in these 'Israel' terms, there is only one reasonable way out of this agonizing situation: that is, to give it an 'Israel' objective. God's purpose in the whole drama does not end with the bringing of Gentiles into the Church. Indeed their entry is meant to provoke Jews to jealousy (Rom. 11^{11}), so that ultimately they too will come into the Church, which will then appear in a straight line of develop-ment, as the true heir of the old Israel (Rom. $11^{25f.}$). If Paul had frankly abandoned 'Israel' as a theologically *fundamental* category and given to Christ alone this status, and if he had been able to escape his deep emotional involvement in the problem, he would have been able to see that in Christ a new and full declaration of God's purpose had been made, and that this created a situation in which all men stood on an equal footing (as he recognizes in Rom. 2), so that while Israel's history had provided the essential preparation, and in Abra-ham, as the man of faith, an anticipation of the new life (Rom. 4), Christ alone was the criterion by which even Israel was to be tested and by which her heritage and the various elements of her theological tradition were to be sifted, some for adoption, others for rejection.

By the time we reach *Ephesians*, the position has been clarified along these lines. Israel is of positive but not of ultimate significance. Gentiles, in becoming Christians, are not simply joining the old Israel; rather in Christ (the *one new man*, v. 15) a new people has been created, to which the image of Israel as the people of God can indeed be applied, as long as its limitations are recognized, and in which Jew and Gentile meet on an absolutely equal footing, as standing in need of a common redemption (2^{1-10}). True, Gentiles are those who hitherto have been *far off* (v. 13) and *alienated from the commonwealth of Israel* (v. 12), but this perspective is swiftly overshadowed by one in which Christ and the *household* (v. 19) created by him occupy the theological centre. Thus we are well on the way to the concept of the Church as the 'third race', neither Jewish nor Gentile, but Christian – the new and perfect instrument of God's purposes, stemming from Christ, the unique centre of all history, a concept first fully explicit in the second-century *Letter to Diognetus* (see E.C.W., pp. 173ff.), which itself uses our passage from *Ephesians*. In other words *Ephesians* has a detachment which on this issue Paul lacked. His usual sharp sense of Christ's unique centrality is blunted by the Jewishness in his bones; and while in Rom. 9–11 the issue is the addition of the Church to a given Jewish base, here the Church is the centre of the scheme, with Jews and Gentiles alike flowing towards her in tributary streams. The personal agony of Paul the converted Jew has gone.

Moreover, there is no explicit statement here that Jewish Christians were, in their pre-Christian days, truly members of God's people. In effect, this passage is simply parallel to its predecessor, only using different terms: the former used the death-life image, this uses the alien-citizen image; the former is chiefly ethical in its purpose, this concerns the community of the Church. But for all practical purposes Jew and Gentile are on equal footing in both, and Christ is the sole basis of the new dispensation. This is hardly Paul's standpoint *tout court*.

That in this passage the author is drawing upon already existing liturgical material is suggested by its structure; it seems to be constructed in a rough chiastic pattern (i.e. with the themes occurring in the sequence *abcde-edcba*), using either corresponding or contrasting ideas in its halves, cf. *in the flesh – in the spirit* (vv. 11 & 22), *alienated – fellow citizens* (vv. 12 & 19), *peace – hostility* (vv. 14 & 16). See Kirby, op. cit. p. 156f. Schille, however, in his identifying of liturgical material in *Ephesians*, isolates 2¹⁴⁻¹⁸ as a unit of a distinct type – a 'song to the Saviour'. In terms of the passage as a whole, this is certainly the core. Vv. 11–13 state the negative situation, vv. 19–22 the positive one (in parallel terms), while vv. 14–18 tell of the act of Christ which produces the one out of the other.

༺༻

11
remember: perhaps in the liturgical sense, amounting to 'praise God because ...' Perhaps rather a reminder of truth in danger of neglect (see above).

the uncircumcision ... circumcision: i.e. 'Gentiles ... Jews'. Cf. Col. 2¹¹, on which this verse partly depends but whose words it nevertheless alters. It also simplifies and changes its sense.

made . . . by hands: the use of this word and its opposite is fairly common in the New Testament (cf. Col. 2¹¹; Mark 14⁵⁸; Acts 7⁴⁸; 17²⁴; Heb. 9¹¹, ²⁴), to contrast the purely physical nature of the institutions of Judaism with the spiritual efficacy of their Christian equivalents.

12

commonwealth: note the contrast with the more intimate *household* which is applied to the Church, v. 19, though the political image is retained in the earlier half of that verse. The word can mean 'constitution' rather than 'state'. If this is the sense, the *covenants* are no doubt seen as the Jews' basic constitutional documents; but in view of v. 19 the other meaning is to be preferred.

strangers: or 'foreigners', cf. *fellow citizens* in v. 19.

covenants: in the plural only elsewhere at Rom. 9⁴. Judaism commonly spoke of a series of covenants made by God, e.g. those with Adam, Noah, and Abraham, as well as the great covenant of Sinai. They are treaties whereby God solemnly takes an individual or a people into relationship with himself, granting them the privilege of his lordship and promising future goods, while requiring faithful service in return (see Exod. 24¹⁻¹¹).

without God: better, 'without any deity'. In fact they had a multitude of deities, but both Jews and Christians regarded these as no gods at all, cf. I Cor. 8⁴ᶠ·; Gal. 4⁸; Isa. 40¹⁸; 46⁵ᶠᶠ·. At best, they treated them as demons masquerading. To trust them is in effect to be adrift and godless in the universe.

13

Cf. v. 17. The background is Isa. 57¹⁹. The original meaning of those *far off* was simply Jews in exile. Rabbis applied the prophecy to proselytes, i.e. Gentile converts to Judaism, and with its help justified their incorporation into Jewry, but now it is applied to Gentiles pure and simple. In the Church they came together with Jews in a new unity. The verse is used also in Acts 2³⁹, in Peter's Pentecost speech. Whatever traditions the writer of *Acts* may have had at his disposal, we take it that the details of the message are his rather than Peter's, so that this reference provides one of a considerable number of parallels between *Acts* and *Ephesians*. As we have seen (p. 254) the two works share not only details of this kind but also certain broad viewpoints which are evidence of their facing common problems with common solutions.

in the blood of Christ: once more *Colossians* is used and at the same time its terms twisted into new patterns. Here the related passage is Col. 1²⁰⁻²² (cf. Rom. 3²⁵; I Cor. 11²⁵). Instead of Christ's *blood* (i.e. his sacrificial death) being seen as the way of reconciling *all things* (in *that* connexion, *Ephesians* makes no reference to Christ's death, cf. $1^{20\text{ff}}$.), it is the way of reconciling Jew and Gentile. And the estrangement (the word in Col. 1^{21} is the same as that translated *alienated* in Eph. 2^{12}) is no longer that between God and sinful man but that between Gentiles and Israel. For this writer the object of Christ's death is (though see also 1^7) the creation of the Church as a Jew-Gentile unity, God's people open to all mankind. A similar – ecclesiastical – turn is given to a central concept in 4^{8-11}, where the chief fruit of Christ's ascension is seen as the Church's ministers, and in 1^{23}, where Christ has been made *head over all things for the Church* (cf. also 5^{25}).

14f.

Cf. Col. 3^{11}; Gal. 3^{28}: though here those more inclusive statements are simplified, so that only the Jew-Gentile division is mentioned. Again, cf. the perspective of *Acts*, especially ch. 10, 11, & 15.

peace: cf. Col. 1^{20}; and perhaps Isa. 9^6, which led rabbis to teach that 'peace' would be the Messiah's name. Vv. 15 & 17 reiterate the word. The Greek stresses the opening *he*: 'Christ and no other'. For this type of statement, cf. Col. 1^{27} (Christ as hope); 3^4 (Christ as life); and the many johannine 'I am' sayings, e.g. John 14^6.

us both one: lit. 'the two things one thing': the Greek uses neuters.

the dividing-wall: lit. 'the dividing-wall of the fence', i.e. two words which are virtually synonyms, joined in typical *Ephesians* style. Or else the second word explains the first – 'the dividing-wall which acts as a fence'. *Hostility*, with a definite article, is placed in apposition to this: 'the dividing-wall, that is, the hostility'. Christ has neutralized the Law *in his flesh:* either, that is, by his becoming man (cf. Rom. 8^3; Gal. 4^4), or, as vv. 13 & 16 imply, by his human (fleshly) death. Cf. Col. 2^{14}. *Law of commandments* may not be just a needless conjunction of equivalents; it draws attention to the fact that the Law's disastrous effects partly result from its consisting of a host of commandments.

The image of the fence is no doubt derived from the wall in the Temple which divided the Court of the Gentiles from the inner parts of the building open only to Jews. To cross the boundary was to merit the death-penalty. It would add to the appropriateness of this reference to our writer's theme if by the time he was writing the wall had been destroyed; this occurred in A.D. 70 at the Temple's destruction by the Romans. But the common rabbinic idea of the fence of the Law (see above) is at least as much to the fore here. There may too be an allusion to Ps. 80, where the breaking down of the walls (v. 12, LXX *phragmos*, as in Eph. 2^{14}) leads on to restoration by the might of the 'man of thy (God's) right hand, the son of man whom thou hast made so strong for thyself' (v. 17): cf. the *one new man* of Eph. 2^{15}. Both here and in Ps. 80 (cf. vv. 1 & 14) 'the man' is a figure with corporate significance.

There is one other strand of thought which probably contributes to the thought of this passage. The speculative Judaism of the first century, so closely allied to the Gnosticism which fully emerges in the following period, had the concept of a wall which divided the spheres of heaven and earth (cf. 1 Enoch 14^9, Charles, II, p. 197), and came to identify it with the Law, seen as the boundary wall between God and man. Similarly, Gnosticism often spoke of the Redeemer-figure as cleaving the wall of heaven, and leading his initiates through to salvation. See also on 3^{18}, p. 304.

All these elements have their part in Eph. 2$^{14f.}$. In the person of Christ, the mythical Saviour has appeared in history (the *flesh*). The fence of the Law, whether standing between Jews and Gentiles or between God and man, or heaven and earth, has been shown up as a barrier. Christ has broken it down and brought all into unity. The writer shares the broad mythological picture of the speculation which we have described, but he sees Christ, who lived and died, as the unique actor in its drama, and as the one who replaces the Law, doing what it could not do and did not even desire to do; that is, reconcile all men to God. Notice that there is no hint of the positive role accorded by Paul to the Law in its proper time and place (e.g. Gal. 3$^{23ff.}$).

one new man: whether there is a conscious reference to Ps. 80 or not, the background here is the common pauline (and New Testament) idea of Christ as the new Adam (e.g. Rom. 5$^{12ff.}$; 1 Cor. 15$^{21ff.}$; Phil. 2$^{6ff.}$; Col. 3$^{10f.}$), which is now applied to the theme in hand. Hence *create*, making the parallel with Gen. 1$^{26ff.}$, the creation of Adam.

16
both: here, masculine, contrast v. 14. The image is of two men, representing Jews and Gentiles, replaced by one man, Christ, representing and summing up in himself the new redeemed humanity. But the idea of our incorporation into Christ goes less deep than in Paul: *in himself* means little more than 'by his agency'.

reconcile to God: Rom. 5^{10}; 2 Cor. 5$^{18ff.}$.

17
preached peace: cf. Isa. 52^7. The image now changes from Christ the reconciler to Christ the preacher, as portrayed in the Gospels. Or, given the mythological idiom here, it may refer to the idea, common in such contexts, of Jesus' preaching at his ascension to the angelic powers, who lie behind the Law and the *hostility* which it represents (p. 164),

2¹¹⁻²²

thus bringing about their submission and opening up the way to heaven (*access*) for his followers; cf. 1 Pet. 3^{18ff.} (Ascension of Isaiah 11, Hennecke, II, p. 662).

those who were near: the writer does not say *us*, to correspond to the *you* of the earlier part of the verse. Some scholars see this as evidence that though the writer adopts the stance of Paul, he is not himself a Jewish Christian and does not naturally identify himself as a Jew, as Paul would surely have done.

18

access: cf. 3¹²; Rom. 5². Contrast *separated*, v. 12. Christ has broken the cosmic barrier, which is identified with the Law.

in one spirit: cf. 1 Cor. 12¹³.

19

strangers and sojourners: i.e. pure aliens (*xenoi*), and aliens enjoying certain rights in the land of their residence (*paroikoi*). Comparison with Heb. 11¹³ and 1 Pet. 2¹¹ shows that these were popular terms for describing the status of Christians in this world, cf. Phil. 3²⁰.

saints: either the angels (see p. 258) or the first Christians already seen as a golden generation (cf. v. 20).

household: cf. 1 Tim. 3¹⁵. It signifies both family and house.

20

While v. 19 simply took up the city-imagery of v. 12, the rest of the passage moves to the related ideas of building and temple. *Household* forms an easy transition. All these images were common in early Christian writing, all received a variety of applications. Some features of their use here are important in trying to solve the problem of the date and setting of *Ephesians*.

foundation of the apostles and prophets: in 1 Cor. 3¹¹, Christ himself is seen as the foundation of the Church, in explicit distinction from apostles like Peter and Apollos. Though obviously there is no intention here of denying or weakening this teaching, nevertheless many scholars see the change of language as significant. It looks as if *Ephesians* comes from a time when the centrality of Christ could be taken for granted in the Church, but when it was already necessary to appeal to the venerable authority of the early leaders of the Church (*prophets* means not those of the Old Testament but early Christian preachers, cf. 1 Cor. 12 & 14; Acts 11²⁷), because this was being threatened by heretical teachers, cf. 3⁵; 4¹¹. Authentic Christian lineage is coming to be seen as a guarantee of true teaching.

built ... structure: cf. 1 Pet. 2⁵; Col. 2⁷.

cornerstone: the stone which completes and holds together the whole building (cf. v. 21). The word occurs again in 1 Pet. 2⁶ in a quotation from Isa. 28¹⁶, a text quoted or alluded to many times in the New Testament. In 1 Pet. 2 it is one of a series of Old Testament texts, all, in one way or another, applying the image of the stone to Christ. It is evident that these texts became associated in Christian apologetic from early days; some of them appear, in closer conflation, in Rom. 9³³. One of them appears again in Matt. 21⁴² and Acts 4¹¹.

21

is joined together and grows: the same verbs appear in 4¹⁵ᶠ· (cf. *building up* in 4¹²), in connexion with the idea of Christ and his body the Church (cf. Col. 2¹⁹). Here we have the parallel image of the *temple*. (Both occur similarly in 1 Cor. 3¹⁶ᶠᶠ· & 12¹²ᶠᶠ·.) Cf. the idea of perfection still to come in 1¹⁴.

temple: this image too received a great variety of uses in the New Testament. Here, as in 1 Cor. 3⁹, ¹⁶ᶠᶠ· & 2 Cor. 6¹⁶, God's holy shrine, replacing the Jerusalem temple, is the Christian people, the Church. They are, as it were, stones in the structure. In John 2¹⁹⁻²¹, Christ himself, in his risen body, is that new temple. Paul would not have quarrelled with that strong application of the idea, for when he thinks in terms of the body of Christ (1 Cor. 12; Rom. 12) Christians and their Lord are strongly identified. They are incorporated in him. It is worth noting that here, as often in *Ephesians*, that idea is not carried so far; Christ is one element in the structure, albeit the vital one. (Note also the strong imagery of Rev. 21²².) Qumran, not suprisingly, shared this image, cf. B. Gärtner, *The Temple and the Community in Qumran and the New Testament* (Cambridge, 1965).

22

in whom: i.e. in Christ = 'by his agency'.

in the Spirit: the new temple is the Spirit-filled community: cf. 1 Pet. 2⁵; Rom. 8⁹; 1 Cor. 12¹³.

With these last verses, compare the Community Rule of Qumran, ch. VIII (Vermes, p. 85):

The Council of the Community ... shall be an Everlasting Plantation, a House of Holiness for Israel ... It shall be that tried wall, that precious cornerstone, whose foundations shall neither rock nor sway in their place. It shall be a Most Holy Dwelling for Aaron, with everlasting knowledge of the Covenant of Justice, and shall offer up sweet fragrance. It shall be a House of Perfection and Truth in Israel.

3 $^{1-13}$ GOD'S GRACE REVEALED IN PAUL'S
APOSTOLATE

[1]*For this reason, I, Paul, a prisoner for Christ Jesus on behalf of you Gentiles –* [2]*assuming that you have heard of the stewardship of God's grace that was given to me for you,* [3]*how the mystery was made known to me by revelation, as I have written briefly.* [4]*When you read this you can perceive my insight into the mystery of Christ,* [5]*which was not made known to the sons of men in other generations as it has now been revealed to his holy apostles and prophets by the Spirit;* [6]*that is, how the Gentiles are fellow-heirs, members of the same body, and partakers of the promise in Christ Jesus through the gospel.*

[7]*Of this gospel I was made a minister according to the gift of God's grace which was given me by the working of his power.* [8]*To me, though I am the very least of all the saints, this grace was given, to preach to the Gentiles the unsearchable riches of Christ,* [9]*and to make all men see what is the plan of the mystery hidden for ages in^d God who created all things;* [10]*that through the church the manifold wisdom of God might now be made known to the principalities and powers in the heavenly places.* [11]*This was according to the eternal purpose which he has realized in Christ Jesus our Lord,* [12]*in whom we have boldness and confidence of access through our faith in him.* [13]*So I ask you not to^e lose heart over what I am suffering for you, which is your glory.*

d Or by   e Or I ask that I may not

Apart from 6$^{21f.}$ (which virtually reproduces Col. 4$^{7f.}$), this passage is by far the most personal in the whole of *Ephesians*. It comes nearer to giving the work the appearance of a genuine letter than any other part. But it has failed to convince many modern critics either that *Ephesians* is an ordinary letter or that it is a work of Paul. On the first issue, though there are a number of references in these verses to Paul's past career and present circumstances, their language is for the most part of a piece with the rest of the work. On the second issue the personal references are all too reminiscent, though the manner is more generalized, of statements in Galatians 1-2 & 1 Cor. 15. The combination of these features seems to many to tell strongly against pauline authorship; others draw precisely the opposite conclusion.

Those who believe that the basis of this work lies in early Christian liturgical material see in our passage an intrusion by the writer made when he put this material into letter-form, presumably in order to circulate it for the edification of the churches. This view is supported by the fact that it leans heavily upon (*a*) the earlier part of *Ephesians* and (*b*) autobiographical references in Paul's undoubted letters. Nevertheless the case cannot be taken as proven. If this is an intrusion, then it has been skilfully done – with one exception: that 3^{14} follows much more naturally from 2^{22} than from 3^{13}. Thematically, the continuity is excellent. If 2^{1-10} has described the fruit of God's work in Christ in terms of man's salvation, and 2^{11-22} has gone on to describe it in terms of the new people of God, open to all men, what could be more fitting in a work of praise by Paul (or by his disciple) than that he should then tell of this work in terms of his own apostolate? That apostolate was God's chosen instrument to bring about the Gentiles' participation in the redeemed community, reconciled to himself. It is not very hard to see *for this reason* in 3^{14} as referring back to the whole of $2^{1-3, 13}$, rather than just to either 3^{13} or the last verses of ch. 2.

Perhaps the chief new point of theological interest in this passage is to be found in v. 9f. The background is the common early Christian mythological conception that at his descent to earth in his incarnation Christ passed incognito through the successive heavens, unrecognized by the various classes of angelic beings who rule and inhabit them. (See J. Daniélou, *The Theology of Jewish Christianity* (London, 1964), ch. 7.) This view was not the only one current in the early Church. Others held the quite contrary doctrine that Christ's appearance on earth took place with the acclaim of the angels, giving cosmic backing to his work (Luke 2^{13}; Heb. 1^6). But our writer chooses the former view, like his master Paul, cf. 1 Cor. 2^8. Only, unlike Paul, he specifies the mode by which the angels are now relieved of their ignorance. Paul, whose concern is with the evil angels who brought about Christ's death, leaves this matter open, though in 1 Cor. 6^3 we find the belief that (presumably at the End) Christians are, by virtue of their association with Christ, even to judge the angels. But, typically, the writer of *Ephesians* both objectifies the Church and heightens its role. The Church, in its preaching, is the instrument by which the angels learn of God's plan, in particular (again typically) his bringing of Jews and Gentiles together in sharing *the unsearchable riches of Christ*. If we ask why Christians believed that the angels (be they, so it seems, good or bad) had been hitherto kept in ignorance, the answer may lie in the need to answer Jewish objections stemming from the earthly obscurity of him for whom Christians made such lofty claims. True, Judaism knew the concept of the hidden Messiah (cf. p. 182), but Christians (cf. e.g. the 'messianic secret' of Mark's Gospel) seized upon this idea and gave it special prominence. Christ had been deliberately hidden from both angels and men – but now the time of proclamation has come and the Church declares him to heaven and earth, all in accordance with God's secret plan. (I am grateful to the Rev. G. C. Stead for suggestions along these lines.)

The passage may also have a more practical aim. Whether Paul wrote *Ephesians* or not, this section unfolds the implication of Paul's title given in 1^1. It constitutes not only a statement of his vocation but also an assertion of his authority, albeit the Christian authority of service and suffering (3$^{7-13}$), like Christ's own (cf. 2 Cor. 12–13). Paul is apostle to the Gentiles, and his passion for the unity of God's people (which ch. 4 takes up again) carries with it a claim that Gentile churches should all look to Paul. In Paul's life-time we already see him facing situations where his universal Gentile apostolate is embarrassed by the activity of others in that field (cf. Rom. 15$^{18-22}$; 2 Cor. 10$^{13-16}$). Both then and later, Paul's Christ-given relationship to Gentile congregations, even those not of his own foundation, needed asserting. The formal and somewhat magisterial way of stating it in *Ephesians* seems to many scholars the mark of a post-pauline ecclesiastical policy.

ॐ

1

For this reason: on any showing it is hard to see here more than the loosest of connexions with what has gone before. This phrase acts as little other than a way of introducing a new section. But if we read v.1 in conjunction with 3^{13}, we may have a reference to the doctrine which we find in Col. 1^{24}: the apostle's sufferings are the way in which he contributes to the divine plan which has just been outlined, the building up of the Church. This view is strengthened (and the grammar improved) if we understand 'am' before *a prisoner*. As the R.S.V.'s literal translation shows, this and the following verses are obscure, not only in their connexion with their context but also in their grammatical structure. A few manuscripts read 'I, Paul ... act as ambassador on behalf of you Gentiles', but this is so obviously an addition designed to smooth the syntax that it can hardly be original.

prisoner for Christ Jesus: cf. Philem. ¹ & ⁹; also on Col. 4¹⁰, p. 219. This reference, that in 6²⁰, and the appearance of composition at the same time as *Colossians*, given by 6²¹ᶠ·, qualify *Ephesians* for inclusion among the Captivity Epistles. In genuine Paul the term almost certainly carries both literal and metaphorical reference. He is captive to Christ for the work of the Gentile Mission (cf. the idea of slavery to Christ, 1 Cor. 7²²). But in a pseudonymous work it may simply be a detail in the pauline façade.

2

you have heard: cf. 1¹⁵. Hardly likely in a letter addressed to the church in Ephesus, so well-known to Paul. Only possible in a later pseudonymous work really addressed to that church, but failing in verisimilitude, or a pseudonymous work addressed more widely, or a genuinely pauline work addressed to Christians whom he did not know personally.

stewardship: Gk *oikonomia*. This is one of the words whose distinctive sense in this epistle is often taken as evidence of non-pauline authorship (cf. D. E. Nineham in ed. Cross, *Studies in Ephesians*, p. 29). It is true that in the closely parallel *Colossians* passage (1²⁵) it bears the sense of 'special task' (R.S.V. *office*), as in the only other pauline use, 1 Cor. 9¹⁷; whereas in Eph. 1¹⁰ & 3⁹ it means something more like 'strategy' or 'planned economy'. Some see this sense here; but there is more to be said for the R.S.V. rendering. Thus the word is used in two different senses even within *Ephesians*, a feature common enough in the word-usage of genuine Paul. The word's basic sense is 'household management', so that there is an echo of the imagery of 2¹⁹ᶠᶠ·. In this case, the meaning is close to that in Col. 1²⁵, the distinction being simply the fine one between the performing of the office (Eph. 3²) and the office itself (Col. 1²⁵). The reader who thinks that in acting thus the author of *Ephesians* shows such incomprehension in his manner of using *Colossians* (assuming that he did), as could hardly occur if it were his own work, will see evidence that he was other than Paul himself. Note that Paul sees apostles under the image of stewardship ('steward' – *oikonomos*) in 1 Cor. 4¹.

given: in Col. 1²⁵ it is the *office* (*oikonomia*) which was given to Paul, here it is *the grace*. This pitches the apostle's role even higher; God's grace has been given to him for their sole benefit, and, conversely, he is the channel of that grace. Cf. Gal. 2^9 for the same word used of Paul's apostolate.

3

mystery: i.e., for this writer, that divine plan, hitherto concealed, which gave to Paul his unique place, the plan of bringing into unity Jews and Gentiles in the one Church (vv. 4–6). In view of the link already noticed, this word probably comes from 1 Cor. 4^1, but the sense is different. Only *Ephesians* uses *mystērion* to signify the Jew-Gentile union. As we saw in relation to 1^9 (p. 268), it is a word about which it is possible to say either 'genuine Paul could not have used it so', or 'genuine Paul already gives the word such a range of senses that he was quite capable of one more' (see Nineham in ed. Cross *Studies in Ephesians,* p. 28).

revelation: cf. Gal. 1^{12}. That verse can be taken in either of two ways. It can mean 'a revelation given by Jesus Christ' or 'a revelation which consisted of Jesus Christ'. Paul almost certainly meant the second. If our writer was using it, he seems to have taken it in the first sense, for its content is *the mystery* (i.e. the Jew-Gentile union), which corresponds to *the gospel* of Gal. 1^{11}. Note: we should say 'a' revelation (the indefinite article cannot be expressed in Greek): it means a particular act of disclosure rather than the mode of operation by which 'Paul' came to know.

I have written briefly: ...er a reference to Gal. 1, or simply back to 1$^{9f.}$, which also speaks of *the mystery.*

4

insight: Gk *synesis.* Cf. Col. 2^2 where again it is used in connexion with *mystērion* (R.S.V. there has *understanding*). From Qumran (Vermes, p. 189): 'In the mystery of thy wisdom, thou hast opened knowledge to me.'

mystery of Christ: cf. Col. 1^{27}: only now the *mystery* is not that of Christ's mystical indwelling of the believer, but the Gentiles' reception into the Church. As we have already seen in this work, the ecclesiastical tends to a degree to displace the purely personal, and doctrine about Christ and his work to displace 'Christ' himself (see note on *revelation,* v. 3 above). The typical pauline mysticism of the believer's incorporation into Christ gives way to language which allows more distinction between them.

5

not made known . . . now been revealed: cf. 3^9; Col. 1^{26}; 1 Cor. 2$^{7-10}$. See above, on *mystery* (v. 3).

to his holy apostles and prophets: cf. 2^{20}; 4^{11}. Notice again the ecclesiastical concern; the parallel in Col. 1^{26} has *to his saints*, i.e. to all Christian believers. This is of course not denied here, but the stress is placed on the proper authority of the Church's foundation leaders – including Paul himself. More than elsewhere in this work, we can sense in 3^{3-13} an awareness of Christians who look to other authorities, and who do not behave as if they had *heard of the stewardship of God's grace that was given* to Paul for them. The reference may be now (contrast $2^{11ff.}$, p. 286) to Jewish Christians who are unwilling to accept Gentiles into the Church on equal terms or to Gentile Christians who are reluctant to assert their equality. For the writer this is the key message of the hour – the heart of his gospel. It was hardly the heart of Paul's gospel. In *Ephesians* Paul's message (of Christ's saving work for all men) has been fused with Paul's role (as apostle to the Gentiles), so that everything revolves round the Church as the point of union of Jew and Gentile.

holy: signifies consecration to God's service.

sons of men: hebraism for 'mankind', cf. Mark 3^{28}.

6

Cf. 2^{19}.

fellow-heirs: cf. Rom. 8^{17}, where all Christians are fellow-heirs with Christ of *his* inheritance as God's Son. Here, Jewish and Gentile Christians are fellow-heirs with one another of the promise of God made through Christ. Once more, the conception is less mystical. The accent is more on Christians as members of the Church. The English conceals three Greek adjectives beginning with the prefix *syn* (= 'with', 'fellow-'): 'inheriting with, embodied with, sharing with'.

in Christ Jesus: probably, as usually in *Ephesians*, instrumental in sense – 'through Christ Jesus'.

7

minister: Gk *diakonos* (= servant); cf. Col. $1^{23, 25}$.

grace given: reiterates 3^2. Cf. Rom. 12^3.

by the working: Gk literally means 'according to the working', so that there are two virtually synonymous phrases introduced by the same preposition *kata* (though depending on different antecedents, as in the translation). These identical words occur in Col. 1^{29} (R.S.V. *with all the energy*).

8

least of all the saints: cf. 1 Cor. 15^9, where Paul describes himself as *the least of the apostles*, because he had *persecuted the Church of God*. Here the context is quite different, though the theme is still the apostleship of Paul. Now there is no question of his needing to establish his claim to that title. The writer of *Ephesians* takes it calmly for granted, though he cannot afford to say anything which might seem to depreciate the authority of Paul the apostle. So an expression of humility in the form he chooses is exposed to fewer risks than an imitation of 1 Cor. 15⁹ would have been. The Pope can call himself 'servant of the servants of God'; he would scarcely substitute 'least of the bishops of Christendom'.

Comparison with 1 Cor. 15⁹ thus affords a typical example of the increased concern in *Ephesians* with the policy and position of the Church and with the way in which she exercises authority. It also exemplifies another not uncharacteristic shift of emphasis: our writer lacks Paul's acute sense of the astonishing paradox of God's action as revealed in Christ. Thus, though both passages share a transition from an admission of being *least* to an assertion of grace received for the office of apostle, the manner differs significantly. In 1 Cor. 15⁹ᶠ·, Paul knows that his being an apostle is a matter of *sheer* grace: everything human stood against it, even to his having been a persecutor of the Church – and yet God (and no other factor whatsoever) has given him this task. Here the contrast is much less radical: between 'Paul's' merits (his disclaimer is almost trite) and his elevation to his great task. *This grace* is more the divine authorization for his office than God's wholly unexpected and spontaneous act. (Note: the oldest manuscript P46 omits *saints*: 'least of all men'.)

riches of Christ: cf. Col. 1²⁷ which *Ephesians* here abbreviates.

Unsearchable: cf. Rom. 11³³.

9
the plan: Gk *oikonomia*, as in 1¹⁰. See on 3².

for ages: lit. 'from the ages, or Aeons'. See on 2² and 2⁷ (p. 281). The sense is as in R.S.V. or else we have the mythological concept of the time that God's plan was hidden from the angelic powers, especially those controlling human history, cf. 1 Cor. 2⁸; Ignatius' *Epistle to the Ephesians*, 19 (E.C.W., p. 81). That plan had now been revealed to the powers (v. 10). There is little to choose between *in* and *by God*: the former is the better text and fits the mythological idiom better.

make all men see . . . created all things: one of the profound simplicities of New Testament teaching. God desires to save all because he has created all. The image of enlightenment may have Gnostic links. To see God's plan is to accept it. Compare the sequence in John 1¹⁻¹⁴, where the creative Word is made flesh and both *enlightens every man* (verb as here) and is seen by men (1^{14}). There may be a polemic in the reference to God as creator in this context: against Gnostics who saw subordinate powers as performing this role. God is the sole author of all things.

10

through the Church: seen in her cosmic role in accordance with God's plan, as expounded in $1^{22f.}$; $4^{15f.}$. The Church is God's mouthpiece in heaven as well as earth, for she already shares in the universal lordship of Christ (cf. 2^6). Events in heaven are the counterpart of events on earth, and the Church, through Christ, spans both realms.

the manifold wisdom of God: wisdom, portrayed in Jewish tradition (e.g. Prov. $8^{22ff.}$; Wisdom of Solomon 9^1) as God's agent in creation, is seen by New Testament writers as embodied in Christ: e.g. 1 Cor. $1^{24, 30}$. He wholly expresses God's creative purpose. Here that wisdom is seen as realized less in Christ's person than in the drama of his redemptive work, when at his final exaltation he was revealed to the cosmic powers as lord of all (cf. $1^{20ff.}$). It is parallel to *mystery*, also referred to as *made known* ($3^{3, 5}$). The use of this term is deliberate in a context which has spoken of God as creator; Christ, not the angelic powers, is God's fully (1^{23}) endowed agent in creation as in redemption, cf. Col. $1^{15ff.}$. God's *wisdom* is *manifold* because it appears in creation, in Christ and his redemptive work, and now in the Church which stems from him.

11
purpose: cf. $1^{5, 9f.}$.

12
boldness: cf. 2 Cor. 3^{12}.

access: i.e. to God; cf. 2^{18}; Rom. 5^2.

13
Cf. Col. 1^{24}. Another reference to Paul's imprisonment.

your glory: cf. 2 Cor. 1^6; 4^{7-15}.

3^{14-21} CONCLUDING PRAYER AND DOXOLOGY

^{14}*For this reason I bow my knees before the Father,* ^{15}*from whom every family in heaven and on earth is named,* ^{16}*that according to the riches of his glory he may grant you to be strengthened with might through his Spirit in the inner man,* ^{17}*and that Christ may dwell in your hearts through faith; that you, being rooted and grounded in love,* ^{18}*may have power to comprehend with all saints what is the breadth and length and depth and height,* ^{19}*and to*

*know the love of Christ which surpasses knowledge, that you may be filled
with all the fullness of God.*

²⁰*Now to him who by the power at work within us is able to do far more
abundantly than all that we ask or think,* ²¹*to him be glory in the church and
in Christ Jesus to all generations, for ever and ever. Amen.*

These verses conclude the first half of *Ephesians*, which has been
characterized largely by thanksgiving to the Father for the vast range
of blessings which he has conferred, in creation, in Christ and in the
Church – *his manifold wisdom* (3¹⁰). As we have seen (p. 259), Jewish
Blessings commonly ended with a prayer that God's gifts might be
rightly received, before the final doxology (cf. Ps. 106⁴⁷), so that
Ephesians follows a customary form. J. C. Kirby (op. cit. pp. 126ff.),
who sees an extensive baptismal *berakah* as forming the basis for these
chapters, regards this passage as part of that formula; it is a prayer
that those baptized may bring forth the fruits of their Christian
profession. If the Blessing form is seen as confined to 1³⁻¹⁴, it is still
true that the rest of ch. 1–3 springs organically from it and develops
its themes in such a way that a conclusion of this kind is entirely
natural.

Mostly, these verses refer yet again to ideas with which we are
now familiar.

ಜಜ

14
For this reason: see above, p. 296.

bow my knees: cf. Phil. 2¹⁰; Rom. 11⁴; 14¹¹. The attitude of homage
primarily, not of prayer. Prayer was usually offered standing and the
synagogue required it (cf. Matt. 6⁵; Mark 11²⁵). By v. 16, homage has
merged into prayer. For occasional instances of kneeling as the posture
of Jewish prayer, cf. Dan. 6¹⁰; Ezra 9⁵; Ps. 95⁶; Acts 7⁶⁰; so our passage
may be another, thus differing from Paul's usage.

15
from whom: not 'by whom', but 'after whom'. God gives his name (i.e.
his presence and power) to all men: cf. Gen. 1²⁶ᶠ·.

family: Gk *patria* means the wider family, the clan, cf. Luke 2⁴. *Patria*
chimes with *patēr* (*father*) in v. 14. Earthly 'fatherships' derive from and
reflect the heavenly prototype, just as (5²²ff·) earthly marriage reflects
the heavenly union between Christ and the Church.

in heaven: the reference is to orders or categories of angels. Rabbis referred to the angels as 'the higher family'. Gnosticism is here implicity excluded; angelic families have no existence that is independent of God, but are wholly derived from him as creator, in precisely the same way as mankind.

16
riches: cf. 1⁷, ¹⁸; Col. 1²⁶.

he may grant: in 1¹⁷, the earlier passage in which the writer prays for his audience, the gift desired is understanding of the doctrine, a petition appropriate to ch. 1–3; now, looking ahead to the second half, he asks for their strengthening in the Christian life.

strengthened with might: this piling up of virtual synonyms, particularly to speak of God's power, is typical of *Ephesians* (cf. 1¹⁹ & 6¹⁰) – and of the Qumran writings ('the might of his power', Vermes, p. 164).

in the inner man: cf. Rom. 7²². Though some scholars would disagree, the phrase is unlikely to reflect any rigid adherence to the dichotomy between the real inner self of man's soul and his fleshly exterior, in the Platonist and Gnostic manner. Rather the inner man is 'what a man is deep down', his basic direction as a person (cf. *hearts,* v. 17), as distinct from his merely external presentation of himself. So Rom. 7²² (*For I delight in the law of God, in my inmost self* – R.S.V.) can almost be rendered, 'What I *really* delight in is the law of God'. Cf. also 2 Cor. 4¹⁶, where the Greek has the same terminology to convey the idea that through his relation to Christ the believer's inner self more and more takes charge of him, as his unredeemed self 'wastes away' (cf. Eph. 4¹⁵ᶠ·). The phrase may refer even more specifically to *baptized* man; see parallel expressions in 4²⁴ & Col. 3⁹ᶠ·.

17
Christ may dwell: this balances the previous phrase. The strengthening by the Spirit and the indwelling of Christ are parallel expressions: cf. Rom. 8⁹ᶠ·. Notice that here (by contrast with Rom. 8¹⁰ & Gal. 2²⁰) the indwelling of the believer by Christ is not something which is part and parcel of the baptismal gift. Rather it is something which one can desire for people who are already Christians. Their faith (in the sense of faithfulness?) will lead to the attaining of this prize. (The pauline teaching of the mystical incorporation of the believer in Christ and Christ's dwelling in the believer is not our writer's commonest way of describing their mutual relation, cf. p. 243.)

The Greek of the latter part of this verse will bear other interpretations than that of R.S.V. First, *in love* may well be meant to go with the first half of the verse: 'that through faith Christ may dwell in your

hearts in love' (N.E.B.). For the linking of faith and love, cf. Gal. 5⁶.
Or else the whole phrase, *being rooted and grounded in love*, may, with
strained grammar (though the same defect applies to R.S.V.'s solution),
go bodily with 17a. This arrangement has much in its favour, especially
from the point of view of sense.

The prayer is that God's action, *through his Spirit*, may meet man's
response (*faith*, in his inner self), and that Christ may thus dwell in man's
inner self (*hearts*). To enjoy such indwelling is to be rooted in the love
of God or of Christ (cf. v. 19). *Rooted and grounded* (N.E.B. 'with deep
roots and firm foundations') carries on the 'depth' idea in *the inner man*
and *your hearts*. Thus the three parts of this first section of the prayer
fit closely together, amounting to a prayer for the Christians' thorough
possession of their new redeemed life. The prayer goes on to ask for
their full awareness of it.

18f.
The sense of 18–19a is brought out thus: 'to grasp . . . what is the breadth
etc. of the love of Christ, and to know that it is beyond knowledge'.

comprehend: the Gk deserves a more vivid translation – 'seize', 'get
hold of', cf. Phil. 3¹².

the saints: either the Christians on earth or the angels to whom the
knowledge of Christ's love has now been revealed (cf. p. 258).

the breadth and length and depth and height: this concept of the extension
of Christ's love in all four directions may have more concrete reference
than at first appears. It may refer to the cross of Christ, symbol of that
love, seen as stretching out towards all points of the universe. The idea
of the cosmic Cross, corresponding to that of Christ as the universal
man (2¹⁵; 4¹³⁻¹⁶), became a favourite one in the more speculative
Christian mythologies (both in the central tradition and among Gnostics) of the succeeding period, and may find early expression here. It
stood for the universality of Christ's redeeming work, acting in two
dimensions; it removed the vertical barrier separating Jew and Gentile,
and the horizontal barrier dividing man from God. *Ephesians* speaks of
both reconciliations: in 2¹⁴ᶠ· & 1¹⁰. In view of the link in 2¹⁴⁻¹⁶ between
the destruction of the dividing wall (*phragmos*) and the cross, it may be
that this use of the symbol of the cross is in mind there too.

Irenaeus, bishop of Lyons towards the end of the second century,
wrote: 'By the Word of God, all things are subject to the influence of
the economy of redemption, and the Son of God has been crucified for
all, having traced the sign of the Cross on all things. For it was right
and necessary that He who made Himself visible, should lead all visible
things to participate in His Cross; and it was in this way that, in a form

that can be perceived, His own special influence has had its sensible effect on all things: for it is He that penetrates that which is beneath; He that traverses the whole vast extent from East to West, and He that covers the immense distance from North to South, summoning to the knowledge of His Father those scattered in every place (*Demonstration of the Apostolic Preaching*, ch. 34). See Daniélou, *Theology of Jewish Christianity*, E.T. (London, 1964), pp. 279ff.

As far as the background of these four terms is concerned, all have a place, together, and some of them singly, in the vocabulary of stoic philosophy, and in the Gnostic speculation and magical formulae of the period.

know ... knowledge: just as Christians are to grasp the true cosmic significance of the Cross, so they are to know that Christ's love there disclosed goes beyond knowledge (Gk *gnōsis*). The context of discourse here is Gnostic; the writer is saying that Christians have a gnosis (i.e. insight into spiritual reality) greater than that of Gnostics themselves, who take pride in their esoteric knowledge of the universe and its secrets. Christ's love shown in his saving death has a simple universality which stands in sharp contrast to the multitude of spiritual agencies in the Gnostic systems, and which gives man direct access to the full indwelling of God (v. 19b; cf. 1^{23}).

filled with all the fullness of God: for a discussion of this language, see p. 277 with reference to 1^{23}.

20f.
The doxology is Jewish in general form, Christian in content. Cf. Rom. 16$^{25-27}$.

in the church and in Christ Jesus: instrumental, probably, in both cases: 'by'.

to all generations, for ever and ever: lit. 'to all generations of the age (*aiōn*) of the ages', a form without *exact* parallel in New Testament or LXX. Sonorous language whose bearing is to be sought in terms of current mythology, but whose precise sense is hard to find. Probably the singular, 'age', indicates that the reference is to the messianic era which has now dawned. (On the word *aiōn*, see p. 281.)

The end of the world and of the Church's historical existence does not seem to be regarded as imminent (cf. 4$^{15f.}$).

Amen: Hebrew solemn ending to prayer: 'so let it be'.

4–6   The Exhortation

CHRISTIAN UNITY AND
                      CHRISTIAN MATURITY

¹*I therefore, a prisoner for the Lord, beg you lead a life worthy of the calling
to which you have been called,* ²*with all lowliness and meekness, with
patience, forbearing one another in love,* ³*eager to maintain the unity of the
Spirit in the bond of peace.* ⁴*There is one body and one Spirit, just as you
were called to the one hope that belongs to your call,* ⁵*one Lord, one
faith, one baptism,* ⁶*one God and Father of us all, who is above all and
through all and in all.* ⁷*But grace was given to each of us according to the
measure of Christ's gift.* ⁸*Therefore it is said, 'When he ascended on high,
he led a host of captives, and he gave gifts to men.'* ⁹*(In saying, 'He ascended',
what does it mean but that he had also descended into the lower parts of the
earth?* ¹⁰*He who descended is he who also ascended far above all the heavens
that he might fill all things.)* ¹¹*And his gifts were that some should be apostles,
some prophets, some evangelists, some pastors and teachers,* ¹²*for the equipment
of the saints, for the work of ministry, for building up the body of Christ,*
¹³*until we all attain to the unity of the faith and of the knowledge of the
Son of God, to mature manhood, to the measure of the stature of the fullness
of Christ;* ¹⁴*so that we may no longer be children, tossed to and fro and
carried about with every wind of doctrine, by the cunning of men, by their
craftiness in deceitful wiles.* ¹⁵*Rather, speaking the truth in love, we are to
grow up in every way into him who is the head, into Christ,* ¹⁶*from whom
the whole body, joined and knit together by every joint with which it is
supplied, when each part is working properly, makes bodily growth and
upbuilds itself in love.*

It is at once apparent that though the main accent of the second half of
the epistle is on exhortation to good Christian life, we have by no
means left doctrine on one side. Nor have we even abandoned the
elevated liturgical style which characterizes the first three chapters.
The combination of moral and theological teaching is common in
Paul's undoubted letters, but the manner now is different. There Paul,
in the course of a series of ethical injunctions, will often intrude a
sudden flash of doctrinal statement, which roots the moral duty in

the very foundations of the gospel. Thus, in 2 Cor. 8:9 almsgiving is urged by reference to the total generosity of Christ in the Incarnation. In 1 Cor. 6:12ff., fornication is condemned on no lesser ground than the believer's incorporation into Christ; immoral unions are frankly adulterous. But here it is not a matter of doctrinal statement coming in to put the moral teaching in its true perspective; rather, the doctrine predominates and the moral teaching flows from it. The opening verses show this procedure at work. The Christian calling to life in the unity and peace of the Church carries with it a duty of mutual forbearance and love.

This passage summarizes the message of the earlier part of *Ephesians* in terms of unity. Christ's work has been, in the view of this writer, to reconcile and unite first, heaven and earth (1:10) and second, Jew and Gentile (2:14ff). Consequently, by this twofold breaking of barriers, man and God are at one (see on 3:18). The fruit of this work is life in unity, to be worked out now by Christians in the Church and ultimately (for it is the work of the Creator of all men, through Christ who is the Lord of the universe) to be realized on the widest scale (3:9; 4:13-16).

The Church therefore is central to our writer's picture. What is the Church for? It exists, subject to Christ, filled with the Spirit, to *grow up into him*. Its evangelistic task, the communicating of the gospel to all, does not exist in its own right, indeed it is never dealt with explicitly at all (apart from hints in 3:9 and 4:11). It is as if it were a by-product of her real *raison d'être*, which is that her members should share with Christ his perfect, mature manhood. The Church looks to Christ. She exists to create true human beings. He is the model. The way is contemplation of him.

This concentration on the Church is not at all generalized. It does not have in mind any loosely organized Christian community. The Church is a society which possesses a definite structure, with various categories of officers whose specific task is to bring about the growing up of Christ's people. Their role is therefore crucial; and so is the source of their authority. It springs from the universal lordship of Christ, which has followed his triumphant work (1:20-23). These officers are in fact the chief gift which flows to the Church as a result of that triumph (4:11f.). Here the writer makes skilful use of a piece of Old Testament exegesis (for which there are rabbinic parallels, see below) to substantiate his point. It is something he takes very seriously. The authority of the Church's accredited officers was something which it had become crucial to uphold before the end of the first century. We can see the question arising in *1 Clement*, in the letters of Bishop Ignatius of Antioch (see E.C.W.), and, within the New Testament, in the Pastoral Epistles and *3 John*. They were one of the Church's best defences against the tendency to split into small groups, whether on personal or on doctrinal grounds. *Ephesians* shares this concern and claims Paul's support for it.

Nevertheless there is no narrow ecclesiasticism here. The writer is not interested in merely keeping the ship on an even keel. He wants his readers to *grow up into Christ*. That is the only thing that matters (4^{14ff.}).

☙❧

1

a prisoner for the Lord: lit. 'the prisoner in (the) Lord'; cf. 3¹ & Phil. 1¹³. In this epistle, it is almost used as a title for Paul. For possible *double entendre*, see p. 219.

beg: Gk *parakaleō*, the common, almost technical word for introducing brotherly exhortation, cf. Rom. 12¹; Phil. 4².

lead a life worthy: cf. Col. 1¹⁰.

calling ... have been called: double statement, particularly common in this work. The word is of great importance in early Christian thought, for it conveys the idea of God's initiative in man's salvation, and also points to the continuity between his relationship with Israel under the old covenant and with the Church through his new work in Christ: cf. Isa. 41⁹; 42⁶; 46¹¹; I Cor. 1^{1f.}; Mark 1²⁰.

2f.

This passage seems to be based on Col. 3¹²⁻¹⁵, which it then proceeds to develop in accordance with our writer's central theme of unity, using the phrase *in the one body* as a starting-point. For particular words, see notes on the *Colossians* passage, pp. 206f. Notice certain significant points of divergence from the parallel statement: there, love is the bond which produces or sustains perfection (Col. 3¹⁴); here, it is peace which is the bond, in accordance with the writer's central concern (cf. 2¹⁴). Meanwhile, the word *love* is transferred to the phrase *forbearing one another* (cf. Col. 3¹³), thereby reinforcing the plea for unity.

bond of peace: i.e. which consists of peace.

4–6

Most of these statements can be paralleled somewhere in Paul's writings, but nowhere else are they heaped together. The nearest comparable passage is 1 Cor. 12$^{4-11}$, and a comparison is instructive. The purpose in those verses is to show that diversity of spiritual talents in the Church is not to lead to envy and strife (such as has arisen at Corinth); all are the gift of the one Spirit of God. Here no particular domestic trouble of this kind is in mind; rather, perhaps, a more general failure to preserve the Church's unity. There the unity is seen in the Spirit who distributes his gifts; here in every feature of Christian life. Unity pervades the whole structure of the faith and is rooted in the oneness of God himself.

Note the rough trinitarian pattern: *one spirit . . . one Lord . . . one God and Father*. Such passages as this adumbrate the later more precise formulation of trinitarian belief, and lead some to see these verses as an early creed-type formula.

one body and one spirit: cf. 1 Cor. 12^{13}; Rom. 12^5.

one hope: cf. 1^{14}, $^{18f.}$.

one Lord: cf. 1 Cor. 8^6. I.e. Jesus. For this title, cf. Phil. 2^{11} & 1 Cor. 12^3, and see p. 78.

one faith: probably the word here has the sense, much commoner later, of 'the Christian faith', i.e. the body of teaching. It is not unknown in genuine Paul, cf. possibly Gal. 1^{23}; 3$^{23f.}$.

one baptism: the mere inclusion of baptism in this list is not enough to buttress the case for the primarily baptismal associations of *Ephesians* or of much of the material included in it. On the other hand 4^1 may well be a reminder of the commitment which baptism involves. The mention of it here is in any case an instance of the strong Church-centredness of the passage.

one God and Father of us all: 1 Cor. 8^6 & 12^6; cf. Eph. 3$^{14f.}$.

above all and through all and in all: as masculine and neuter have in these cases the same form in Greek, it is impossible to tell whether *all* means 'everybody' or 'everything'. Almost certainly it is the latter, cf. 1^{23}. This is a piece of simple stoicism set in a Jewish-cum-Christian frame. The Stoics saw divinity as a quality pervading all existence. For the Jewish tradition, however, God was transcendent, distinct from his creation (*above all*).

7

Here the passage comes closest to its parallel in 1 Cor. 12$^{4ff.}$, in particular to v. 11; also cf. Rom. 12^6. The idea of *Christ's gift* is now taken up in the quotation that follows and in v. 11.

8–10

The quotation from Ps. 68^{18} and the comment which follows raise
many questions. To begin with the quotation itself is inaccurate.
The original of the second half of the verse is cast in the second (not
the third) person singular, and its sense is the exact opposite of our form,
'Thou didst receive gifts among man(kind)'. That an Old Testament
passage should be used so cavalierly (there is no need to suppose that
the alteration was other than deliberate) need occasion no surprise.
Jewish exposition at this time made use of a set of elaborate methodolo-
gical principles, which permitted modifications of the text when overriding 'meaning' dictated it. So here the fact that Christian events
tuned in better with the word *gave* than the word *received* not merely
permitted but even demanded the change. In this particular case there is
a point of comparison with the thought of the Jewish rabbis. At a
somewhat later period if not as early as the writing of *Ephesians*, they
used this text in roughly this form to signify the giving of the Jewish
Law by Moses (*on high* means on Mount Sinai). Where Moses had
given the Law, Christ, the new and greater Moses (as often in the New
Testament, e.g. 2 Cor. 3$^{7ff.}$), had given the leaders of the Church, who
were guiding her to full maturity in Christ.

The writer provides his own exegetical comment on the quotation,
in v. 9f., before going on to describe these gifts. The meaning of his
comment is not entirely clear. Traditionally the reference to *the lower
parts of the earth* has been taken to describe the descent of Christ to the
place of the dead between his crucifixion and resurrection, an idea
found in Rom. 10^7, and perhaps existing behind Matt. 27^{52} and
in 1 Pet. 4^6 (though see J. N. D. Kelly, *The Epistles of Peter and Jude*
(London, 1969), p. 174). Another view, one already held by Calvin in
the sixteenth century, who compared 4^9 with John 3^{13}, is that the phrase
means the earth itself (the genitive being in apposition), and that we
have here an assurance of the reality of the incarnation: the word
ascended positively entails a previous descent (the scripture had to be
fulfilled). No doubt there were already Christians who doubted the
full genuineness of the incarnation, holding that Christ's humanity was
only an appearance or a temporary disguise for his divinity. The currency of such ideas, which stem from the extreme pessimism about the
material world, including bodily nature, can be seen from the efforts
to combat them in *1 John* and perhaps in Phil. 2$^{6ff.}$.

Accepting this meaning for that particular phrase, some scholars take
a quite different approach to the passage as a whole. It stems from the
fact that in Jewish liturgical use, this psalm is associated with the Feast
of Pentecost (fifty days after Passover, christianized and anglicized as
Whit Sunday). Thus G. B. Caird has convincingly argued that as-

sociations with that festival were carried over into Christian use, and suggests that the descent of Christ referred to is neither at the incarnation nor at the crucifixion but after his ascension. It is his return 'at Pentecost to bestow his spiritual gifts upon the Church'. (We need to omit the *had* from R.S.V. v. 9, the Greek does not justify it.) The explanation in v. 9f. then corresponds precisely to the order of events in the psalm: ascent, then (descent and) giving. That the spiritual gifts were conferred by the self-same Jesus who had recently been on earth in the flesh is a point made elsewhere in the N.T.; cf. Acts 2^{33}, and John $14^{16, 18}$ where Christ and Paraclete are identified. Paul too in a passage like Rom. $8^{9f.}$ fails to make any neat distinction between Christ and the Spirit. (Dr Caird thinks that Eph. 2^{17} also refers to the post-crucifixion work of Christ, but it is not clear that the verse demands this sense.)*

How typical is the presentation we find here? In fact this distinction between the 'moments' of Christ's ascension and the bestowing of the gifts of the Spirit, both of them seen as separate from the resurrection (see on $1^{20ff.}$, p. 276), occurs in no other writer apart from the author of *Luke-Acts*. In the undoubted letters of Paul, we find these distinctions are not drawn in terms of successive temporal events. The exaltation of Christ and the presence of the Spirit are rather alternative ways of describing the outcome of Christ's work.

While differing from *Ephesians* and *Luke-Acts* on this point, other New Testament books associate the risen and/or exalted Christ with the giving of a solemn charge to the disciples. In particular, Matt. 28^{16-20} has several points of contact with our present passage. Matthew often sees the disciples of Jesus' life-time as models for disciples of any time, but in some passages – and this final scene is probably one of them – they appear rather as prototypes of the Church's leaders. On the mountain, in solemn meeting with the exalted Lord, they are enjoined to 'go', to 'make disciples', to 'baptize' and to 'teach', a list of tasks which corresponds closely to the list of offices mentioned in Eph. 4^{11}. In John 20^{21-23}, the presentation is much less vivid, but looks as if a related tradition may lie behind it. The commissioning of Peter as shepherd of the Church in John 21^{15-17} is also comparable: *pastors* in Eph. 4^{11}. The work of the Church's ministers is in all these passages the gift of the risen Lord.

led a host of captives: lit. 'captured captivity', with abstract noun used for concrete. The prisoners are the (evil) angelic powers: cf. Col. 2^{15}.

all the heavens: the current belief in a series of heavens, one above the

* G. B. Caird, *The Descent of Christ in Ephesians 4^{7-11}*, in *Studia Evangelica II* (1964), pp. 535ff.

other, usually believed to be seven in number (but sometimes three, cf. 2 Cor. 12²), each with its angelic rulers.

fill all things: this argues for an interpretation of 1²³ which takes *him* to refer to Christ (see p. 277). See also on 3¹⁹.

11

What are we to make of this list of the Church's ministers? It will be helpful to understand its status as a whole before turning to the titles which it includes. A good starting-point is to compare it with the list to be found in 1 Cor. 12⁴⁻¹¹, ²⁷⁻³⁰. The first three titles in v. 28 reappear in our present verse, but this similarity is overshadowed by important differences in both content and meaning. First, the list in *1 Corinthians* is much longer and more diverse. Second, it is a list of spiritual gifts exercised in the Church; whereas Eph. 4¹¹ speaks of offices provided for the Church. In other words, in the eyes of the writer of *Ephesians*, the organization of the Church is both simpler and more formal than it was in the Corinthian congregation of Paul's day. Such a view of the ministry is entirely typical of what we know of the developments after Paul's time. *The Pastoral Epistles* (e.g. 1 Tim. 3), *1 Clement* (E.C.W., pp. 44–6), and *The Epistles of Ignatius* (e.g. E.C.W., p. 95), all from the late-first or early-second century, show the same picture – a small number of ranks of more or less official clergy, rather than a multiplicity of freely exercised gifts. The situation envisaged in *Ephesians* in this respect supports the case for a post-pauline date.

Did the writer then simply describe the ministry of his own day or was he saying what he thought it consisted of in Paul's day, i.e. was he being deliberately anachronistic? In one respect at any rate he probably was. Most of the evidence we have suggests that the title *apostle* was confined to the Christian witnesses and missionaries of the first generation. In the eyes of some, Paul himself was too late and insufficiently qualified (cf. 1 Cor. 9¹ff.; 15⁷ff.). It is true that in the little treatise called *The Teaching of the Twelve Apostles* (*the Didache*), dating from late in the first century or early in the second, we read of itinerant missionaries who bear this title. (Cf. E.C.W., pp. 232f., where *apostoloi* and *prophētai* are rendered 'missioners' and 'charismatists'!) But that is hardly what *Ephesians* has in mind. Here the writer refers to *apostles* as founding fathers and as the seat of authority, cf. 2²⁰ & 3⁵. In his own day their position would probably be reflected by the Church's chief leaders, whatever title was then given to them (probably *episcopos*, 'overseer', cf. already Phil. 1¹, or *presbyteros*, 'elder').

That *apostle* is here chiefly associated with rule and authority is made likely, not only by the other references to the apostles in this writing, but by the fact that the title is explicitly differentiated from that of *evangelist.* An *evangelist* is presumably one whose task is to spread the gospel. In Paul's undoubted letters the title never occurs, for the very good reason that this was precisely the work of an apostle (cf. 1 Cor. 9^{16}). By the time *Ephesians* was written, however, the associations of apostleship had altered. It is not hard to see how this may have happened. In pauline circles it probably started with the view taken of Paul himself. A generation for whom his memory was chiefly preserved in his letters and in the existence of churches founded by him would naturally look at his apostolate in this changed light. For the letters are much more concerned with his pastoral oversight than with his evangelistic work; and his churches would look back to him with all the reverence due to a founder's authority. It is part of a more general process in the Church of this period of seeking bases of orthodoxy; the apostles' authority soon came to be seen as crucial in this. In other words, when Paul at the beginning of his letters claims the title *apostle of Jesus Christ*, there is no doubt that he intends it in the sense of missionary (*apostolos* = one sent out). When 'Paul' in Eph. 1^1 claims it, he is more concerned to assert authority, to exercise the apostolic office in Paul's name (cf. p. 253). See H. von Campenhausen, *Ecclesiastical Authority and Spiritual Power* (London, 1969).

His gifts were: refers back to v. 8b.

prophets: in 2^{20} and 3^5, they are linked with *apostles* as belonging to the Church's earliest days, and Masson (op. cit., p. 193) thinks that in the light of those references we are to understand that meaning here: only the last three ministries belong to the churches of the writer's own time. But *prophets* (like *apostles*, see above) may have remained a distinct group in the Church's ministry in some places at least. In one of his letters, Bishop Ignatius of Antioch (*c.* A.D. 110) describes himself preaching in exactly the manner signified by this title (E.C.W., p. 113).

evangelists: cf. Acts 21^8 and 2 Tim. 4^5, both works which probably belong, like *Ephesians*, to the post-pauline period.

pastors: lit. 'shepherds'. Cf. John 21$^{15\text{ff.}}$. There is no other New Testament example of the use of this term as a title for Church leaders. As the johannine passage shows, it stems from the common application of this image to Christ: cf. John 10; Matt. 18$^{12-14}$; Luke 15$^{3-7}$; 1 Pet. 2^{25}; Heb. 13^{20}. Presumably it meant much the same as *bishops* or *overseers* in Phil. 1^1, i.e. men who had charge of a local congregation. Our writer, having in mind an audience consisting of a number of churches, and in this passage thinking of the universal Church, has no difficulty in moving from offices (like apostle) which were general in scope to those exercised on the purely local scale.

teachers: the instructors of new members. They are regarded with the *pastors* as a single group.

As we now look back over this list again, we can hardly deny that it gives the impression of a more established and regularized community than the comparable list in 1 Cor. 12. This is true whether we decide that all, or only some, of these offices belonged to the churches of the writer's time. They are designed to meet the needs of the Church rather than to respond to the free operation of the Spirit. The passage goes on to describe what those needs were. Notice that all these minist-ries (except that of the *evangelists*) look primarily to the internal life of the Church rather than to her mission to those outside. As we saw above (p. 307), the Church exists first to *grow up into* Christ.

12

In Gk the first *for* differs from the other two. This might lead us to modify the sense given by R.S.V. – in either of two ways. We could omit the comma after *saints*, thus reducing the role of the leaders and extending that of believers in general. Or we could omit the comma after *teachers*, seeing the equipping of the saints as the task of the pastors and teachers, and the wider ministry, of service and edification, as the work of all the groups mentioned. This latter interpretation (cf. Masson, op. cit., pp. 192f.) is not a very natural one.

equipment of the saints: cf. the extended use of the similar image in 6$^{10ff.}$.

ministry: i.e. service. Cf. 3^7. 'Paul' is the servant of the gospel, and the Church's officers are also dedicated to service – whether of the gospel, of Christ, or of the Christians is not made explicit (probably the last, to judge from the two parallel phrases).

building up the body: combines the images of 1^{23} and 2^{22}.

13

until we attain: this verse certainly seems to envisage a certain period of time to develop, lying ahead of the Church – the end of the world is less imminent than it was for Paul, cf. 6^4.

all: who are meant by this? Either all mankind, cf. 3^9; or all Christians, in which case we have an instance of the common pauline principle of believers needing to realize and work out what is already their possession (for there is already, objectively, *one faith*, v. 5), cf. 1$^{14, 19}$; Col. 3$^{1, 5}$.

Having described the work of the Church's leaders, the writer now goes on to tell of its ultimate purpose. He does this in two ways, first in terms of doctrine and knowledge which Christians are to acquire, then in the wider terms of their whole direction of life. Believers are to grow into their status as Christ's body, under his headship, cf. 1$^{22f.}$.

Manhood is too abstract: the Gk means *man* (*anēr*), in the sense of 'the male of the species', not *anthrōpos*, the more general word for *man*, which can mean 'mankind'. The fully-grown man is Christ, the Church's exemplar and goal, cf. v. 15; 22–24. It is a combination of the two ideas of Christ as the new Adam (cf. Rom. 5$^{12ff.}$; 1 Cor. 15$^{22, 45}$) and of the Church as his body. Note (see p. 243) that the degree of incorporation of the believers into Christ is less complete than in 1 Cor. 12 and Rom. 12: Christ retains headship, and so a measure of distinctness from his people.

mature: cf. Col. 1^{28}. Typically, *Ephesians* shifts the application of the word; from *every man*, incorporated into Christ, to Christ, into whom we are to *grow up*.

fullness of Christ: cf. 1^{23}. Either the fullness which comes from Christ to his body, or the fullness which Christ has received from the Father. In either case Christians are to share the *stature* of the *fullness*, and it may be that the sense is concrete, in mythological Gnostic terms: Christians are to indwell the great cosmic Man, who is Christ. The language has spatial as well as relational overtones.

14

children: immature Christians, as in 1 Cor. 3^1 (where R.S.V. has *babes* for the same Gk *nēpios*). There the reason for the description is that the Corinthians, or some of them, are bickering childishly among themselves. Here it is a much less domestic matter; the sign of immaturity is being easily swayed from sound doctrine. The message is for a period when heresy is beginning to be recognized as a danger. Many think that this threat and this recognition of it belong to the years after Paul rather than to his own day.

The Pastoral Epistles presuppose the same danger: 1 Tim. 1$^{3f.}$; 6$^{3, 20f.}$; and the speech which contains Acts 20$^{28f.}$ may have been composed with it in mind.

15f.

These verses are very close to Col. 2^{19} (see p. 198), but, as usual, there are alterations. There the growth comes from God, through Christ, the head. Here Christ is the source of the growth, as he is also its goal – it is growth *into* him. As in 4^{12}, the images of building and body are combined, with the latter greatly predominating. This writer adds his characteristic *in love* at the end. Indeed the phrase occurs twice even in these two verses, reiterating the dominant concern for unity, which love among Christians safeguards and develops.

On grammatically purist grounds, some reverse the usual view that *Ephesians* depends on *Colossians*, feeling that Col. 2^{19} is a somewhat inexpert copy of these verses; both have a masculine relative pronoun (*from whom*), but in Col. 2^{19} it refers to *head*, which is a feminine noun (*kephalē*). This is the strongest item of evidence for the view that at least some parts of *Colossians* depend upon *Ephesians* (see p. 138). But as *the head* clearly is Christ, the masculine pronoun need not be due to slavish copying but simply to the force of the sense.

4$^{17-24}$ THE OLD LIFE RENOUNCED

^{17}*Now this I affirm and testify in the Lord, that you must no longer live as the Gentiles do, in the futility of their minds;* ^{18}*they are darkened in their understanding, alienated from the life of God because of the ignorance that is in them, due to their hardness of heart;* ^{19}*they have become callous and have given themselves up to licentiousness, greedy to practice every kind of uncleanness.* ^{20}*You did not so learn Christ!* – ^{21}*assuming that you have heard about him and were taught in him, as the truth is in Jesus.* ^{22}*Put off your old nature which belongs to your former manner of life and is corrupt through deceitful lusts,* ^{23}*and be renewed in the spirit of your minds,* ^{24}*and put on the new nature, created after the likeness of God in true righteousness and holiness.*

From now on the ethical note is sounded more firmly, but echoes of the teaching and the actual language of the doctrinal chapters are still frequent. On the whole there is less discontinuity here than there is between the doctrinal and hortatory sections of, for example, *Romans* and *Colossians*. There the ethical teaching is indeed theologically orientated, but it is less closely integrated with the themes and words of the earlier parts of the epistle.

Notice that whereas in 2^{12} the Gentiles are *alienated from the commonwealth of Israel*, now in 4^{18} they are *alienated from the life of God*: the aspect of alienation mentioned is in each case appropriate to the context. Another important link with the rest of *Ephesians* is disguised by R.S.V.: *old nature* (v. 22) ... *new nature* (v. 24) are literally 'old man' ... 'new man'. It is a case of the familiar pauline parallel between the first Adam, seen as the inclusive representative of sinful humanity, and Christ, the new Adam. It looks back particularly to 4¹³⁻¹⁶, but more generally to the rule of Christ expounded earlier. Now we see its ethical implications. Above all, this image maintains the thread of the unity theme through this section.

This passage illustrates another feature which we shall find throughout these three chapters (apart from 6²¹f.). We do not feel that any specific moral crisis is demanding urgent action. This is general Christian ethics, the only distinctive note being that the teaching is for Gentile Christians. In this respect too, these ethical chapters are at one with ch. 1-3. The audience is a wide group of such Christians, who indeed have certain needs and weaknesses, but about whose detailed circumstances we are told nothing. It is true that in the undoubted letters of Paul we find in the ethical sections a certain amount of general teaching which appears to be in the nature of an early Christian 'hand-out'. Parts of Col. 3-4 can be seen in this light, for example. But it is equally true that there is nearly always a plausible case for seeing here and there the reflection of quite specific situations (see on Col. 3²²⁻4¹). This does not happen in *Ephesians*.

ගිඟි

17-19
in the Lord: by these words the writer claims Christ's authority for his teaching.

as the Gentiles do: this description of the pagan way of life is closely paralleled in Rom. 1²¹, especially the reference to its *futility,* and to the *darkened* state of their minds (v. 18). In both passages, though more clearly in Rom. 1, pagan immorality is seen as wilful and culpable; it is *due to their hardness of heart* (cf. Rom. 2⁵ which uses a different Gk word). That is, it was not inevitable (e.g. as part of the divine plan), but was the result of their deliberate refusal of the moral light available to them in their own thought and conscience. In one respect *Ephesians* states this more explicitly than *Romans*. In Rom. 1²⁴,²⁶, Paul says that after their refusal to infer the patent truth of God from the created order, God himself *gave them up* to moral perversion; here (v. 19) it is their own doing. Cf. 5³ and Col. 3⁵.

futility: Gk *mataiotēs;* a common LXX description of the condition of those who reject God.

greedy, etc.: lit. 'for the working of all impurity in covetousness (or greed)'. It is the same three-fold group of cardinal sins as in 5³, ⁵; see note pp. 324f.

20f.

Christian discipleship is the exact opposite of the way of life which has just been described. Whereas that is vain and futile, this centres on Christ; whereas that is characterized by mental darkness, *the truth* is to be found in Jesus, and (5^{14}) he is the giver of light.

learn Christ: in contrasting his position with that of the pagan, a Jew might have said that he 'learnt the Law'. The Christian way is to *learn Christ*, that is to accept him fully as guide. He is the source not only of new relationships with God and man, but also of a new way of life. (See Rengstorf in T.D.N.T., 4, p. 410.)

The two phrases in v. 21 (*heard about him*, lit. 'heard him', and *were taught in him*) both repeat the same idea. To hear carries with it, as commonly in the Old Testament, the idea of obedient acceptance. Presumably the reference is to the tradition of Jesus' teaching, either still in oral form or already in the written Gospels, and to his living authority.

as the truth is in Jesus: i.e. almost, 'in the authentic Jesus-way'; though perhaps, like v. 20, this expression too carries an implicit contrast with the Jewish Law, cf. John 14^6. There is no call to look for a philosophical reference here; it is the Old Testament sense of *truth* – that which stands and can be relied upon.

22–24

In Gk there is no new sentence here and the discarding of *the old nature* and donning of *the new* are presented as the content of the teaching referred to in v. 20f. This enables us to see more force in the expression, to *learn Christ*. For *the new nature* is literally 'the new man'; it is an instance of the Adam imagery that is applied to Christ in, for example, Rom. 5^{12} and 1 Cor. 15 (see on 4^{13} and general notes above). For Paul, he is the inclusive new Man, who incorporates within himself those who come to him. But as we have often seen already, the writer of *Ephesians* adopts a less thoroughgoing concept of incorporation: he prefers to keep Christ to a degree above or distinct from his people, who *grow up into him* (4^{15}). So here the new humanity, created like the old (cf. Gen. 1^{26}) *after the likeness of God*, is not identified outright with Christ (cf. v. 13), whereas in Gal. 3^{27}, which also uses the image of donning clothes, the identification is explicit.

put off . . . put on: the parallels in Col. 3$^{9f.}$ and Gal. 3^{27} use these verbs to refer to the act of baptism. Here the reference is rather to the process which flows from *learning Christ*, following his teaching; for this use, cf. Col. 3^{12}.

is corrupt: lit. 'is being corrupted', i.e., probably, as in death, cf. Rom. 6²¹ff..

deceitful lusts: lit. 'the desires of deceit', cf. *do not lie to one another,* in Col. 3⁹.

in the spirit of your minds: it is tempting to regard this, like some other phrases in *Ephesians,* as vague with the sonority of rhetoric, and so simply making a contrast with the condition of the Gentiles as described in v. 17f., in words reminiscent of Rom 12². But *spirit* needs to be looked at more closely. In all other uses of *pneuma* in *Ephesians* (except 2²) the reference is to the Holy Spirit of God, and presumably the same is true here. The Spirit is the agent of renewal. The genitive, *of your mind* (Gk *nous,* meaning here the inner self), will then indicate the place where, from baptism, the Spirit acts and dwells (cf. 1 Cor. 2¹⁰ff.); his action there is to be fully accepted. If, as it appears, the writer is adapting Rom. 12², he has simply inserted the reference to the agency of the Spirit (see Masson, op. cit., p. 202). Translate: 'Be renewed by the Spirit in your mind'.

created: the tense implies single action, i.e. it refers to baptism. As in 2 Cor. 5¹⁷, this language stresses the utter incompatibility between the old way and the new. It is as if the new self, made on the perfect model of Christ, is presented to the new Christian at baptism, like a set of clothes. He must then grow up until he fits the new self.

holiness: Gk *hosiotēs,* i.e. devotion, piety.

righteousness: here, the moral quality – uprightness, justice. Cf. p. 98.

These two words are together again in Luke 1⁷⁵ (as several times in LXX), and the former occurs nowhere else in the New Testament.

true: lit. 'of truth', a semitism. The word modifies both nouns; these qualities stem from God, the genuine and reliable one. Contrast *deceitful* in v. 22, and cf. v. 25.

4²⁵–5²   THE ETHICS OF UNITY

²⁵*Therefore, putting away falsehood, let every one speak the truth with his neighbour, for we are members one of another.* ²⁶*Be angry but do not sin; do not let the sun go down on your anger,* ²⁷*and give no opportunity to the devil.* ²⁸*Let the thief no longer steal, but rather let him labour, doing honest work with his hands, so that he may be able to give to those in need.* ²⁹*Let no*

evil talk come out of your mouths, but only such as is good for edifying, as fits the occasion, that it may impart grace to those who hear. [30]And do not grieve the Holy Spirit of God, in whom you were sealed for the day of redemption. [31]Let all bitterness and wrath and anger and clamour and slander be put away from you, with all malice, [32]and be kind to one another, tenderhearted, forgiving one another, as God in Christ forgave you.

5 [1]Therefore be imitators of God, as beloved children. [2]And walk in love as Christ loved us and gave himself up for us, a fragrant offering and sacrifice to God.

The writer has just stated the basis of the new life contrasting it with his readers' background in paganism; its source and sole authority is Christ. Now he goes on to state its moral implications in some detail. Later he will turn to questions of family relationships, but he begins with certain rules of Christian living. Two features deserve special notice. First, all the qualities enjoined here are aspects of that unity in the Church which it is our writer's prime concern to elucidate and to foster. To this matter he deliberately gives pride of place (cf. the brief treatment of it already in 4^{1-3}). Similarly, the evils to be avoided (v. 31) are all destroyers of human harmony. Second, the impulse towards the new way, summed up as *walking in love*, comes directly from Christ (4^{32} & 5^2); our writer never goes far without returning to that centre of his teaching.

The content of this passage is to be chiefly accounted for by reference to the author's own thought; but there may be some deliberate dependence upon the latter half of the Ten Commandments, cf. also 5^3 & 6^2. There are too strong echoes of the tradition of Jesus' teaching, as we find it in the Gospels; cf. $4^{20f.}$. See the notes for details.

ನ್ನ

25

putting away: the same verb as in v. 22 (and Col. 3^8). We now see something of the kind of behaviour characteristic of *the old nature*. The link is explicit in Col. 3^9.

falsehood ... truth: cf. v. 21.

let every one ... neighbour: an almost exact quotation from Zech. 8^{16}. Notice that here (see the rest of the verse) the *neighbour* is almost certainly the fellow-Christian. This is in line with the Jewish tradition whereby Lev. 19^{18}, for example, the command to love one's neighbour as oneself, applied only to relations with fellow-Jews. Jesus' teaching, as found in Luke 10^{25ff}; Matt. 5^{43ff}; and (implicitly) Mark 12$^{28ff.}$ breaks out from this narrow definition.

members one of another: these words occur also in Rom. 12^5. But there they are preceded by the statement that *we, though many, are one body in Christ.* And in 1 Cor. 6^{15}, the believers' bodies are described as *members of Christ.* Here there is no reference to Christ. In terms of his image of head and body for Christ and the Church, our writer can consider the body independently (cf. 5^{30}), and use the idea to urge mutual charity among Christians. In other words, as usual, he avoids the deeper incorporation imagery which is characteristic of Paul (see p. 243).

26

be angry but do not sin: from Ps. 4^4; cf. Col. 3^8; Jas. 1$^{19f.}$. See Matt. 5$^{21f.}$ for the evaluation given to the sin of anger in the teaching of Jesus.

do not let the sun go down upon your anger: for the principle, cf. Deut. 24^{15}. The expression here is paralleled in Plutarch, writing a little later than Paul, and cited by him as a pythagorean maxim.

anger: parorgismos, found only in the LXX, usually means 'provocation to anger', but see Jer. 21^5 for the same sense as here.

27

no opportunity to the devil: cf. 2 Cor. 2^{11}; and see p. 338.

28

let the thief no longer steal: there is no reason to think that here any more than elsewhere the writer is addressing himself to the specific circumstances of his audience. The occurrence of this at first sight random injunction, without any close connexion with the main theme of these verses (the avoidance of strife in the Church), is evidence that some stereotyped list of moral rules, perhaps based on the Ten Commandments, lies somewhere in the background (cf. Exod. 20^{15}; then compare the equation of anger, v. 26, with murder in Matt. 5$^{21ff.}$, and the sixth command of the Decalogue, 'you shall not kill', Exod. 20^{13}). Cf. Rom. 2^{21}.

but rather let him labour: the commendation of honest toil, either in himself or in others, is common in Paul; cf. 1 Cor. 4^{12} for the former; 1 Thess. 4$^{11f.}$ for the latter; see also 2 Thess. 3$^{6-12}$. It is generally thought that reluctance to work among the Thessalonian Christians was the result of a state of high spiritual enthusiasm engendered by the expectation of the speedy End to all things. The scandals and difficulties to which this gave rise are countered by Paul with the remedy of hard work. Here work is the antidote to the more commonplace evil of theft (a sign of a later date for *Ephesians*?).

to give to those in need: the idea that the profits of labour are to lead to generous giving (especially to the poor among one's fellow-Christians, cf. v. 25; Gal. 2¹⁰) recurs in 2 Thess. 3¹²ᶠ·; cf. Rom. 12¹³; Gal. 6¹⁰.

29
no evil talk: cf. Col. 3⁸; Matt. 5²². Jas. 3⁶ᶠᶠ· is the most extensive example of New Testament teaching on the theme of the control of speech. For the latter part of the verse, cf. Col. 3¹⁶; 4⁶; 1 Cor. 14²⁶; also Eph. 5⁴, ¹⁹.

30
grieve the Holy Spirit: cf. p. 270. Here the Spirit is personified more than elsewhere in this writing. Though the believer has the Spirit dwelling in him, by God's gift, he still has to allow the full penetration of the Spirit, just as he has to *grow up into Christ* (4¹⁵); cf. 1¹³ᶠ·; 4²³. This process can be halted by the believer's sinful behaviour: cf. 1 Thess. 4⁸ & 5¹⁹, though in the latter passage the reference is more specifically to the Spirit's activity in inspiring preachers.

sealed: see on 1¹³, p. 270: it is evidence that this instruction *may* be addressed originally to the newly baptized.

day of redemption: i.e. the Last Day. In 1⁷ *redemption* is the believers' present possession, here the word is used for the completion of the work already begun (*salvation* would be the usual pauline word, though in 2 Cor. 6² it carries the former sense).

31f.
bitterness etc.: for lists of this kind, see on Col. 3⁵, p. 204. Cf. Col. 3⁸, ¹²ᶠ·.

in Christ: i.e. by Christ's agency.

forgave: i.e. at baptism; cf. the baptismal reference in v. 30.

5¹
be imitators of God: cf. 1 Cor. 11¹ & 4¹⁶. The latter verse, while urging imitation of *Paul*, follows on his addressing the Corinthians as his *beloved children,* as here.

2
love: Gk *agapē*, the generous self-giving love of God, which is to be the quality chiefly characterizing his people. It sums up all the qualities enjoined in the earlier verses.

5³⁻²⁰

loved us and gave himself up for us: cf. 5²⁵ & Gal. 2²⁰.

a fragrant offering: the Gk phrase rendered *fragrant* means literally 'for an aroma of fragrance'. It is a Hebraism, made up of two virtual synonyms, a commonplace of sacrificial terminology in the LXX (cf. e.g. Exod. 29¹⁸; Lev. 2⁹). While here it refers to Christ's offering of himself to God, in Phil. 4¹⁸ Paul can use it to refer to the presents he has received from the congregation at Philippi.

offering and sacrifice: the two words here, as a pair, may be taken from Ps. 40⁶ (a text used prominently in Heb. 10⁵ᶠᶠ·).

5³⁻²⁰   CHRIST THE GIVER OF LIGHT

³*But immorality and all impurity or covetousness must not even be named among you, as is fitting among saints.* ⁴*Let there be no filthiness, nor silly talk, nor levity, which are not fitting; but instead let there be thanksgiving.* ⁵*Be sure of this, that no immoral or impure man, or one who is covetous (that is, an idolater), has any inheritance in the kingdom of Christ and of God.* ⁶*Let no one deceive you with empty words, for it is because of these things that the wrath of God comes upon the sons of disobedience.* ⁷*Therefore do not associate with them,* ⁸*for once you were darkness, but now you are light in the Lord; walk as children of light* ⁹*(for the fruit of light is found in all that is good and right and true),* ¹⁰*and try to learn what is pleasing to the Lord.* ¹¹*Take no part in the unfruitful works of darkness, but instead expose them.* ¹²*For it is a shame even to speak of the things that they do in secret.* ¹³*But when anything is exposed by the light it becomes visible, for anything that becomes visible is light.* ¹⁴*Therefore it is said, 'Awake, O sleeper, and arise from the dead, and Christ shall give you light'.* ¹⁵*Look carefully then how you walk, not as unwise men but as wise,* ¹⁶*making the most of the time, because the days are evil.* ¹⁷*Therefore do not be foolish, but understand what the will of the Lord is.* ¹⁸*And do not get drunk with wine, for that is de-bauchery; but be filled with the Spirit,* ¹⁹*addressing one another in psalms and hymns and spiritual songs, singing and making melody to the Lord with all your heart,* ²⁰*always and for everything giving thanks in the name of our Lord Jesus Christ to God the Father.*

The moral qualities that make for unity were the writer's first concern, and he has summed them up in the idea of love modelled on that of Christ. Now he turns to purity of desire – both in the sexual area and more generally (vv. 3 & 5). Even lighthearted talk about sex is to be avoided and to be replaced (rather surprisingly at first sight) by thanksgiving. This does not mean that he is merely enjoining that pious talk should take the place of dirty talk. His point is that whereas sexual impurity and covetousness both express self-centred acquisitiveness, thanksgiving is the exact opposite, and so the antidote required; it is the recognition of God's generosity. It is also in point of fact the dominant note in prayer in the Jewish tradition: to pray *is* to praise God. Thanksgiving means recognizing not only God's gifts but God himself, so that in this respect too it counters covetousness, which, by elevating the desired object to the centre of one's life, is as good as idolatry.

Just as the virtues of harmony are rooted in the love of Christ, so purity is rooted in Christ as the giver of light (vv. 8–14). Once more we return quickly to the doctrinal basis of morality. This image points once more to the incompatibility between Christ and evil of any kind.

The last part of this section (vv. 15–20), much of it closely modelled on *Colossians*, takes up the theme of 4^{29} and 5^4. Christian talk is to be sober, serious, and edifyingly earnest. The writer thinks especially of gatherings of Christians at which the Spirit inspires them to utterance that bears these marks.

৩৩

3
immorality: i.e. sexual misconduct. Christian writers saw this as the characteristic pagan sin (cf. e.g. Rom. 1^{24-32}), but attacks on it come as much from pagan writers as from Jews and Christians (see on Col. 3^5, p. 204). Sexual *impurity* and *covetousness* are no doubt linked because both involve inordinate desire, but there may also be continued dependence on the Ten Commandments (cf. $4^{26,\,28}$ & 6^2). Here and in v. 5f. we are close to Col. 3^5.

saints: i.e. Christians, as in 1^1. *Impurity* carries ritual associations; Judaism sometimes saw the three chief sins as greed for riches, fornication and profanation of the Temple (Vermes, p. 101), a group of three very close to that in our present passage, cf. also 4^{19}.

4
Cf. Col. 3^8. The Qumran Community Rule makes the same contrast between foolish talk and thanksgiving (in the sense of the praise of God), see Vermes, p. 91; it also punishes the former severely (Vermes, p. 83f.).

5

that is, an idolater: cf. Col. 3⁵. *The Testament of Reuben* (4⁶, Charles, II, p. 298) says that fornication leads to idolatry, in that 'it deceiveth the mind and understanding'.

has any inheritance: cf. Gal. 5²¹ and 1 Cor. 6⁹. Both those passages cast the 'inheriting' into the future, at the Last Day. Here, in the light of 1¹⁴, ¹⁸, the Christian's hope already gives him a title to this future possession. The immoral man has no such assurance.

kingdom of Christ and of God: this is the only explicit reference to the kingdom in *Ephesians*, though the idea is present in 1²⁰ᶠ·; and it is the only use of this double expression in the New Testament. *The kingdom of God* is overwhelmingly the commonest form, but the idea of Christ's kingdom is to be found in (e.g.) Col. 1¹³ and Matt. 25³¹ᶠᶠ·. In 1 Cor. 15²⁴⁻²⁸ we see Paul's view of the relationship between the two. Here they are simply set down in parallel.

6

deceive: cf. Col. 2⁴.

the wrath of God comes: i.e. at the Last Day, when God's Judgement takes place. Cf. Col. 3⁶. Rom. 1¹⁸ regards the wrath of God as already being revealed, in the dispensation set in motion by Christ's life and death and indeed in man's conscience, alongside the righteousness of God.

sons of disobedience: there are Gk examples of this kind of phrase, but it is typically semitic (cf. 2²). The Dead Sea Scrolls speak of the 'sons of darkness'. Here the contrast is with *the children of light* (v. 8).

8–14

darkness … light: a commonplace of religious imagery. But whereas in much oriental and Hellenistic religion (e.g. Gnostic sects) it described a fundamental cleavage of the universe between two powers, in Judaism and early Christianity it was, despite elements of the other view, much more a division between two ways of life. Our passage well illustrates this ethical orientation (v. 9). *Light* stands for good life in obedience to God, *darkness* for its opposite. Yet light is above all associated with the sphere in which God dwells (e.g. 1 Tim. 6¹⁶), and he (or Christ) is the source of light (e.g. John 1¹⁻⁵; so here, *in the Lord*). All this is paralleled in the thought of the Qumran sect: 'Those born of truth spring from a fountain of light, but those born of falsehood spring from a source of darkness. All the children of righteousness are ruled by the Prince of Light and walk in the ways of light; but all the children of falsehood are ruled by the Angel of Darkness and walk in the ways of darkness ... The God of Israel and his Angel of Truth will succour all the sons of light' (Vermes, pp. 75f.).

8

now: this is sometimes taken as evidence for the original use of this material in the instruction of the newly baptized; but it equally well applies to Christians of longer standing.

children of light: cf. Col. 1^{12}; 1 Thess. 5^5; and Qumran parallels, above.

9

The trio of virtues balances the trio of vices in vv. 3 & 5. The Gk uses abstract nouns not adjectives, and their sense is chiefly practical: doing good, dealing justly, acting truly or loyally. Like the vices, these qualities too have their parallels in the Dead Sea Scrolls; the members of the community are to 'practise truth, righteousness, and justice upon earth' (Vermes, p. 72). (Cf. also Mic. 6^8.)

11

works of darkness: cf. Rom. 13^{12}.

expose: Kuhn (N.T.S., 7) compares this with passages in the Community Rule of Qumran (Vermes, p. 80) which speak of the duty of members of the community to rebuke (another possible sense of the Gk *elenchō*) one another for their faults, sometimes publicly 'before the Congregation'. Both the prominence of affinities with the Rule throughout this part of *Ephesians* and the general Church-directedness of the writer support the view that this practice is in mind here; it means that already before v. 19 the writer probably has Christian assemblies in mind. On the other hand, the *sons of disobedience* are surely non-Christians, and it would need a change of direction for *the works of darkness* to be the acts of members of the Church. 1 Tim. 5^{20} and 2 Tim. 4^2 are closer parallels with this aspect of Qumran life. Here it is more likely that the reference is still to the sins of the pagan world, with *expose* as correct.

13

Cf. John $3^{20f.}$. This verse seems at first reading to be simply a general statement about the action of light, to support the use of the image in v. 11. But the end of the verse has the highly concrete expression, *is light,* used in v. 8 to describe the status of Christian believers. It may therefore be that the *exposing* of v. 13 refers to the convert's confession of his sins and the latter part of the verse to the act of becoming a Christian (though it is true that we might expect 'anyone' rather than *anything*). If this is so, the quoting of what is probably a baptismal hymn in the next verse follows easily. So does the next step, into v. 15 (also logically connected, by *then*); to become a Christian is to 'be' light in the midst of the dark, heathen world, visible to all. Therefore the

Christian must be careful about his manner of life. If this is the right interpretation, the author is taking advantage (probably unconsciously) of some of the width of meaning which the verb *elenchō* can bear; it can mean not only 'expose' (which fits the light-imagery well) and 'rebuke' but also 'convict' (which suits the reference to the acknowledgement of sin).

14

Therefore, it is said: as in 4⁸ (and Jas. 4⁶), the formula introduces a quotation, there from the Old Testament, here from a Christian hymn.

Awake: Gk *egeire*, lit. 'arise', one of the two common words for resurrection (the other follows). So this fragment uses the idea of Paul – to be baptized is to share in Christ's resurrection (cf. 2¹; Rom. 6⁵⁻¹¹; Col. 3¹). For the linking of resurrection with the coming of light, cf. Isa. 26¹⁹. For the description of the unconverted state as sleep, cf. Matt. 25¹ff.. Though the hymn originally spoke of baptism and the status which it confers, the purpose of its inclusion here is rather to urge the ethical realization of that status; there is an easy shift from the one to the other, also in Paul's undoubted works; e.g. compare Rom. 6⁵⁻¹¹ with 13¹¹ff., and Col. 3¹, ⁵. C. F. D. Moule (*The Birth of the New Testament* (London, 1962), p. 25) notes similarities between this verse and the story of Peter's release from prison in Acts 12⁶ff., e.g. *sleeper, light, arise,* (*anasta*, this form only in these two places), as well as the Easter and so baptismal allusion. 'Is this ancient hymn', he asks, 'built round the Peter story?' It may be more likely that the author of Acts uses current paschal and baptismal terms to give a death-and-resurrection sense to his story (there are numerous similarities with Luke 22–24), and the writer of *Ephesians*, working at much the same period, is familiar with the same vocabulary.

Christ . . . light: cf. *light in the Lord* (v. 8). Cf. Deut. 33²; Ps. 50²; and the idea of the divine glory shining forth at the End (cf. Col. 3⁴).

15

Look carefully then: on Kuhn's view (that v. 11ff. refers to the practice of Christian brethren rebuking one another as an intra-Church discipline) the force of this verse is 'Be careful how you behave in order to avoid being exposed to rebuke'. In commenting on v. 13 we have already given another view.

wise: to be wise is to know *what the will of the Lord is* (v. 17). This is the Jewish tradition of 'wisdom' whose heart is 'the fear of the Lord', e.g. Ps. 111¹⁰. Cf. Col. 4⁵; Matt. 10¹⁶.

16

Cf. Col. 4⁵, see p. 217.

17

will of the Lord: the way to discover the Lord's will is to *be filled with the Spirit,* especially as it is experienced in the Christian assemblies (v. 18f.). For the link between Christian wisdom and the Spirit, and an exposition of how the Spirit enables the Christian to *comprehend the thoughts of God,* see 1 Cor. 2⁶⁻¹⁶.

18

drunk with wine: in view of the following contrast the reference here may be to the practice in some esoteric sects of using alcohol to induce ecstatic behaviour. The practice may have crept into Christian congregations, and 1 Cor. 11²¹ may be evidence of it. The parallel is strengthened if *giving thanks* (v. 20) refers to the holding of the Eucharist (= 'the Thanksgiving'). We do not know whether the verb *eucharisteō* could already carry this specialized sense. For the association of the ecstatic behaviour brought about by the action of the Spirit (see 1 Cor. 14) with drunkenness, cf. Acts 2¹³. It must have been a familiar gibe, probably with a grain of fact to justify it. (Cf. also Rom. 13¹³ and 1 Thess. 5⁷.) The words here are taken from Prov. 23³¹ LXX. Cf. Prov. 20¹.

19f.

Cf. Col. 3¹⁶ᶠ·, p. 208. See Mitton, op. cit., p. 253: 'The way in which Col. 3¹⁶⁻¹⁷ is reproduced in Eph. 5¹⁹⁻²⁰ is very peculiar. The phrase "in the name of Jesus" is wrenched from the word to which it appropriately belongs in *Colossians* . . . and is artificially associated with "giving thanks", a verb which is adjacent to it in *Colossians,* but not attached to it by any sense-link at all . . . An imitator might be guilty of this, but it is not what Paul would have done.'

5²¹⁻³³   CHRIST AND CHRISTIAN MARRIAGE

²¹*Be subject to one another out of reverence for Christ.* ²²*Wives, be subject to your husbands, as to the Lord.* ²³*For the husband is the head of the wife as Christ is the head of the church, his body, and is himself its Saviour.* ²⁴*As the church is subject to Christ, so let wives also be subject in everything to their husbands.* ²⁵*Husbands, love your wives, as Christ loved the church and gave himself up for her,* ²⁶*that he might sanctify her, having cleansed her by the washing of water with the word,* ²⁷*that he might present the church to himself in splendour, without spot or wrinkle or any such thing, that she*

might be holy and without blemish. ²⁸*Even so husbands should love their wives as their own bodies. He who loves his wife loves himself.* ²⁹*For no man ever hates his own flesh, but nourishes it and cherishes it, as Christ does the church,* ³⁰*because we are members of his body.* ³¹*'For this reason a man shall leave his father and mother and be joined to his wife, and the two shall become one.'* ³²*This is a great mystery, and I take it to mean Christ and the church;* ³³*however, let each one of you love his wife as himself, and let the wife see that she respects her husband.*

From the unity and purity of God's people, the writer turns to their domestic life. Once more, familiar features recur; harmony, guaranteed by the submissiveness of wives (v. 22) and the love of husbands (v. 25), is paramount; and this is rooted in the significance of Christ. In fact marital unity only reflects the greater unity that binds Christ and his Church, yet for that very reason the status of marriage is for the Christian enormously enhanced.

Together with the section which follows (6¹⁻⁹), this passage forms a unit which is comparable with passages in several other New Testament epistles. These counsels for the conduct of Christian households (often called by the German technical term, *Haustafel*) were, to a degree, set pieces of ethical instruction, found in Jewish and pagan sources alike. We discussed them more fully in relation to the parallel passage in *Colossians* (3¹⁸ff.) on pp. 209ff. In examining that passage we found that though it had a bearing on the circumstances of Paul's relationship with the congregation at Colossae, it was not integrated with the doctrinal teaching which forms the bulk of *Colossians*. Our present section is quite different. It is clearly based on Col. 3¹⁸f. and, in common with that parallel, follows the reference to the singing of hymns and psalms at Christian meetings; but in expanding those two verses it transforms them and, as with most of the other ethical material (6¹⁻⁹ is an exception), thoroughly 'christens' them. That is to say, the marriage relationship is seen as determined by the central doctrinal teaching of the epistle: the lordship of Christ and his intimate love for his people who exist in union with him, as body to head. Thus marriage is not only a beneficent disposition made by God in creation (v. 31), but also an expression of and way of participating in the new redeemed order which flows from the triumph of Christ. All this represents a striking doctrinal development from the teaching in *Colossians* (and for that matter in other parallels

such as 1 Pet. 3$^{1\text{ff}}$.). It is not to be regarded as a self-contained development in marriage-doctrine; rather, as a setting of marriage
within the writer's general teaching.

At the same time this passage is more abstract than its *Colossians*
equivalent in another respect too. There is no sign here of any reflection of specific circumstances in the situation of those addressed.
The teaching is for general consumption.

As he is discussing marriage the writer is led to vary the image of
the Church as the *body* of Christ (cf. 1^{23}; 4^{16}) and to present it also as
Christ's *bride*. V. 28 shows how easily the one idea merges into the
other, especially in the light of the traditional Jewish teaching that
marriage creates a complete union (*one flesh*) between the partners
(v. 31; Gen. 2$^{23\text{f}}$.).

But the idea of the Church as Christ's bride does not spring simply
from the fact that human marriage is under discussion. Its roots lie
far deeper. From earliest times and in many different cultures,
sexual union has been of the greatest significance in forming religious
thought and practice. Fertility of man, beast, and field has been
commonly seen as depending upon the union of father-god with
mother-goddess or else of divine beings with humans (cf. a reflection
of this in the story in Gen. 6$^{1-4}$), and upon its ritual enactment.
(See H. Frankfort, *Before Philosophy* (Pelican, 1949), e.g. pp. 214f.)
What mythology told in story, the cult expressed in action.

The institution of 'sacred marriage' (between king and queen or
priest and sacred prostitute), often referred to by the Gk term *hieros
gamos*, was at the heart of the religion of the peoples of the ancient
Near East among whom Israel dwelt. The infiltrations of fertility
religion into Israelite worship went deep. Of that the prophets'
constant attacks on the cult of Baal and Asherah, god and goddess
of Israel's immediate neighbours, are sufficient evidence. But the
'pure' tradition of the worship of Yahweh (the Old Testament name
of God), represented in the great bulk of the writings of the Old
Testament, resisted the central features of this religion, while at the
same time incorporating its imagery into its own system. The dominant interest in fertility gave way, in orthodox Yahwism, to the motif
of the covenant or bond which Yahweh had established with his
people at the time of the liberation from Egypt under Moses. To that
covenant his faithfulness was assured and theirs demanded. The image
of Israel as the bride of Yahweh became one of the commonest

and most vivid ways of speaking of it. It dominates most movingly the prophecy of Hosea, and is to be found in numerous other places (cf. Exod. 34¹⁵; Jer. 31³¹ᶠᶠ·; Isa. 54⁵). Often Jerusalem, the cultic centre of Israel, appears under the same guise, e.g. Zeph. 3¹⁴ᶠᶠ·; Zech. 9⁹. The city is symbolized as the daughter of Zion.

It is then not surprising that the early Church, conscious of herself as the new Israel, enjoying the life of God's new covenant with his people through Christ, should have spoken of herself in terms of this image, and the Old Testament tradition is sufficient explanation of it. In some passages this is clear, e.g. Rev. 19⁷⁻⁹; 21², ⁹; in other cases some scholars believe that other sources have contributed. Thus in the Mediterranean world of the first century, with its widely syncretistic religion, blended of many Hellenistic and oriental ingredients, the 'sacred marriage' persisted, often in a different key. No longer only concerned with a people's prosperity, it was now a question of the union of the individual's immortal soul with the deity, in order to assure his salvation from the world of matter and exposure to fate. In the mystery cults of the time, orgiastic rites, expressing this union, were an important element (perhaps they are what Eph. 5¹² has chiefly in mind). *Ephesians* went out to people to whom such rites were familiar, often no doubt from personal experience before their conversion to Christianity. What could be more appropriate than to present the relationship of Christ to the Church under the image of marriage? What more necessary than to counter immorality with a true doctrine of the union of man and wife? In the relationship of Christ to his bride, faithful and eternal, were to be found both the assurance of genuine salvation (v. 23) and the model of all true human love. All licentiousness was thereby rigorously excluded (cf. 4¹⁹; 5³ᶠᶠ·).

This image received wide and varied expression in the Church's early days. In the Fourth Gospel it appears in 3²⁹ and, subtly and allusively, in the story of the Marriage at Cana (2¹⁻¹¹) and in the conversation with the Samaritan Woman (4¹⁶⁻²⁶): see J. Marsh, *Saint John* (Pelican, 1968) pp. 142ff. It appears again in Jesus' parabolic teaching in Mark 2¹⁹ᶠ·; Matt. 22¹⁻¹⁰; 25¹⁻¹³. Christ is the bridegroom, corresponding to the God of Israel in the Old Testament, who has come or will return to his people. Elsewhere not the Church as a whole, but a particular Christian congregation can be seen as Christ's bride, cf. 2 Cor. 11² and, probably, 2 John 1 & 13. In 1 Cor. 6¹⁵ it is the individual Christian. And in Luke 1^{26ff} Mary fulfils the prophecies about the virgin daughter of Zion to whom God would come (cf. Zeph. $3^{14ff.}$; R. Laurentin, *Structure et Théologie de Luc I-II* (Paris, 1957)). But here in *Ephesians* we have its most natural Christian application, set in relation to ethical teaching and thereby giving to that teaching a new profundity. The union of man and woman in marriage receives 'cosmic' roots; it is as deep and indestructible as Christ's God-given union with his people.

ॐ

21
Be subject: in Gk this is a participle so that many take this verse as appended to the preceding sentence. This is quite possibly right, but the parallel in *Colossians* (3^{18}), which has been doubled into a general and then a particular statement (vv. 21 & 22), points to the R.S.V. arrangement; in Gk the verb is left to be understood in v. 22. And, as urging good order, this verse makes a natural bridge from the preceding passage. (Cf. Gal. 5^{13}; I Pet. 5^5.)

out of reverence for Christ: lit. 'in fear of Christ'. The *Colossians* parallel has *in the Lord*. The change is small but significant; it is typical in replacing the language of indwelling with that of looking up to Christ, seen as distinguishable from his people, however intimately he is joined to them (though cf. Col. 3^{22}).

22
The writer sees in the social conventions of his time a parallel with the eternal hierarchy: God-Christ-Church. For him both are permanent dispositions of God, and the subordination of women in marriage is mysteriously built into the framework of the universe. It is apparent to us that he over-estimated the permanence of the conventions of marriage as he knew them, and in this respect was carried away by the beauty of his scheme. Though Christians feel a constant obligation to see social relationships in the light of relationship with God, there is nothing sacrosanct about their transient features, even though, while they last, they may serve as useful illustrators in matters of morals and doctrine.

23
head ... body: cf. 1^{22} (see p. 277); and I Cor. 11^3, where, however, the point is rather different: to present God-Christ-man-woman as a chain of authority. I Cor. 11^8 shows the basis of the wife's subjection to her husband: it is rooted in nature, in creation (Gen. 2^{21-3}), just as the marriage union is (cf. I Cor. 11^9; 7^{39}; v. 31). In commenting on 1^{22}

and on Col. 1^{18} we have discussed the more speculative associations of the term *head*, but in the simple sense of 'ruler' or 'superior' in its first occurrence here, it looks back to LXX usage, cf. Deut. 28^{13}; Isa. $7^{8f.}$; Jud. 10^{18}. On *body*: see on 1^{23}, p. 278.

Saviour: this is not a regular pauline title for Christ. He uses it only in Phil. 3^{20}. In line with Paul's normal use of words of this family it refers there to Christ's role at the Last Day. Here this need not be so, in view of the use of the verb 'to save' in the past tense in $2^{5, 8}$. In this writer's vocabulary Christ's already accomplished work is the 'saving' of his people and he is already their saviour. In accounting for the use of this title reference is often made, especially in view of some of the associations of *body*, to Hellenistic religions in which *saviour* (*sōtēr*) was a frequent title for a divine redeemer; but there is also strong Old Testament background for the term. It is used in the LXX for God as the rescuer of his people: Deut. 32^{15}; 1 Sam. 10^{19}; Ps. $24(25)^5$; cf. Luke 1^{47}.

25
Cf. Col. 3^{19}.

gave himself up for her: nowhere else in the New Testament do we find in so many words the idea that Christ's sacrifice of himself was for the sake of the Church, and that the Church was the object of his love. Paul speaks rather of Christ giving himself *for our sins* (Gal. 1^4; cf. Rom. 4^{25}), or *for me* (Gal. 2^{20}), or *for us all* (Rom. 8^{32}). John on the other hand says that it was God's love for the world which prompted the giving of his only Son (John 3^{16}). However, in neither of these writers does the teaching effectively diverge from that of our present passage. The persons referred to in Paul's statements are the Christians, and in John 3^{16} it is believing in the Son (i.e. entering the Church) which alone leads to eternal life, the fruit of Christ's self-giving. At the same time, in all three, the Church's mission has a universal destiny (cf. Eph. 1^{10}), so that this passage does not at all bear witness to parochialism. That our writer chose to express himself in this more 'institutional' language, as it seems to us, is entirely characteristic of him. He lives at a time when it has become a little more natural than in Paul's time to objectify the Church as a society ('the Church' rather than 'us'); yet his vision has no narrowness, nor is he at all pre-occupied with the Church as an earthly organization. Quite the contrary, he is concerned with it as the divine instrument of Christ's redemptive purpose for the world.

26f.
So strong is his sense of the Church as a community that he speaks here of baptism as a corporate act, done to the Church. It may be that he sees lying behind the baptism of individuals, in an archetypal (quasi-

Gnostic? cf. 4¹³, p. 315) way, the death of Christ, of his body (cf. v. 30), as the fount of saving action. In Mark 10³⁸ Jesus refers to his coming death as his *baptism*, and it is likely that the writer of that gospel saw Jesus' baptism in Mark 1⁹⁻¹¹ as prefiguring his death. (The association of suffering with immersion is common in the Old Testament, cf. Ps. 69¹; 130¹.) Moreover, in the Fourth Gospel, Christian baptism is seen as springing from the death of Jesus and being an effective sharing in the benefits of his passion (19³⁴; 4¹⁴; 7³⁷⁻⁹). Rom. 6³ᶠᶠ· moves in the same field of ideas. So here the Church is seen as a totality, already existing in principle in that saving death which was the moment of her birth. All Christian life rests upon that act. Yet her full growth remains in the future and her glorious perfection is still to be realized (v. 27; cf. 1¹⁸, ²¹; 4¹³⁻¹⁶; Col. 1²², where we note *you* rather than *the Church*). Only then will she be the unblemished sacrificial offering, matching, by his grace, Christ's own self-offering. (Paul can already speak of the Corinthian congregation in similar terms, 2 Cor. 11², when he thinks anything but good of much of her behaviour; the Church is God's people, objectively, taken into relationship with him.) Here the images of the pure sacrifice and the young maiden (symbol of Israel in the Old Testament, cf. Zech. 2¹⁰; Zeph. 3¹⁴) join. They are applied to God's *new* people.

In the early second-century writing by Hermas, *The Shepherd* (Lightfoot, *Apostolic Fathers*, p. 412), the Church, under the image of a tower, is seen as 'builded upon the waters' and 'founded by the word of the Almighty and Glorious Name' (see below).

with the word: either the preaching which evokes the faith in Christ's saving death (cf. John 15³; Rom. 10⁸), or the words of baptism which apply that act to the individual believer, or, perhaps, more specifically, the actual name of Jesus, pronounced in the rite as the means of entering into his life and power (cf. 1 Cor. 6¹¹; Acts 2³⁸).

28–30
The bride image now fuses into the body image, in order to demonstrate the intensity and strength of the unity between man and wife, Christ and Church.

nourishes it: possibly a reference to the eucharist.

members of his body: cf. 1 Cor. 6¹⁵, *members of Christ:* here, as usual, the language shows Christ as more detached – he is the head (cf. v. 23), joined to yet distinct from the body. (Cf. 4¹⁶, ²⁵.)

31
From Gen. 2²⁴. This verse was commonly quoted in early Christian

teaching on marriage and divorce, cf. Mark 10$^{7f.}$; Matt. 19^5. Its use
here may mean that the idea of Christ as the new Adam plays its part
in the imagery of this passage. If so, it is not the 'inclusive' Adam of
Paul (I Cor. 15^{22}), in whom the believers are incorporated, but Christ
married to his Church as Adam to Eve, in union but still distinguishable.

32

mystery: see on 1^9, p. 268. The writer sees the Old Testament passage
as having now received a new meaning, or rather its true meaning
has at last been disclosed, in the union of Christ and the Church (cf. 3$^{9f.}$).

6$^{1-9}$ CHILDREN AND PARENTS, SLAVES
                AND MASTERS

^{1}*Children, obey your parents in the Lord, for this is right.* ^{2}*'Honour
your father and mother'* (*this is the first commandment with a promise*),
^{3}*'that it may be well with you and that you may live long on the earth.'*
^{4}*Fathers, do not provoke your children to anger, but bring them up in the
discipline and instruction of the Lord.*

^{5}*Slaves, be obedient to those who are your earthly masters, with fear
and trembling, in singleness of heart, as to Christ;* ^{6}*not in the way of eye-
service, as men-pleasers, but as servants^f of Christ, doing the will of God
from the heart,* ^{7}*rendering service with a good will as to the Lord and not
to man,* ^{8}*knowing that whatever good any one does, he will receive the same
again from the Lord, whether he is a slave or free.* ^{9}*Masters, do the same to
them, and forbear threatening, knowing that he who is both their Master
and yours is in heaven, and that there is no partiality with him.*

f Or slaves.

For the most part this passage diverges little from its parallel in Col.
3^{20}–4^1, and the notes on that passage should be consulted (pp. 210ff.).
However, the instruction to children adds a reference to the Ten
Commandments, strengthening the view that our writer has had
them consciously in mind through much of his ethical teaching (cf.
on 4^{26}; 5^3). Fathers are to be more didactic than in Col. 3^{21}: in line
with our writer's emphasis on harmonious order among Christians.
In addressing slaves, the writer oddly leaves aside the word *inheritance,*
by which Paul (Col. 3^{24}) describes their future reward for faithfulness,

despite the fact that this is a favourite word of his, cf. 1$^{14, 18}$. For this general and rich term for the heavenly consummation which awaits the believer he substitutes a more quantitative approach to the matter (v.8). (It is one that sounds un-pauline, but see 2 Cor. 5^{10}.) Here masters rather than slaves (cf. Col. 3^{25}) are warned that God is impartial in his judgement. Clearly, masters are likely to stand more in need of this warning, and the difficulty is to account for the statement in *Colossians*. J. Knox suggests that it has an eye on the circumstances in which that letter was written, the case of the slave Onesimus, whose master needed reassuring that despite his pleading in *Philemon*, Paul was still able to take a proper and dispassionate view of the due rights of slave-owners (see p. 125).

ॐ

1

in the Lord: these words do not occur in some of the best manuscripts and should perhaps be omitted. The *Colossians* parallel has *in everything, for this pleases the Lord* (lit. 'is well-pleasing in the Lord'). Our sentence, as often, shifts words and meaning but roughly preserves the shape. If *in the Lord* is to be kept in, the sense is 'as Christians should'.

2

Cf. Exod. 20^{12}, as in LXX, but omitting the words which refer the promise to the land (= *earth*, Gk *gē*) of Israel; now it can apply to all men. That this commandment carried a promise from God is important to the writer because he is aware that he lives in the era, ushered in by Christ, when God's promises are being fulfilled.

first: probably 'first in importance'. None of the later commandments in the Decalogue carries a promise, and Exod. 20$^{4-6}$, which does, precedes this one.

4

discipline and instruction of the Lord: fathers are to give their children a Christian education and training. Gk *paideia* (*discipline*) is training with the accent on the correction of the young. This mention of education (contrast Col. 3^{21}) may indicate a long-term view – the End is no longer seen as imminent, as in earlier days.

8

whether he is a slave or free: a common pauline phrase, but elsewhere always in connection with the universality of Christ's work, cf. 1 Cor. 12^{13}; Gal. 3^{28}; Col. 3^{11}.

^{10}*Finally, be strong in the Lord and in the strength of his might.* ^{11}*Put on the whole armour of God, that you may be able to stand against the wiles of the devil.* ^{12}*For we are not contending against flesh and blood, but against the principalities, against the powers, against the world rulers of this present darkness, against the spiritual hosts of wickedness in the heavenly places.* ^{13}*Therefore take the whole armour of God, that you may be able to withstand in the evil day, and having done all, to stand.* ^{14}*Stand therefore, having girded your loins with truth, and having put on the breastplate of righteousness,* ^{15}*and having shod your feet with the equipment of the gospel of peace;* ^{16}*above all taking the shield of faith, with which you can quench all the flaming darts of the evil one.* ^{17}*And take the helmet of salvation, and the sword of the Spirit, which is the word of God.* ^{18}*Pray at all times in the Spirit, with all prayer and supplication. To that end keep alert with all perseverance, making supplication for all the saints,* ^{19}*and also for me, that utterance may be given me in opening my mouth boldly to proclaim the mystery of the gospel,* ^{20}*for which I am an ambassador in chains; that I may declare it boldly, as I ought to speak.*

In coming to the end of his work the writer returns to the fact which lies behind the whole of his message, the triumphant lordship of Christ, and sees its bearing on the life of the Christian in the world. His words form an inspiring exhortation, so much more extended than anything in Paul's undoubted writings that they help to put *Ephesians* into the category of liturgy or oratory rather than epistle, at least as far as most of its material is concerned. Some scholars see vv. 10–18 as having a more specialized place in early Christian use; they were addressed to those who had just been baptized and were embarking on the serious struggle of the Christian life.

The writer assumes the victory of Christ over the evil powers of the cosmos. He spoke of that in 1$^{20-23}$, and the theme is shared with many other New Testament writers. The victory is for the time being chiefly a heavenly one. Christ has established his rule, under God, over the angelic powers of the universe. On earth his authority over them, though assured, is not yet fully realized. Those who join themselves to him in the Church share in the assurance of that victory (1^{14});

but as well as beginning to share its fruits they must face its serious implications. They must take their part in continuing and completing the struggle. This is the outward-looking task, which correspond to their task within the Church of growing up into Christ (4¹⁶), or *building up the body of Christ* (4¹²). Notice that this work is only presented secondarily in terms of evangelism or persuasion. First and foremost it is warfare. That warfare is specifically not directed against human beings (v. 12) but only against the cosmic powers. Men are under their enslaving power needing liberation. The Christian is then to be, to his fellow-men, the bringer of release, salvation, such as he himself already enjoys (v. 17). He does that by proclaiming Christ's victory, that is the gospel (vv. 15, 19). Men who accept that message and believe it can come into the Church and find freedom from the oppression under which they have laboured. The Christian's resources for extending this freedom to others (which is equivalent to prosecuting the fight against the powers) are his own inner qualities (v. 14 *righteousness*) and the message committed to him (vv. 15, 17). This corresponds to the dual content of *Ephesians* – the doctrine, and its moral application. Meantime the Christian is to be constant in articulating the life to which he has come, in prayer to God.

⁊⁊

10
be strong in the Lord: cf. 1¹⁹. The Christian's strength is derivative. It depends upon God's infinite power. So, v. 11, the armour is provided by God. Cf. also 1 Cor. 16¹³; 2 Tim. 2¹⁻³.

11
Put on the whole armour of God: cf. Rom. 13¹²; 1 Thess. 5⁸; also Col. 3¹²; Gal. 3²⁷.

whole armour: Gk *panoplia*, the full armour of a heavy-armed soldier. For the use of this image, apart from the references above, see Wisdom of Solomon 5¹⁷ᶠᶠ·; Ecclesiasticus 46⁶; and Ignatius' Epistle to Polycarp 6 (E.C.W., p. 129). In Isa. 59¹⁷ (as in the much later *Wisdom* passage) it is God who wears the armour, and it is detailed in language which at two points is reproduced here: *the breast-plate of righteousness* (v. 14) and *the helmet of salvation* (v. 17). It is then literally God's armour, which he hands over to the believer; just as in 1 Cor. 2¹⁰ᶠᶠ· it is God's own Spirit which comes and indwells him.

the devil: i.e. the head of the opposing army, the chief of the evil powers. *Diabolos,* used here and in 4²⁷, never appears in Paul's undoubted writings.

338

12

contending: for the idea of the Christian's warfare, cf. 2 Cor. 10³ᶠ·;
2 Tim. 2³. There is ample background in the Old Testament for the
notion of Yahweh, the God of Israel, as a warrior, with his people
fighting his battles under him. The familiar title, 'Lord of hosts'
(= armies), going back to Israel's early days, witnesses to this. It is,
for that matter, a commonplace of religion to see the deity as a warrior
and his followers as the soldiers in his army. In Judaism it was still a
living tradition. It had been revived in the revolts of the Maccabees
in the second century B.C., and was in the forefront of the minds of
the many in Israel, who were engaged in the struggle against the Romans
and had been savagely defeated in A.D. 70. Sometimes it appeared in a
context closer to that of *Ephesians*, in relation to the final cosmic struggle
between God and evil. *The War Rule* of the Qumran sect (Vermes,
pp. 122ff.), a work of considerable length and intricacy, well illustrates
its importance. There, as in *Ephesians*, it is a matter of the struggle
between two universal powers for the spiritual mastery of all things.
For Qumran this battle still lies in the future, for the Christian writer
it is already fully engaged and Christ has won the decisive victory.

flesh and blood: i.e. human beings, cf. Matt. 16¹⁷; Gal. 1¹⁶; or human
nature, cf. Heb. 2¹⁴.

principalities . . . powers: see p. 163.

heavenly places: cf. 1²⁰, p. 276.

13

the evil day: i.e. the expected day of trial when the struggle of God and
the devil reaches its decisive climax.

14

Cf. Isa. 11⁵; 59¹⁷. *Truth* (= genuineness, reliability) and *righteousness*
(= uprightness, justice) are both attributes of God which man is
bidden to imitate: cf. Exod. 34⁶ (LXX); Ps. 40¹¹; Isa. 5¹⁶.

15

This verse seems to be based on three verses from *Second Isaiah:* 40³, ⁹;
52⁷. The word translated *equipment* (which is its sense in modern Greek)
means literally 'preparation', which corresponds to the verb in Isa. 40³.

17

Cf. Isa. 59¹⁷; 11⁴; 49². Salvation *is* the Christian's helmet, the indwelling
Spirit *is* his sword. The Spirit gives him the word to speak, cf. Mark 13¹¹,
and Isa. 51¹⁶.

18

pray . . . in the Spirit: cf. Rom. 8²⁶ᶠ·, for the idea of the Spirit forming the Christian's prayer. On this and the next verse, cf. Col. 4²ᶠ·; Phil. 4⁶.

19

mystery of the gospel: i.e. the mystery (see p. 268) which consists of the gospel, that is, the doctrine set out particularly in the opening Blessing of this writing.

20

ambassador in chains: cf. 2 Cor. 5²⁰; Philem. 9; Acts 28²⁰.

as I ought to speak: cf. Col. 4⁴.

6²¹⁻²   A PERSONAL MESSAGE

²¹*Now that you also may know how I am and what I am doing, Tychicus the beloved brother and faithful minister in the Lord will tell you everything.* ²²*I have sent him to you for this very purpose, that you may know how we are, and that he may encourage your hearts.*

These two verses virtually duplicate Col. 4⁷ᶠ·. In *Ephesians* they stand alone in their mention of an associate of Paul's and in their sense of intimacy with those who are to receive the letter. They are closely bound up with the question of the nature of *Ephesians* as a whole, so they come into the discussion in the Introduction (p. 239). Here we may notice two points. First, in quoting from *Colossians* (if that is, as is most likely, what he has done), our writer stopped short in the middle of a sentence. He left out the reference to Onesimus. If the writer was Paul this is easy to explain; Onesimus was of interest only in Colossae whereas Tychicus was Paul's messenger and known in all the churches he visited. But if the writer was not Paul (this is our second point) then he may have included this fragment because he had read 2 Tim. 4¹², which speaks of Paul sending Tychicus to Ephesus. It added verisimilitude to his pseudonymous work. The problem of how this is related to the (perhaps later) address of this work to Ephesus (1¹) allows several solutions; either may have led to the inclusion of the other, both may have come into the work together after the writing of the main work.

FINAL GREETING

²³*Peace be to the brethren, and love with faith, from God the Father and the Lord Jesus Christ.* ²⁴*Grace be with all who love our Lord Jesus Christ with love undying.*

Paul's farewells take many forms and are much less stereotyped than his openings. This one is longer and more formal than that which ends *Colossians*, but most of it finds a parallel somewhere in the undoubted epistles. It includes many of the great qualities which the apostle and any Christian pastor would wish God to pour upon his people: peace (cf. 2¹⁴), love, faith, and grace. All are his gift, and his people's place is to make the return of love.

with love undying: lit. 'in immortality (or incorruptibility)', either his or theirs; or else regarded as the goal of their love. It is not a common New Testament word and is more characteristic of Hellenistic than Jewish future expectation. But these two spheres knew no rigid segregation of ideas at this time, and we find the word in Paul, in Rom. 2⁷ and 1 Cor. 15⁴²,⁵⁰,⁵⁴, in relation to the coming glorious age. It is a final reminder of the consummation so often referred to in *Ephesians* as the ultimate hope.

Index of References

OLD TESTAMENT

APOCRYPHA

NEW TESTAMENT

Index of Names

Index of Subjects

Acts of the Apostles, 34ff., 122f.
Adam, speculation concerning, 73ff., 79, 201, 205, 206, 291, 315, 318
Angels, 163ff., 175, 186ff., 190, 192, 194, 197, 275, 276, 295, 300
Apocalyptic, 23, 151, 177, 274, 281
Apostle, 91, 93, 145ff., 242, 292, 300, 312
Authenticity, of *Philippians*, 38f.; of *Colossians* 134f.; of *Ephesians* 240f., 249ff., 255

Baptism, 188, 251, 302, 327, 333f.
Body of Christ, 181, 243, 321, 332, 334

Caesarea, 44, 60
Church, 135, 171, 181, 244, 295, 330ff.
Colossae, 119ff.
Colossians and *Ephesians*, relationship, 138, 246ff.
Computer studies, 39f., 135

Dead Sea Scrolls, 17, 23, 49, 182, 193ff., 252, 261, 268f., 276, 281, 303, 324, 325, 326, 339
Death, 62

Ephesians and *Colossians*, relationship, 138, 246ff.
Ephesus, 42, 60, 121, 139, 255
Eschatology, 61f., 97, 102, 110, 177, 201, 205, 305, 322, 325, 333
Ethics, 204, 209ff., 320ff., 323ff., 329ff., 335ff.
Eucharist, 328

Fullness, 172, 185, 277f.

Gnosticism, 22, 84, 127f., 133, 140, 153, 172, 266, 291, 303, 304, 305, 315, 333f.
Gospels, 19f.

Holy, 48, 148

Imprisonment, place of, 41ff., 90f., 112f., 139
Integrity, of *Philippians*, 40f., 89, 95; of *Colossians* 137f., 210
Israel, Church and, 286ff.

Jerusalem, fall of, 20
Judaism, 16, 33, 96, 97ff., 103ff., 121, 128ff., 163, 173, 193ff., 204, 210, 244f., 270, 274, 286, 290, 310f.

Kingdom of God, 220

Law, Jewish, 18, 99f., 186ff., 190, 191, 291
Lord, 78, 215
Love, 150f., 207, 213, 322

Marriage, 27, 209ff., 329ff.
Ministry, 49, 145ff., 311, 312
Mystery, 178f., 182, 195, 216, 268, 298
Mythology, 22, 295, 304

Pharisaism, 16, 107
Philippi, 31ff., 66
Pre-existence of Christ, 75f., 140, 178, 245
Pseudonymity, 240f.

Resurrection, 97
Righteousness, 97ff.